The Essential

Guide to Living in Mérida

The Essential
Guide to Living in Mérida

Tons of Useful Information, Including Information on AirBNB Stays, "The Best of Mérida," and Dog Culture

Edited by Eduviges Montejo

The Essential Guide to Living in Mérida, 2016: Tons of Visitor Information, Including Information on AirBNB, Stays, "The Best of Mérida," and Dog Culture

Publication date: January 2016.

Published by Hispanic Economics, Inc.
P.O. Box 140681
Coral Gables, FL 33114-0681
info@hispaniceconomics.com
HispanicEconomics.com

ISBN: 978-1-939879-22-6

Cover and Interior Design by John Clifton
john@johnclifton.net

Complete Quick Find

TABLE OF CONTENTS

Editor's Note

With the publication of the 2016 edition, we are now into our sixth year of providing the most comprehensive information about living in Mérida.

We are delighted that this has now become to "go to" guide about moving and living in Mérida, especially now that Mérida has been voted the third "most livable" city in the entire country of Mexico—only Querétero and Monterrey are ahead of us!

It is also gratifying to know that the first four editions of this book sold out. It's a testament to the interest in Mérida and the demand for an up-to-date guide that aids visitors and expatriates alike. It is also wonderful to know that this *Essential Guide* provides comprehensive information that is proving to be an invaluable resource to so many.

Remember, every day, somewhere in Mérida, a business opens its doors. Every day, somewhere in Mérida, an establishment closes theirs for good. Every day, someone calls the telephone company to set up service and others are calling to disconnect their numbers.

In a book this comprehensive something, somewhere will inevitably be out of date, or incorrect. No matter how much care and diligence has been exercised in compiling the information in this book, dear reader, there will be errors and omissions. This is why it's our continuing commitment to update this book annually in order to deliver the most current information available anywhere. We want to continue to be the essential guide to visiting Mérida and living in this wonderful city.

So, consider this an invitation. If you have any information, whether it is a correction or any recommendation, to improve this guide, please send me an email and let me know about it. I want to know about it! And remember, in a book this ambitious in scope, there are hundreds of companies and business that were not included. This is, after all, a city of almost one million people! That said, an omission is not to be construed as a negative recommendation!

With that, enjoy this book, and may you find it instructive, illuminating, and useful to you.

Eduviges Montejo
Mérida, Yucatán

Email: *EssentialMerida@gmail.com*

Acknowledgments

This book represents the collaboration, contributions, and opinions of many people. The 2016 edition includes what readers have requested, including a broad guide to the social media for the expat livingin Mérida, comprehensive information on the new immigration laws, rules for importing motor vehicles, and the exploring food and local-sourced food scene. As Editor, I would like to thank the following for having contributed, made suggestions, offered information, or provided material quoted about Mérida, which makes this the most comprehensive guide to living in Mérida ever published.

My thanks go to the following contributors, writers, reviewers, and advisors who have enriched this book: Miguel Aguayo de Pau, Karín Alvarez, Ricardo Ancona, Francisco Arrigunaga, Mark Arbour, Tony Burton, Emilio Guadalupe Chan, Claudia Guerrero, Vanessa Hernández, Alberto Huchim, Thomas Lloyd, Gerardo Martínez, Concepción May, Louis Nevaer, Zenaida Pantaleon, Glynna Prentice, Dan Prescher, Diane Provenzano, Robert Provenzano, Reed Robertson, Pete Sigal, and María Luisa Uc.

—E. M.

In Memoriam

Edward Vincent Byrne died on March 24, 2015. He was diagnosed with Hepatosplenic T-Cell Lymphoma in June 2014. Despite an aggressive treatment program that declared him 100% in remission by December 2014, his recovery was short-lived. He was able to attend his only child's wedding, Sarah Lillian, on February 28, 2015 in Las Vegas, Nevada. The following week, however, he was hospitalized. Less than a month later, he died.

During his time in Mérida, Ed was a strong and vital presence. He loved this city and its people and he bravely defended the integrity of the Mexican people rogue elements. If one looks through his website, *http://www.mexicogulfreporter.com/*, one is struck by his fierce political and social principles. He was not afraid to call it as he saw it—especially when he saw things that were morally wrong. Ed, for example, reported extensively on gay American men living in Mérida who who sexually molested Mexican youngsters.

As the editor of this guide, I reached out to Ed and we had coffee. He was delightful and charming, a gentleman in ways not often seen nowadays.

This edition of *The Essential Guide to Living in Mérida* is dedicated to him. It is our hope that his daughter, Lillian, and her husband, Marc, know full well how much Ed was loved and how much he is missed. Mérida was a better city when he was a resident here, and Mérida remembers—and misses—our Mexico Gulf Reporter, Ed V. Byrne.

Fare thee well, our friend.

—E. M.

Part I
Welcome to the Yucatán!

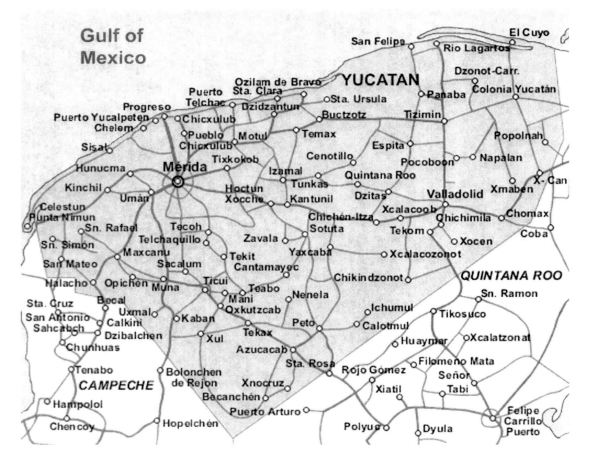

Where in the world is Mérida?

By Louis Nevaer

"YUCATECANS are fiercely proud of their culture, sprinkling their Spanish with Mayan words and quick to recount the stories of resistance and revolution that set this region apart from the rest of Mexico for centuries. Somehow, those tales seem a little distant now in Yucatán's capital, Mérida, a languid city of pastel mansions and evening promenades. The city, now one of the safest in Mexico, is an architectural jewel, and has one of the country's largest historic centers outside Mexico City. Block after block of houses dating to the mid-19th century and earlier are in the midst of a restoration boom, and the city's cultural and restaurant scenes are flourishing," Elisabeth Malkin, New York Times, December 2, 2011.

Mérida, with just fewer than one million residents, is the largest city in the Yucatán. It is the capital of the State of Yucatán.

It is also one of the oldest cities established by the Europeans in the Americas. Founded by Francisco de Montejo "El Mozo" in 1542, at that time a scant 70 Spanish families formed the "city." It was an ambitious effort, a small European enclave in the heart of a vast wilderness, surrounded by scores of Maya communities, many of which did not know what to make of these foreigners in their midst. It was this uncertainty and precarious nature of their small community that led Montejo to choose this precise location for the city: ruins offered ready-cut stones for building the initial structures of the new settlement.

Mérida was therefore established amid the ruins of the abandoned Maya city of T'ho, which itself was built on the site of an even earlier abandonded Maya ceremonial center, Ichcaanzihó. (When the Spaniards asked the Maya who had built the crumbling temples of T'ho, the answer  given was: Who knows?) The name "Mérida" was chosen because it reminded the Spaniards of the Roman ruins found in Mérida, Spain. And so, ruins from one ancient civilization inspired the Spaniards to name their new city in honor of the ruins of another ancient civilization.

From that humble—and audacious—beginning, Mérida has become what it is today: a cosmopolitan, vibrant city, one of the fastest-growing in Mexico, with a rich history stretching from the 16th century to the present one. Often described as a "colonial gem" and "unspoiled," Mérida has become a "tropical paradise" in the world's imagination, especially since it stands in sharp contrast to glitzy Cancún and the disjointed resorts of the Maya Riviera. Where Cancún boasts beaches and a climate of excess, Mérida boasts opera, museums, symphonies, culture, and the tranquility in which to enjoy it all. It is a community of storied waves of immigrants and a metropolis of distinctive cuisines that reflects influences from exotic sources, from the Maya to the Middle East.

It also has some of the more riveting history to be found anywhere in the Americas. It is, for instance, the only place in the hemisphere where an uprising of the First Peoples, the Maya, almost led to the complete expulsion of all the Europeans. The War of the Castes in the 19th Century was so ferocious that the Governor ordered the evacuation of the city of Mérida. Mexico, Cuba, Spain, the United States and the United Kingdom sent ships to help rescue the fleeing refugees. The circumstances that led to this uprising, which are discussed briefly later on this book, itself is a fascinating study of the Maya religious beliefs and the consequences of the mercantile system imposed under Colonialism.

Mérida is also the place that welcomed Fidel Castro (who resided in Mérida for months) on his quest to foment revolution in his homeland. It is also where Pan Am World Airways built, with CIA money, Mérida's international airport, partly in order to check on Soviet ambitions in the region. Charles Lindbergh surveyed the peninsula from the air and discovered unknown Maya ruins. Another Charles, Charles Duller, used NASA satellites to penetrate the forest canopy and "see" the remains of Maya ceremonial centers. Louis C. Tiffany made a small fortune designing stained glass windows for the grand homes of Mérida's wealthy. Cuban poet and liberator José Martí spent months here, growing inspired by the Maya. A few decades before his arrival, John Lloyd Stephens and Frederick Catherwood embarked on a grand journey of exploration that resulted in a landmark book, *Incidents of Travel*, which brought the achievements of the Maya civilization to the consciouness of the world and launched the field of Maya studies.

The list goes on and could fill a book. Suffice it to say that Mérida is an oasis of history and culture, with a distinct set of values, sensibilities and affections that are not quite Mexican and which set the Yucatán as a region apart. This difference has led to misunderstandings across the centuries, much the same way that the differences between the Maya and the First Peoples from central Mexico led to conflicts between them centuries before any European set foot on this continent. The Maya, after all, saw themselves as a kind of chosen people: the very word "Maya" means just that!

This history of Maya Exceptionalism, in fact, created obstacles to the fledging colony of Spaniards in the Yucatán. Of the Maya settlements within a couple of days' distance from Mérida, some were openly hostile to foreigners settling in the Yucatán. A few welcomed the Spaniards, seeing them both as accomplished in military skills and a people who arrived with astonishing goods; the Maya had never seen horses or hammocks, and they went wild over the Spaniards' foods: oranges, lemons, cinammon, pork. Most of the Maya, however, were indiffirerent. To them, the Spaniards had as much right to make themselves at home in the ruins of an abandoned city as much as anyone else did!

Montejo, for his part, was careful, having studied the lessons of the Spanish reconquest of the Iberian Peninsula from the Muslims. It is not a coincidence that when Mérida was founded, it was dedicated to *Nuestra Señora de la Encarnación*, Our Lady of the Incarnation. This is the name of a church in Álora, a village in southern Spain, today part of Málaga, which was liberated from the Muslims after several unsuccessful attempts. Montejo saw this isolated outpost of New Spain as surrounded by threats and he was determined to provide for the safety of families under his responsibility. Since there was no natural protection for the city, such as a river, or cliffs, or outcroppings, a wall would have to be built to protect the residents. More to the point, Mérida was declared a "Ciudad Blanca," a "White City."

I would be willing to bet that somewhere you've read, or someone has told you, that Mérida is the "White City" because the buildings are painted white—very few are, really—or that the name reflects the "cleanliness" of the city. Both of these stories are nonsense, merely myths propagated by tourism officials and the uninformed who repeat what they've been told. Apart from the Museum of Anthropology and the Casa Montes Molina on Paseo de Montejo, what other landmark building is painted white? (And these are painted shades of eggshell, not white!) Indeed, the liming that is widely used to whitewash the buildings was unknown until the mid 17th century. Also, consider the first buildings that still stand today: The Casa de Montejo and the Cathedral, each of which displays its natural stone and were never whitewashed.

The Montejos explicitly sought to make Mérida a "White City" for the safety of Spanish residents. Michel Antochiw Kolpa, a Mexican historian who is an authority on first decades of Mérida's existence, confirms that Mérida was a city where only Europeans could live. Others would visit and work in Mérida proper during daylight hours, but they could not spend the night. This was seen by the Maya as reciprocity: they had restrictions on Spaniards living in their communities since the Maya believed they were an excitable and dangerous people by nature.

5

It was this exclusion that created the need to establish "Colonias"—Santiago, Santa Ana, San Sebastián, and so forth, which were designated as residential communities for other peoples. Santiago was established for the Maya who had business in Mérida and as residential neighborhoods for Europeans who had business in town, primarily Portuguese and Italian merchants. Santa Ana was established for mixed race people and blacks who were brought in to augment the labor force and mitigate the Spaniards' fear of skirmishes with the Maya. All the Colonias were considered "extramuros," meaning they were "outside the walls" of Mérida proper. The chapter on the Colonias of Mérida offers a broader discussion, but for now, it's important to note the ambivalence of Spaniard and Maya from the very beginning.

In the early decades, in fact, the same way that Montejo established Mérida as the "White City," the Maya referred to the growing Spanish settlement as "Chak T'ho," meaning, "Red T'ho," or "Red Mérida." Why did the Maya call Mérida the Red City? Well, from the Maya perspective, the Spaniards turned "red" in the tropical sun, much the way native Floridians ridicule snowbirds that arrive every winter and in a few days are red as lobsters for not knowing how to enjoy the sun without getting burned. To the Maya, Mérida was a city of people who turned "red" at the slightest exposure to the sun. (And fear of skin damage is one reason that so many "proper" Yucatecans today are heliophobes!)

It is clear to see that this mutual exclusion and mistrust gave rise to prejudices and misgivings. This is instructive. It reveals that that the history of Mérida over the centuries has been the struggle for social justice and inclusion.

Mérida is located 198 miles west of Cancún. This is both a blessing and a curse, depending on your perspective. For those who treasure Mérida as a "gem" and "unspoiled" and a "respite" from the world, it is great to be removed from the hustle-and-bustle of Cancún. On the other hand, there are those who lament that Mérida has been eclipsed by Cancún, and that it has been economically marginalized, with most people pointing to the relative difficulty of air travel in recent years as proof of that isolation. A little over a decade ago, Mérida boasted two daily flights to Miami, with regularly scheduled service to Guatemala City, Havana, Houston, New Orleans and Orlando. (Many Yucatecans remember fondly, and proudly, that in the 1980s Eastern Airlines had a direct flight from Mérida to New York City!) In 2011, by comparison, the only commercial international flights are to Havana, Houston and Miami. Local authorities are pushing for increased nonstop service between Mérida and other cities. Maya Air has been encouraged to provide daily service to Cancún and Cozumel; it was a major setback when Delta Airlines suspended its flights to Atlanta a couple of years ago.

6

Whether one considers it good or bad, the result is that Mérida lives in a splendid isolation, a metropolis of tranquility, filled with museums, galleries, exuberant cultural calendars where opera, symphony and concerts take place almost year-round. In 2000, Mérida was designated "American Capital of Culture," which has fostered international conferences and meetings ever since, highlighting the city's unique cultural heritage and vibrancy. That Mérida is a pedestrian-friendly city is an added attraction, although in all fairness, the sidewalks can be in various states of disrepair. Beware as you walk! Not unlike most colonial cities in Mexico, Mérida affords residents a city where it's possible to enjoy early morning brisk walks and leisurely strolls in the late afternoons and early evenings. (In no time, new residents learn that it's best to know where you want to be between 11 AM and 4 PM to avoid being caught under the unforgiving sun!) It is a city of Old World charm, yet almost every park has free Wi-Fi and youngsters sit on the benches with their elders. Their elders enjoy the afternoons, reminiscing about the good old days, while in the company of their grandchildren—who are busy on Facebook, Tumbler, Twitter, and whatever youthful folly they are intent on pursuing right then and there.

A tranquil, safe and pleasant metropolis, Mérida feels like a small town, while offering the amenities of a major metropolitan center. Montejo's little colony of 70 or so families has been a successful experiment, one that has flourished across the centuries!

This is Mérida, where you can discover the truth that so often eludes us in our world today: *Life is good.*

A Question of Safety in Mexico

How Safe is Mérida?

Concerned about Safety? Try Living in Yucatán, Mexico

By Thomas Lloyd

Although media images have caused many people to be concerned about safety when considering living in Mexico, statistics, as well as testimonials from Americans living here show that safety is actually a good reason to leave the U.S. and move to Mexico. This is especially true for many of Mexico's favorite tourist areas with significant expat communities, such as the colonial city of Mérida and the surrounding state of Yucatán. If you are considering buying Yucatán real estate, you will actually be improving the level of safety and the resulting comfort in your lifestyle.

Mérida is not only safer than the image people have of Mexico, but it is actually safer than most places in the U.S. According to statistics, aggravated assault, rape, theft, automobile theft, and burglary are all considerably lower in Mexico overall than in the U.S., each rate for Mexico being around 50% of the rate for the U.S., and Yucatán falls well below the national average. In terms of the murder rate (per 100,000 inhabitants), the U.S. was at about 4 for 2009, while Yucatán's rate was 2.5. …

Besides the stats, Americans who live in Mérida will consistently attest to the fact that they actually feel safer. "Truthfully," says one American, "My wife and I feel safer walking to and from our midtown home in Mérida to parks, restaurants, and evening events than we did in Omaha."

Five Reasons Why Mexico is Safer than You Think

By MexExperience

News headlines reporting drug-related violence in Mexico have caused people to question safety and security in Mexico by default. To provide some perspective, listed here are five reasons which demonstrate that Mexico's drug-related issues, although real and in need of addressing by governments, do not make Mexico wholly unsafe, nor do they foretell a collapse of the Mexican State.

Visitor numbers are rising: The Bank of Mexico is responsible for collating and publishing foreign visitor statistics. Earlier this year, the figures showed that over 22 million foreign visitors arrived in Mexico in 2010—a rise on 2009's figures and one of the highest recorded numbers since these records began. Despite the swine-flu of 2009, the global economic crisis, and the drug-violence, people keep coming to Mexico. Statistics from foreign consulate records show that the overwhelming majority of visits to Mexico are trouble-free.

No expat exodus. In decades past, when Mexico's economy was less certain and less stable, foreign expats would often flee home in the event of a peso crisis. Today, even with the drug-related violence playing out, no such exodus is taking place and, furthermore, interest in relocations *to* Mexico is rising. Mexico's government is fully expecting its expat communities to grow over the coming decade and beyond, and has been working to facilitate this process, as the financial and cultural benefits it brings are significant. If Mexico is a wholly dangerous place to be, why are existing expats staying put and inquiries for relocations to Mexico increasing?

Most people remain unaffected by the drug-related violence. Recent figures published by the Mexican government showed that most of the homicides in the country over the last few years have comprised of gang members killing other gang members. Tourists, business visitors, and foreign expats are not being affected by the drug-gangs, and statistics show that the overwhelming majority of visits to Mexico pass by trouble-free.

Mexico matters: the neighbor to the south of the U.S. is one of the world's most important nations—poised to play a major role in world affairs during the 21st century. Its shared land border with the States is a primary reason why drug lords want control of the overland trade routes into seemingly insatiable U.S. narcotic markets, where the illegal substances they peddle are readily available to those who seek them. For these reasons and others, the matter will not be resolved by Mexico alone, but by Mexico and the U.S. working in partnership.

Mexico's underlying story is strong and getting stronger. Notwithstanding the current drug-related violence, the country's macro economics are in good shape; Mexico has substantial oil and gas reserves as well as considerable mineral and precious metal wealth; foreign visitors keep coming back to visit despite the unsavory news headlines; foreign governments are actively courting trade and commerce with Mexico; expats living here are going about their lives normally; statistics continue to show that Mexico's levels of general crime and violence continue to be lower than those of most large U.S. cities; foreign expats we talk with say that they feel safer here in Mexico than they do in their home country.

For more information, please see: *http://www.mexperience.com/blogs/mexicoliving/?p=119*

1 The Beauty of Living in the Yucatán

Mérida is a splendid city, almost paradise in many ways. But is it right for you?

An even more important question: Are you ready to become an expatriate? Do you have the fortitude to live in a country that is fundamentally different from the United States or Canada? Are you prepared to be a "minority"—a native English-speaker in a Spanish-speaking country?

The truth of the matter is that Americans who move to Mérida (or anywhere in Mexico for that matter) freely choose to become instantly a minority! That seldom occurs to them and it is a fact of life that affects you in ways that you can only appreciate once you do, in fact, become part of Mexico's English-speaking minority.

It could be liberating—how wonderful to be in a place where there are virtually no expectations of you, other than to abide by the law, and to be a good neighbor. No one expects you to form an opinion about what city officials are doing or not doing. No one cares to hear what you think about the Governor's position on this or that. No one expects you to volunteer to help the local school with that or the other. No one, really, cares what you think or what you do or what your opinion is about anything.

In many ways, you are invisible, and that affords a certain amount of privacy and the freedom to live life without civic obligations, or responsibilities, or social expectations. It is for many Americans just what they want: the luxury of being left alone so they can pursue their happiness as they see best! This is undoubtedly one of the great pleasures that Mérida affords you as an expatriate that has grown ever so elusive in the United States: *the pursuit of happiness*.

In fact, city officials are so determined to safeguard Mérida's international reputation as a city that is safe and family-friendly that city government is relentless in addressing quality of life issues, regardless of which political party is in charge of City Hall, called the Ayuntamiento. It is as if the "Department of Ambiance" worked round-the-clock to make things even more family-friendly and to enrich the amenities afforded citizens, whether it is closing major thoroughfares on Sundays so families can ride bicycles together, or subsidizing the symphony so anyone can enjoy a world-class concert for the equivalent of a few dollars.

This concern for "quality of life" issues extends to Mérida's disparate expatriate communities, with major overtures being made to the resident Cubans, Lebanese and now Americans residing in the city. It has to be said, however, that the Cubans and the Lebanese have been very successful at integrating themselves into the mainstream life of the Yucatán—a Cuban couple's Yucatecan-born son started the city's largest newspaper mid-twentieth century; the offspring of Lebanese immigrants have successfully entered political office, as is the case with Mérida's former mayor who was of Lebanese descent. The Americans, for whatever reason, have failed to be as successful. Apart from businessman Thomas Kelleher, archaeologist James Callaghan and the family of E. Wyllis Andrews, Americans have not been seamlessly integrated into the social, economic or political life of the Yucatán. For now they remain sidelined on the public stage of civic life.

There are profound reasons for that, which are described when the history of the Colonias is discussed in the next chapter (see the history of the Centenario District). For now, suffice it to say there is beauty in this isolation. It affords a certain degree of anonymity, and it allows you to build a parallel community, one that is not consumed by the demands of the "real world."

Living in Mérida can be as wonderful as it gets: Life is good in a world where many bad things happen.

The Beauty of Living in Mérida: The Best Place to Retire in North America

Mérida has been voted the third most liveable city in Mexico!

Only Querétaro and Monterrey rank higher. This is according to *MEX DF Magazine*. We all knew Mérida was special—and the only thing that held the city back from being #1 is its failure to have more international flights to the U.S.

MEX DF Magazine is not alone in singing Mérida's praises. Every year, *International Living* magazine surveys 194 countries around the world, and guess what? Mérida is the best city for Americans to retire to in the whole of North America!

This is how Glynna Prentice, the Mexico Editor at *International Living* describes Mérida:

> **"Mérida, capital of the Yucatán Peninsula, is a happy combination of old and new: a gracious, historic colonial city with modern conveniences like shopping malls, an international airport, and excellent hospitals. You can enjoy a relaxed life here, with friendly locals, music in the streets almost every night, and several thousand expats to make adjusting easy."**

11

Almost 25,000 foreign expatriates must agree with Dan Prescher, since they make their home, year-round, in Mérida. That explains the Cubans speaking their rapid-fire Cuban Spanish, and the Arabic-language magazines (published in Mexico City!) with the social goings on of the wealthy Lebanese of Mexico that one finds at the authentic Lebanese restaurants around town. (Did you know more Yucatecans speak Arabic at home than speak English?) It also explains the breathtaking diversity of Mérida's cultural scene, where art exhibitions, festivals, and cultural events reflect the interests of the diverse communities. (Did you miss last year's Catalan-language film festival? Or the Korean high tea ceremony? Don't miss the Cuban celebration of Santería next time around!)

You get the idea.

For Americans, there are tremendous opportunities. City government remains sensitive to certain issues. Officials, for instance, have gone out of their way to discourage a backlash against Americans in Mérida that has arisen not only as a consequence of the situation in Arizona where recent legislation there is perceived as being "anti-Mexican," but also at a number of scams that American expatriates in town have carried out in recent years. This is a far cry from the United States where Mexicans are vilified and, according to FBI statistics, are five times more likely to be the victims of hate crimes as non-Hispanics. Mérida offers civility and respects the right of all its residents to live their lives in peace.

How *International Living* Assembles its Numbers

To rate and rank the 194 countries considered in this year's **Quality of Life Index**, the Editors of *International Living* take into account:

Cost of Living (15% of the final ranking)   **Health** (10%)
Culture and Leisure (10%).   **Infrastructure** (10%)
Economy (15%)   **Safety and Risk** (10%)
Environment (10%)   **Climate** (10%)
Freedom (10%)

Source: InternationalLiving.com

The Curious Stigma of Being an Expatriate

In Paris, when friends get together and one mentions that he or she is moving overseas to become a "francais de l'etranger," or a "Frenchman in a foreign land," the first reaction is this: *"What are you running away from?"*

To be a stranger in a strange land may sound romantic and adventurous, but it is also fraught with implications. The French are always suspicious of their fellow countrymen they encounter overseas. There is a saying in Paris that the person most likely to swindle you is a fellow Frenchman overseas. Parisians warn each other, with horror stories about their experiences, or those of acquaintances, when dealing with other Frenchmen living in foreign countries. In France, the stereotype of a French expatriate is of a middle-aged man, who was never too successful in France, who decides to leave France in order to start fresh, in a place where he can reinvent himself.

Often he is also said to be looking for "a less assertive" woman, easily deceived, younger and less experienced in life, with whom to have children. He is also on the prowl for susceptible locals willing to believe in the integrity of a European, or other Frenchmen innocently believing the naive notion that a fellow Frenchman would have his best interests at heart in a foreign land.

Then the story ends in disappointment: the local who was swindled, the fellow Frenchman who was betrayed. The French, in other words, are advised to stay clear of any financial dealings with fellow Frenchmen in foreign lands.

What of Americans in foreign lands? What of Canadians in foreign lands? What are the assumptions that others will make of you?

Will they see you as friend or foe?

Quality of Life in Mérida

The City of Mérida maintains a hotline that anyone can call to report a quality of life issue.

What quality of life issue? Street lights that are burned out, pot holes on city streets, a pile of garbage someone left on the side of the road, excessive noise, a dead animal, fallen tree limbs on sidewalks, and so forth.

The office is **AYUNTATEL** and the number is (999) **924-6962**.

2 AN IDEAL WEEK IN MÉRIDA

Before you decide if Mérida is right for you, shouldn't you spend some time here? This is an ideal week-long stay in Mérida, one that is designed to let you get a feel for the place, the people and the options available to you, should you decide to live in this splendid city!

"The cultural scene in Mérida is top notch! The soul must be fed and Mérida serves up a stellar menu of arts, dance, symphony, jazz, recitals, poetry readings, theatre, cinema, markets, parks, fairs, and bazaars. The government and local residents patronize the arts. Culture is important and art galleries are flourishing. Every night of the week there is something 'happening' in Mérida. Street dances or singing, art openings, wine tasting, music recitals, poetry readings, discussion groups, professional baseball and soccer games, annual festivals, color and fun. ... In the year 2000, Mérida was named the first American Capital of Culture," Mitch Keenan, proprietor, Mexico International

For most of the 20th century, Mérida was the gateway to the Maya World; this was the city that was served by Pan Am World Airways. It has hosted everyone from Katherine Hepburn to the Duke and Duchess of Windsor. Cancún changed all that, for the better or worse depends on your perspective. But the wonderful things that made Mérida a treasure then still makes Mérida an exceptional cultural Mecca today. It is, in essence, quite possible to spend a week in this city and be fascinated by the wealth of activities and day-trips available.

Seven Days in Mérida

Day 1: Upon arrival, it's time to get your bearings and enjoy the city for the cultural treasure that it is. Start by going to the Main Square, also known as the Zócalo. This is the heart of the colonial city, flanked by the oldest cathedral built on the mainland of the American continent and the **Casa Montejo**, the grand architectural gem that was the city's founder's home. The Cathedral (**Catedral de San Ildefonso**) was begun in 1561 and completed in 1598. It celebrated its 450th anniversary in

2011, and an exhaustive narrative of the cathedral's history was published to commemorate this milestone. *Mérida: Biografía de Una Catedral*, written by Miguel Bretos, is the authoritative book on the cathedral. One of the more interesting facts about the cathedral is the crucifix, known as the Cristo de la Unidad (Christ of Unity), which symbolized the reconciliation between Christians and the Maya. Throughout much of of Latin America, rather than focusing on the negative aspects of the encounters between the peoples of the Old and New worlds—How can blame be assigned to a value-neutral fact that, centuries before science discovered the existence of germs and bacteria, were the culprits in the massive loss of life throughout the continent in the first century following contact between the peoples of the Old World and the New World? As a result, there is a consensus on the *positive* aspect: the arrival of Europeans brought Christianity to the New World and the promise of everlasting life to First Peoples of the Western Hemisphere. Make of that what you will, but this is how the social contract works in Latin America for the most part.

Of Mérida's cathedral, the noted architectural historian Richard Perry writes, "During the infamous *noche triste* of September 24, 1915, an anticlerical mob inflamed by misplaced revolutionary zeal burst into Mérida cathedral and set about destroying its priceless contents. These included the gilded 18th century main altarpiece, which, along with several other side altars, was ripped from its supports in the cathedral apse, stripped of its gold leaf, crudely dismembered, then carried out into the street and burned. Only a few decorative fragments survived the destruction, notably a pair of beautifully crafted relief panels from one retablo illustrating scenes from the Nativity of Christ. Both panels, carved from mahogany and painted in exquisite *estofado* style, have been recently restored. One of these panels, showing the **Adoration of the Shepherds**, is currently displayed in the **Mérida City Museum**, located just beside the Cathedral. The second relief, shown above and now in the collection of the museum at **Dzibilchaltún**, illustrates the **Adoration of the Magi**, rendered as an affecting folk tableau. The Holy Family is shown facing the richly costumed Three Kings. The figures are simply but sympathically portrayed against a minimal but conventional classical background. Note the folkloric touch of the heads of the ox and ass, poking out between columns reminiscent of the cathedral portals."

It is a breathtaking structure; it rivals the grandest cathedrals of Europe.

As for Casa Montejo, Richard Perry describes it as, "the finest civil example of the Spanish Plateresque style in Mexico or indeed in the New World." He then elaborates: "The lower facade surrounding the doorway is outlined in elegant Renaissance fashion, with fluted columns, classical entablatures and coffered paneling. The inner panels are neatly carved with grotesques, and enlivened with inscribed plaques and medallions enclosing sculpted heads. The two large flanking

15

busts above the doorway are traditionally thought to be portraits of the Adelantado Montejo and his wife. Atop this decorous scheme, however, a frieze of horned cherubs and grotesque animal heads strikes a jarring note, and above the doorway, a bowed figure wearing sheepskins holds up the corbelled second floor balcony, which sets the fantastical tone of the upper tier. While contemporary with or later than the lower facade, the more sculptural upper tier nevertheless harks back to the medieval and Moorish antecedents of the Plateresque, and although the stonecarving is less accomplished, it holds greater sculptural and textural interest. A large shield of the Montejo coat of arms stands above the window surmounted by an armorial helmet upon which an eagle is perched, signifying the heroic nobility of the owner. The escutcheon is set against a stone tapestry of stylized floral motifs hung with rattle-like fruits. Giant figures of Spanish halberdiers flank the entire upper level, their feet resting upon the heads of the vanquished - popularly thought to be Mayan Indians but more likely demonic heads in the European tradition." (Please note that Richard Perry has written a wonderful book on the colonial architecture of the Yucatán, *Maya Missions*, and it is well worth getting a copy.)

In 2011, the building, owned by Banamex, was restored and opened as a museum. It is a must visit, especially since one sees the grandeur and proportion of the architectural style and the integrity of the building. Known as the **Casa de Cultura Banamex**, the building is open to the public and showcases rotating and permanent exhibitions that are lovingly curated by the staff. One of the more engaging aspects of the Casa Montejo is that their gift store highlights the artisanal handicrafts of Maya who participate in the Fundación de Haciendas en el Mundo Maya, A.C., a nonprofit organization dedicated to nurturing artisanal excellence in craftsmanship and bringing these works to the market. Website: *www.museocasamontejo.com*.

The other building of note is the **Governor's Palace**, which is the seat of State Government and is open to the public during normal business hours. The current building was constructed in 1892 on the site of the former palace of colonial governors. The grand building is characterized by murals painted by Fernando Castro Pacheco. Completed in 1978, the artwork depicts the history of Yucatán. The murals begin with two grand paintings titled *Social Evolution of Man in Yucatán*, which are based on the Maya teachings found in the Chilam Balam, the book of their sacred myths. These works depict prophesies that a race of mankind would arrive from the east and conquer their land. As you climb the grand staircase, there grand murals representing the Maya cosmology. Each of the four cardinal points are associated with a specific color and myths. According to the Maya, the gods made several versions of mankind, none of which were entirely satisfactory, until the present race of humanity: *We are made of corn, which is nurturing, and in our ability to love and create culture, we are pleasing to the gods.*

16

The second floor is graced by additional murals depicting the history of Yucatán from the colonial period to the mid-twentieth century. To the credit of the people of Yucatán, the paintings accurately depict shameful periods of history, such as *Guerra de Castas*, which tells the tragedy of the War of the Castes (Maya versus European) during the second half of the 19th century, and *Venta de Indios*, a brief time when European colonial elites sold the Maya as slaves to Cuban slave traders, beginning in 1849. These murals, housed in the History Room, looks over the Main Square, and it is a magnificent vantage point from which to contemplate the street life below.

If you cross the street towards the Cathedral, you will notice a glass-enclosed atrium on the south side that has public art. This is the new gateway to the **Museo de Arte Contemporáneo**, known as the MACAY. It is housed in the building originally constructed as the residence of the Archbishop. It has been repurposed as a contemporary museum showcasing both a permanent exhibition of noted local artists as well as revolving exhibitions of contemporary art. Website: *www.macay.org*.

With these three magnificent structures and the MACAY museum viewed, you are ready to take in Mérida's city life. Walking north 60th Street you will encounter the **Church of the Third Order** (also known as the **Iglesia de Jesús**), the small park with a statue to Motherhood, and the beautiful Opera House, the **Teatro Peón Contreras**. Opposite the opera house is the main campus of the **Universidad Autónoma de Yucatán**, known as **UADY**. The Teatro Peón Contreras was built between 1900 and 1908 and reflects the craze for all things Italian during that decade. Its main staircase is of Carrara marble, and there are frescoes by Italian artists who were invited to decorate the interior of the building. The theater has an active schedule, hosting symphonies, dramatic recitals, operas, and musicals. It is also the venue for public events, from graduation ceremonies to political ceremonies. It is always a good idea to check out the schedule, since local and state governments take an active role in promoting culture. It's not unusual to find performances ranging from the Prague symphony to Cuba's National Ballet throughout the year. The programming is exceptional and the ticket prices are government-subsidized.

A break might be in order. Be aware that, as is the case the world over, where tourists stroll, tourist traps abound. Fortunately, there are a few recommendations on places to eat, or have coffee, depending on your mood. For coffee, try **Café Pop** (Calle 57 #501, between Calle 60 and 62 Street) for breakfast and lunch. For a charming break, order up something while seated in the interior garden of the **Hotel Casa del Balam** (on the corner of Calle 60 and Calle 57, just across the street from the Teatro Peón Contreras) which serves breakfast or lunch. If you want a more extensive lunch, or supper, there are three recommendations. **La Chaya**, serving Yucatecan food (on the corner of the Calle 62 and Calle 57 and also on Calle 55 between Calle 60 and 62 Street);

17

Restaurante Bar Amaro, which boasts and extensive vegetarian menu (located on Calle 59 #507, between Calle 60 and 62 Street); and **Pancho's**, which serves the kind of Mexican food most foreigners associate with Mexico (located on Calle 59 #509, between Calle 60 and 62 Street). If all you want something refreshing, right on the north side of the Main Square is **Sorbetería Colón**, which has sorbets and sweets. It is consistently written up in publications such as *Food & Wine* and *Travel & Leisure* (located on Calle 62 #500, under the arches just west of the Governor's Palace).

To continue getting these "must see" sights out of the way, you can continue walking north along Calle 60 until you reach Calle 47, then head east to **Paseo de Montejo**. Or you can take a taxi straight to the Museum of Anthropology on Paseo de Montejo.

The **Museo Regional de Antropología e Historia** is housed in the massive Palacio Cantón, which took two years to build (1909-1911). The home of General Francisco Cantón Rosado (1833-1917), the house is testament to the wealth that flowed through Yucatán during the last decades of the 19th century and the beginning of the 20th century, most of it arising from the sisal (henequen fiber) exports to the world. Today, the museum provides a wonderful introduction to the Maya civilization. The permanent collection is sweeping in scope. Its collections ranges from massive funerary urns and imposing stone monoliths decorated with hieroglyphics to delicate jewelry and items made of jade and obsidian. The displays of ornately-decorated ceramic pottery and history of the Maya calendar are exceptional. The museum includes a vast historical record of the Yucatán's history, from the earliest arrival of the Maya to the region to contemporary Yucatán. There is one period that is remarkably missing: the colonial period. Call it political correctness, or ambivalence, but the museum's extensive holdings on colonial artifacts are stored away from public view and this is the one criticism that can be levied against it.

If your thirst for archaeological wonders has not been sated, then take a cab (or drive) to the **Gran Museo de la Civilización Maya**, adjacent to the Siglo XXI Convention Center. This is the largest museum dedicated to the Maya civilization in Mexico. In the short time it has been opened, it now attracts more visitors than all the other museums in the city. It is also a work in progress because the museum is still assembling its collections and exhibitions. It is housed in a world-class installation that will serve generations of visitors to come. Its Gift Shop has an interesting collection of gift items as well. Afterwards, head back to Mérida proper and enjoy an extended stroll along **Paseo de Montejo**, Mérida's grandest boulevard.

There was a time when Mérida had more millionaires in the world than any other city in the world (1890s and the 1990s) and it was known as the "Paris of the West." The grand mansions that still line the boulevard were built by the landed *hacendados* whose control of the sisal industry—known as the "Green Gold"—brought unimaginable wealth to the region. Many of those fortunes have long been squandered, although there are some Yucatecan families who still live off the fortunes built more than a century ago. Almost all the remaining mansions have been bought by large corporations for their regional offices and many of the gardens were sold off to build smaller "commercial" centers. The slow migration of well-off residents to the northern suburbs that ring the city being what it is, it's a shame that many of the commercial life along the Paseo de Montejo is lacking. What could be a vibrant district of cafes, restaurants, shops, and galleries is a melancholy venue of "For Rent" signs and closed storefronts. Most of the commercial activity is found where Avenida Colón and Avenida Cupules run into Paseo de Montejo, since that's where the **Hyatt**, **Holiday Inn** and **Fiesta Americana** hotels are located. A few blocks further north, the Monument to the Flag is surrounded by a few restaurants of interest. The monument itself was built by Rómulo Rozo, a Colombian immigrant to Mérida.

As you take in this beautiful boulevard, depending on which end you find yourself, and what you are in the mood for, consider the **Hotel Casa San Angel** or the boutique hotel **Rosas & Xocolate** for a drink or meal. If you are at the northern end of the boulevard, **Slavia** or **Cubaro** are recommended restaurants, and so is **Tobago** for coffee or a drink.

Afterwards, it's time to head back to your hotel or B&B. This first day provided a comprehensive understanding of Mérida, its history and it makes one wonder how such a special place has managed to remain so hidden from the world. In the days to come, you will discover many hidden gems!

Day 2: This is the day when you can get the unique cultural institutions out of the way, an opportunity to expand your perspective and take in the rich cultural heritage of the Yucatán peninsula. First stop is **La Quinta Montes Molina**, originally known as Villa Beatriz, located on Paseo de Montejo. The mansion was built by don Aurelio Portuondo y Barceló, a Cuban immigrant to Mérida, during the Porfirio Díaz period (1876-1911). The building, with its lavish furnishings, including Tiffany stained glass windows, has been preserved and this structure is one of the finest examples of the architecture and furnishings of the period. This home is larger than the Frick Museum in New York City! Tours in English are available Monday through Friday at 9 AM, 11 AM and 3 PM Admission is $50 pesos. Website: *www.LaQuintaMM.com*.

Afterwards, hop in a taxi to Barrio Santiago to visit two extraordinary cultural centers. The first is **Casa Catherwood**, which houses a complete set of Frederick Catherwood's original lithographs of the Maya ruins and ceremonial centers published in 1844. Catherwood is the architect and illustrator who, in the first half of the 19th century, accompanied John Lloyd Stephens, author of the best-selling *Incidents of Travel*. If you've traveled this far, you owe it to yourself to take in Catherwood's stunning lithographs, especially if you intend on visiting any of the ruins. To see how the Maya ceremonial centers were when they were discovered in the first half of the 19th century and how much has been restored is an extraordinary comparison. Casa Catherwood itself is the only gallery in Mérida that has been featured in *Hemispheres*, the in-flight magazine of United Airlines and in *the Wall Street Journal*. Address is Calle 59 #572, between Calle 72 and 74 Street, Centro. Admission is $50 pesos. Website: *www.casa-catherwood.com*.

Housed adjacent is **Casa del Chocolate**, Mérida's only cultural and educational center devoted to chocolate! With a wide selection of books on chocolate, as well as artisanal items made from the cacao tree—writing journals made of cacao tree paper, lamps whose shades are made from cacao leaves, and spa products made from cacao butter. There is a Discovery-channel worthy documentary (52 minutes long) that's played in various languages, including Spanish, English, and French. Did you know that the **Ki Xocolatl** brand of chocolates sold at the Casa del Chocolate is the best-selling chocolates sold at the Smithsonian Institution in Washington, D.C.? Well, now you know. Address is Calle 59 #572-A, between Calle 72 and 74, Centro. Admission is free.

This is a great opportunity to explore Santiago, with its charming park and beautiful church. After taking in the area, there is a taxi stand on the corner of Calle 59 and Calle 72, which is very convenient.

You are ready for lunch, and there are wonderful choices available, and with what you've seen at the Quinta Montes Molina, Casa Catherwood and Casa del Chocolate, there will be plenty for engaging conversation. After lunch, do what Yucatecans do after their midday meal: retire to your hotel for a siesta, or spend some time in a pool. This rest will recharge your batteries for the rest of the day, which should begin around 4 PM or 5 PM

Start by treating yourself to some wonderful sorbets at Sorbetería Colón, one is located on the Main Square and the other on Paseo de Montejo. Then make your way to Santa Ana and, inspired by this morning's cultural immersion, head over to **100% Mexico**, housed in the lobby of the Hotel Casa San Angel, located a Paseo de Montejo #1, Remate. This store, which has extraordinary handicrafts from every state in Mexico, is owned by Homa Abhari. You will surely find something extraordinary. The shop also has been extended to include a collection of Pineda Covalin's silk scarves, shawls, purses, and other items. Website: *www.hotelcasasanangel.com*.

Afterwards, walk over to **Tataya Gallery** where Francois Valcke has a shop with a fascinating selection of works by contemporary Mexican artists and artisans, as well as a good number of mid-career Cuban painters. Collectors from New York, Los Angeles, and as far away as London routinely drop by to make purchases, and they are experts of shipping anywhere. Address is Calle 60 #409, between Calle 45 and 47 Street. Website: *www.tataya.com.mx*. The final place to stop is **Casa de las Artesanias**, an initiative of the State of Yucatán that showcases the work of emerging Yucatecan artisans, this shop has a charming selection of regional handicrafts. Address: Paseo de Montejo, between Calle 41 and 43 Street. Website: *www.artesanias.yucatan.gob.mx*. While visiting Tataya Gallery and 100% Mexico, you will have an opportunity to explore Santa Ana, with its elevated square built on the ruins of a Maya elite residential compound, and beautiful church built in 1733.

Now you are ready for dinner, drinks, and, depending on the day of the week, one of the free concerts that take place around town. After the musical concert or dinner (or both), call it a night with cocktails at a lobby bar, or at one of the hip restaurants along Prolongación Montejo and Circuito Colonias. The concierge or host at your hotel or B&B can make recommendations based on your personal preferences.

Day 3: The earlier you get out of town, the better it will be! Yes, it's a day for Indiana Jones meets Chocolate, since today we suggest you visit Uxmal, nearby Maya ceremonial centers, and the Eco-Museo del Cacao. We recommend you return to Mérida by way of two Maya towns, where you will enjoy the small-town charm of the contemporary Maya, and a visit to two beautiful haciendas. After a hearty breakfast head out (or be picked up by a driver) and head towards Uxmal.

The **Ruta Puuc**, or Puuc Route, is a sweeping journey through the Maya heartland, consisting of the sites of Uxmal, Kabah, Sayil, Xlapak, and Labná; the Eco-Museo del Cacao; the underground caverns at Loltún; tours of the Maya towns of Ticul and Oxkutzcab; and, finally, visits to the former haciendas of Ochil and Temozón. Leave Mérida no later than 8 AM and return around 6 PM It's important that you are prepared: comfortable shoes, a hat, sunscreen, water, loose long-sleeved shirts, and insect repellant are necessary. Be sure to tackle Uxmal bright and early, since this will give you an opportunity to enjoy the site before the heat of the day—and busloads of other visitors—arrive.

First stop: **Uxmal**, pronounced "Oosh-mahl," is a World Heritage site, and one of the most majestic ceremonial centers of the Maya civilization. There are books written about Uxmal and you are well-advised to read up on it. Suffice it to say that it became the center for the Puuc region between 850 A.D. and 950 A.D. The most impressive structure is the Pyramid of the Magician which, legend has it, was built in one night. Near this pyramid one finds the Nunnery complex, a vast residential compound believed to have functioned as training facilities for astrologers, priests, and the children of the elite. The Governor's Palace, which occupies five acres, has some of the most compelling mosaic sculpture and arresting representations of the rain god Chaac found anywhere. There are a dozen other structures of note, including ball courts which give a visitor the chance to understand the gradual and natural evolution of Maya architectural scale when this ball court is compared with the one found at Chichén Itzá.

Depending on the time of day, and how much time you spent at Uxmal, one recommendation is to enjoy lemonade, sorbet or a light meal at the Lodge at Uxmal. Part of the Mayaland family of facilities, this lodge serves some of the best meals in the area. If you didn't pack a lunch, then this is your chance to enjoy something light and delicious before continuing onward.

Second stop: **Kabah**, an intimate Maya center, it is best known for the "Palace of the Chaac Masks." The site is noted for its well-preserved *sac-be*, or stone road, that linked it to Uxmal. Other buildings of interest are the House of the Witch, the Temple of the Columns, and the Codz Pop. The slender stone Arch building is believed to be the "gateway" to the *sac-be* leading to Uxmal.

Third stop: **Sayil**, which means, curiously enough, "The Place of Ants." The most compelling sculpture is the stelae located in a thatch-roof building. Sayil is believed to have been at its apogee during the Terminal Classic period (200 A.D. to 1000 A.D.). Take note of the Great Palace which has an 85-meter façade and is built on a two-terraced platform. Archaeological analysis of ceramic remains confirms extensive trade with the southern cities in the Petén region of Guatemala.

Fourth stop: **Xlapak**, a modest site consisting of three partially restored pyramids and about a dozen unexcavated mounds. This site is worth a visit because it gives you a new appreciation for the work archaeologists perform when restoring ruins. The notable features of this site are the beautiful karst limestone used in the facades of the structures. It is believed that, lying in the flat valley suitable for agriculture, some of the structures were elite household compounds, and contained ceremonial centers designed to ensure bountiful harvests.

Fifth stop: **Eco-Museo del Cacao**. This eco-friendly nature park is the gateway to understanding the Maya civilization through chocolate. Who can argue with that? The Eco-Museo del Cacao represents years of hard work to make this working cacao groves and plantings into a world-class eco-museum and educational center devoted to the cacao tree and its role in the life of the Maya—and chocolate lovers around the world today. The brain child of Eddy Van Belle, the Eco-Museo del Cacao opened to the public in July 2011 and it is winning rave reviews from visitors from around the world. One reason is that it is a partnership that includes master chocolatiers from Belgium and Mexico. Dominque Persoone, perhaps the most well-known Master Chocolatier in Belgium, and Yucatán's own adopted son Master Chocolatier Mathieu Brees, are intimately involved in planning the Eco-Museo. Their authoritative expertise is well evident.

After visiting three important Maya ceremonial centers, the Eco-Museo brings the Maya fascination and discovery of chocolate to life. Consisting of several thatched-roof structures, the Eco-Museo tells the story of the Maya, the cacao tree, and the evolution of how chocolate became the delectable delicacy that it is today. Each thatched-roof hut centers on a specific exhibition; they are connected by a winding stone path flanked by tropical foliage and the spices that are used in making chocolate. The first exhibition focuses on the Maya cultivation of cacao and chocolate culture. It shows how chocolate was used in ceremonies, rituals, and daily life. It was considered a sacred ingredient. The second exhibition is a faithful reproduction of a Maya home, including a working outdoors kitchen, an orchid garden, and the indigenous melipona bee. Maya bees have no stingers—hence you won't be stung!—but they play an essential role in the cacao tree's life cycle. The winding path passes a small enclosure with rare animals, turtles, and reptiles of the region. There are also numerous spice plants—cinnamon, all-spice, cardamom, and the vanilla orchid. (If you didn't know that vanilla comes from an orchid, you do now!)

The next thatch-roof hut is a test kitchen. The exhibition explains how many cacao pods are required to make specific quantities of chocolate, the roasting process, and the various ingredients used to make distinct chocolate foods. But the best part is yet to come! Maya artisanal chocolate makers demonstrate how cacao is toasted, peeled, ground several times, and how spices are infused to make a chocolate beverage for you. What would you like in your chocolate? Cinnamon? Cardamom? Coffee? Ask, and one of the chocolate makers will prepare the chocolate to your specifications.

Where else in the world are you going to have a Maya artisanal chocolate maker prepare a chocolate beverage for you?

Afterwards, the last area is a petting-zoo, where the prime attraction is the native white-tail deer, which is a diminutive animal. There is a cafeteria, which has salads, Yucatecan foods, and, of course, lots of chocolate! There is also a play area for children and the opportunity to wander through the cacao groves in a nearby orchard. A hiking area is also in the works and there is also the opportunity for a horseback ride among the grounds (seasonably available, since several months of the year it is too hot for the horses). A final note: Given that this "jungle" eco-park is located in the heart of the Maya tropical forests, it can be very humid, which is why their gift shop only carries a limited supply of items. (Books, cacao-paper products, and other souvenirs wither in the humidity.) In consequence, their entire line of gifts is available in Mérida at the Casa del Chocolate, Calle 59 #572-A, between Calle 72 and 74 Street.

The **Choco-Story Mexico** is one of those treasures that will remain with you for years to come. It relocated to its new location, steps away from the ceremonial center of Uxmal. Website: *http://www.choco-storymexico.com/uxmal/.*

Sixth stop: **Labná** is the next and final archaeological stop. Although it is a small site, Labná is famous for three things. One is its two-story palace, which boasts one of the longs continuous facades, measuring 120 meters, nearly 400 feet, in the Maya world! Another is its grand *sac-be*, which links this center to Uxmal, a testament to the audacity of the Maya to build roads through the tropical forests that have managed to survive for centuries after being abandoned. The third reason for notoriety is the Gateway at Labná, an impressive arch that is a passageway between public areas in this ceremonial center. It was immortalized by Frederick Catherwood in the first half of the 19th century. A lithograph of this Arch, Plate 19 of "Views of Ancient Monuments in Central America, Chiapas & Yucatán," was published in 1844. This image is on view at Casa Catherwood in Mérida, and when you compare your own experience of Labná with the image from 1844, it is spellbinding to appreciate the historical legacy that unites us all across the ages.

Now, you have a choice. You can either back-track your steps, returning to Mérida and stopping at the former Haciendas of Ochil and Temozón, or you can continue forward to the caves of Loltún and the Maya towns of Oxkutzcab and Ticul before heading towards the former haciendas. If you are headed back, you are advised to have a late lunch at either Hacienda Ochil or Hacienda Temozón, since you would be returning to Mérida around 3 or 4 PM, when the city is taking its midday siesta from the heat of the day. If you are moving forging ahead, be sure you have water, since the caves at Loltún are hot.

Seventh stop: **Loltún Caves**, which are among the most extensive cave systems in Mexico, are an amazing natural wonder. One of the most startling things about the Loltún Caves is that there is archaeological evidence of human occupation dating back 10,000 years, which is astounding. Among the more riveting aspects of the Loltún Caves are the paintings, sculptural images, and geometric shapes. There are also "negative" human portraits that are wonderful. What is also fascinating is learning that, apart from primitive tools, the bones of mammoth, bison, and jaguars have been found in the cave. Its continuous importance as a sanctuary for people fleeing turmoil is confirmed by the remains of horses—which were brought over by the Spanish— and literature documenting that these caves were used by the Maya in the 19th century to hide during the War of the Castes, a civil war that raged throughout the peninsula.

Eighth stop: **Oxkutzcab**. From ancient history to the contemporary Maya, indeed! A small town of 22,000 people, Oxkutzcab is known as the "citrus" capital of Yucatán. As you enter the town's main square, you will be astounded to see so many oranges, lemons, mandarins, grapefruit, and other tropical fruits on sale. People from Mérida drive to Oxkutzcab just to load up on citruses, at the town's market: **Mercado de 20 de Noviembre**, facing the **Templo Ex-Convento de San Francisco**. The town dates back to the 1440s, about a century before the arrival of the Spaniards. The city preserves its Maya character, and in fact, the Spaniards recognized it as a regional capital during colonial times. The Xiu family ruled as governors. (Legend has it that the Xius are the descendants of the last royal family to rule over Uxmal.) Today, the town's identity is so closely linked with the Maya love for and skill at agriculture that Oxkutzcab is renowned throughout Mexico for its "Orange Festival," a two-week event that takes place in late October or early November.

Ninth stop: **Ticul**. After enjoying a glass of orange juice in Oxkutzcab, of course, it's time to head out to Ticul, a Maya town near Santa Elena. Ticul's main attractions pay homage to both its Maya and Spanish heritage. On the Spanish side of the town's identity one finds—what else?—a church. The 18th century church has a stunning stained-glass window over an arched doorway. It is in the simple style for which the Franciscans are renowned. The church is adjacent to the monastery built two centuries before the present church. The other attraction is the Galería de Arte Juanita Canche de Manzanero, who was the mother of Armando Manzanero, one of Mexico's most famous crooners and songwriters. The gallery has a lovely collection of photographs and paintings, but its very existence is homage to the Maya people. It should be noted that Ticul is famous for its clay pots and pottery. Most of the red clay planters that you see everywhere in Mérida come from Ticul, and many people for Mérida make day trips to Ticul specifically to shop for pottery—and shoes, since the town boasts a vibrant shoe-making cottage industry. If you are loathe to haul back a red clay pot, you might want to opt for a pair of shoes. How many times will you be able to boast that you have a pair of shoes made by a Maya craftsman from Yucatán?

What time is it? It all depends on how long you've taken on this route. If it's getting late, and you think you may want to have overnight accommodations, we recommend the **Lodge at Uxmal** (*www.mayaland.com*) and the **Flycatcher Inn** (website: *www.flycatcherinn.com*). Either one has terrific rooms at fair prices. A place to eat is **The Pickled Onion**, run by a rather eccentric Brit (Scottish by birth, formerly a long-time Canadian resident) by the name of Valerie Pickles who does more than her fair share to reaffirm the notions most people have about the British. Website: *www.thepickledonionyucatan.com*.

If it is mid-afternoon and you are ready to start heading back, then do so by way of two former haciendas: Ochil and Temozón.

Tenth stop: **Hacienda San Pedro Ochil**. As you head back towards Mérida, follow the signs to the former hacienda San Pedro Ochil. Website: *www.haciendaochil.com*. Hacienda Ochil participates in the Fundación de Haciendas en el Mundo Maya, A.C.'s program to showcase Maya craftsmanship. After you park your car, you can either walk to the hacienda—an easy 5 or 7 minute stroll—or take the ride on the rails. Along the way you will see a series of "shops" that feature Maya artisans and their work. Take a look around. The hacienda itself is known for its restaurant that features Maya and Yucatecan cuisine. On weekends, they have a buffet, which allows you an opportunity to enjoy various Maya delicacies that you would otherwise not have an opportunity to sample. The hacienda itself now boasts an amphitheatre that resembles the open areas known throughout the Mediterranean for plays and performances. Of greater interest is the small museum dedicated the henequen (sisal) industry. It is rather amazing to see the actual machinery (in ruins) that was used at the height of Yucatán's economic notoriety and wealth.

Eleventh stop: **Hacienda Temozón**. This hacienda-turned-boutique-resort is amazing. With Lebanese-inspired floors, hand-carved furnishing and somber paintings, it is like stepping back in time. It boasts a world-class full-service spa. There are 28 rooms and suites—starting at $375 USD! The grounds are manicured. There are walking trails, stone pools, and stables. Hacienda Temozón gives you a glimpse of the spectacular and opulent lives of the Yucatán's wealthy during the Gilded Age—and at the unimaginable wealth generated by the export of sisal. Enjoy a cocktail, or a glass of lemonade—or better year, an ice-cold beer. How exclusive is this place? Consider that it has a heliport, for guests who arrive by helicopter. Website: *www.thehaciendas.com*.

As you head out for the rest of the trip back to Mérida, there will be much to think about on this extraordinary "day trip" that, in many ways, is a trip of a lifetime!

Depending on the time you return to Mérida, and how tired you are, you may be ready for an early evening—or a night on the town. If you are in the mood for a night out, you may want to consider some of the restaurants that are found in Colonia Mexico or along Prolongación Montejo. Your hotel or B&B will be able to offer suggestions.

Day 4: It's another day to get out of town, at least for half the day. Less than an hour south of Mérida you can travel back in time, to the 19th century when large plantations, called haciendas, were economic powerhouses in the Yucatán. The agave cactus, known as *Agave fourcroydes*, was the source of henequen, or sisal, fibers from which twine was spun. At a time before petroleum-based plastics had been invented, twine was used in all manner of products. The henequen industry was so lucrative that Mérida was one of the wealthiest cities in the world during the Edwardian Age. Indeed, Mérida was the ~~first~~ city in Mexico to have electricity!

At the height of production in 1915, more than 1.2 million bales of twine were exported to International Harvester in Chicago, enough to make about 45 million miles of twine. The henequen cactus was the "Green Gold" of the Yucatán. With the introduction of petroleum-based synthetics, however, the henequen industry collapsed within a decade. Abandoned, the haciendas fell into disrepair. It has only been since the late 1980s that they have been restored, often transformed into exclusive boutique hotels and spas.

Hacienda Sotuta de Peón, remarkably, has been resorted as a working hacienda, one that gives visitors an idea of the era when these large plantations were the source of tremendous wealth. Visitors are invited to take the mule-drawn ride along wooden rails on the 382-acre plantation. One can see how the henequen was planted, harvested, and transformed by workers into sisal fiber, ready to be shipped. The equipment is the original, meticulously restored, and each machine is capable of processing 100,000 cactus leaves in an eight-hour shift. The tour begins in the main house. Victorian and Edwardian furniture showcase the conspicuous consumption and opulence of the hacienda owners, who imported much of their furnishings from France, England, and the United States. The high-ceilinged rooms and exquisite tiles are breathtaking. After touring the house, the production facilities are next, where every step in the process of turning henequen cactus into twine rope is explained. (Your hotel or B&B can make arrangements, or you can contact them directly: **Hacienda Sotuta de Peón**, Municipio de Tecoh. Telephone: (999) 941-8639. Email: *info@haciendatour.com*. Website: *www.haciendatour.com*.)

For Americans, this day trip is particularly poignant: Substitute henequen for cotton and the Maya workers for slaves, and you have an arresting idea of what how the plantations in the

American South looked like on the eve of the Civil War! For the modern visitor, Hacienda Sotuta de Peón has a remarkable *cenote*, or natural sink hole, where you can swim, before enjoying a lavish traditional Yucatecan lunch. The *sopa de lima* (a citrusy lime soup with chicken), guacamole, and *poc chuc* (a traditional Maya pork dish), are excellent. The Neapolitan flan is famous throughout the region. The tour concludes with a cool taste of Mexican tequila.

By the time you return to Mérida, it is time for a siesta, rest at your accommodations and a late afternoon swim—or all three. When you are ready for an evening on the town, there is nothing better than checking out the social scene. Depending on the day of the week, there may be a free concert that will get things rolling or perhaps there is something at Peón Contreras. Mérida city government subsidizes most events at the theater and opera. Tickets are unbelievably inexpensive. Then perhaps for dinner, you might want to sample some Yucatecan cuisine—most guidebooks have terrific recommendations—or some of the international cuisines that continue to be consistently good. There are a fair number of very good Argentine, Lebanese, and Italian restaurants.

Day 5: One more day of adventure, but to the shore! Heading west towards the Bay of Campeche (Gulf of Mexico), one finds the Celestún nature reserve, one of the most cherished national parks in Mexico. Home to more than 300 different species of birds, including the pink flamingo, Celestún is an easy drive from Mérida. Once you arrive there at Celestún, crossing the bridge into town, immediately to your left is the tour area where you can hire a boat trip into the estuaries. The trip is reminiscent of similar rides along the Florida Everglades and Florida Keys—exhilarating and astounding in the sheer variety of birds and water fowl one can see. There are sea hawks, herons, eagles, pelicans, mot-mots, and, during the winter months, tens of thousands of migratory birds. And, of course, the flamingo! When birds fly south for the winter, the Yucatán peninsula is the "south" where they winter! Thousands of bird watchers descend on Celestún in January and February each year. The place is remarkably peaceful; the reserve is that expansive.

The **Celestún Biosphere Reserve (Parque Natural del Flamenco Mexicano)**, is a 147,500-acre wetland reserve is unique in that it is both a fresh water and salt water estuary. Fresh water flows up from the underground river systems that run through the limestone landmass. Salt water comes from the Gulf of Mexico. Celestún is also one of the few places in the world where endangered sea turtles come to lay their eggs. There is an active program to protect, rescue, and ensure that the hatchings are released as nature intended.

After the tour, don't miss the opportunity to enjoy the mangroves by navigating through them in a kayak! This is a great adventure, and it is quite something to see fresh water gush from underground success, creating a cool and refreshing place to swim. Several tour operators offer kayaking in Celestún, but one of the more established outfits is **Ecoturismo Yucatán**, owned by the husband-and-wife team of Alfonso Escobedo and Roberta Graham. Their team offers exceptional guides and very knowledgeable staff. Website: *www.ecoyuc.com.mx.*

Is it time for lunch? There are several restaurants along the beach in Celestún town proper. With views of the Bay of Campeche—the waters are a translucent shade of green and almost bathwater warm—seafood is whatever the fisherman brought in that morning. That includes lots of shrimp, octopus, along with the catch of the day.

There is also a wonderful gem nearby: **Ecoparaíso**, a boutique spa resort, located a short drive north. If you head over to the Ecoparaíso, you will enjoy a wonderful meal and drinks in the comfort of an enormous palapa-shaped restaurant. This resort offers full spa services, in case a massage is in order after a busy morning of holding binoculars in your hands—or paddling in your kayak! Website: *www.ecoparaiso.com.* Afterwards, head back to Mérida and arrive in time for—yes, you guessed it—a siesta and rest before taking on the evening.

This is a good time to continue exploring Mérida's colonial past—or its 21st century future. By this we mean, you may want to return to the historic center and meander about, exploring the neighborhoods around Santa Lucía, Santa Ana, Mejorada or Santiago. Each church has its own history, and each neighborhood has its own vibe. If you are curious about contemporary Mérida, this might be an opportune moment to see where the city is gravitating towards: sprawl and high-tech excess. A visit to the **Siglo XXI Convention Center**—adjacent to two shopping malls—will give you an understanding of the ambitious **Museo Maya de Mérida**. This museum, whose construction was filmed by National Geographic for its "Megastructures" cable television show, is one of the anchor projects shifting the city's cultural centers closer to the suburban communities. The **Palacio de la Civilización Maya** opened in 2012 adjacent to the new Museum. Address for both museums: Calle 60 Norte #299-E, Ex-Cordemex, Colonia Revolución. Telephone: (999) 942-1900. It's fascinating to check out the Facebook page for the complex:

http://www.facebook.com/media/set/?set=a.441003493679.229309.277869003679#!/ph oto.php?fbid=441016848679&set=a.441003493679.229309.277869003679&type=3&theater.

And what can be said of the malls? There's one with an ice rink—Galerías de Mérida—where Liverpool, the upscale Mexico City-based department store, is located. The one with Sears and Comercial Mexicana, on the other hand, offers a variety of goods and services for the majority of Mérida's residents. If nothing else, a visit to these malls will give you insights into the lives of contemporary Yucatecan residents.

As for dinner, there are some lovely restaurants along Prolongación Montejo as you head back towards your hotel and B&B, or throughout the Historic Center. Make sure to ask your concierge for recommendations before heading out—either to the historic center or towards the Siglo XXI Convention Center.

Day 6: This is a day for staying in town, or close enough to it. After breakfast, it's time to explore the area in the eastern part of the historic center. Start at the **City Museum,** housed in the former Federal Palace of Post and Telegraphs. The post office and telegraph center were inaugurated in 1908. Address: Calle 56 #529-A, between Calle 65 and 65-A Street. This museum has an extensive collection of artifacts and exhibitions that document the city's history on the ground level. The upper floors house rotating exhibitions of artwork by contemporary Yucatecan artists. The museum is free and open every day, except Monday.

Across the street is the historic central market, one of the largest such markets remaining in Mexico. A virtual labyrinth of stalls and buildings, this is the kind of market that evokes the Maya tradition. After visiting ancient Maya ceremonial centers, it's not difficult to imagine being transported back in time a thousand years when the similar market stalls and vendors—selling honey, fruits, vegetables, spices, meats, textiles, jade, cacao beans, feathers, salt, animals, hides, pottery, and everything else imaginable—were installed at Uxmal or Chichén Itzá. For many visitors it is a revelation to see a market of this size, with Maya vendors going back and forth, Yucateca Maya being spoken nearly as much as Spanish. Others are fascinated by the sheer variety of products—from tomatoes grown in the backyards of small villages near Mérida to butter imported from New Zealand. There is a Municipal Artisanal Market, called **Lucas de Gálvez**, which may be of interest, one block south of the City Museum.

When you are ready, head three blocks north back to Calle 59, then west, walking towards **Mejorada Park**, which is often neglected by most visitors. Mejorada Park is dominated by a large statue honoring the "Niños Héroes," who are remembered for sacrificing themselves protecting Chapultepec Castle in Mexico City during the American military occupation of the nation's capital. There are two museums worth a quick visit. One is the **Yucatán Museum of National Folk Art**, located at Calle 50-A #487 on the corner of Calle 57. This museum houses more than 1,800 pieces of Mexican Folk Art, with an emphasis on folk art from the Yucatán. A visit here is all the more reason to appreciate what the offerings at the Casa de Cultura Banamex and 100% Mexico. The other museum is the **Museum of the Yucatecan Song**, located on Calle 57 #464, corner of Calle 48. Trova is the music more closely associated with the Yucatán and there is a rich history of composers, musicians, and singers from Mérida who have contributed to Mexico's repertoire of music. The museum houses memorabilia from such well-known and renowned artists as Ricardo Palmerin, Guty Cárdenas, Armando Manzanero, Pastor Cervera, and Juan Acereto, among others. If the names don't ring a bell, their music will probably do!

One thing to do—which almost no one does—is walk around the corner and visit the **Architecture School**. Why? Since the school is housed in a former convent, one of the most spectacular colonial buildings in Mérida. The former "Convento de la Mejorada"—located on Calle 50 between Calle 57 and 59 Street—is a work of art, with its magnificent courtyard and the multi-storied structure, which dates back to the early 1600s. Although it is a school, and not technically opened to the public, during regular hours it's possible to stroll in and take a look around. On the third floor is the architectural library which is open to everyone (and a great resource for finding information on specific houses or buildings in town; many expatriates enjoy learning the history of their homes). The **Convento de la Mejorada** served as the principal hospital during the city's early life, where the wounded were tended to after the many and frequent skirmishes between the Spanish and the Maya as the Spanish moved eastward across the peninsula. Indeed, the former military barracks on Calle 59 between Calle 50 and Calle 48 is now a center for children's activities and school programs.

Time for lunch? There are several choices: on the western side of Mejorada Park are two well-established eateries. One is a Spanish restaurant, **Mesón del Segoviano**, and the other is a Yucatecan one, **Los Almendros** (website: *www.restaurantelosalmendros.com.mx*). Another option is lunch at the nearby Hacienda Misné. Take a short taxi ride and you will be amazed that, after driving through nondescript working-class neighborhoods, you enter a compound that is an oasis. The **Hacienda Misné** has an exceptional restaurant, and it is a remarkable spot in the middle of this busy urban center. Website: *www.haciendamisne.com.mx*. Indulge in a leisurely lunch, and then head back for a nap or a rest or an afternoon swim.

Another option to explore is an evening of fine wines and a gourmet meal, there are two places for that. One is **Trotter's**, on Circuito Colonia near Prolongación Montejo or to head down to Santa Lucia and indulge in a great culinary experience at **Apoala**, a contemporary Mexican/Oaxcan restaurant. An entire gastronomic evening, on the other hand, can be making arrangements for dinner at the **Hacienda Teya**, a short drive from the Histor

Renowned for hosting visiting dignitaries, from Queen Sofía of Spain to Secretary of State Hilary Clinton, the Hacienda Teya has an excellent kitchen, and they are authoritative in pairing meals with wines, tequilas and mescals. Go for it, for a memorable evening. Website: *www.haciendateya.com.*

After the open-air cinema, or a culinary adventure with wine—or both, head back for a well-deserved rest after an exceptional day in Mérida.

Day 7: This is a good day to recollect your thoughts over breakfast. Is there something you wanted to buy at the **Eco-Museo del Cacao** and regret no having done so? (The Eco-Museo del Cacao's merchandise is available at the Casa del Chocolate, Calle 59 #572-A, between Calle 72 and 74 Street, Centro.) Have you loaded up on **Ki Xocolatl's** award-winning chocolate? (They have two shops: Downtown at the shops of Santa Lucia, on Calle 60 between Calle 53 and 55 Street; Uptown: Calle 49 #215 by Calle 32, Local 17, Colonia San Antonio Cucul.) Coffee and dessert at **Botella Verde**, next door to Ki Xocolatl, is a grand expat treat. Additionally, their chocolates are available at **Rosas & Xocolatl** on Paseo Montejo—their website is *www.rosasandxocolate.com*—as well as at the **Casa del Chocolate**. Have you had a chance to buy something from an up-and-coming Mexican artist or artisan? (Drop by **Tataya Gallery** and **100% Mexico** for one more tempting visit.) If you're not sure what to take home, consider meandering through the tourist-boutiques on the ground-level shopping center of the **Fiesta Americana**, which has a good number of shops selling sun dresses (*huipiles*), men's *guayabera* shirts, and Mexican silver.

That doesn't mean there isn't a great deal left to do. After a hearty breakfast, it's time for an archaeological adventure—one that's close by. **Dzibilchaltún** is about 12 miles north of Mérida, an easy trip. The name means "writing on the stones"—and there are a lot of carvings! It's a great archaeological site to visit in the morning, wandering around the open spaces, imagining what life must have been like for the approximately 2,000 years it was occupied. It was settled around 500 B.C. it remained inhabited until the arrival of the Europeans around 1540. It is believed that at its height, Dzibilchaltún was home to about 40,000 people, making it one of the largest metropolitan areas in New World. The Temple of the Seven Dolls (also known as the Temple of the Sun) is the center of the site. The temple is characterized by *sac-bés* (white limestone elevated roads) that connected Dzibilchaltún to nearby communities in antiquity.

There is a lovely, modern **Museum of the Maya People** nearby, which tells the history of the Yucatec Maya from their arrival on the peninsula—technically known as the "Northern Maya Lowlands"—to the present time. Much of what is known about the site was a result of the pioneering work of E. Wyllis Andrews. His body of work work is closely linked to the field of Maya studies in this part of the peninsula.

There are two other reasons for visiting Dzibilchaltún. First, it's possible to head to **Xlacah**, which has a wonderful *cenote* (sink hole) for a late morning swim. Second, should you prefer a round of golf, there's the **Yucatán Country Club** nearby, where visitors, who have made reservations, are welcome to play a round of golf. (The Yucatán Country Club is a gated community, and is becoming one of the more exclusive places where foreigners and well-heeled Mexicans from Mexico City and Guadalajara are purchasing retirement homes and investment properties.) Website: *www.yucatancountry.com*.

Regardless of your preferences, taking a swim in a *cenote* or playing a round of golf (or both), it will soon be time for lunch—and perhaps a massage. As you head back towards Mérida, you are advised to have lunch at the **Hacienda Xcanatun**. One of the most beautiful haciendas within a short distance of Mérida, lunch is a wonderful affair. Their spa services are exceptional. It's a good idea to schedule a day beforehand which can be arranged by your hotel or B&B. Website: *www.xcanatun.com*.

By the time all this concludes, it will probably be mid-afternoon, and the Yucatecan ritual of returning for an afternoon rest is in order. This will help solidify your plans for your final evening in town. What will it be? A quiet, simple meal over drinks? An upscale restaurant for a great meal? Perhaps you may want to check out the exuberance of youth that descends on **City Center**, an open air shopping mall—that boasts a number of fine wine bars, and an exceptional coffee house in **Café Punta del Cielo** (City Center Mall, San Ramón Norte, Tel. 999-913-9090.) Or maybe this is the time when you do get those last-minute gifts and prepare for tomorrow's departure.

Departure: Was yesterday really your last day in Mérida? If it was, you might be on the first flight to Houston or Mexico City, or you might be on the last flight out—or free to drive out at your discretion. That means you may have enough time for breakfast, or half a day, or almost an entire day. If you are in town for half a day, then this is a great opportunity to visit some of the areas of town that give you a glimpse into the daily lives of Mérida's people. A visit to the **Parque de la Americas** in Colonia García Ginerés is worthwhile. There is a children's library, a children's playground, and an elementary school nearby, giving you a glimpse into family life in Mérida. The park itself is an Art Deco-inspired tribute to Maya aesthetics and charming. Another area of interest is the new zoo, the **Animaya**. Clever name, right? It's a great zoo, a short taxi ride away. It affords the visitor with an up-close opportunity to interact with Mexican families—their well-behaved and charming children in tow—as they have fun at the zoo. You are bound to walk away with as many photographs of young Maya families as you are of the zoo's residents.

If you are heading out of Mérida south, a stop in **Campeche** is recommended. Its historic center has been faithfully restored and it is a wonderful opportunity to learn about the legacy of pirates—and how pirates raided this fortress city. Campeche is such a gem that it is becoming a "hot" destination for the *uber*-hip. (Did you miss American pop star Katy Perry's tweets from Campeche in the summer 2011?) If you are headed east, towards Cancún, a brief two-hour stop in **Izamal** is recommended before continuing onto the toll highway that will whisk you to the Maya Riviera. A week has passed, and you have only begun to explore—and delight in—Mérida.

A Note on the Weekly Free Concerts Around Town

Mérida city government sponsors concerts every day of the week around town, free of charge. Depending on the days of the week that you are in Mérida, you will be able to enjoy these events.

Monday: Regional dancing in the Main Plaza, known as the "Vaquería Regional," 9 PM

Tuesday: Big Band music of the 1940s in Santiago Park, Calle 59 and Calle 72, 8:30 PM

Wednesday: Musical show at the Olimpo Cultural Center, Main Plaza, 9 PM

Thursday: Yucatecan Serenade at Santa Lucía Park, Calle 60 and Calle 55, 9 PM

Friday: University Campus Serenade, Calle 60 and 57, 9 PM (Note that these concerts conform to the school schedule; please call (999) 923-1198 to confirm.)

Saturday: "Mexican Night," or "Noche Mexicana," at Paseo de Montejo and Calle 47, 8 PM Afterwards there is the "Heart of Mérida" festival, Calle 60 between the Main Plaza and Calle 53, 10 PM

Sunday: "Mérida on Sunday," with street closures and free music concert along the Main Square (Calle 60) to Santa Lucía Park (Calle 55), 9 AM to 9 PM

Not all concerts are created equal, however. **The "Mexican Night" on Saturday and the "Yucatecan Serenade" on Thursday are the best ones.** These are the two concerts that no one should miss. The others are pleasant enough, but not that exceptional. If you have flexibility in your schedule in terms of days of being in town, make sure that you're here for the Thursday and Saturday concerts.

A Warning about "Tourist Guides" in Mérida

The American Business Media publishes an Editorial Code of Ethics. This Code of Ethics states, in part, that: *Editors must make a clear distinction between editorial and advertising. Editors have an obligation to readers to make clear which content has been paid for, which is sponsored and which is independent editorial material. All paid content that may be confused with independent editorial material must be labeled as advertiser-sponsored.*

In Mérida there are three tourist guides. **Yucatán Today**, **Yucatán Living** and **Explore Yucatán**. The first two violate the standard Code of Ethics for the publishing industry.

Yucatán Today (*www.yucatantoday.com*), under the direction of Juanita Stein and Judy Abbot Mier y Terán, operates its tourist guide as a way of promoting the interests of friends and family. Consider that under "International Restaurants" it lists McDonald's. Would that happen to be because McDonald's advertises in their magazine or is it because people fly to Mérida from the world over to taste a Big Mac? Or what can one say about a magazine that omits listing Casa Catherwood, the only gallery in Mérida to be featured in *Hemispheres*, the in-flight magazine of United Airlines, or Casa del Chocolate, which was mentioned in *Departures* magazine published by American Express? Perhaps they are omitted because neither advertises in *Yucatán Today*. Take *Yucatán Today* for what it is: a publication where the editorial content promotes advertisers, without any regard for ethical guidelines separating editorial from advertising.

Yucatán Living (*www.yucatanliving.com*), founded by James Fields and Ellen Fields, also uses its online magazine to advance their commercial interests and those of their friends, without adhering to the ethical guidelines separating Editorial and Advertising. "When I complained to Ellen that they didn't include my company in their article on real estate agencies," Jim Mann reports, "Ellen told me it that was because I didn't have a banner ad on her website. She smiled." Take Yucatán Living for what it is: an online publication where the editorial content promotes advertisers, without any regard for ethical guidelines separating editorial from advertising.

Make of it what you will, but be aware of the controversy surrounding the articles that appear in both **Yucatán Today** and **Yucatán Living**. You are advised to stick to **Explore Yucatán**, which abides by Ethical Guidelines.

For more information on ethical guidelines, please refer to the American Business Media, *www.americanbusinessmedia.com.*

3 THE COLONIAS, OR NEIGHBORHOODS, OF MÉRIDA

By Louis Nevaer

Now that you have given the matter serious thought and have decided to become an expatriate, or are contemplating becoming one, it's time to understand the "lay of the land," so to speak. What are Mérida's neighborhoods like?

Mérida is a city comprised of neighborhoods, called Colonias, which fan out, encircling the Main Square, or Zócalo. On official maps the Main Square is still the "center" of the city, although so much development has taken place north and northeast that, relatively, the Zócalo is no longer in the middle of the city—it's slightly to the south and west. If you ignore residential neighborhoods built, say, after the 1960s, then, yes, the Zócalo would be the bull's eye of the city. It certainly is the heart of the Colonial district, known as the Historic Center, or Centro Histórico.

One reason Mérida has been able to grow into the metropolis that it is, with about one million residents and Los Angeles-style sprawl, is geography. Unlike other colonial cities, such as Oaxaca, Guanajuato, San Miguel, Cuernavaca, and so forth, which were built in plateaus ringed by mountains and ranges, the Yucatán peninsula, a vast limestone land mass, is flat as a pancake. The Yucatán, in fact, is the "sister" peninsula of Florida—another flat-as-a-pancake land mass.

Another reason Mérida is able to sustain growth is its ample water supply. What water supply you ask? If you look at globe, you will see that all the great cities in the world reside near water—by the sea, adjacent to rivers, on lakeshores. People simply need water, and waterways offer means of transportation: One can travel from London to Venice by vessels; one can journey from New York to Buenos Aires by sea. Mexico City once existed as a series of islands in a vast lake, now almost long gone. And Mérida sits atop what is believed to be one of the world's most extensive underground freshwater river systems. All those cenotes, or sink holes, and all those pozos, or wells, offer an almost unlimited supply of freshwater—and all easily accessible throughout the region.

This continues to fuel ever-growing and ever-ambitious developments. New neighborhoods are announced, ground-breaking ceremonies take place, and the city continues its expansion. And this is the way it has always been. How many times have people mentioned how lovely Colonia Itzimná is, with its charming church around the square surrounding by impressive mansions? Well, that was a town, far removed from Mérida, a couple hundred years ago. But somehow, the distance grew shorter as the vacant land between "Mérida" and "Itzimná" was developed. Today Itzimná resides properly within Mérida's city limits, a once-small town happily incorporated as one of the city's neighborhoods.

With this in mind, consider that as the city "proper" grew, so did the neighborhoods. The first was Santiago, built in the 17th century and named after St. James—Santiago is Spanish for James, by the way. It was designed to be self-sufficient. It had a Church, a public park, a market and grand buildings for important residents of the neighborhood. Santa Ana, to the north of the Zócalo was first a 16th century plantation and then established in the 18th century as a "colonia." It was subsequently incorporated into the city proper by official decree.

Unlike other cities which have razed their colonial centers to reinvent themselves in subsequent centuries, the almost limitless supply of vacant land has afforded Mérida the ability to grow without having to tear down what is already there. One result is the absence of high rise buildings, and the other is spread of urban sprawl. Another result is more charming: Mérida boasts the second-largest declared Historic Center in Mexico. Only Mexico City has more colonial buildings! When you consider that Mexico City is more than twenty times as large as Mérida, it says somethingabout this city.

Most expatriates still prefer to find something within the "Centro Histórico," although that definition keeps expanding as Mérida is marketed by realtors. If you want to be technical about it, the "colonial" era ended in 1810, when Mexico declared it independence from Spain, meaning that anything built after 1810 is not "colonial." It can be colonial in design, or ambiance, or style. But it is not a colonial building! (The same is true in the United States—after 1776, America's "colonial" era ended!) Anything built during the Victorian or Edwardian times is definitely not a colonial anything. Most of the grand homes along Calle 59, for example, were built to celebrate Mexico's Centennial celebration of its independence, which was commemorated in 1910! And neighborhoods that, a generation ago no one would have considered "colonial"—such as Paseo de Montejo or Colonia García Ginerés, both of which were considered the height of modernity when they were build in the late 19th and 20th centuries—are now marketed as part of the "Historic Center" filled with grand "colonial" homes.

In broad terms, however, when realtors discuss Mérida, and they speak of the "Historic Center," what they refer to is the series of neighborhoods that immediately radiate from the Main Square, and which are graced with homes that are either from the Colonial period, or were built during the Victorian and Edwardian times. They also refer to areas that are so unlike contemporary suburban living in the United States and Canada that they have an undeniable appeal to American and Canadian buyers, since it excites their imagination about what living in "Mexico" should be, and the kinds of homes in which they envision living.

To understand how these neighborhoods came into existence, it's important to know a few things. Almost every Colonia, or Barrio, within the Historic Center is built around a church. It is each church that is the anchor of the neighborhood, built in the center. There is often a small market adjacent to the church where vendors sell fresh produce and products brought in from neighboring towns and villages. There is often a public gathering place, or playground, across the way. School or government buildings flank the streets around the church. The name of the church is almost always the name of the neighborhood. Santiago is the name of the church in Barrio Santiago. Santa Ana is the name of the church in the Colonia Santa Ana. So it goes. There are no defined boundaries for the "colonias" in city-center, since they were not designed as formal developments past a dozen or so blocks that radiate from the anchoring church.

The Main Square, or Plaza Grande, or Zócalo

When the Spanish arrived, they decided that the abandoned Maya city of T'ho would be an ideal location for their settlement. It was named "Mérida" because the Maya ruins reminded the Spaniards of the Roman ruins that abound in Mérida, Spain. And in the same way that Europeans had long used Roman ruins as ready-cut building blocks for their own buildings—think how much of the abandoned Coliseum in Rome ended up being used to build palazzos and churches in Rome! —the Spaniards set out to use the Maya ruins for their own construction.

The Cathedral of San Idelfonso, for instance, still has Maya carvings on some of the stones visible on its massive walls. The Cathedral, along with the MACAY museum of contemporary art, flank the Zócalo on the eastern side. The Governor's Palace is on the northern side, and moving counter-clockwise, the Olimpio Cultural Center and City Hall, or Ayuntamiento, flank the Zócalo on the western side. Moving along, the Casa de Montejo, where the Conquistador Francisco de Montejo lived, is on the south side. The descendants of the Montejo family still lived there through the mid-1980s, until Banamex, today a subsidiary of Citibank, acquired the massive structure for its regional offices. There are numerous business that also ring the Zócalo, from bookstores to video game parlors, pharmacies to coffee shops.

The main square itself is a massive public gathering area. On any given day one finds protestors mounting a sit-in in front of the Governor's Palace and shoe-shiners buffing clients' boots. Vendors sell elotes—state fair-style corn on the cobs—and balloon vendors add color to

39

the plaza. Children run around after the pigeons and tourists sit reading up on Mérida from their guidebooks under the shades of the imposing laurels that dominate the park. At night, the Zócalo, unfortunately, takes on an unsavory atmosphere, a place where, not unlike the Ramblas in Barcelona, with disreputable elements. This is one reason city government upgraded the Main Square's infrastructure to make it more pedestrian- and family-friendly.

Although the Zócalo is a grand, open plaza today, it bears in mind that for much of its life, it was a gated park. Only Europeans—whites—were allowed to enter. It is also interesting to see how much misinformation there is about the Coat of Arms sculptures that flank the entrance to the Casa de Montejo. Depicted, in carved stones, are two conquistadors, fully attired in their battle outfits, standing on the heads of two Maya individuals. In the sixteenth century, the most effective way of communicating that the Spanish were in charge was to use imagery that was familiar to the defeated Maya.

To our sensibilities this comes across as racist, but in the context of it time, it was, in fact, a culturally-sensitive way of conveying vital information to the civic body. In the monumental architecture and bas-reliefs of the Maya, the conquering rulers where always depicted as standing on the heads of the vanquished. Imagine Churchill depicted in a statue as standing on the head of Hitler, or Bush standing on the head of Gore. That's how the Maya made political points. One of the most riveting examples comes from the reconstructed stelae in Copan, where the Maya rulers are depicted as crushing the heads of the defeated rivals. However unfortunate it may seem to us today, those sculptures on the facades convey the message that, henceforth, the guys in the pointy metal headgear are the ones calling the shots.

The last point to consider is that there are few private residences near the Zócalo today. One of the last remaining homes—a home so grand and massive that it has a working elevator!—is owned by the Rosel family. If you walk half a block south on Calle 62, between 61 and 63 Streets, there is a small shop with the simple sign "Joyeria Rosel." To the side is a small passageway, discreet and unassuming. But if you cross to the other side of the street, and look up, you will see how massive the building is in fact. That entire structure is a private residence, with salon after salon, wide terraces and an open air central plaza. The house has not been restored or updated since electricity was introduced back in the 1910s! And it boasts a series of tunnels, a few of which are believed to be connected to neighboring buildings, and then through passageways to the Cathedral.

Santiago

Barrio de Santiago, one of the most desirable and established Colonias in Mérida, lies five city blocks to the west of the Zócalo. The Church of St. James the Apostle was built in 1637, although it was subsequently damaged during various uprisings. The church that we see today is the one rebuilt in the mid-19th century. It was originally established as a neighborhood where mestizos, people of mixed European and Maya heritage, and the Maya who had business in the city, could live. Mérida, being the "White City," only allowed people who were either European (Spaniards) or their New World-born children (criollos) to spend the night in Mérida proper.

In consequence, Santiago became one of the fastest-growing districts during the 17th century, with artisans, vendors, household help, construction workers, and working-class people resided. Many foreigners who had business dealings with Mérida, but who were not able to afford to live in Mérida proper, opted to live in Santiago. One of the more famous families, the Salazars from Portugal, still have descendants in the neighborhood who own small businesses there. It became a favored shopping area for residents of nearby Colonias of Ermita and San Sebastián, who may not have felt welcome in Mérida proper. Along with Portuguese, the other dominant foreign community was the Germans who arrived in the 19th century, mostly because they supplied machinery to the haciendas, and they introduced pharmaceuticals to the peninsula. The Farmacias Canto chain of pharmacies began when representatives of German manufacturers arrived to expand their sales in Mexico. Around the same time, this was the area where the first Koreans arriving in Mérida lived, before they moved to Colonia Chuminopolis. There is a monument in the northwest corner of the park (across from the Monte de Piedad pawn shop) that commemorates "Chemulpo Street," formerly known as "Calle Incheon," the first community district for Koreans in the Yucatán. Other immigrants last century also have left their mark, and maintained their presence. In the early part of the 20th century, Cuban émigrés settled here, a trend that was accelerated after the Cuban Revolution of 1959. In recent decades, American and Canadian expats have discovered Santiago and it is one of the preferred Colonias in Centro.

With such a curious past, it's no wonder that some of the more noteworthy residents were born, or lived in, Santiago, including Manuel Cepeda, one of the more famous governors, who was in office in the 1860s. He allowed safe passage and gave sanctuary to Americans (and American slaves) fleeing the wreckage of the American Civil War. Other luminaries range the spectrum of life, from composer Guadalupe Trigo to chess Grand Master Carlos Torre Repetto, from Bishop Crescencio Carrillo Ancona to educator Rodolfo Menéndez de la Peña.

A century ago, Calle 59, which runs through Santiago from the Centenario to downtown, was the most fashionable place to live. Many of the grand residences along this boulevard were built between the 1890s and 1910, just in time for Mexico's Centennial. Many of the homes, which were built in the Victorian and Edwardian styles fashionable during the era of Porfirio Díaz, are in the process of being restored. Today Santiago boasts an active little community, with a lively market, filled with cocinas económicas, fresh produce, a section for meats and chicken, and various sellers of everything from tortillas to spices.

There is a small park in front, with a playground for children, and an area that is used for public dances on Tuesday (and skateboarding at all other times!). One legacy of the German presence is the various number of small hardware shops. The Flor de Santiago, one of the oldest cafés in town which itself is an institution, was in fact founded by Cubans, and it is named for Santiago de Cuba! (Yes, there are dozens of Cubans and Cuban-Yucatecan families still in Santiago, and the probably out-number of other foreign residents in the Colonia!)

Across the church, originally opening in 1914 as "La Frontera," was the first "moving pictures establishment" located on the western side of the plaza, and it was adjacent to a hotel, now long-gone. A year later, another movie house, "El Salón," opened on the north side of the plaza. It evolved into the "Apolo," an establishment that specialized in Spanish zarzuela musical theater, and Portuguese operettas. During the Roaring Twenties, it was rechristened as "Cinema Rivoli," and has continued to be a movie house ever since. There are also three large schools in Santiago: Nicolas Bravo, Colegio América, and Primaria Vincente Guerrero.

Cultural Activities of Interest

Bailes Musicales, Big Band orchestra music at Santiago Park, on Calle 72 between Calle 57 and 59 Street, every Tuesday at 8:30 PM. It's a very family-oriented event, and it's wonderful to see older couples dancing cheek-to-cheek to the great sounds of the big band era!

Casa Catherwood, Calle 59 #572, between Calle 72 and 74 Street, exhibits a collection of Catherwood's lithographs of the Maya ruins from 1844 which were originally published in the legendary book *Incidents of Travel*, by John Lloyd Stephens. There is a small shop with showcases crafts from women's cooperatives around the world, from Kenya to Thailand, Madagascar to Haiti. There is also a small café in the courtyard.

Website: *www.casa-catherwood.com*

The Diplomat Mérida, Calle 78 #493-A, between Calle 59 and 59-A Street, has become the city's premier boutique guesthouse. Canadian owners Sara deRuiter and Neil Haapamaki have transformed a colonial place into an inviting refuge, the quintessential Yucatán experience. This place has invigorated Santiago as the Historic Center's most desireable neighborhood.

Website: *www.thediplomatmerida.com*

Santa Ana

Here's some perspective: Santa Ana is older than Jamestown!

The charming church facing Calle 60 at 45 Street dates back to the 16th century, and was subsequently rebuilt in the 1776 after it was destroyed in an uprising. (Is there a theme going on with anti-clericalism in the Yucatán? No comment!) Excluded from Mérida proper, the residents of Santa Ana were Maya, blacks, mulattos (people of European and black parentage), and *chinas cambujas* (people of black and Maya parentage).

The area that today comprises Santa Ana was farmland. It extended from Santa Ana to the north and east. These plantations supplied Mérida with most of its produce. Santa Ana park itself (and where the church is built on the north end) is an elevated platform. The reason for this is simple: it is believed to have been an ancient Maya platform that once supported an important ceremonial center, probably in the 13th and 14th centuries. It was a sizeable community at the end of the Colonial period and it is believed that just over 10% of the Mérida's population lived in the Santa Ana area.

Today, as is the case with Santiago, Santa Ana is a thriving neighborhood. It has a small market filled with fresh produce shops, and other vendors selling condiments. There is a lively set of *cocinas económicas* and a great deal of artisanal businesses. Because Calle 60 is such a busy thoroughfare, and cars headed west on 47 Street are often on their way to Paseo de Montejo, there is less pedestrian activity compared to Santiago. In fact, negotiating the streets can be a bit arduous. Parking is difficult. Santa Ana's proximity to the wealth of architectural structures along Paseo de Montejo further undermines it as a destination in and of itself, which is unfortunate.

Suffice it to say that on the southeast corner of Santa Ana, adjacent to the market and the tourist-shops is a Pemex gas station, which has detracted from the park's appeal. This is a pity, since most people drive by quickly, or simply don't notice, the Centro Cultural Andrés Quintana

Roo, or the Andres Quintana Roo Cultural Center, right on Calle 60, across from the church, which boasts extensive galleries and some rather fine art exhibitions throughout the year.

Santa Ana, which is roughly defined as the area encompassing Calle 60 to the east, Calle 66 to the west, Calle 45 to the north and Calle 55 to the south, retains a slightly bohemian, artistic sensibility. Many of the expatriates who have moved to the area are artistically inclined—painters, photographers, musicians, and writers. The city's impressive Museo de Arqueología is a little more than block from Santa Ana church, draws tens of thousands of visitors to the area. There are always interesting cafés and small galleries popping up along Calle 60 and the adjacent streets. The Casa de los Artistas, owned by the husband-and-wife couple, Abel Vázquez and Melba Medina are accomplished émigrés from central Mexico who have made a wonderful contribution to the artistic community.

Cultural Activities of Interest

Noche Mexicana, or "Mexican Night," this is a free concert of Mexican music, featuring mariachi sounds and ballads from central and northern Mexico, reminiscent of American cowboy and Western music. It is accompanied by street vendors, in a festive atmosphere, at the foot of Paseo de Montejo, between Calle 47 and 49 Street, every Friday at 7 PM.

100% Mexico, a store located in the lobby of the Hotel Casa San Angel, Montejo #1, by Calle 49 in the Remate. This store operates as a franchise of Fonart, Mexico's federal agency that promotes artisanal excellence throughout the entire country. This shop has museum-quality pieces from every state in Mexico. It is quite simply one of the city's most important treasures!

Website: *www.hotelcasasanangel.com*

Galeria Tataya, Calle 60 #460, between Calle 45 and 47 Street, has one of the city's best collections of contemporary Mexican paintings, selected handicrafts from renowned artisans and an extension offering of contemporary works from Cuba.

Website: *www.tataya.com.mx*

Casa de los Artistas, Calle 60 #405, between Calle 43 and 45 Street, is the home, studio and classroom of Abel Vázquez and Melba Medina. They offer art classes, and have an extensive collection of their work for sale.

Website: *www.artistsinmexico.com*

A Note About Santiago and Santa Ana

Santiago and **Santa Ana** comprise the heart of the American expatriate community within the Historic Center.

English speakers call it "Gringo Gulch," and Spanish speakers informally call it "Gringolandia." This is both good and bad.

It is good because it gives a geographic identity to the growing American and Canadian expatriate community.

But it is bad because, as discussed in the chapter on Real Estate, since 2005 Americans have been their own worst enemies, distorting the housing market and creating a bubble the likes of which Mérida has never seen before.

Also, the Mérida English Language Library, which straddles the "border" between Santiago and Santa Ana, lies dead center between these two Colonias drawing still more Americans to the area.

This is either good or bad, depending on your perspective of things!

Following are the other Colonias that comprise the Historic Center.

Santa Lucía

Santa Lucía boasts a special history, one that is invisible to the casual passerby: it is the neighborhood that was populated primarily by Mérida's black community. The Church of Santa Lucía was built as a place of worship for the city's black residents. They were forbidden to set foot in Mérida proper at first, and then, along with the Maya, to spend the night in the city. The courtyard of the church, today covered in cobblestones, was the city's only cemetery for the black community.

Its close proximity to the Main Square, and its rather small geographic area, however, are the two reasons why there are few residences in the Santa Lucia area available. To the west of Calle 60 one finds business and government offices, from Internet cafés to the city's public library, from small hotels and parking lots to the broadcasting offices of radio stations. To the east, similarly, the first two blocks are full of businesses, offices, small hotels, and only then are there a few blocks of residential houses, and most of these are occupied by local families who have lived there for decades, if not generations.

A further impediment to the area, of course, is that the buildings surrounding Santa Lucia Park itself were closed until the fall 2014. City officials worked for various decades to come up with a redevelopment plan, but for a variety of reasons progress was slow. That the Global Recession of 2008 hit many of the smaller business that lined Calle 60 from 47 to 53 Streets has only added to the sense of abandonment one feels along this stretch of Calle 60. Many storefronts were shuttered, and it seems that people briskly walk from past Santa Lucía, which only is active on Sundays, when vendors set up their stalls for "Mérida en Domingo" and Calle 60 is closed off as a pedestrian and bicycle thoroughfare. With the opening of exciting shops and restaurants under the arches of Santa Lucia it is hoped that this renaissance will reverberatet throughout the entire community. And it has! By the time 2015 arrived great restaurants—and Ki' Xocolatl—transformed the entire plaza into a vibrant space. Bravo!

Cultural Activities of Interest

Serenade is an evening of traditional Yucatecan song and dance, featuring the "Jarana" dance and Trova music, with young Maya ladies dressed in elaborate dresses and Maya gentlemen in traditional costumes. The free concert takes place every Thursday, on the corner of 60 and 55 Streets, 9 PM.

Ki' Xocolatl, Calle 60, Portales de Santa Lucia, between Calle 53 and 55 Street, is the city's premier chocolate shop. Owned by the Master Chocolatier, Mathieu Brees, these award-winning chocolates have found a tremendous following around the world. The chocolates, which are the only bean-to-bar chocolates made from cacao beans grown in the Yucatán, are the most popular Mexican chocolates sold at the Smithsonian in Washington, D.C. and at The Chocolate Room in New York. That says it all.

Website: *www.ki-xocolatl.com*

Botella Verde, Calle 60, Portales de Santa Lucia, between Calle 53 and 55 Street, is the "in" spot for the expat community of in the Santa Lucia area. With its provisions and "comfort" lunches, this place has managed to speak to the local community. Robert Klie and his partner Michael Berton are on top of every detail.

Website: *https://www.facebook.com/profile.php?id=100004876939427*

Coqui Coqui, Calle 55 #513, between Calle 62 and 64 Street, this is a world-renowned shop specializing in scents and perfumes. Often profiled by international magazines, and with locations in Valladolid and Tulum, the perfumes created here reflect the bounty of the tropical forests and

Italian techniques in developing fragrances. Beatrice Rugai will be more than happy to assist you. Their telephone is is (999) 923-0216.

Website: *www.coquicoquiperfumes.com*

Artisan & Souvenir Store

Artesanaria offers an exceptional collection of artisanal handicrafts from all over Mexico. The shop is a favorite among many designers who are decorating homes in Mérida. The pottery selection is splendid, and the collection is worthy of several visits. Artesanaria is located at Calle 60 #480, on the corner of Calle 55. Telephone is (999) 252-3736. Hours are: 11 AM to 10:30 PM, daily. Email is *artesanaria@hotmail.com*. Website: *www.artesanaria.com*.

Portales de Santa Lucia

After decades of neglect, Santa Lucia is now a jewel! It has been revitalized into a series of wonderful shops with ample parking in the rear (accessible on Calle 53) and reflects the movement of young, entrepreneurs into the neighborhood, many embarked on exciting ventures. From La Tratto, an Italian-inspired bistro with a Mexican accent to La Recova, Argentine steakhouse and wine bar with a Mexican twist; from Ki Xocolatl to the Tequila Factory Store, the Portales de Santa Lucia is now a "must" destination. In addition, the new Apoala, a contemporary Oaxcan/Mexican restaurant, offers a wonderful menu. These are further complemented by splendid shops selling Mexican crafts.

Many of the young entrepreneurs are from the "interior" of Mexico and they are determined to transform the historic center into a vibrant cultural, culinary, and commercial area fashioned along the lines of Oaxaca City or Puebla. Hector Ruiz de la Vega, of the Tequila Factory Store, is the unofficial "mayor" of these new exciting collections of shops and he is an invaluable resource about Santa Lucía. Indeed, what is most exciting is that many of these shops and restaurants reflect the commitment of young, urban sophisticates in reshaping and reimagining what Mérida's historic center can become: alive with life!

Bienvendios!

Mejorada

To the slight northeast of the Zócalo, running along Calle 59, one enters Colonia Mejorada, anchored by the church located at the intersection of Calle 59 and 50 Street. This church was constructed in 1562, just two decades after the city itself was founded. Why so massive a church so soon after the city's founding?

There are two reasons. First, the Cathedral itself would take decades to build. Second, and more importantly, the Spanish had a mandate to Christianize the Maya. This meant having facilities from which to organize the program of establishing a network of "missions" in every Maya community. At that time, a massive wall was being built around Mérida proper to protect the Spaniards from constant attacks from the Maya. The same year in which construction of the Mejorada church began is also the year when Mérida's first hospital was built across the plaza. The ambivalent nature of Spaniard-Maya relations explains the other structures built in this area: a military fort, or *cuartel*, occupies the entire city block south of the church; and the first Franciscan convent was built adjacent to the church, since nuns were needed to run the hospital, attend to the needs of the Mérida community, and provide administrative support for the Franciscan missionaries.

Many of the first residences in the area were the homes of military officers and high-ranking ecclesiastical authorities, two divergent communities that more often than not were at odds with each other. The political rivalries between the armed forces (state) and the Franciscans missionaries (church) made for an interesting dynamic, particularly in the vast, distant, and resource-poor province of Yucatán. It was the backwater of New Spain. The three conquistadors named Francisco Montejo—Francisco de Montejo "El Adelantado" (father), Francisco de Montejo y León "El Mozo" (the son) and Francisco de Montejo "El Sobrino" (the nephew)—were exasperated by the waves of defections among the early settlers. About the same time that Montejo founded Mérida, Francisco Pizarro arrived in Peru, and in short order news spread of vast gold mines in New Granada (South America).

Scores of settlers, realizing that the Yucatán was mineral-poor, left, hoping to find their fortunes in lands further south. They made their way to San Francisco de Campeche, seeking passage to Havana and from there to New Granada (Cartagena). This weakened the Montejos and it only strengthened the Church in the Yucatán, giving greater prominence to the Colonia Mejorada, since this was the seat from which the early missionary initiatives were launched.

After Mexico's independence, however, the Church's profile diminished, as did the importance of the military in Mérida. The Franciscan convent was relocated elsewhere and the military was moved to the opposite part of town, where the Centenario Park is presently located at Calle 59 and Avenida Itzaes. The former convent was donated to the Universidad Autónoma de Yucatán (UADY) by the State government in 1970 and today it is the campus for the School of Architecture. The school houses a research library where, incidentally, the histories of many of the grand homes around town can be located. The campus is open to the public. Feel free to wander and admire the beautiful building, imagining what it must have been like when they was a convent. The barracks is also a public building today. It houses various educational organizations, the most important of which is dedicated to children's education. The Centro Cultural del Niño Yucateco (CECUNY), or Cultural Center of the Yucatecan Child, is a nationally-recognized educational center that feature classes, workshops, and cultural activities to promote childhood development and encourage "classroom skill sets" to less privileged youngsters.

A few blocks to the north and one block west is a vast area under redevelopment—the Victorian railroad station, one of the grandest ones built in Latin America. Portions of the railroad station have been refurbished and house the Escuela Superior de Artes de Yucatán, or ESAY, and it is expected to become a lively community for the visual arts. The railroad tracks themselves remain littered with trains, engines and railcars, a still unorganized "railroad museum" where it's possible to ask permission from the attendants to wander around. As recently as the mid-1980s, trains left the station at sunset and arrived at Palenque at dawn, all in the frayed comfort of antique Pullmans. It was all more romantic that comfortable.

As for Mejorada Park itself, it is one of the more secluded ones in Mérida. There is a large sculpture honoring Mexico's Niños Heroes de Chapultepec. On the western side of the plaza are two time-honored institutions: Los Almendros, a legendary restaurant specializing in Yucatecan cuisine, and El Segoviano, what many considered to be the best Spanish restaurant in the city. To the north one finds a closed movie house, which dates back to the first half of the 20th century. There are charming buildings on either side, some of which have been recently restored. On the northwest corner is the Museo de Arte Popular, which carries a varied collection of populist handicrafts. On Calle 57 by 48 Street (northeast corner of the plaza) one finds the Museo de la Canción Yucateca, or the Museum of the Yucatecan Song, which honors the trova music of Yucatán and the world renowned Yucatecan musicians, such as Ricardo Palmerín, Guty Cárdenas, Pastor Cervera and Juan Acereto. Both museums are free.

San Juan

Thus far we've discussed the Colonias in the Historic Center that are north of the Zócalo. Now we turn our attention to the ones that lie south of the Zócalo, beginning with San Juan, which is located a few blocks south of the Plaza Grande and a block west. This is one of the older Colonias established once Mérida itself was founded. Its location was rather accidental: it straddles outside the gates that connected Mérida to Campeche.

Campeche was Mérida's lifeline to the rest of New Spain, its link to a seaport where commerce could come and go and where people could more easily find passage to the other two great colonial seaports of New Spain: Veracruz and Havana. The splendid archway was

49

constructed in 1690, an architectural flourish to the growing importance of Mérida as the Spanish stronghold on the peninsula.

It was here, near the entrance that the Maya, who worked as day laborers in Mérida proper, were allowed to live. In time, ecclesiastical authorities built the Church of San Juan Bautista, St. John the Baptist, in 1769. It was an odd church, since it served two very distinct constituencies. Foremost, it served as a welcome to travelers arriving in Mérida and it was also here that an extensive campaign to Christianize the Maya who lived to the south of Mérida in the Puuc hills was carried out. The name of the church reflects the mission to baptize the Maya into the Christian faith. As a curious aside, this is the only church in Mérida that bears the influence of Islamic architecture, since the single long corridor speaks of the Muslim legacy.

In recent years, the Church of San Juan has been refurbished and the park in front of it has been remodeled. It now includes a charming children's playground and the statue—commissioned in Paris and endearingly called "La Negrita," or "the little black lady"—that rests at the center of the fountain is back in place. There are plans to make the streets around the church a pedestrian zone with the focal point being the new statue of Benito Juárez.

Its close proximity to the vast central market—and all the bus routes that ferry people from neighboring communities in and out of Mérida—make it more difficult to carry out plans for a pedestrian thoroughfare, however. Where, city planners wonder, could so many buses be re-routed? Consider that Colonia San Juan is adjacent to the CAME bus station, with buses operating all hours of day and night, making the challenge greater.

But there are civic leaders involved in cultural and urban affairs who want to restore San Juan's history as a center for liberal thinking and European culture. One of the more intriguing historical figures to emerge from this Colonia is Vicente Velasquez, who founded the Sanjuanistas in 1808. Velasquez, who had been educated in Europe, established a salon in the Hermitage of the Church where he taught the liberal ideals of European philosophers such as Montesquieu and Voltaire. When the imperial crisis erupted in Spain, it was the Sanjuanistas who voiced their support for the liberal reforms introduced by the Cortés and pledged their support for the Constitution of 1812. A year later, when the first printing press arrived in Mérida, they were at the forefront of printing political literature championing their cause. It is a legacy of the Sanjuanistas that most of Mérida's newspapers are located in the immediate neighborhoods to the south of the Zócalo.

As a Colonia suitable for residences, most of the buildings surrounding the Church of San Juan Bautista have been converted to commercial spaces and offices. There is a large Pemex gas station located on the northwest section. Through the southern gates, the cobblestone streets are residential—and among the oldest remaining structures—but, until recently, have been deemed less desirable. Most lack ample backyards on which to build additions, pools or other amenities. Only a few enterprising foreigners have ventured to restore homes in this area, if for not other reasons than given their historical importance, there are strict conservation and restoration laws.

San Cristóbal

The Colonias discussed so far reflected the natural evolution of life in Mérida with the Maya, the arrival of the Spaniards, and the introduction of a significant black labor force that was deemed necessary in the 17th and 18th centuries. There is another constituency, however, that has long been overlooked: indigenous peoples, or First Peoples, from other parts of Mexico.

Why? Divide and conquer. The restlessness of the Maya proved a constant challenge to the Spanish. Montejo resolved that the only way to subjugate the Maya was to bring their traditional enemies to Mérida and let the ancient animosities between the Maya and the "Aztecs"—the Maya used the derogatory term "uach," pronounced, "watch" for "foreigners" from the Valley of Mexico.

It proved a strategic move and soon old grudges and rivalries went far in pacifying the Maya. Compared with the conduct of their indigenous peoples from Central Mexico, the Maya found the Spaniards "reasonable." For church authorities, on the other hand, the rivalries only made their task more difficult. It was as if old scores that needed settling took precedence over everything else. The Church of San Cristóbal—Cristóbal means "Christ-bearer"—sought to bring peace to everyone. The Colonia San Cristóbal was constructed beginning in 1757 and it was dedicated to the Virgin of Guadalupe, who appeared on the outskirts of Mexico City. The Virgin of Guadalupe continues to hold special meaning to the indigenous people that Montejo brought from the Valley of Mexico. As if to underscore the need for cooler heads to prevail, the fortress-like church has an inscription over the nave that reads: "This is the House of God and the Gate of Heaven." That's how people in the 18th century said, "Chill out and sit down."

Although the Colonia is surrounded by shabby buildings and the inhabitants of the neighborhood are definitely working-class families, the Church of San Cristóbal looms large in Mérida's life. As the only church dedicated to the Virgin of Guadalupe, it is the center of the city's life every December 12, the Day of the Virgin of Guadalupe. It seems everyone in town pays homage to the Virgin of Guadalupe and one would think that everyone wants to do so by physically visiting this one church. If ever there is any doubt about where the passion of the Mexican people lies, forget soccer, it's the Virgin of Guadalupe!

One native of San Cristóbal of note was Manuel Crescencio Rejón, who worked for greater social justice and whose family was renowned during Mexico's struggle for independence. If the name sounds vaguely familiar, it should: Mérida's international airport is named after him.

At present, the largest expatriate community in San Cristóbal are Europeans—mostly Spanish, Czech and Croatian—and with a certain hipster sensibility. What does this mean? Oh, that their idea of interior design runs more along the lines of graffiti on the walls and Mexican license plates nailed on doorways, and not Talavera tiles in the kitchen. Where Santa Ana affects an artistic flair, the expatriates of San Cristóbal, with their trademark complete abandon, are the kind of people who sweeten their espressos with Xtabentun. (If you are not familiar with this liquor, this is how Gary Regan described it in the San Francisco *Chronicle*: "The producers of d'Aristi Xtabentun say that the drink is based on balche, a magical potion said to have been consumed at ancient Mayan [sic] rituals, though balche was made from water, honey and tree bark, so honey is the only ingredient common to both beverages. Nonetheless, d'Aristi Xtabentun is a fairly stunning liqueur."[1] Yes, the expatriates here reflect a more Eastern European aesthetics, which is in keeping with the more cultish nature of Christian sects favored in the more superstitious areas of Europe. Think of the ambivalence that surrounds lands where the Roman and the Cyrillic alphabets meet, and now you can image a neighborhood where a few Nahuatl (Aztec) words have intermingled with the indigenous Yucatec Maya.

In some ways, San Cristóbal is not unlike the Confederacy in the American South: folks who cling to their liquors and centuries-old grudges, while wrapping themselves in the flag, and vowing allegiance to one patron saint or another, whether it is Robert E. Lee, the Virgin of Guadalupe or the European pursuit of Epicureanism.

San Sebastián and Ermita

In keeping with norms of the time, Francisco Montejo "El Adelantado," gave a vast parcel of land to his son, Francisco Montejo "El Mozo," south of Mérida proper. "El Mozo" proceeded to establish a grand estate, with the church of San Sebastián at the center of it. It was a curious development, simply because of a crushing lack of funds. The constant skirmishes with the Maya and the absence of valuable minerals made public finances a constant battle for Mérida.

It would be more than a century later before the present Church of San Sebastián that we see today was finally constructed. Indeed, it took a concerted political effort to finance the 1706 structure. Only after city officials reluctantly extended certain privileges to the Church. During his

---

[1] See: *www.sfgate.com/cgi-bin/article.cgi?f=/c/a/2007/02/02/WIGK9NRPNI1.DTL#ixzz1ATMeeP72*

lifetime, "El Mozo," one has to bear in mind, was only able to build his estate by availing himself to the poorest of the Maya, many from outlying, desolate places. He resettled them in Colonia San Sebastián, almost as indentured servants, with the hopes that their closer proximity to Mérida would afford them greater economic opportunities. This set the precedent and San Sebastián became known as the "colonia" for the most "desamparados," literally, the most helpless of people. This reputation, throughout the centuries, continued, and seemed a self-fulfilling prophecy: society's most disenfranchised found itself scratching a living in San Sebastián, from destitute Maya in the 17th century to aging foreign never-do-wells in the 21st century who are making their home here.

Attempts to improve the lot of the residents through education, greater integration with the whole of Mérida's society, and recruiting young men for the military did little to reverse the district's reputation. That San Sebastián was the site of the city's first *Rastro Municipal*, or meat-packing district, did little to enhance the area's reputation. Located on the outskirts of Mérida proper, incoming cattle from Campeche was butchered for Mérida's populace, and the sight of vultures circling overhead, which could be seen in the distance from the entire city, was a constant reminder that death was ever-present in San Sebastián. (The *ex-Rastro Municipal* is now a sports complex, with soccer fields and a baseball diamond, adjacent to the Chedraui supermarket, which faces Avenida Itzáes as one travels towards the airport.)

If Montejo established Colonia San Cristóbal for Central Mexican thugs he brought in to keep the Maya in line, then the nearby Colonia of San Sebastián is the place, long known as the "Barrio Bravo," for home-grown toughs. In fact, in less dramatic terms, the "gangs of Mérida" of the 20th century resided principally in San Sebastián. During the final years of the Porfirio Díaz dictatorship and throughout much of the Mexican Revolution (1910-1917), the fiercest turf wars took place in San Sebastián. Legendary "guerras de barrios" ("wars for the neighborhoods") and "guerras de esquinas" ("wars for the street corners") left the place the most dangerous Colonia in Mérida. It is said that from sunset to sunrise, not even the police dared venture into San Sebastián.

The cultural influence of the Maya, however, prevailed and violence became an institutionalized pastime. Rules were established, and the "turf" wars among members came to be supervised by referees who enforced a code of conduct. In other words, Mérida's tradition of *boxing as a spectator sport* emerged from the gritty streets of San Sebastián. As Mérida grew wealthy between the 1880s and 1910s, gentlemen indulged the vicarious pursuit of violence by sponsoring boxing matches. It was not unheard of to have lavish dinner parties in the grand houses of Santiago, Santa Ana or Paseo de Montejo that did not include the spectacle of a boxing match. (In the parlors the ladies would amuse themselves with cards, dominoes, and backgammon, while the men smoked cigars, drank liquors, and went outside for whatever entertainment the host had arranged for the evening.)

The other saving grace of Colonia San Sebastián is the Ermita de Santa Isabel Church, on the corner of Calle 77 and 66 Street, which is dedicated to Nuestra Señora del Buen Viaje, or Our Lady of the Good Voyage. As attacks against Campeche by English and Dutch pirates intensified in the late 1600s, people in Mérida grew concerned for their safety. The Ermita de Santa Isabel Church, built in the early 1700s on a small grotto overlooking the Camino Real, was established for voyagers to offer one last prayer before embarking on a trip to Campeche. It was also a place to give thanks for those who had arrived safely. Even today, Yucatecans are fond of saying, "Que llegues con toda felicidad," or "May you arrive with complete joy," to those who are about to embark on a journey.

The area of San Sebastián closest to the Ermita de Santa Isabel is currently in the throes of urban renewal. The church itself has been restored. So has the nearby park. The streets are being rebuilt and the original bricks were re-installed. The expatriates moving into the area are primarily Western Europeans with some Americans. Many intellectuals, artists, and hipsters from Mexico City have discovered the area. So have Spanish immigrants to Yucatán. Occasionally one encounters aging American self-styled "refugees" who fancy themselves being "of the people"— advocating causes as disparate as "ritual" alcoholic enemas (to cleanse your body and mind) or supporting the almost-forgotten Zapatistas rebels. On late afternoons, one can stroll from the Ermita de Santa Isabel up Calle 66 towards San Juan Bautista and it's possible to see the vultures hovering over the intersection of Calle 81 and 70 Street. This is the only Colonia considered dangerous because of the petty street crime and gangs in the area engaged in "turf" battles. It is considered the least desireable area of the Historic Center in which to invest.

The cultural center of the community, however, is **ULE**, located on Calle 64 #560, between Calle 71 and 73 Streets, which is the brainchild of Eugenia Montalván Colón. The Ermita de Santa Isabela and ULE are the two reasons tourists are making the effort to this Colonia. But the neighborhood remains marginal and city officials are working on improving the municipal services and police vigilance in the district.

 Cultural Activities of Interest

ULE Centro Cultural
Calle 64 #506, betweeen 71 and 73 Streets
Telephone: (999) 120-4210

Website: *www.unasletras.com*

Summing up the "Centro Histórico, these are the Colonias that constitute the Historic Center proper. They also represent the principle districts where most expatriates long to find a home. It is also the area where, as is amply discussed in the Real Estate chapter, the basic laws of supply and demand have been undermined by a real estate frenzy and hype. With this caveat, what follows is a description of attractive Colonias that ring the Centro Histórico, where value is still to be found and where more expatriates are discovering splendid residences away from insular world of "Gringo Gulch." These Colonias are all an easy five to fifteen minute drive to the Zócalo and all are widely served by city buses and commuter vans.

Now we turn our attention to the Colonias around the "Centro Histórico."

García Ginerés

There is a consensus that Colonia García Ginerés, with its stately Avenida Colón, is the most gracious of Mérida's neighborhoods. It is also one of the more storied one. For as long as there are records, the entire area that comprises García Ginerés was part of an "Hacienda" known as Dátil y Limón, or Date and Lemon, which was abbreviated as "Datilimón." The earliest known records date back to the 17th century and they identify this vast estate as bordered by the following properties: Tanlum to the north, Santa Catarina to the south, and San Juan Bautista de Xoclam to the east. It fell within the ecclesiastical jurisdiction of Santiago, and the earliest recorded names as proprietors are the Maya family that was recognized by Mérida as head of the indigenous communities in the northwestern outskirts of Mérida proper: Santiago Euan and, after his death in 1762, his widow, Isabel Ku. In due course, the property passed into the hands of the Lorenzo de Lorra, the Majordomo of Rents for the Nun's Convent.

The entrance to the Hacienda was located on the corner of where today Calle 62 runs into 35 Street. For many years the Hospital del Niño stood there; today it is the location of the Civil Registry. During the intervening years, the residence was home to military, political, and religious leaders. Some of the more distinguished names include José Estanisalo del Puerto, a military captain credited with putting down various rebellions. He built his home there in the 1760s, a grand structure named "Nuestra Señora del Loreto." Other luminaries included Manuel Artazo y Barral, who served as Governor (1812-1815); the military leader General Antonio López de Santa Anna, who also served as Governor (1824-1825); and the Bishop José María Guerra y Correa (1834-1863). It was during this time that the Hacienda was called the "Quinta del Obispo," or the

Bishop's Quinta. In time, it was sold to Alvaro Peón de Regil, the Count of Miraflores, in the second half of the 19th century.

The Hacienda entered the modern era when Cosme Angel Villajuana y de la Paz, who had served as mayor of Mérida, purchased it in the 19th century. He renamed the vast estate in honor of his patron saint. The vast stretch of land lay fallow, until Joaquin García Ginerés, a native of Tarragona, Spain purchased it in 1904. He proceeded to develop San Cosme into the first real estate development venture on a modern scale, but encountered resistance. There was skepticism because his first real estate venture had not been as successful as he had hoped: the Colonia Itzimná. (On Calle 17 of Itzimná one can still see some of the buildings he constructed, but which did not convince families to leave Mérida proper for these outskirts so far removed from the Zócalo.) At first, investors were reluctant to share his optimism that a parcel of land, however vast, could prosper, since it was also so far removed from the Plaza Grande.

He was adamant: with the "Colonia" San Cosme, he hoped to have more than enough land at his disposal to build a modern community, one that would rival the Belle Epoque divisions that were being built on the outskirts of major European cities, from Barcelona to Paris. His efforts paid off. The grounds of the vast Hacienda were urbanized with modern boulevards, wide streets, and generous plots to build gracious residences, obliterating all reminders of the Hacienda's agrarian past. (Today, the last remaining vestige of the original property is located on the grounds of the Jenaro Rodríguez Correa School: a well that was used to water the groves of dates and lemon trees.) Joaquin García Ginerés died in March 1915, and later that same year, by official proclamation, the City of Mérida renamed the district in his honor: Colonia García Ginerés.

With such pedigree, it is not surprising to learn that many of the notables of the 20th century who made their way to Mérida spent time in the gracious homes of García Ginerés. At the center is Parque de las Américas, or Park of the Americas, which boasts a stela for each nation in the Western Hemisphere, and Puerto Rico.

The architecture of that park is astounding. The fountain at Parque de las Américas is a singular example of the Maya Revival style pioneered by Frank Lloyd Wright became associated with the Art Deco movement in the mid-twentieth century. This fountain was designed by Manuel Amábilis in 1946 and a comparable example of a similar style is found in the United States in the Federal Building in Balboa Park, San Diego, designed by Richard Requa in 1935. Manuel Amábilis was a famous architect, his international notoriety having been secured when he designed the Mexican Pavilion for the World's Fair in Seville, Spain in 1929. What is also intriguing is that this park was the center of the cultural links between Havana and Mérida before the Cuban Revolution. The royal palms were a gift of the Rotary Club of Havana in the 1950s and the children's library across from the park is dedicated to nineteenth century Cuban liberator José Martí.

The homes that flank the streets adjacent to the park are filled with history. One home, on the corner of Calle 24 and 23 Street, with its Art Nouveau windows, hosted Gloria Swanson when she was in town, as well as Charles Lindbergh, Joan Crawford, Octavio Paz, and Truman Capote. Another house, on the corner of Calle 20 and 17 Street, was built by radio magnate don Perfecto Villamil, who hosted just about everyone interviewed on the radio (as was the custom) when they were in town in the 1930s, 1940s, and 1950s, including Pedro Infante, Dolores del Rio, Diego Rivera, Frida Kahlo, Louise Nevelson, and Gabriel García Márquez. Further afield, the luminaries continue. The house on the corner of Calle 26 and 9 Street hosted Fidel Castro, and two corners away on Calle 26 and 13 Street, that has been a gateway for distinguished intellectuals in the arts and sciences from the world over, everyone from archaeologist Michael Coe to chef Diana Kennedy, from National Geographic's George Stuart to designer Bill Blass, and a list of American and Mexican diplomats, businessmen, and politicians too long to enumerate.

It is possible to become dizzy with excitement at the thought of singular families who have been privileged to share this Colonia with so many distinguished men and women from around the world. But, as is often the case, as families of means have left for more contemporary homes, many of the grand mansions along Avenida Colón and the adjoining streets, have come on the market, many of which are corporate offices, but not a few remain private residences.

Itzimná

Colonia Itzimná was a charming Maya village for centuries, an easy horseback ride from Mérida. Although there are scores of Maya towns and villages in the greater environs of Mérida proper, Itzimná held special importance to the Maya. It was a place of pilgrimage to render homage to Itzimná, the Maya deity who ruled over heaven, day, and night. Often associated with the points of the compass, and the colors associated with these cardinal directions—east, red; north, white; west, black; and south, yellow—it was a logical place for the Spanish missionaries to build a church to carry out their campaign of converting the Maya to Christianity.

In 1572 they constructed a small fortress-like church, and it was dedicated to Archangel Michael, who is viewed as the "field commander" in the Army of God. The Spanish believed that the pantheon of Maya deities were nothing less than Satan's ploy to deceive humanity and that the Spaniards would need to enlist guidance from Archangel Michael if they were to triumph and win over the Maya.

That Itzimná resides northeast of Mérida also made it a coveted town, charming and closer to the Gulf's sea breezes, which offered respite during the sweltering summer months. As a rule, the further south one travels from the Zócalo, the hotter it becomes, and the natural growth of upscale communities has been to expand northward, towards the beaches and the sea breezes. Mérida's more privileged families began to build summer homes in the area. The presence of the missionaries had made the area safe from the threat of Maya attacks and the geography does lend itself to ameliorate the summer heat.

At the end of the 19th century, our illustrious Catalan, Joaquin García Ginerés, envisioned an extensive community with the church of Itzimná at the center, but it was hard to convince investors that people from Mérida would be prepared to live year-round in the *afueras*, or outskirts. What did they mean by this? Simply that there was a reluctance to live *beyond* the newly-installed railroad track! If one had to cross the railroad track, then one was not in a fashionable area.

Many historians credit the success of Colonia García Ginerés to this one simple fact: it resides entirely within the railroad track that then surrounded Mérida, defining "city limits." That was then, of course, and today the gracious, beautiful homes built by Mérida's wealthy are full-time residences and many comfortable homes (and sought-after schools) are found on the streets that flank the church. It is a very fashionable neighborhood, one where a good number of expatriates are finding homes and are building lives just beyond "walking distance" of downtown.

Miguel Alemán

Directly to the southeast of Itzimná one finds Colonia Miguel Alemán—a place virtually empty of American expatriates. Named after Mexican president Miguel Alemán, this Colonia was the first U.S.-style suburb, and it dates back to 1957.

With broad avenues defining the Colonia, Miguel Alemán boasts one of the most tranquil and family-oriented public squares in town. The center of the Colonia is the vast park, Parque Miguel Alemán, which encompasses an entire city block. In the late afternoons, families gather to socialize with the neighborhood's children playing. There are plenty of teenagers on skateboards, inline skaters and hipsters hanging out, often sharing iPods and texting each other surreptitiously while their grandparents look on, pretending not to see how they are flirting. There is an amphitheater, similar to the one found in Colonia García Ginerés, and on weekends high school bands make a ruckus not far from the children's playground. There are vendors selling all manner of foods and families coming in and out of the Sacred Heart of Jesus Church, or Iglesia del Sagrado Corazón de Jesús, which has services every morning and evening.

Over the decades, families have bought adjacent plots and today most of the homes are comfortable, two-level residences with enclosed parking and open-floor layouts, very similar to the layouts one finds in Florida and California, with kitchens opened to dining areas and "Florida" rooms. There is no significant business or commercial district, other than pharmacies, corner stores and a few services (dry cleaning stores, sundries shops and small restaurants). There really is no need, since it is a short drive to major shopping malls and supermarkets.

There is a distinct residential feel to the place and the residents, mostly middle- and upper-middle Yucatecan families like it that way. The park is located on the intersection of Calle 31 and 20 Street. If you go to YouTube.com and search "Miguel Alemán" and "Mérida" you'll find video clips showing teenagers break dancing, skateboarding, and carrying on the way the young and hopeful are inclined to do.

Centenario

To the west of the Centro Histórico lies a vast district that really isn't a "colonia" in and of itself, but an area broadly defined as the "Centenario." It's comprised of sections of primarily working-class colonias of Sambula, San Lorenzo, and Carrillo Ancona. It's called "Centenario" because at the heart is not a church, but a park, formerly the city zoo, which is bound by Calle 65 to the south, Avenida Itzáes to the west, Calle 59 to the north and Calle 84 to the east. It is also called "Centenario" because the buildings that surround the vast park, "Parque de la Paz," were constructed to commemorate Mexico's centennial in 1910. Before the construction that was carried out anticipating Mexico's Centennial, the area was designated as Santa Catarina.

The Hospital O'Horan, which at the time was en par with any other hospital in the world, also contained an asylum for the insane. The penitentiary was world class, and the broad extension of Calle 59 from the Historic Center to Avenida Itzáes marked a new, formal entry to the city. The grand homes that front that street were built in a real estate frenzy as Yucatecans of means vied with one another for a place along that street, knowing that it would be officially inaugurated when Porfirio Díaz came to Mérida for the Centennial celebrations. (When he did arrive, he also inaugurated state-of-the-art facilities, including the Post & Telegraph offices, which today house the Museum of the City; the Nicolas Bravo school on the intersection of Calle 59 and 72 Street; and the State Department of Health, located Calle 72 and 53 Street.) The grand urban expansion program extended the vast area that fell under the ecclesiastical jurisdiction of "Santiago."

Today, when we refer to the Centenario District, we mean the Parque de la Paz, at Avenida Itzáes and Calle 59, to Calle 76, south to Calle 65 and north to Calle 59-A, which runs into Jacinto Canek at Avenida Itzáes. The homes within this area are in a flux, with some rather modest homes where older people live, their children long moved to other, more prosperous parts of town, and where some grand structures have been rebuilt or refurbished. To give you an idea of the kind of homes located in this area, consider the boutique hotel, The Villa, which, up until a few years ago, was a decrepit structure in a state of near collapse. If you peruse the images at *www.villahotelmerida.com*, you'll understand the wealth that Mérida enjoyed during the Edwardian time.

The Centenario district, however, is also remembered for one of the darkest episodes in Mexican history: it is where Henry Lane Wilson, an American ambassador to Mexico spent considerable time, before taking his post in Mexico City. As is well-remembered, Wilson was implicated in the assassination of Mexican president Francisco Madero on February 22, 1913, and many loyalists came to believe that Wilson had conspired with conservative elements in the Yucatán who were against Madero's liberal reforms. The entire matter festered, particularly when Wilson published his memoirs, *Diplomatic Episodes in Mexico, Belgium and Chile* in 1927. In that memoir he alluded to his contacts in Mérida and of his admiration for Mérida. This is the primary reason that, even to the this day, Mérida officials are reluctant to accept overtures from American citizens, or to involve them in any official capacity, simply because of the lingering mistrust of their motives, or how associating with American citizens will be interpreted should some untoward event—a *"gringada"*—result as a consequence of any collaboration with U.S. citizens.

The Centenario area is under a slow, but steady, redevelopment. Electric cables are being buried under ground, new lamp posts are being installed, the Centenario has been repurposed as a family-oriented park, several museums, including the Museum of Natural History, or Museo de Historia Natural, located on Calle 59 #648, between Calle 84 and 84-A Street are at the center of activities. In addition to The Villa, there is another boutique hotel a block east, the Casa de las Columnas (*www.casadelascolumnas.com*) and the tourist-class hotel, the Hotel Residencial (*www.hotelresidencial.com.mx*). Scattered between are homes, some of which have been restored, and many others that are in need of restoration, or have been repurposed into commercial use.

Chuminopolis

Finally, to the east of the Centro Histórico one finds the Colonia of Chuminopolis, which is a working-class and warehouse district. It is also the site of the city's Korean neighborhood. This is a rich background, made more intriguing by the charming history of Chuminopolis, starting with its ridiculous name! What in the world does it mean? The suffix is easy enough; "polis" is Greek for "city," hence "metropolis." But what of "Chumin"? Well, "Chumin" is a nickname for someone named "Domingo," the same way that "Pancho" is a nickname for someone named "Francisco," and "Nacho" is a nickname for someone named "Ignacio." Mexican revolutionary hero and outlaw "Pancho Villa" was really "Francisco Villa," and "Nacho Figueras," the world-famous polo player, who is the model in the Ralph Lauren Polo advertising campaign, is really "Ignacio Figueras."

"Chuminopolis" is the name given to this Colonia by José Domingo Sosa, a wealthy landowner who was very well-respected during the Belle Epoque. Most of Colonia Chuminopolis occupies lands he owned, and as commerce with farming communities to the south increased, so did the expansion of the Colonia, with massive warehouses and transportation offices. The construction of the railroad in the 19th century further fueled activity and not just in shipping, but in the diversity of the communities and immigrants living in the neighborhood. It was officially recognized as a Colonia in 1904, after José Domingo Sosa petitioned city officials.

When it was officially established, the Hacienda of Pat San Pedro Noh was annexed into the Colonia. The Hacienda had been a Franciscan monastery with its renowned House of Christianity, or Casa de la Cristianidad, so named because it lay on the road that led to Valladolid. It was the last place of prayer before missionaries embarked to their missions that stretched from Mérida to the eastern portions of the peninsula. The Franciscans took their tasks seriously, and were very meticulous about prayer. The Hacienda Pat San Pedro Noh boasts several icons associated with missionary work: in each of the small chapels on the property one finds wooden shelves with several illustrations: Christ of the Blisters, Dedications to the Sorrowful Mother, Our Lady of Fatima, Our Lady of Perpetual Help, and Our Lady of Lourdes.

One of the more colorful characters to move into Chuminopolis was Rafael Quintero, an engineer best remembered for paving the major thoroughfares of Mérida proper. He grew rich, and he indulged in one extravagance: Quinta del Olvido, his "Quinta of Oblivion." It's open to conjecture precisely what Quintero intended with such a peculiar name, but in his "quinta" he built a chapel dedicated to Nuestra Señora del Carmen, Our Lady of Mount Carmel, who is associated with the search for inner peace. Historians speculate that the fame and notoriety he received for his work on behalf of Mérida made him weary. Fr. Gabriel of St. Mary Magdalene de' Pazzi, one of the leading authorities on Our Lady of Mount Carmel explains, "Our Lady wants us to resemble her not only in our outward vesture but, far more, in heart and spirit. If we gaze into Mary's soul, we shall see that grace in her has flowered into a spiritual life of incalculable wealth: a life of recollection, prayer, and uninterrupted oblation to God, continual contact, and intimate union with him. Mary's soul is a sanctuary reserved for God alone, where no human creature has ever left its trace, where love and zeal for the glory of God and the salvation of mankind reign supreme." Quintero in his later years became a recluse.

In the meantime, other, more urgent, interests were moving into the neighborhood: German brewers. The first brewery had its origin in this area, and it was José Ponce who launched, in 1869, what would become Cervecería Yucateca. And a notorious Juan Martínez is credited with starting Mérida's first "professional"—however that is defined—house of ill repute in this Colonia. German biermeisters, and Yucatecan recluses, beer drinkers, and pimps were joined by the arrival of another significant foreign community: Koreans.

Koreans were lured to the Yucatán to work the henequen fields and to build the railroad, and today there is a museum dedicated to their presence in the Yucatán. The Korean Museum, located on Calle 65, between Calle 44 and 46 Street, tells the history of their arrival in the peninsula and their contributions to Yucatecan society. In a charming event held the last Sunday of each month, the museum holds a children's hour called "Cuentame un cuento, Jalmoni," or "Tell me a story, grandmother." ("Jalmoni" is Korean for "grandmother.") A Korean grandmother tells Korean stories and recounts legends. On occasion the event is also held at the children's library in Parque de las Américas in Colonia García Ginerés.

 Cultural Activities of Interest

Korean Museum (Museo Coreano)
Calle 65 #397-A, between Calle 44 and 46 Street
Hours: Monday-Friday: 10 AM to 2 PM, and 3 PM to 6 PM
Saturdays: 9 AM to 2 PM
Facebook: *www.facebook.com/pages/Museo-Conmemorativo-de-la-Inmigracion-Coreana-a-Yucatan/153347068015960*

The preceding shares a bit of the history of the more popular Colonias in Mérida. In recent years, however, another number of neighborhoods are becoming destinations for expatriates. Many of these have been "discovered" accidentally. Most of these are on the way to and from the Star Médica medical complex—and medical tourism is a rapidly expanding industry in Mérida!

Be mindful that almost all of these districts were built after 1950 and except for the occasional older structure, these are two-story homes, designed in styles that were fashionable in the 1960s through the 1990s. What they lack in colonial "charm" they more than make up in modern plumbing, family rooms, and two-car garages. Most have small, but well tended gardens, and many have high walls, offering privacy, since they lack room for gardens to separate the sidewalks and the actual residence.

Here is a list of the Colonias, in alphabetical order, which may be worth driving through, and most of these lie northeast of Colonia Miguel Alemán:

Altabrisa	Montecristo
Brisas	Prado Norte
Buenavista	San Antonio Cinta
Chuburná	San Antonio Cucul
Jardines de Mérida	San Esteban
Jardines del Norte	San Lorenzo
La Florida	San Miguel
Los Pinos	Vista Alegre

What's the Story on "Colonia"?

Colonel Who?

Did you hear about the Londoner who visited Mérida, fell in love with the place, but shared with a compatriot her reservations about moving here?

"I'm afraid I'm torn," she said. "This is such a lovely place, but I can't see myself living in a place that's so militaristic!"

"Militaristic," a fellow Briton replied.

"Why, yes, all the neighborhoods are named after colonels!"

She had presumed that "Col. García Ginerés" was named after Colonel García Ginerés, "Col. Itzimná" was named after Colonel Itzimná, and that "Col. Santa Ana" was named after Colonel Santa Ana, and so forth.

In Mérida, "Col." stands for "Colonia," not "colonel," as in a military rank!

An Important Note about Owning Real Estate in Mérida!

If you decide to purchase property in Mexico, take note that Mérida resides almost entirely in what is called a "restricted zone," and foreign citizens will need a trust, known as a Fideicomiso.

Q: Why does Mexico have "restricted zones" when it comes to owning property?

A: Once upon a time Mexico made a mistake that it regrets to this day. That mistake was trusting American immigrants. Back in the first half of the 19th century Mexico, like many other countries throughout the hemisphere, encouraged immigrants, simply because there were vast stretches of land that needed to be settled. It was in this spirit that it welcomed Americans who bought land in the northern areas, a vast landscape known as "Tejas." These American settlers proceeded to establish prosperous enclaves, but, in defiance of Mexican law, they insisted on importing America's "peculiar institution"—slavery.

Mexico, aghast that these renegade immigrants were trafficking in human beings, proceeded to put an end to it. Americans, enraged, then declared their independence from Mexico, creating the Republic of Texas.

From that bitter mistake, Mexico has put strict restrictions on the ability of foreigners to own land outright along the borders and within 50 kilometers of the coastlines. The rationale is to prevent foreigners from conspiring or colluding in the purchase of land along the border or the coastlines for nefarious purposes. Of course, through bank trusts, foreigners can own properties anywhere—from a house in Mérida, or a condo in Cancún—which are protected from expropriation or nationalization through international treaties. The mere existence of these restrictions is a reminder of Mexico's insistence on taking precautions on the potential threat that foreigners pose to the Mexican nation.

With this in mind, it's amazing to see how many Americans are indifferent to Mexican sensibilities and, either out of ignorance or arrogance, proceed to behave as if they were of political consequence in Mexico. **Never forget that, unless and until you become a Mexican citizen, you are a guest of the Mexican nation, and are expected to act accordingly.**

Part II
Mérida's Amenities

4 THE ABCs OF MID

That should be enough history as a general introduction to Mérida for the time being. This chapter is dedicated to answering the most often asked questions about Mérida that newcomers have. The questions range across the board: Why is Mexico so bureaucratic? Where are the non-Catholic churches located? Is there a cooking school I can sign up? Are there other expat communities in town? Why do the addresses in Mérida have the letters "x" and "y" in them? Can you recommend a guidebook for the Yucatán peninsula that includes the Maya Riviera? Where can I sign up for Spanish classes? Is birding all that popular down here as I've heard? Why are the floors described as "pasta"? Is there a source for heirloom tomatoes?

By answering these questions now, you can learn a good deal of general information that will give you insights into the unique and wonderful aspects of living in Mérida. It also will give you a firm background on culture and society, which will help you understand the chapters that follow—chapters that deal with the more mundane realities involved in everything from opening a bank account to how to get the CFE to put your name on the electric bill! Finally, "MID" is used in the title of this chapter because it is the airport code for Mérida—and how your luggage ended up arriving with you!

It's going to be a fun chapter!

Why is Mexico so bureaucratic?

One thing that expatriates moving to Mérida (or Mexico for that matter) for the first time find is ... exasperation! Why in the world is everything so bureaucratic?! Why is everyone always asking for some paper, receipt, document or whatever?! Why do you find yourself walking around with a folder filled with little papers?!

Little papers! *Papelitos!*

It makes you want to scream. Really, it does. But there's a reason to this, and it has nothing to do with sadistic bureaucrats trying to make your life inconvenient. On the contrary, it is designed to make sure that serious matters are handled in a serious way and that, by being handled correctly, there won't be problems down the road. Mexico, unlike the United States—until recently—has always been adamant about "not trusting and always verifying."

You want to change the name on the electric bill over the phone? No way, José. You have to come down and prove that you are who you say you are and that you are authorized to change the name on the electric bill. Unlike the U.S., Mexico is very meticulous about its official documents. It is very demanding with its documentation and extremely thorough about verifying the validity of paperwork presented for official business.

"All those little papers!"

One of the more exasperating things about Mexico for Americans are all pieces of identification required for just about everything—from setting up an account with the power company to opening a checking account. It seems that "official" papers, identifications, passports, and utility receipts are always needed to satisfy requirements for just about anything. This is in stark contrast to the United States where, for instance, in most places all you have to do is call the utility and, over the phone, change billing address or even the name on the account. That's impossible in Mexico, where many transactions require that they be done in person, not over the phone, and with supporting documentation.

Why?

Unlike the U.S. where, for instance, banks sent out pre-approved solicitations for credit cards as if they were confetti on New Year's Eve, Mexico is a place where there are multiple steps, and every step of the way is designed to minimize the possibility of identity theft or fraud. (The research firm of Javelin Strategy reported that identity theft cost American consumers more than $68 billion in 2012.)

The incident of U.S.-style identity theft is almost unheard of in Mexico, but the price is the redundancy built into the system, just to make sure that documentation matches with all the other documentation, but also to make sure that you are who you say you are, and are doing this transaction—whether is setting up a new account with the water company, or transferring a million pesos to a stranger in Nigeria—is being done of your own volition.

But lest you become flustered, it's good to realize that the annoyance is a one-time deal required during the initial set-up of accounts (and for subsequent changes). The benefit is that, once it is done, you have the peace of mind that comes from knowing your business is well protected. You also have confidence that you can expect superior customer service because officials at the bank, tax office, Power Company, and so on, have met you, and they know who you are. In Mexico, it's almost impossible to be just a name associated with an account number— simply because a real human being is the one who sets up every account!

Is there is a list of churches?

The vast majority of people in Mérida are Catholic, including the sizeable Arab Marist community, immigrants from Lebanon. Fewer than 10% are Protestant. Another 6% is estimated to be other Christian denominations. There are a few Yucatecan Jews and practicing Muslims.

Catholic Church

Website:*arquidiocesisde yucatan.com.mx*
Please note that there is an English-language mass on Sundays at 9:15 AM in the Cathedral on the Main Square. *This mass is Christian, not Catholic.*

Baptist

"El Mesías"
Calle 28 by 16 Street
Colonia Morelos Oriente

Berea
Calle 35 Diag. #361, between Calle 46 and 48 Street, Centro

Jesucristo es El Señor
Calle 22 #108, Locals 2 and 3, between Calle 29 and 31 Street
Colonia México

First Baptist Church
Calle 62 #538, between Calle 67 and 69 Street, Centro

Jehovah's Witnesses

Salón del Reino de los Testigos de Jehová
Calle 90 #482-B between Avenida Jacinto Canek and 47 Street
Colonia Inalámbrica.

Methodist

La Rosa de Saron
Calle 62 #300-F, corner of Calle 35
Centro

Evangelical Christian

"Emmanuel"
Calle 112 #425-A, corner of
  Calle 59-H
Colonia Bojórquez

"Príncipe de Paz"
Avenida Itzáes, between Calle 71 and 73 Street, Centro

Centro de Fe "Sinai"
Calle 66-B #889, corner of
  Calle 109-D
Colonia Obrera

Centro Cristiano "La Nueva Jerusalén"
Calle 20 #106, between Calle 23 and 25 Street
Colonia Chuburná

Church of Jesus Christ of Latter-Day Saints

Calle 65 #527, between Calle 70 and 72 Street, Centro

Presbyterian

Shalom
Calle 26 #215 by 27 Street
Colonia García Ginerés

El Verbo de Dios
Calle 20, between Calle 21 and 19 Street
Colonia Chuburná

El Divino Salvador
Calle 66 #520 by 63 Street, Centro

Antioquía
Calle 74 #468, Centro

Episcopal

Saint Mark's Anglican Church
Calle 21 #116, between Calle 58 and 60 Street
Progreso

Where can I take cooking classes?

There are a good number of cooking schools in Mérida, and a fair number of tour operators offer cooking workshops—everything from using chocolate in the kitchen to how to make Mexican and Yucatecan marinades. Here is an alphabetical listing of recommended cooking schools. Bon Appétit!

Cocina + Arte

Calle 20 #99 between Calle 19 and 21 Street, Colonia Itzimná
Telephone: (999) 671-8686
Website: *www.coninarte.edu.mx*

Colegio Gastronómico del Sureste

Avenida Cámara de Comercio
Calle 49 #303, between Calle 46 and 48 Street
Frac. Villas la Hacienda
Website: *www.cgscaribe.com*

Chef Internacional

Calle 24 #210-B, by Circuito Colonias
Colonia Mexico Oriente
Telephone: (999) 938-0018
Website:
www.chefinternacional.com

Culinaria del Sureste

Calle 19 #34, by Calle 1-H
Fracc. Montecristo
Telephone: (999) 948-2681
Website: *www.culinaria.edu.mx*

Are there other Expat Communities in Mérida apart from Americans?

Americans think they are the largest community of expatriates living in Mérida. They are mistaken. There are more Cubans and there are more Lebanese in Mérida than there are Americans. That makes Americans a minority within a minority!

Canadians in Mérida—and Progreso

Canadian expat Mark Arbour is a stellar example of how moving to another country can be a successful venture, especially with enough planning, appreciation of another culture, and the determination to make it work. Here he shares his perspectives on living and working in Mexico, the businesses he and his business partner are running there and what he and his wife think are the ups and downs of expat life in Mexico:

"Do you have any tips for our readers about living in Mexico?

Embrace the culture and don't try to force your values and beliefs on them. Remember you are a visitor to their country. Most important please do not believe all the negative press in North America about how dangerous Mexico is. Yes, Mexico has a drug war happening. It is the Narcos killing Narcos. It is mostly around the US border where the drugs are destined to go to in the first place. I was a RCMP (Royal Canadian Mounted Police) for 12 years. I can tell you that you have a 4 times greater chance being murdered in the US than in Mexico. Use common sense, there are bad places in Canada and the US, if you go to those kind of places you risk a violent crime happening. Mexico is no different."

To contact Mark, email him at: *marka@inversafe.com.mx*

Source: *www.expatinterviews.com/mexico/mark-arbour.html*

If you are interested in reaching out to the other expatriate communities, consider doing so:

Other Expatriate Communities

Catalan Society

Joséph Ligorret Perramon
Director
CASAL CATALÁ
Calle 14 #187, between Calle 23 and 25 Street
Colonia García Ginerés
Telephone: (999) 925-1155
Email:
casaldeyucatan@yahoo.com.mx
Website: www.casaldeyucatan.cat
The Catalan community operates a Catalan-language library, the "Biblioteca L'Alba de Ferran de Ral."

Cuban Society

Pedro Juan de la Portilla Cabrera, President
Asociación de Cubanos Residentes en México "José Martí" A.C.
Website:*cuba-mexico.org*

Centro Cultural José Martí

Avenida Colón and Calle 20 (in Parque de las Americas)

Colonia García Ginerés
Hours: Monday to Friday, 8 AM to 7:30 PM; Saturday, 9 AM to 4 PM
Director: Ana Georgina Várguez Pérez
Email: *ana.varguez@merida.gob.mx*

Centro
Telephone: (999) 927-2403
Francophile Website:
www.quoideneuf-merida.com
Email:
quoideneuf_merida@live.com.mx

French Society

L'Alliance Francaise
Uptown Location:
Calle 23 #117 by Calle 24
Colonia Mexico
Downtown Location
Calle 56 #476, between Calle 55 and 57 Street

Lebanese Society

Centro Social & Deportivo Libanés de Yucatán, A.C.
Calle 1-G, #101, between Calle 14-A and 16 Street
Colonia Mexico Norte
Telephone: (999) 948-0408

How do you make sense of the addresses?

Yes, at first it's odd to see an address that goes something like this, Calle 59 #503 x 64 y 66. In Mérida, the addresses are both addresses and directions. To understand how this nomenclature evolved, you have to go back to language and grade school and the multiplication tables.

In elementary school, kids are taught that 2 x 3 = 6. When read out loud, it's two *times* three *equals* six. In Spanish, it is dos *por* tres *son* seis. But in Spanish, "por" means both "by" and "times" when used to refer to multiplication. This becomes engrained in how we speak throughout our entire lives. So the mystery of Mérida's addresses is now solved. Calle 59 #503 x 64 y 66 is read: "Number 503 on 59th Street, by 64 and 66 streets." The address includes the direction on how to get there!

On a rare occasion, one will see the address "Calle 59 #503 entre 64 y 66," or "Calle 59 #503 ÷ 64 y 66." In these cases "entre" means "between" and the division symbol is read "divided by" the cross streets.

Where are the grocery stores and supermarkets?

Bodega Aurrera (2 locations)
   1. Avenida Itzáes by Calle 90
   2. Calle 86-A, #644-E, between Calle 90 and 92 Street, Colonia Los Reyes
Chedraui (4 locations)

1. Paseo de Montejo, by Monumento a la Bandera
2. Avenida Itzáes at Calle 86-B #544
3. Plaza las Américas and Norte (across from Gran Plaza)
4. Caucel, off square

73

Costco
Calle 60 #220, Fracc. del Norte
ISSTEY
Calle 60 #480 between Calle 49 and 51 Street (Reopened after remodeling but now requires ID cards certifying employment as civil servants)
Mega Comercial Mexicana (2 locations)
1. North Calle 60 and Circuito Colonias
2. Gran Plaza (Ground level)
Mercado Grande (traditional market)
Calle 56 at Calle 65, right downtown
Pacsadeli
Calle 56 #368, between Calle 37 and 39 Street, Centro
Sam's Club

Prolongación Montejo, right before Gran Plaza, on Calle 10 #312
Soriana
Avenida Jacinto Canek, by Calle 12-B #277, Fracc. Yucalpeten
Super AKI
Calle 59 #646, between Calle 82 and 84 Street
Superama
Prolongación Montejo going north, before the Club Campestre, on Calle 30 #500
Wal-Mart (2 locations)
1. Paseo de Montejo and Avenida Pérez Ponce
2. Plaza Dorada (Ground level)

Are there any Good Bakeries?

Wheat doesn't grow in the Yucatán. As a result there is not a strong cultural tradition of fined baked goods. Corn is the carbohydrate of choice, but that said, there are a small number of artisanal bakers working to provide good breads and pastries. These are the best in town, so be sure to become familiar with them.

For an authentic French bakery, head to Escargot or Petit Délice. Even French expats rave about thes places. And Pistache is an excellent choice for fare that is as close to Paris as possible.

Escargot
Calle 58 between Calle 57 and 59 Street, right across from the Congress Hall building
Website:
https://www.facebook.com/pages/Escargot-Panaderia-Francesa/1431551083732544?ref=hl

Petit Délice
Victory Plaza (Avenida García Lavin #352)
Website:
https://www.facebook.com/PetitDeliceMx/timeline?ref=page_internal

Pistache
Paseo de Montejo #470, between Calle 37 and 39 Street
Hours: 8 AM to 10 PM
The owners are French and they have created a wonderful Parisian-style bakery. Their pâte sable is as good as anything in France.

For everyday breads, however, expats who have lived in Mérida for a long time continue to praise the bakery at both Superama and Costco. Here are their addresses:

Superama
Prolongación Montejo going north, before the Club Campestre, on Calle 30 #500

Costco
Calle 60 #220, Fracc. del Norte

Apart from Superama and Costo, here is a chain of the locations of a local bakery that continues to win consistent praise from expatriates: El Retorno. There are four convenient locations.

El Retorno
Calle 67, between Calle 68 and 70 Street
Centro
Telephone: (999) 928-4836

El Retorno Plaza Dorada
Calle 50, between CAlle 15 and 21 Street, Dept. 30
Colonia Miguel Hidalgo
Telephone: (999) 987-1379

El Retorno Oriente
Calle 66, between Calle 6 and 8 Street
Colonia Cortés Sarmiento
Telephone: (999) 929-2829

El Retorno Oficinas
Calle 8, between Calle 63-C and 63-D Street
Colonia Cortés Sarmiento
Telephone: (999) 929-3413

In addition there are two wonderful bakers in Mérida who make artisanal breads: Sofía Burckle and Monique Duval. Sofía Burckle provides bread-making workshops (some of which are designed for parent-child classes, others for adults-only sessions, mentioned on page 98) Monique Duval is active in the Slow Foods Market.

To contact Sofía Burckle, email her at *sofiaburckle@hotmail.com*.

Hipster Tour Guide

Do you know about *Baktún Maya*? Well, you should. Written and compiled by a Yucatecan staff of young people, this hipster guide covers Mérida from the optimism of young people. That's refreshing.

Website: Baktún Maya Magazine: www.baktunmaya.com.mx

Convenience Stores

There are three comprehensive convenience store chains in Mérida: Oxxo, Extra and 7-11. The last one most Americans will recognize. The other two are national chains. Oxxo, which is owned by Coca-Cola, has almost 10,000 stores throughout Mexico. The other, Extra, is smaller, but they are competitive and expanding rapidly throughout Yucatán.

Oxxo's website: www.oxxo.com

Extra's website: www.extra.com.mx

7-11's website: *www.7-eleven.com.mx*

German Deli

There is one terrific German Deli in town that German expats—and just about everyone else—raves about: Rommel.

Rommel: Rincón Alemán

Calle 49, #212 between CAlle 30 and 32nd Street
Colonia San Antonio Cucul
Monday—Friday: 7 AM to 2 PM and 4 PM to 9:30 PM
Saturday: 9 AM to 2 PM
Email: *especialidades@jerommel.de*

German Sausage

Interest in all things German continues to go. Here is the the German Sausage Lady, which garners rave reviews.

The Sausage Lady

Avenida Reforma at Calle 33-D
Colonia Centro
Wednesday—Friday: 9 AM to 5 PM
Facebook:
https://www.facebook.com/pages/The-Sausage-Lady/338830192950784?sk=info&tab=overview

Canadian Restaurant: Caribou

Finally, a restaurant that speaks to the Canadian soul—and in the heart of Mérida. It features that Quebec delicacy: poutine!

Caribou Montreal Smoke House

Prolongacion Montejo and Calle 35
Colonia Centro
Hours: Tuesday-Sunday, 7 PM to 3 AM
Telephone: (999) 944-0295

Best Bars in Town

There are two great bars in town, the kind of laid-back places that have no pretensions, great drinks, and fun crowds.

El Cardenal Cantina

Corner of Calle 70 and 63 Street
Colonia Santiago
Hours: Daily, 1 PM to 11 PM
Telephone: (999) 923-3955
Facebook:
https://www.facebook.com/elcardenalcantina/

La Negrita

Corner of Calle 62 and 49 Street
Colonia Centro
Hours: Daily, Noon to 10 PM
Telephone: (999) 187-7615
Facebook:
*https://www.facebook.com/LaNegri
taMerida/?fref=ts*
Website:
http://www.lanegritacantina.com/

Car Repair Shop

If you don't have a favorite mechanic, then go to Overhaul, which continues to get great reviews.

Overhaul

Calle 10 #341 Bis, between Calle 7 and 7-A Street
Colonia Díaz Ordaz
Telephone: (999) 943-9141

Best Cafés in Town

There are three coffee and breakfast places that have earned remarkable accolades and a warm following.

Orgánico Mérida

Calle 53 #502-D between Calle 60 and 62 Street
Colonia Centro
Facebook:
https://www.facebook.com/profile.
php?id=100008139434074
Telephone: (999) 345-7818

Café Montejo

Calle 55 #584 between Calle 72 and 74 Street
Colonia Centro
Facebook:
*https://www.facebook.com/CafeMo
ntejoMerida/?fref=ts*

Casa Catherwood Spa Boutique

Calle 59 #572 between Calle 72 and 74 Street
Colonia Centro
Facebook:
https://www.facebook.com/pages/C
asa-Catherwood-Spa-boutique-
Restaurante/653407858081298
Telephone: (999) 908-6802

Disabled Visitors

Mérida is at the forefront of providing services to disabled and differently-abled visitors and tourists. "Acompáñame a Sentir," or "Come Feel With me," is a free tour for blind and wheelchair-bound visitors conducted by the city. Departing from the Peón Contreras Theater, it ends at the Government Palace.

Please visit the following website: *http://sefotur.yucatan.gob.mx/noticia/ver/8 5*

Holistic Festival

Colonia Itzimná now has a holistic fair to promote wellness. The Feria Sabia Itzimná brings together various wellness practices and practioners to create a sustainable, natural, and life-affirming community. It is certainly well worth checking out if you're interested in yoga, mediation, massage, organic foods and making like-minded friends. Do note that this fair is primarily Spanish-speaking with a number of French and Italian expats as participating members.

Feria Sabia Itzimná

Calle 21 by Calle 20
Colonia Itzimná
Telephone: (999) 114-2810
Facebook:
https://www.facebook.com/groups/
50142217184

Local Newspapers

There are two local newspapers, *Diario de Yucatán* and *Por Esto!* They are owned by the same extended family. They offer competing social visions and opposing political perspectives. One is more conservative, pro-Catholic and pro-PAN. The other one is more liberal, pro-indigenous rights and pro-PRI.

Diario de Yucatán: *www.yucatan.com.mx*

Por Esto!: *www.poresto.net*

Drinking Water

DO NOT DRINK TAP WATER. Almost everyone in town buys purified water for drinking. It's not that the water is unsafe, but that it's treated and leaves a chlorine aftertaste. The truth of the matter is that there are very few cities in the world where it's perfectly safe to drink the water right out of the faucet. Fortunately, there are plenty of companies that supply purified water. Most peole have 20 liter (5.25 gallon) dispensers in their kitchens and water is found in every supermarket, or routinely delivered by various water companies.

Hipster & Counter-Culture Hangout

There are two hipster hangouts in Mérida. The first is for monied hipsters, a very young and hip crowd, more into artisanal craft brews, tapas, and gourmet foods. The other place is a tattoo and body modification (piercing) establishment for the Modern Primitive in all of us. Both cultivate their respective audiences. Both are frequented by friendly young men and women.

Malta Cerveteca & Gastropub

Calle 1-B #270
Plaza Carillón
Colonia Campestre
Centro
Telephone: (999) 142-9599
Website:
http://www.maltacerveteca.com.mx

Steel & Ink Studio

Corner of Calle 55 & 62 Street
Centro

Website:
https://www.facebook.com/pages/S

teel-and-Ink-Tribal-Gear-Merida-Yucatan/211890018923564

How do I make phone calls?

Dialing a local number in Mexico

Mérida is in the Mexican area code [*Lada*] 999. If you are in 999 and want to call another number in 999 dial just the final seven digits, such as 944-0000.

Exception: to call a local cell phone from a local land line, add 044 to the start of the number, ten digit number, 044-999-260-0591.

It's not usually necessary to dial 044 in front of a local cell phone number when calling it from another local cell phone. In that case you would just dial 999-260-0591.

Dialing long distance within Mexico

To dial a land line outside of your area code in Mexico, prefix the ten digit number with 01.

A Progreso number 969 934-4567 becomes 01 969 934-4567 from elsewhere in Mexico.

To dial a long distance cell phone from a land line, prefix the number with 045 instead of 01.

To dial long distance from cell phone of one area code, to a cell phone of another code, just dial the full ten digit number like 999-260-0591.

Dialing the US and Canada from Mexico

The international access code from Mexico is 00, and the country code for the US is 1 (the same as the long-distance code in the US and Canada).

To dial a US number from Mexico, just add 00-1 to the start. For example, to reach 656-636-0114, dial 00-1-656-636-0114.

The same applies to call any numbers in the "1" country code. An exception: US 800 numbers are dialed differently. US 800 numbers are NOT free from Mexico and you need to alter the area code to make them work.

An 800 number is dialed as 001 880 followed by the number: 800-555-8648 becomes 001-880-555-8648.

For other toll-free numbers, replace the area code 888 with 881, 887 with 882, and 886 with 883.

Dialing other countries from Mexico

To call any other country from Mexico, it's the international access code (00 followed by the country code and the local number.

For many countries like the UK and Australia, first drop the leading zero on the local number.

Dialing Mexico from the US or Canada

To call a Mexican land line from the US or Canada, dial the international access code (011 from those countries), then the country code 52 for Mexico, followed by the Mexican area code [*Lada*] such as 999, then the local number: 011 52 999-944-000.

However, it is different if you are calling a Mexican cell phone number. You add a 1 after the country code and before the area code. Calling a Mexican cell phone from the US is 00 52 1 999 260-0591.

Dialing Mexico from other counties
When calling Mexico from countries outside of North America, the rules are the same: the international access code, then 52 then the area code then the number.
To call a Mexican cell phone you need to insert the 1 after the country code.

By Jane Grimsrud

Are there online resources for expats living in Mérida?

How times change! A few years ago there were scores of blogs by expats living in Mérida. But social media is a fickle thing. Blogs are out and Facebook Groups are in! Here is a list of the most popular Facebook pages, a few blogs, and some websites that are indispensible.

Facebook Groups of Note

Merida Epicure

Run by Patricia Cuadros Westrick, this is the most authoritative Facebook group for foodies. This is one of the most popular Facebook groups about Mérida and visitors can count on daily specials posted every single day by some of the most popular restaurants in town.

https://www.facebook.com/groups/553 753508009166/

Support Your Local Small Business

Run by Jennifer Underhill, this Facebook group helps expats support local business, both Mexican-and expat-owned.

https://www.facebook.com/groups/463 666080430232/

Mérida Antiques Market

This Facebook group is a place for buying and selling antiques as well as being a site for the exchange of useful information about antiques.

https://www.facebook.com/groups/314 365115387568/

Yucatán Association of Gardeners

This Facebook group is a community of gardeners. The group strives to share ideas of what works best for gardeners and their gardens in Yucatán's tropical environment.

https://www.facebook.com/groups/YA Garden/

Arts and Crafts Yucatán Mercado

This Facebook group showcases local artisans, their handicrafts, and fosters a community to promote local artisans to nurture an artisan community in town.

https://www.facebook.com/groups/ArtsandCraftsYucatanMercado/

Yucatán Animal Lovers

This Facebook group is a networking place to try and find homes for animals in the Progreso area.

https://www.facebook.com/groups/180598995379101/

Traveling Around Yucatán

Run by Brent Marsh, this group shares tips and offers advice about wonderful places throughout the Yucatán peninsula.

https://www.facebook.com/groups/297183957143153/

Expats Living in Mexico

This Facebook group is a friendly place where expats, wannabe expats, and former expats can share stories, ask for advice and give advice to support one another. It is for people who truly love Mexico, the culture and the people.

https://www.facebook.com/groups/100321184028/

Canadians Living in Mexico

This Facebook group is for Canadians, friends of Canadians, and other foreigners who live in Mexico who can offer a Canadian perspective about life in Mexico.

https://www.facebook.com/groups/4868463748/

Mérida Food Hunt

This Facebook group offers assistance in locating those hard-to-find grocery and cooking items. A spreadsheet is provided to make it easier to locate specific food items! Happy Hunting!

https://www.facebook.com/groups/284458208396105/

Yucatán Online Garage Sale

Run by Jennifer Underhill, this Facebook group helps expats and residents alike run an online garage sale exchange.

https://www.facebook.com/groups/yucatanonlinegaragesale/

Yucatán Beach Friends

This Facebook group is a forum for all those who are living in one of the many beach communities that dot the Yucatán coast.

https://www.facebook.com/groups/yucatanbeachfriends/

Vegging Out in the Yucatán

This Facebook group is for vegetarians in Mérida, and environs, and designed to foster their lifestyle.

https://www.facebook.com/groups/709235805767099/

Mérida Casitas for Rent and for Sale

Run by Jennifer Underhill, this Facebook group helps expats find homes to rent or buy by bringing people together, commission free.

https://www.facebook.com/groups/284978388304546/

Progreso Post-It

This is the Facebook version of the Welcome Wagon for expats living in the greater Progreso area.

https://www.facebook.com/groups/progresopostit/

Yucatán Literary

This Facebook group requires that you speak Spanish and are interested in literary pursuits. This is a great group to find out what's going on with the local literary scene.

https://www.facebook.com/yucatan.literario?fref=ts

Wholefood Market

This Facebook group offers information on the whole foods market near Progreso.

https://www.facebook.com/groups/704401749638699/

Door 54 Garage Sale Warehouse

Run by Chris Kibler, this Facebook group is a marketplace for the Garage Sale Warehouse located on Calle 54 downtown.

https://www.facebook.com/groups/463791483767226/

Yucatán Vegetariano

A Spanish-language Facebook group for vegetarians and their friends.

https://www.facebook.com/groups/50142217184/

Festival Gastronómico Vegetariano

A Spanish-language Facebook group about the annual Mérida vegetarian festival for everyone.

https://www.facebook.com/festivalvegetarianomerida

Yucatán Yogis, Spirituality, Holistic

A Yucatán gathering place for all things Yoga, organic and natural, spirituality, holistic health and sustainability.

https://www.facebook.com/groups/601811936503731/

Mexico Travel Writers

This Facebook group is networking group of writers, editors, journalists, authors, publishers, bloggers, photogs and those in the travel industry in order to showcase your writing and photos of Mexico travel, culture, and lifestyle.

https://www.facebook.com/groups/324652589443/

Mexico Budget Travel

This Facebook group is for everyone who likes to travel to Mexico on a budget. This group is an ideal forum to exchange information and tips for discounts, specials, and promotions.

https://www.facebook.com/groups/338385549622490/

Blogs and Websites of note in an alphabetical lising

Bicycle Yucatán

www.bicycleyucatan.blogspot.com

Casa Catherwood

www.casa-catherwood.com

Crazy Gone Native

www.ldorton.blogspot.com

Critica y Punto

www.criticaypuntro.wordpress.com

Diario de Yucatán

www.yucatan.com.mx

Explore Magazine

http//yucatan.revistaexplore.com

Galeria Tataya

www.galeriatataya.blogspot.com

Inside Mex

www.insidemex.com

Inspiring Expatritism

www.expatify.com

Instituto de Desarrollo de la Cultura Maya

www.indemaya.gob.mx

Jim Conrad's Naturalist Newsletter

www.backyardnature.net/n/11/110313.htm

Lawsons Yucatán

www.lawsonsyucatan.com

Mérida Hideaway

www.blog.meridahideaway.com

The Mérida Initiative

www.themeridainitiative.blogspot.com

Mexico Bob

www.mexicobob.blogspot.com

Mexico Cooks

www.mexicocooks.typepad.com

Mexico Gulf Reporter

www.mexicogulfreporter.com/

Moving to Mérida

www.movingtomerida.com/

On Mexican Time

www.on-mexican-time.blogspot.com/

The Pickled Onion

www.thepickledonion.com

Primera Lluvia

www.primeralluvia.wordpress.com

Proceso

www.proceso.com.mx

Que Comer en Mérida

www.quecomerenmerida.com

La Revista Peninsular

www.larevista.com.mx

Surviving Yucatán

www.yucalandia.wordpress.com

The Yucatán Times

www.theyucatantimes.com

 ## Do you have a list of recommended travel books on Mérida, the Yucatán and Mexico?

Here is a list of our recommended books. Please note that the description of each book is provided by the publisher.

Moon Yucatán Peninsula (Moon Handbooks)

By Liza Prado, Gary Chandler
Experienced travel writers Liza Prado and Gary Chandler offer up their best advice on Mexico's Yucatán Peninsula, from exploring Mayan ruins and Caribbean beaches to visiting hotspots like Mérida, Cancún, and Playa del Carmen. Prado and Chandler include unique trip ideas for a variety of travelers, such as Pyramids and Palaces, Diving and Snorkeling, and A Family Affair. With essentials on dining, transportation, and accommodations for a range of budgets, Moon Yucatán Peninsula gives travelers the tools they need to create a more personal and memorable experience.

Yucatán Pocket Adventures (New Pocket Adventure)

By Bruce Conord, June Conord
Need information while you're on the go? Tired of guidebooks that don't fit in your pocket? We hear you. If you're visiting for just a week or two, perhaps you don't need the in-depth history section or geographical details that can make a book cumbersome. Check out this brand new series of portable travel guides designed to be used while you're on

the move. Their handy, pocket-sized format means they'll slip into your pocket or fanny pack while you focus on what you came for - whether that's hiking in Belize's rainforest with binoculars in hand, exploring Maya ruins in the Yucatán or taking in historic town sights. Adventures covered are anything from town walking tours and beachcombing to white-water rafting and organized horseback riding excursions. These guides still contain all the practical travel information you need - places to stay and eat, tourist information resources, travel advice and more. The text is filled with interesting factoids, while town and regional maps make planning day-trips or city tours easy. Best of all, these books are affordable. Maps, index

The Rough Guide to Yucatán 2 (Rough Guide Travel Guides)

By Zora O'Neill, Rough Guides

The Rough Guide to Yucatán is bursting with inspirational ideas for your trip to this balmy Caribbean paradise. The guide covers activities for all travelers, from scuba diving at Cancún to exploring the Mayan ruins at Uxmal. There are detailed entries on the must-see attractions, from the wilds of the Sian Ka'an Biosphere Reserve to Chichén Itzá, one of the New Seven Wonders of the World. There are hundreds of up-to-date reviews for accommodation, restaurants, markets and music venues, and plenty of practical tips for adrenalin seekers. With dozens of user-friendly maps, The Rough Guide to Yucatán will guide you through Yucatán's tumultuous history, pre-Colombian cultures, unique environment and diverse wildlife. Make the most of your time with The Rough Guide to Yucatán.

A Tourist In The Yucatán

By James McNay Brumfield

Journey to the sun washed resort of Cancún and follow a young American couple, Jack and Josephine Phillips, on an adventure into the jungles of Mexico's Yucatán Peninsula. Adventure turns to terror when Josephine disappears and Jack finds himself on the run from mysterious assassins, the Mexican Federales, and possibly even his own government. The Phillips have unwittingly become entangled in the Mexican underworld, a complicated web that stretches from the Caribbean coast line of Quintana Roo to the upper reaches of the United States Government. In a land where the line between the law and the outlaw is blurred, can Jack survive long enough to solve the mystery of his wife's disappearance?

Must Sees Cancún + The Yucatán, 1e (Michelin Must Sees Cancún & the Yucatán)

By Michelin

Cancún is a sun-drenched playground of transparent coastal waters, white-sandy beaches, water sports, vast resorts and golf courses, with bars and nightclubs moving to the sounds of salsa and rumba. Away from the hubbub of the town you head inland to the

Mayan relics of the Yucatán, such as mighty Chichén Itzá, offering even the weariest revelers some respite. Sights within must sees Cancún and the Yucatán are grouped according to Michelin's time-honored star-rating system, which for more than 100 years has guided travelers to the best a place has to offer. The Michelin Man symbol represents the top picks for activities, entertainment, where to eat and where to stay.

Lonely Planet Cancún, Cozumel & the Yucatán (Regional Guide)

By Greg Benchwick

Lonely Planet knows Cancún, Cozumel and the Yucatán. This 5th edition helps you build the perfect itinerary, whether it includes visiting ancient Maya ruins, people watching in an open-air café on Mérida's Plaza Grande or heading to Cozumel to dive into the coral gardens of the Great Maya Barrier Reef. Lonely Planet guides are written by experts who get to the heart of every destination they visit. This fully updated edition is packed with accurate, practical and honest advice, designed to give you the information you need to make the most of your trip.

Frommer's Cancún and the Yucatán Day by Day (Frommer's Day by Day - Pocket)

By Joy Hepp

These attractively priced, four-color guides offer dozens of neighborhood and thematic tours, complete with hundreds of photos and bulleted maps that lead the way from sight to sight. Day by Days are the only guides that help travelers organize their time to get the most out of a trip.

- Full-color package at an affordable price
- Star ratings for all hotels, restaurants, and attractions
- Foldout front covers with maps and quick-reference information
- Tear-resistant map in a handy, re-closable plastic wallet
- Handy pocket-sized trim

Mexico (Eyewitness Travel Guides)

By Marlena Spieler

Recognized the world over by frequent flyers and armchair travelers alike, Eyewitness Travel Guides are the most colorful and comprehensive guides on the market. With beautifully commissioned photographs and spectacular 3-D aerial views revealing the charm of each destination, these amazing travel guides show what others only tell. Includes beautiful new full-color photos, illustrations, and enhanced maps, with extensive information on local customs, currency, medical services, and transportation New "Discovering" feature helps decide which regions are best suited to the trip.

Pauline Frommer's Cancún & the Yucatán (Pauline Frommer Guides)

By Christine Delsol

Spend less, see more. This is the philosophy behind Pauline Frommer's guides. Written by travel expert Pauline Frommer (who is also the daughter of Arthur Frommer), and her team of hand-picked writers, these guides show how to truly experience a culture, meet locals, and save money along the way.

- Industry secrets on how to find the best hotel rooms
- Details on alternative accommodations, great neighborhood restaurants, and cool, offbeat finds
- Packed with personality and opinions

Mexico (Insight Guides)

By Insight Guides

This brand new edition Insight Guide to Mexico features outstanding full-color photography, alongside illuminating explorations of all the places to go in a region-by-region format, covering everywhere from Mexico City and the Gulf Coast to the less well known tourist areas in the North of the country. Major attractions, such as the Maya ruins and the Copper Canyon are highlighted to help you plan priorities for your trip; all places of special interest are cross-referenced on full-color maps throughout the guide, so they can be quickly pin-pointed as they are mentioned in the text. Additional maps of Mexico and Mexico City can be found within the front and back covers, to provide instant orientation and easy navigation. Clear, color-coded sections include in-depth features on Mexican history and culture, fiestas, art, food and the local people, alongside a detailed look at the Day of the Dead festival celebrated each November. Also included is a section of practical advice covering accommodation for all budgets, transport, eating out and much more. Useful contact information and many other travel tips are also provided. The unique combination of insightful exploration alongside practical advice means that this guide truly is a pleasure to read before, during and after your visit.

Where can I sign up to take Spanish language classes?

L'Alliance Francaise

Address: Calle 23 #117 by Calle 24
Colonia México
Ask for: Diana Castillo
Telephone: (999) 927-2403

Instituto Benjamin Franklin

Address: Calle 57 #474-A, between
Calle 52 and 54 Street
Centro
Ask for: Rosy Cetina
Telephone: (999) 928-6005
Website:
www.benjaminfranklin.com.mx

CIS: Centro de Idiomas del Sureste

Address: Calle 52 #455, between Calle 49 and 51 Street, Centro
Telephone: (999) 923-0954

Address: Calle 11 #203-C by Calle 26, Colonia García Ginéres
Telephone: (999) 920-2810

Address: Calle 14 #106 by Calle 25, Colonia Mexico
Telephone: (999) 926-9494
Ask for: Chloe Pacheco
Website: *www.cisyucatan.com.mx*

ECORA—Instituto de Idiomas y Centro Cultural

Address: Calle 50 #361, between Calle 53-B and 53-F Street
Colonia Francisco de Montejo
Ask for: Susana Villanueva
Telephone: (999) 953-4974
Website:
www.spanishschoolecora.com

Habla: The Center for Language and Culture

Address: Calle 26 #99 B, between Calle 19 and 21 Street
Colonia México
Telephone: (999) 948-1872
Website: *www.habla.org*

Instituto de Lengua y Cultura de Yucatán

Address: Calle 13 #214, between Calle 28 and 30 Street
Colonia García Ginerés
Ask for: Cecilia Novelo
Telephone: (999) 125-3048

Website: *www.ilcymex.com*

Institute of Modern Spanish

Address: Calle 15 #520B, between Calle 16-A and 18 Street
Colonia Maya
Ask for: Miguel Ceron
Telephone: (999) 911-0790
Website: *www.modernspanish.com*

Lengua Alternativa

Address: Calle 37 #539 between Calle 72-A and 74 Street
Colonia García Ginéres
Telephone: (999) 943-9181
Website: *www.lengualternativa.com*

MJ International

Address: Calle 13 #214, between Calle 28 and 30 Street
Colonia García Ginéres
Ask for: Gabriela Bojorquez
Telephone: (999) 925-4692

Spanish Center Mérida

Address: Calle 13 #108, between Calle 18 and 20 Street
Colonia Itzimná
Telephone: (999) 926-6819
Email:
info@spanishcentermerida.com

UNAM: Centro Peninsular de Ciencias Sociales y Humanidades de la UNAM en Mérida

Address: Calle 43 s/n, between Calle 44 and 46 Street
(Ex Sanatorio Rendón Peniche)
Colonia Industrial
Telephone: (999) 922-8446, Ext. 115

A Note on Language and Accent

Please note that Spanish spoken in the Yucatán is a different and distinct regional accent within Mexico. It is influenced by the Spanish colonial legacy and the Yucatec Maya language, which has its own cadence. (Remember, a third of the population of the Yucatán State speaks Maya!) Yucatec Maya, which is the most-widely spoken indigenous language in Mexico, is harshly melodic, and filled with "sh" sounds (which represented by the letter "x" in the Mayan language). That sid, the Spanish spoken in Yucatán is *grammatically and syntactically proper Spanish*, but it is spoken in a *regional accent*.

If you are curious about the emerging "pan-American" standard Spanish, tune in to Univision. Its newscasters are at the forefront of speaking "universal" Spanish, which is fast-becoming the standard for business and news broadcasts. In fact, Univision in Mexico City has courses where broadcasters from other parts of Latin America come to learn this "neutral" speech.

What's the point of this? It is simply to be mindful to ask your instructor to distinguish between a Yucatecan Spanish word or inflection and the "Univision standard Spanish"! After all, you wouldn't want to learn English with a Southern accent if you were in the U.S.—or speak as if you learned in English in Montreal!

Is birdwatching an avid pastime here?

Yes, bird watching and birding are world-class pastimes in the Yucatán and Mérida is the heart of the birding community. But it is Hacienda Chichén, on the outskirts of the ruins of Chichén Itzá that has year-round activities. The annual TOH Bird Festival in Mérida, do note, draws birders from the world over.

TOH Bird Festival

www.yucatanbirds.org.mx
Email: *info@yucatanbirds.org.mx*

Hacienda Chichén

Chichén Itzá, Yucatán
Website:
www.haciendachichen.com

Driving directions from Mérida to the Hacienda Chichén: As you stay in the toll Federal highway #180, exit at Pisté/Chichén Itzá, it is right at the first toll booth. Make sure you drive to the Chichén Itzá toll booth side of the highway. Once you pay (less than $8 USD) turn right to go towards the town of Pisté. In Pisté, the road will dead end with the old church on your right near the village's main square. When the road dead-ends, turn left and drive pass the first road sign indicating the archaeological site. Follow the road looking for signs for the "Zona Hotelera" exit. When this road turns to the left towards Xcalacoop, you will see signs indicating the "Zona Hotelera" drive slowly now as you are to take the sharp right turn into the Zona Hotelera road and Chichén Itzá's south entrance; continue on this road until you see the Hacienda's entrance.

Closer to Mérida, there's the wonderful park/sanctuary of Sihunchen:

Parque Ecoarqueológico Sihunchen
Address: Posada Punta del Cielo
Website: www.parquesihunchen.com
Email: *parquesihunchen@gmail.com*

For information on what's going on, there's a great blog that has current information on goings on about town and the state: *https://yucatanbirdclub.wordpress.com/*

And here is a listing of organizations of interest to bird watching enthusiasts in Yucatán. Most of these organizations have activities in Mérida:

- American Birding Association (ABA): *www.aba.org*
- American Bird Conservancy (ABC): *www.abcbirds.org*
- National Audubon Society: *www.audubon.org*
- Cornell University: *www.cornell.edu*
- BirdLife International: *www.birdlifeinternational.com*
- Iniciativa para la conservación de las Aves de América de Norte (ICAAN): *www.conabio.org*
- North American Bird Conservation Initiative (NABCI): *www.nabci-us.org*
- CIPAMEX, Organización de Ornitólogos de México:*www.iztacala.unam.mx/cipamex*

Food Delivery in Centro?

Where did the day go? It's time to eat … and there's nothing cooked … and you don't have time … but you don't want junk food!

Anita and Messina's are two food vendors that deliver in the downtown area. Anita specializes in rostisserie and grilled chicken. (It also has a simple seafood items for delivery.) Messina's, on the other hand, is an excellent local chain of pizzas with 20 locations in Mérida. With a small brigade of mopeds, their deliverymen are fast and their pizzas are very, very good. Although nothing is as good as homemade meals, if you're in a crunch and are loathe to east junk food from fast food chains, these are fine choices for those living in the heart of Centro.

Anita Pollos & Mariscos
Calle 68 #465, between Calle 55 cand 53 Street
Colonia Centro
Telephone: (999) 279-7428

Messina's
Calle 57 #514-A, Corner of Calle 64
Colonia Centro
Telephone: (999) 924-9899
Website: *www.messinaspizza.com/web/*

Are there alternative film houses?

Yes, there are three wonderful art film houses in town.

Cairo Cinema Café
Ricardo Ancona, Director
Calle 20 #98A between Calle 15 and 17
Street, Colonia Itzimná
Telephone: (999) 926-5718
Email: *cairocinemacafe@gmail.com*
Website: *www.cairocinemacafe.com*

El Nuevo Teatrito
Miguel Elenes Inchaurregui, Director
Calle 25 #91, by Calle 14
Colonia Chuburná de Hidalgo
Email for current films:
miguel.elenes@gmail.com

In addition, the State's Instituto de Cultural de Yucatán, known as ICY, sponsors wonderful film festivals throughout the year, and all are free and open to the public. To check out the current cultura programming, visit: *www.culturalyucatan.com*.

Air Travel Consumer Protection—U.S.

The wave of airline consolidation in the U.S. in recent years has prompted a sharp increase in consumer complaints. In response to the conduct of U.S. carriers, the U.S. Department of Transportation has compiled a consumer rights brochure for the general public. For expatriates living in Mérida the single-most complaint voiced concerns the United Airlines hub in Houston. Complaints center of missed connections in Houston coming and going to Mérida through Houston. There are also complaints on how luggage is handled in Houston. Mérida-bound travelers often complain about American Airlines out of Miami and Dallas.

Know your rights. For a copy of "Fly-Rights: A Consumer Guide to Air Travel" please visit this website: *http://airconsumer.dot.gov/publications/flyrights.htm*.

There is also important information on traveling with pets.

If the floors are made of pasta, can you eat them?

If we had a peso every time someone referred to the paste tile floors as "pasta" floors, we could retire!

In Spanish, "pasta" means both "pasta"—as in spaghetti or linguine—and it also means "paste," as in a kind of pasty clay. Those beautiful tiles are *paste* tiles, made of *paste* that is colored before it is fired. Talavera tiles are kind of glazed tile, where paint is applied to the clay tile. The origins of the paste tiles so familiar in Spain and Mexico have their origins to the Muslim occupation of the Iberian Peninsula for about eight centuries prior to the discovery of the Americas. Throughout the Middle East beautiful paste tiles, usually with cobalt and turquoise colors, are ubiquitous. *Paahhhstaahhh* tiles? Really? Linguine or angel hair? If you're speaking English, say "paste tiles."

Mérida is so close to Cuba—Can I travel to Cuba?

Yes, there are lots of options to travel to Cuba from Mérida and many Mexican, Canadian, and European nationals living in Mérida do travel to Cuba.

But if you are a U.S. citizen or Resident Alien please heed the following warning!

American Citizens and Resident Aliens who wish to travel to Cuba:

On December 17, 2014 President Barack Obama announced that the United States and Cuba had reached an agreement on reestablishing diplomatic relations after more than fifty years.

This process is expected to take almost two years before each nation opens an embassy in each other's capital and ambassadors are appointed.

That said, as of now, concerning travel to Cuba by U.S. citizens, here is an important notice, so important it's capitalized and in bold letters. Read it!

U.S. CITIZENS AND RESIDENT ALIENS MUST BE IN POSSESSION OF A VALID LICENSE TO TRAVEL TO CUBA. LICENSES CAN BE SECURED BY WRITING MR. JEFFERY BRAUNGER, OFFICICE OF FOREIGN ASSETS CONTROL, CUBA DESK, TREASURY DEPARTMENT, WASHINGTON, D.C. 20220. IT IS A FEDERAL CRIME FOR U.S. CITIZENS AND RESIDENT ALIENS TO TRAVEL TO CUBA WITHOUT A LICENSE FROM THE OFFICE OF FOREIGN ASSETS CONTROL

With this warning, please be advised that the administration of Barack Obama modified restrictions on travel to Cuba in the summer 2011, and it is now easier for U.S. citizens and Permanent Residents to travel to Cuba. Following is a list of planned people-to-people trips to Cuba compiled by Michelle Higgins of the *New York Times.*

HARVARD UNIVERSITY'S ALUMNI ASSOCIATION, (www.alumni.harvard.edu), will take a group of 35 to Havana for five days in late October, led by Julio Cesar Pérez Hernández, the Cuban Loeb Fellow at Harvard University Graduate School of Design, to explore the city and meet professionals, including local artists and enjoy a private concert at the Ceramics Museum with guitarist Luis Manuel Molina.

INSIGHT CUBA, insightcuba.org, is offering several trips that include a weekend in Havana that costs $1,795 and visits an orphanage; Callejon de Hammel, a community project promoting art, music and culture; the Instituto de Cubano de Amistad con los Pueblos (Cuban Institute of Friendship With the People), an international Cuban organization that promotes cultural relations between the United States and Cuba; and an eight-night Cuban Music and Art Experience, where visitors meet the staff at Egrem, the Cuban state record company, participate in a percussion and dance workshop, visit local music schools and talk to musicians during rehearsal at a famous Havana jazz club.

CORCORAN GALLERY OF ART AND COLLEGE OF ART AND DESIGN, corcoran.org, plans to offer an eight-day trip in November, pending a license. The trip, led by Mario Ascencio, the museum's library director, will explore the art scenes of Havana and Trinidad, a Unesco World Heritage Site. Guests will attend a cocktail reception at the Ludwig Foundation, which promotes Cuban contemporary artists, and meet local curators, artists and gallery owners.

Source: "New Ways to Travel to Cuba—Legally," by Michelle Higgins, *New York Times*, June 30, 2011.

ONE FINAL WARNING: When you arrive in Havana, even if you ask that your U.S. passport not be stamped, this does not mean that your arrival is not reported to the U.S. government. **Cuba and the U.S. cooperate with each other and the State Department receives a monthly report of EVERYONE arriving in Cuba with a U.S. passport.**

Why? Because governments cooperate with each other and Washington and Havana have an interest in monitoring who is coming or going, regardless of what is stamped or not in your passport.

Pets and Traveling: Are there Pet-Friendly Hotels?

If you're traveling to Mérida with pets, you're not alone. Fortnuately, there are three places that welcome pets.

La Pantera Negra
Calle 67 #547-B, between Calle 68 and 70 Street, Colonia Centro
Mérida, Yucatán
Telephone: (999) 126-9796
Email: *posadapanteranegra@gmail.com*
Website: *www.lapanteranegra.com*

Casa Esperanza Bed & Breakfast
Calle 54 #476, between Calle 55 and 57 Street, Colonia Centro
Telephone: (999) 286-7316
Email: *info@casaesperanza.com*
Website: *www.casaesperanza.com*

Hotel Dolores Alba
Calle 63 #464, between Calle 52 and 54 Street, Colonia Centro
Telephone: (999) 928-5650
Email: *info@doloresalba.com*
Website: *www.doloresalba.com*

Hacienda San José
Km. 30 Carretera Tixkokob-Tekanto
Mérida, Yucatán
This is a Five-Star resort, with full amenities.
Reservations, calling from the U.S, are required: 1 (888) 5STAR-11

The Most Pet-Friendly Cafes in Town

If you want to take your dog for a walk and enjoy a peaceful time at a café, then consider these two places, the most pet-friendly spots in town.

Botella Verde
Address: Santa Lucia Park, Calle 60 and 55 Street

Casa Catherwood Spa Boutique
Address: Calle 59 #572 between Calle 72 and 74 Street, Santiago

The Most Bicycle-Friendly Cafes in Town

If you want to take ride your bike somewhere and enjoy a peaceful time at a café, then consider these two places, the most bicycle-friendly spots in town. (Amanda Aragón at Casa Catherwood is one of the organizers of a civic bicycle club!)

Bistro Cultural
Address: Calle 66 #377-C, between Calle 41 and 43 Street

Casa Catherwood Spa Boutique
Address: Calle 59 #572 between Calle 72 and 74 Street, Santiago

Is it Possible to Learn the Maya Language?

Not only is it possible to learn Yucateca Maya, it is encouraged! Yucatec Maya is one of the most widely-spoken indigenous languages in the New World. If you are living in Mérida, then this is a great opportunity to learn the language that surrounds you.

There are three Maya Language schools that offer classes to help beginning students learn Spanish. In addition, INDEMAYA, the agency run by the Yucatán State, also offers classes. Some of the introductory courses are available on CDs and are posted on YouTube. When the time comes to expand your horizons, just drop by each of these schools and see which schedule is the right one for you.

Academia de Lengua Maya de Yucatán A.C
Address: Calle 44 # 452, between Calle 73 and 73-A Street, Centro
Telephone: (999) 924-8591
Email: *diccionariomaya@yahoo.com.mx*

Academia Municipal de la Lengua Maya "Itzamná"
Address: Calle 64-A #536 between Calle 77 and 79 Street, Colonia La Ermita
Telephone: (999) 924-0841

Unidad de Ciencias Sociales UADY
Address: Calle 61 # 525 between Calle 66 and 68 Street, Centro
Telephone: (999) 924-2767
Email: *mcolli@tunku.uady.mx*

Iguala – Ayotzinapa – 43

This guide makes no political comments. It is important, however, to explain an unfortunate situation that took place in September 2014.

On September 26, 2014, forty-three students from the Raúl Isidro Burgos Rural Teachers' College of Ayotzinapa were abuducted in Iguala, a town in Guerrero State. An official investigation confirmed that the students had commandeered several buses and drove themselves to Iguala that day with the intention of holding a protest in front of a conference led by that town's mayor's wife. When authorities learned of this, the mayor ordered the local police to intercept them before they entered Iguala proper. A confrontation followed. The exact details of that encounter remain unclear, but the investigation conducted by federal authorities has determined that once the students were in custody of the local police, these law enforcement officials handed the students over to the Guerreros Unidos ("United Warriors"), a criminal organization associated with drug trafficking. Guerreros Unidos then murdered the students.

Mexican federal authorities have concluded that Iguala's mayor, José Luis Abarca Velázquez, and his wife María de los Ángeles Pineda Villa, ordered the police to intercept the students and to hand them over to Guerreros Unidos. The couple, when accused, fled, as did Iguala's police chief, Felipe Flores Velásquez. The mayor and his wife were subsequently arrested after they were found hiding in Mexico City.

The massacre of the forty-three students outraged the Mexican public. This mass murder has led to protests, attacks on government buildings, and mass rallies throughout the country. Guerrero State Governor, Ángel Aguirre Rivero, was forced to resign in the wake of civil unrest. The death of the students, who were studying to become teachers, has created the most vexing challenge to Mexican President Enrique Peña Nieto's administration.

This may be the one incident that forces Mexico to reflect at the cost the War on Drugs and the corrupting relationship between public officials and the drug cartels.

Don't be surprised if "43," "Iguala," and "Ayotzinapa" continue to heard throughout 2016. It was a subject brought up when Pope Francis visited Mexico in 2016. People in Mérida—and throughout Mexico—continue to demand a full investigation into this incident that has garnered international condemnation and brought heartache to the Mexican people.

Are there other Foreign Consulates in Yucatán?

Austria

Alberto Bulnes Gueda
Av. Colón #501-C, Centro
Mérida
Telephone: (999) 925-6386
Email: bulnesa@prodigy.net.mx

Belgium

Rafael Baekeland
Av. Tulum "Plaza Tropical" #192
Local 59 SM 4, Manzana 17
Cancún, Quintana Roo
Telephone: (998) 892-2512

Belize

Miguel Alfredo Dutton Delorme
Calle 53 # 498, between Calle 56 and
58 Street, Centro
Mérida
Tel: (999) 928-6152
Email: Consbelize@dutton.com.mx

Canada

Alie Bourgeois
Centro Empresarial, Local E7
Zona Hotelera Km12
Cancún, Quintana Roo
Telephone: (998) 883-3360
Email: cncun@international.gc.ca

Cuba

Jesús Manuel García Rodríguez
Calle 1-D #320 x 42 y 44
Colonia Campestre
Mérida
Tel: (999) 944-4216
Email:
conscubamer1@prodigy.net.mx

France

Mario Ancona Teigell
Calle 60 #385, between Calle 41 and
43 Street, Centro
Mérida
Telephone: (999) 930 1542
Email: consulado@sipse.com.mx

Germany

Johannes Rommel
Calle 49 # 212, between Calle 30 and
32 Street
San Antonio Cucul
Mérida
Telephone: (999) 944-3252
Email: konsulat@jerommel.de

Honduras

Suzette Gavidia Arias
Instituto Monte Libano SCP
Calle 54 #486, between Calle 57 and
59 Street, Centro
Mérida
Telephone: (999) 924-3986
Email: consulhonyuc@hotmail.com

Netherlands

José E. Gutiérrez López
Calle 64 # 418, between Calle 47 and
49 Street, Centro
Mérida
Telephone: (999) 924-3122
Email: pixan2003@prodigy.net.mx

Spain

Victor Manuel Gómez Rodríguez
Calle 38 No. 31-A, Interior 31
Colonia Campestre
Mérida
Telephone: (999) 948-3489
Email: consulado.es.mid@gmail.com

97

Are there Day Spas?

Of course there are! And there are world-class day spas! The resort Haciendas throughout the Yucatán offer thrilling spas but closer to town, here is a list of day spas to consider.

Boho Spa Center

Calle 33 #343, between CAlle 36-C and 36-D Street
Colonia San Ramón Norte
Telephone: (999) 941-6029
Website: *www.bohospa.com.mx*

Hacienda Xcanatún

Carretera Mérida-Progreso
 Street, Colonia Itzimná
Telephone: (999) 941-0213
Website: *www.xcanatun.com*

Rosas & Chocolate Spa

Paseo de Montejo #380, corner of Calle 41
Colonia Centro
Telephone: (999) 924-2992
Website: *www.rosasandxocolate.com*

Sak Beh Spa

Calle 53, between Calle 62 y 64 Street

Colonia Centro
Telephone: (999) 923-0323
Email: *sakbehspa@gmail.com*
Facebook:
https://www.facebook.com/pages/Sak-Beh-Spa/181160318685749

The T'ai Spa

Avenida Shután Medina (Calle 4) #138, between Calle 11 and 13 Street
Telephone: (999) 944-5063 & (999) 944-7063
Website: *www.thetaispa.mx*

Yaxkin Spa

Located at the Hacienda Chichén at the ruins of Chichen Itzá
Telephone: (999) 920-8407 & (999) 925-3952
Email: *info@yaxkinspa.com*
Website: *www.yaxkinspa.com*

Astrological Readings

Sonya Kralova, who divides her time between Mérida and her native Prague, is renowned for her astrological readings and consultations. "The horoscope of each person is as different as his or her fingerprints. And in the [astrological] chart, which is a wheel, astrologers can see what is happening at the time, but at the same time, they can read what happened since you were born until the cycles are concluded," she told the *Diario de Yucatán* when a reporter for the newspaper interviewed her in February 2013.

She is fluent in Spanish, English, Czech, and German.

To make an appointment, call her at (999) 155-0340.

Telephone: (999) 928-6382

Shopping Centers & Anchor Stores

If you take public transportation—buses or taxis—to the shopping malls, here is a list of the anchor stores at the principal shopping centers:

Altabrisa Shopping Center: Sears, Sanborn's, Suburbia, and Soriana
City Center Shopping Center: Wal-Mart and La Europea
Galerías Shopping Center: Liverpool Department Store
Gran Plaza Shopping Center: Sears, Sanborn's, and Comercial Mexicana

Home Decorating: Urban & Chic Home

The "it" home décor shop for 2016 has to be Urban & Chic Home. In a short time, this has become the place for expats. It has that authentic feel of "shabby chic" with repurposed and upcycled products. If nothing else, it certainly is worth a look for great ideas and wonderful inspiration.

Urban & Chic Home
Address: Calle 28 #98-A between Calle 17 and 15th Street, Colonia Itzimná
Website: *https://www.facebook.com/UrbanAndChicHome*
Website: *www.cirsociales.uady.ms/servicios.php*

Who are the Elected Public Officials?

Who are the public officials?

Please note that Mexicans went to the polls in July 2012 and elect new officials. As a result of elections held in 2012, the PRI controls the statehouse but the PAN won Mérida city hall.

Governor (State)
Rolando Zapata (PRI)

Municipal President (Mayor of Mérida)
Renán Barrera (PAN)

Senators (Federal)

Daniel Ávila Ruiz (PAN)
Adriana Díaz (PAN)
Angélica Araujo (PRI)

Government Websites
State: *www.yucatan.gob.mx*
City: *www.merida.gob.mx*

Interested in following the campaigns?

Foreigners are prohibited by law from participating in Mexico's electoral process, but if you are curious about Mexico's political discussions, a nonpartisan site worth visiting to learn more is: *www.mexicodebate.org.mx.*

Where can I catch the local buses?

Mérida has a wonderful and extensive intercity bus system. The bus fare for adult is seven pesos, and three pesos for senior citizens (provided they have a Senior Citizen discount card, which are available, free of charge, at City Hall). Most people who live in town use public transportation, which consists of both buses (*autobuses*) and vans (*colectivos*). For pennies, buy a copy of the *Guía de Rutas de Autobuses*, which is the bus line route map, available from kiosks all over Centro. If you want to become familiar with a specific route, one easy way is to hop on the bus and see exactly where it goes.

Most buses run their entire route in just under an hour. One of the more popular lines for expatriates is Bus 52, Norte, Ruta 2. This line departs from Calle 59 between Calle 58 and 56 Street, runs north along Calle 56 before turning onto Paseo de Montejo. It continues north, turning to the left at the Monument to the Flag, and continues to a very popular supermarket: Mega (Comercial Mexicana). If you want to go to the main shopping areas, take the bus that runs on Calle 60, which goes to Costco, Sam's Club and the three major shopping centers: Gran Plaza, Chedrauí Norte and Liverpool (Plaza Galerías).

Current information about changes and updates is always available from *Plano de la Ciudad y Guía de Transporte Urbano Mérida*, Fansa Editores. Their telephone number is (999) 285-4226. Their email is: *fansaeditores@yahoo.com.mx.*

Here are a few of the more popular bus routes, which connect the Historic Center with the various areas where expatriates live and shop:

100

DESTINATION	BUS LINE	VEHICLE	ROUTE NAME & NUMBER	ORIGIN (CENTRO)
Plaza Galerías Mall	Minis 2000	Minibus	69 Tapetes	Calle 58 between Calle 59 and Calle 61
Gran Plaza Mall	FUTV	Colectivo	163 Tapetes	Calle 61 between Calle 58 and Calle 60
Gran Plaza Mall	FUTV	Colectivo	172 Dzitya - Las Americas	Calle 58 between Calle 57 and Calle 59
Gran Plaza Mall	FUTV	Colectivo	173 Komchen - Maquiladoras	Calle 58 between Calle 57 and Calle 59
Gran Plaza Mall	FUTV	Colectivo	175 Chablekal	Calle 58 between Calle 57 and Calle 59
Walmart Paseo de Montejo	FUTV	Colectivo	164 Itzimná - Águilas	Calle 58 by Calle 59
Plaza Altabrisa Mall	FUTV	Colectivo	164 Itzimná - Águilas	Calle 58 by Calle 59
Plaza Altabrisa Mall	Expreso	Bus	129 Carranza	Calle 59 between Calle 56 and Calle 58
Airport (Avenida Itzaes)	Alianza de Camioneros de Yucatán	Bus	1 Circuito	Circuito Colonias
Itzimná (Zócalo)	Expreso	Bus	129 Carranza	Calle 59 between Calle 56 and Calle 58
Itzimná (Zócalo)	Modernos	Bus	130 Monterreal	Calle 59 between Calle 54 and Calle 56
Parque Las Américas	Minis 2000	Bus	74 Pensiones	Calle 56 between Calle 59 and Calle 61
Star Médica	Expreso	Bus	128 San Lucas	Calle 59 between Calle 56 and Calle 58

DESTINATION	BUS LINE	VEHICLE	ROUTE NAME & NUMBER	ORIGIN (CENTRO)
Centro Médico Las Américas (CMA)	Expreso	Bus	128 San Lucas	Calle 59 between Calle 56 and Calle 58
Centro Médico Las Américas (CMA)	Expreso	Bus	129 Carranza	Calle 59 between Calle 56 and Calle 58
Centro de Especialidades Médicas (CEM)	FUTV	Colectivo	162 Chuburná	Calle 61 between Calle 58 and Calle 60
Clínica de Mérida	Minis 2000	Bus	75 Inalámbrica	Calle 56 between Calle 59 and Calle 61
Clínica de Mérida	FUTV	Colectivo	160 Pensiones - Chenkú	Calle 56 between Calle 61 and Calle 63

A complete list of all the bus lines provided by the City of Mérida appears here: *http://www.merida.gob.mx/transporte/paraderos.htm*

Organic Coffee Suppliers

In Centro, **Riqueza de Chiapas** offers an excellent selection of organic and high-quality coffee beans. Proprietor Julia Vinanco Sabido has among the best gourmet coffee beans downtown. Best part of all? They deliver to you!

Riqueza de Chiapas
Calle60, Corner of Calle 49
Col. Centro
Telephone: (999) 928-2864
Email: *caferiqueza@hotmail.com*

Which is the Best Boutique for Local Products?

Esencia Maya has, in a few years, taken the entrepreneurial spirit of young Mérida and transformed it into a chain of outstanding boutiques. This represents the best of local artisan, sustainable, and community-based capitalism. Shop on!

Esencia Maya Platino

Avenida 56-A #499, between Calle 47
and the corner of Calle 58
Colonia Centro
Telephone: (999) 287-1104
Website: *www.esenciamaya.com*

Esencia Maya Factory

Avenida 47 #500, between Calle 58 and
60 Street, Department 1
Colonia Centro
Telephone: (999) 923-0040
Website: *www.esenciamaya.com*

Esencia Maya Elsy

Avenida 47, between Calle 58 & 60 St.,
Interior of Santa Ana Market, Local 5
Colonia Centro
Telephone: (999) 928-8124
Website: *www.esenciamaya.com*

Esencia Maya Montejo

Avenida 56-A #462, between Calle 35
and 37 Street
Colonia Centro
Telephone: (999) 924-6968
Website: *www.esenciamaya.com*

Women's Artisanal Boutiques

Tejón Rojo (The Red Badger) is an intimate T-shirt and souvenir shop owned Annie Farias and Erika Canto Rejón, two young women who creates her own designs. Located downtown, it continues to generate interest among many young women who find it empowering to see female creativity thrive.

Tejón Rojo
Calle 53 #502-E, between Calle 60 and 62 Street
Col. Centro
Telephone: (999) 287-3617
Cell: (999) 956-3558
Website: *www.tejonrojo.com*
Facebook: *https://www.facebook.com/TEJONROJO*

Color Amor is a wonderful shop showcasing local talent. Another woman-owned enterprise, this shop has an eclectic and enticing selection of gifts.

Color Amor

Calle 55 #510-D, between Calle 60 and 62 Street
Col. Centro
Telephone: (999) 923-0944
Facebook: *https://www.facebook.com/coloramortalentstore/timeline*

Casa del Bosque focuses on locally-made accessories by women designers. The small shop has a charming display of clever and unusual items.

Casa del Bosque
Calle 55, between Calle 62 and 64 Street
Col. Centro
Email: *la_casadelbosque@hotmail.com*

Kukul Bout'ik offers a splendid selection of handmade cultural gifts. The items are thoughtfully chosen and the entire offering reflects contemporary sensibilities on sustainable and responsible gifts.

Kukul Bout'ik
Calle 44 #513, between Calle 60 and 62 Street
Col. Centro
Telephone: (999) 923-2240
Facebook: *https://www.facebook.com/KukulBoutik/timeline*

María Bonia is dedicated to feminine, if not girly, aesthetics, showcasing accessories and handmade products that reflect exuberant optimism. It's the most recent arrival to the shops in the area launched by young women.

María Bonita
Calle 4 #467 Dept. 3, between Calle 62 and 64 Street
Col. Centro
Facebook: *https://www.facebook.com/Maria-Bonita-485063478285419/?fref=ts*

Tamales

Can you believe people have been known to drive from Campeche for tamales from this place? It's true. That's how wonderful these banana leaf-wrapped tamales are! **Los 4 Hermanos**, or The Four Brothers, is a family-run business. There are two locations in town.

Los 4 Hermanos
Calle 15 #210-C, between Calle 26 and 28 Street
Col. García Gineres

Telephone: (999) 925-5273

Los 4 Hermanos
Calle 21-C #310, between Calle 34 and 34-A Street
Col. Chuburná
Telephone: (999) 981-6259

Chicharrón—Pork Rinds

Yes, it is a guilty pleasure. Yes, George H.W. Bush and his son George W. Bush both introduced pork rinds at official White House summer events. Yes, it makes people think twice … but on a hot summer day, with a cold beer, sitting on the terrace, even vegans are tempted. In answer to the often-asked question, "Where can you find the best *chicharrón* in town?" Here is the answer: **El Campeón**.

A family-run business for three generations, there are four locations in town. For delivery, telephone orders are taken by calling: (999) 970-0379.

Super Chicharronería "El Campeón"
Calle 7 #188 by 32nd Street
Col. García Gineres
Telephone: (999) 920-6487

Super Chicharronería "El Campeón"
Calle 16 #150, between Calle 7 and 9th Street
Colonia Mulsay

Super Chicharronería "El Campeón"
Calle 35, Diagonal #355-A, between Calle 38 and 40th Street
Col. San Luis de Chuburná

Super Chicharronería "El Campeón"
Calle 59-A #697, between Calle 114 and 116 Street
Avenida Jacinto Canek

Corn in Yucatán

In Yucatán State, corn is part of the basic regional cuisine and enjoyed every day. In fact, regional dishes in Yucatán take this basic carbohydrate as the basis for the preparation of traditional dishes such as *vaporcitos* (tamales), *salbutes* (a corn-tortilla regional dish), "Queen's Arm"" (a tamale prepared with chaya, similar to spinach, filled with ground pumpkin seeds, hard

105

boiled eggs and tomatoes), *Mukbil* Chicken (a regional dish in which shredded chicken meat is stuffed in corn meal, along with tomatoes and onions, wrapped banana leaves and baked), *panuchos* (a tortilla and black bean-based regional dish), *papadzules* (a vegetarian taco, made of hard boiled eggs, tomato sauce and garnished with crushed pumpkin seed sauce), and *joroches* (a tamale, stuffed with ground meat or chicken, and cooked in black bean sauce) among others.

Be aware that, unlike the U.S., corn tortillas—not flour ones—are the staple in Yucatán!

Basil Varieties

What began as a bet has now turned into a successful, sustainable enterprise: basil varities in Mérida. Mediterranean (sweet) basil, Lemon basil (*Ocinum americanum*), African Blue basil, Thai basil (Siam Queen), and Spice basil are now available year-round. David Joralemon has decided to let his basil herbs be sold in town. He is still working on his salad greens—arugula, red mustard, radicchio, and Royal Oak Leaf lettuce—before making those available. For now, Mérida has a new source of five wonderful basil herbs to enjoy.

If you are interested, send him an email at *david.joralemon@hotmail.com*.

Heirloom Tomatoes

Finally! Exquisite heirloom tomatoes are available in Mérida. Thanks to the initiative of Reed Robertson and his Maya associates near Conkal, the following heirloom tomatoes are grown in his orchard: Black Crimson, Brandy Wine, Bull's Heart, Cherokee Purple, Evergreen, Goldie, Great White, Pineapple, Tangerine, White Cherry, and Yellow & Red Stuffer.—*Eduviges Montejo*

Their harvests sell out—last year there was a waiting list. If you are interested, send him an email at *RABNYC@hotmail.com*.

Organic Maya Honey

The Yucatán produces some of the best honey in the world. It's not surprising that Yucatán exports honey to Germany—and Frida Kahlo coveted its honey for her home in Coyoacán in Mexico City. Now, thanks to two entrepreneurial Maya gentlemen, Guillermo and Julián, anyone can get their hands on extraordinary Maya honey.—*Eduviges Montejo*

For more information, visit: *http://www.gandjhoney.com/*.

Pizza & Breadmaking Workshops

Sofía Burckle is a force of nature! A single mother who is as devoted to her daughter as she is to the artisanal craft of dough, bread and pizza-making, she is a baker who conducts monthly workshops. With her German and Mexican heritage, she has cultivated a loyal following among expats who count on her to deliver bread and impart baking advice. The handmade bread workshop focuses on artisanal breads influenced by European baking traditions. Her recipes focus on wholewheat breads with pecans, almonds, pumpkin and sunflower seeds, oats, and amaranth. Her pizza workshops, likewise, focus on locally-procured ingredients and are artisanal. With the exception of outstanding imported cheeses, the pizzas are gourmet and are made from scratch.

Sofía Burckle's workshops are limited in size, no more than eight or so participants, and some of them are family affairs, with parents learning the art of bread- and pizza-making with their children. Workshops usually take place the last weekend of the month.

Sofía Burckle
Telephone: (999) 905-9220
For more information, please visit:
www.casa-catherwood.com/puertascerradas/pizzaworkshop.html

Gourmet Salt

Yucatán has always been famous for its salt. And as part of the cultural initiatives of Fundación Haciendas del Mundo Maya, we now have the best gourmet salt available anywhere in Mexico. Flor de Sal, Sal Rosa, and Espuma de Sal are available at the shop located in the Banamex Cultural Center downtown. Marketed under the name **TRASPATIO MAYA**, indulge!

Tienda Mérida Casa Montejo
Address: Calle 63 #506, between Calle 60 and 62 Street
Historic Center

Gelato

Sorbets are wonderful—but so are gelatos! The best two gelato places in town are Argentine- and Italian-style.

Domo Blanco Gelato (Argentine-style)
Address: Prolongación Montejo, Playa Mayor (Segafredo)
Facebook: *https://www.facebook.com/domoblanco.merida*

Pola Gelato Shop (Italian-style)

Address: Calle 55 #467-D between Calle 62 and 64 Street
Website: *www.polagelato.com*
Email: *polahelados@gmail.com*
Telephone: (999) 330-3441

Slow Food Yucatán

Products available: Organic produce, organic eggs, organic coffee, organic dry foods, organic artisanal cheeses, homemade organic bread, artisanal organic pastas, organic sauces, organic preserves, organic marmalades, natural honey … and lots more!

Every Saturday, from 9 AM to 1 PM

Address: Avenida Reforma (Calle 72) and Avenida Colón (just to the north of the CFE offices)

Website: *http://www.facebook.com/pages/Slow-Food-Yucatan/368398226531989*

Organic Market: Les Terrasses de Frida

Bistro Cultural has partnered with local growers and cooks to bring you a cornucopia of natural and holistic products. Held each Thursday, Johann's Green Market at Les Terrasses de Frida complements—and in many ways surpasses—the offerings of the Slow Food Market.

Every Thursday, from 8 AM to 3 PM

Address: Calle 66 #377-C between Calle 41 and 43rd Street

Website: https://www.facebook.com/groups/462691573872219/

The Best Belgian Waffles … in all of Mexico

Yes, believe it or not … many Belgian expats in town now claim that the best Belgian waffles found in Mexico are right here in Mérida. Where? Why, at the **Le Café de Bruxelles**. Caroline Aebi is the gifted young woman behind this delectable café.

Le Café de Bruxelles
Calle 42 #176 by Calle 40, Local 15
Plaza Altana
Col. Pinzón
Fraccionamiento Francisco de Montejo

Mérida, Yucatán
Telephone: (999) 289-5583
Cell Number: (999) 243-8355
Email: Caroline_Aebi@hotmail.com

The Best Artisanal Pasta ... in all of Mérida?

Oliva, located on the corner of Calle 49 and Calle 56, offers the best artisanal pastas in Mérida. The fettucini and ravioles continue to garner rave reviews from locals and visitors alike. An intimate place—seating accommodates barely a dozen guests—it is another example of the growing sustainable movement in Mérida. Fortunately, they deliver.

Oliva
Corner of Calle 49 and Calle 56
Centro
Mérida, Yucatán
Telephone: (999) 923-2248

The Best Belgian Biergartens ...

Over the past few years there has been a revival of the influence of German culture. Oh, yes, back in the 19th century, German immigrants brought beer culture to the Yucatán—and the largest German community is comprised of Mennonites in Campeche State.

But in Mérida, there are now wonderful biergartens. Here are the best:

Biergarten Parque Cervecero
Carretera Mérida-Progreso
Catastral #14714, Lote 9, Manzana 1
Xcanatún, Yucatán
Telephone: (999) 347-6985
Website: *www.cervezapatito.com*
Facebook: *https://www.facebook.com/Biergarten-Patito-1133066120037806/info/?tab=overview*

La Bierhaus
Calle 23 between Calle 18 and 20 Street
Colonia México
Mérida, Yucatán
Telephone: (999) 928-0333
Facebook: *https://www.facebook.com/labierhausmx#_=_*

The Best Food Trucks

No culinary scene today is complete without food trucks, right?

These are the two best food trucks in town.

Truck Chef
Avenida Cámara de Comercio and Calle 45
Fraccionamiento Montecristo
Mérida, Yucatán
Telephone: (999) 947-0359
Facebook: *https://www.facebook.com/TruckChef/#_=_*

Escolar Food Bus
Calle 20 #46-A, between Calle 4 and 5 Street
Colonia México
Mérida, Yucatán
Telephone: (999) 122-0950
https://www.facebook.com/Escolar-Food-Bus-762674797154392/

The Favorite Hair Salons in Town Are …

Robert Abuda Salon remains the favorite salon among ladies who lunch. Operated by Robert Abuda, with a convenient location on Paseo Montejo, this salon continues to build a loyal following and elicit tremendous accolades among the expat community.

Robert Abuda Saon
Paseo de Montejo #470-C, by Calle 39
Centro
Telephone: (999) 926-3015
Email: robertabudasalon@gmail.com
Website: *www.robertabudasalon.com*

Alternative Hair Salon & Spa
Calle 38 #466-B between 35th and 37th Streets
Colonia Jesús Carranza
Telephone: (999) 740-3302 and (999) 155-7307
Email: robertabudasalon@gmail.com
Website: *https://www.facebook.com/AlternativeHairSS*

The Best Pubs to Drink ... in all of Mérida?

Nothing is as refreshing as a few cold beers in this tropical heat. Cool off in style at these great pubs:

Bierhaus
Calle 62, between Calle 57 and 59 Street

La Fundación Mezcalería
Calle 56, between Calle 53 and 55 Street
Noon to 10 PM

La Negrita
Calle 62 and Calle 49
Noon to 10 PM

Mayan Pub
Calle 62 between Calle 55 and 57 Street

Sales Taxes Returned ... Yes!

If you are in Mérida, as a tourist, and you return to your home country, it's possible to get the sales taxes (Impuesto al Valor Agregado, or IVA) returned to you. The bonus, of course, is that it's possible to get the IVA back as you make several trips back and forth before your move to Mérida—and purchase of a residence has been finalized!

For more information, please visit: *www.taxback.com.mx*

The Best Florist Shop ... in all of Mérida?

Providing both flowers that are grown by local growers and representing the extensive selection from Mexico City's exclusive Chiltepec Florists, this is an excellent resource for all the floral needs of gracious hosts and hostesses throughout town.

Chiltepec
Paseo de Montejo #470-A, by Calle 39
Centro
Mérida, Yucatán
Telephone: (999) 938-1508
Website: *www.chiltepec.com*

The Best Restaurant … in all of Mérida for 2016?

Everyone wants to know the answer to this question. And after we surveyed 168 expats and local gourmands … it has come down to two choices:

Chef Roberto Solís
Nectar
Avenida A García Lavín
Plaza Jardín Mérida
Mérida, Yucatán
Telephone: (999) 938-0838
Website: *www.nectarmerida.com.mx*

Chef Sara Arnaud
Apoala
Santa Lucia Square
Colonia Centro
Mérida, Yucatán
Telephone: (999) 923-1979
Website: *www.apoala.mx*

The molecular menu at **Ku'uk is** undeniably the most innovative restaurant, but these two are more approachable.

Amateur Theatre

A charming new development in Mérida is the "Mérida Mystery Theatre," which larks back to the dinner theater tradition of mid-century Americana. Amateurs and theater-buffs are invited to participate in the "murder mysteries" that are staged.

For more information, please email: *info@meridamysterytheatre.com*

Expat Hangout for the Drinking Crowd

In Key West, Florida, it's the Green Parrot Bar on Whitehead. In New Orleans, it's Molly's on Toulouse. It seems every town has a place favored by resident "committed drinkers." Mérida is no different: **Hennessy's Irish Pub,** on Paseo de Montejo, is the preferred place for expat hardcore drinkers. The food is mediocre and the mixed drinks, some complain, are watered-down. But the bottles of beer are cold and the clientele consists primarily of American expats. If you want to get down with this crowd, it can be rather amusing to watch them as their eyes become glassy and their speech slurred as the evening progresses. The conversation invariably turns to where you can get bargain Botox shots or discounted Viagra. In fact, this place has the aura of an "upscale" "Margaritaville" hangout; there are even brawls that conclude with bar stools being smashed! Yes, it can be tawdry and low-life but that's part of its thrill! Don't forget your camera but remember to keep your distance from the frolicking expats!—*Eduviges Montejo*

Hennessy's Irish Pub
Address: Paseo de Montejo #486-A
Telephone: (999)923-8993
Website: *www.hennessysirishpub.com*

English-Speaking Dentists

There is a list of dentists in Mérida who have complied with the requirements established by the U.S. Embassy in order to be recommended to American citizens living in Mexico in the chapter on doctors and dentists. In addition, here are five dentists who do not appear on that list, but who are both fluent in English and continue to be praised by expats living in Mérida.

It would be prudent to consider ALL the dentists who are available to you, but if you hear recommendations about these five dentists, here is information on how to reach them.

Dra. Ligia Maldonado
Address: Circuito Colonias #73 between Av. Alemán and Calle 6
Col. Felipe Carrillo Puerto
English-speaking dentist: Yes
Telephone: (999) 926-7531
Email: *ligiamaldonado@prodigy.net.mx*
Website: *www.dentaleman.com.mx*

Dra. Diana Navarro
Address: Calle 15 #491 by Calle 22, Fracc. Altabrisa, Edificio 1000enium
English-speaking dentist: Yes
Telephone: (999) 907-1834
Email: *diana@meridadentist.com*
Website: *www.meridadentist.com*

Dra. Gabriela Novelo
Address: Calle No. 31-A Interior 417, by Calle 6, Col. Nuevo Yucatán
English-speaking dentist: Yes
Telephone: (999)986-4155
Email: *odontologika_saludbucal@hotmail.com*

Website: *http://www.odontologika.com*

Dr. Jesús Manuel Sánchez
Address: Calle 53 #518-13, between Calle 64 and 66th Street, Centro
English-speaking dentist: Yes
Telephone: (999) 924-9895
Email: *yucatandental@hotmail.com*
Website: *www.yucatandental.com*

Dra. Cecilia Vazquez
Address: Calle 21 by Calle 10, Edificio Interplaza, Local 14, 2nd piso, Col. México
English-speaking dentist: Yes
Telephone: (999)121-6934
Email: *cvn25@hotmail.com*

Adventure Travel: Mérida

With so many younger couples and young families moving to Mérida, one question keeps coming up: Which are the best "adventure" travel outfits? There are several, and here are four that are exceptional:

Catherwood Travels
Website: *www.meridadentist.com*

Aventura Maya
Website: *www.aventuramaya.com.mx*

Ecoturismo Yucatán
Website: *www.ecoyuc.com*

Maya Amazing Adventures
Website: *www.mayaamazing.com*

Promoting Mérida

Interested in helping promote Mérida? So are the folks at Real Life in Mérida. More information on this group is available here:

Real Life in Mérida
Website: *http://www.reallifeinmerida.com/*

Zombies in Town

Believe it or not, "The Walking Dead" has inspired Yucatecans for form their own "zombie" club … a chance to have the living dead wander about town. Interested in joining these faux zombies about town?:

Mórbido Mérida: Zombies
Website: *http://zombiewalkmerida.com/*

Adventure Travel Agent: USA

If you are interested in high-end custom vacations, Helena Iorio, recipient of the Silver Magellan award, the most prestigious such recognition in the travel industry, caters to Americans and Canadians who want tailor-made extraordinary trips in Yucatán:

Helena Iorio
HMI Travel Consulting
Website: *www.hmitravelconsulting.com*
Email: *HMItravelconsulting@gmail.com*
Telephone: 781-475-2005

Cenotes—Sinkholes

A *cenote* is a natural pit, or sinkhole, characteristic of Mexico's Yucatán peninsula, that is created from the collapse of limestone bedrock. Usually, a *cenote* exposes groundwater that flows from the fresh water acquifer that characterizes the peninsula. The word is not Spanish, but Yucatec Maya; it derives from the *Ts'onot*, used to denominate any location with accessible groundwater. There are thousands of *cenotes* throughout the Yucatán peninsula. A good number of these are open to the public. It's possible to swim in them and explore these cool, refreshing pools. At the request of readers, what follows is a list of some of the most accessible *cenotes*:

CENOTILLO
This name of this village is derived from the large number of *cenotes* located both in town and its environs. By one count there are just over 150 *cenotes*! The three *cenotes* more often used for recreation are Kaipech, Xayin and Ucil.

CHIHUAN
Just over 50 miles from Mérida on the "Libre" (toll-free) road to Cancún, this *cenote* remains popular and it is easy to access. There are dressing rooms, parking, a few restaurants serving local

dishes. One reason for its popularity is that overnight camping is allowed. Horseback riding is available. More information at: *www.cenotechiuanvillaspa.mex.tl*.

CUZUMÁ

The town of Cuzamá is well known for the large number of *cenotes* located there. There are three *cenotes* and tours are available that will take you to all of them. These are: Chelentún, Chansinic'che, and Bolonchoojol. The *cenotes* boast stalactite and stalagmite formations. All three are suitable for swimming. More information at: *www.balamkaan.com*.

DZUL HA

Dzul-Ha is the *cenote* located on the grounds of the Hacienda Sotuta de Peón. The hours of operation are every day, including holidays. The entrance fee includes: Tour of the compound aboard a "truck," a visit to Casa Maya, where traditional Maya life is recreated, and for those going to the *cenote*, they provide both life jacket and visor. Optional: Restaurant service. More information at: *www.haciendatour.com*.

IK KIL

A few minutes from Chichén Itzá and the town of Pisté, this *cenote* is famous because it is shaped in an almost-perfect circle and boasts a natural waterfall. There is a fee of $70 pesos to enter. The *cenote* has a solid stairway that leads you down the steps into the water. Open daily, from 8 AM to 6 PM. An adjacent restaurant offers a buffet style meal service. There are bungalows for overnight stays.

SAN IGNACIO

Less than 20 minutes from Mérida on the highway to Campeche, this *cenote* is adjacent to the village of Chochola. It is ideal for swimming is renowned for its transparent, turquoise waters. There are palapas, bathrooms, public showers, dressing rooms, a play area for children, wading pools, restaurant, and spa nearby. More information at: *www.cenotesanignacio.com*.

XLACAH

North of Mérida, near the ancient Maya ceremonial site of Dziblichaltún, this is one of the most charming *cenotes* around. Open to the public to coincide with the ruins' schedule, you can enjoy this *cenote* from 8 AM to 4 PM.

YAXUHAH

New stairs have been installed and there is access to a picnic area. It is located a short distance between Chichén Itzá and Yaxcabá and it is famous for its clear waters and lush surroundings. More information at: *www.yaxunahcentrocultural.org*.

YOKZCONOT

This *cenote* is only minutes from Chichén Itzá and is adjacent to the popular Ecohotel & Camping facility. Set amid the tropical forests, it is also a terrific place for birdwatching. Tours are available for any size group. It is open every day, year round except Christmas Day and New Year's Day. More information at: *www.yucatanmayanretreat.webs.com*.

KANKIRIXCHE

This is one of those *cenotes* that are large and offer a spectacular sub-aquatic cavern with crystal clear waters. The visibility is astounding. It is one of the favorites for snorkeling or scuba. The *cenote* also features stalactites and several Alamo trees whose roots form an impressive formation from the ceiling to the water. This *cenote* is accessible only in organized tours. More information at: *www.mayanecotours.com*.

ZACÍ

This world-famous *cenote* is located in the heart of Valladolid. With a diameter of 150 feet and a depth of 260 feet, it is one of the most popular cenotes in the entire state. It is a great place for a refreshing swim. There is also a lovely restaurant on the property.

Day Trips: Campeche, Izamal & Isla Holbox

What are the "can't miss" day trips from Mérida? Many have asked. Here are three popular excursions that many expatriates in town enjoy tremendously. Indeed, they often become "overnight" trips—and reasons to explore places that are removed from the hustle and bustle of busy lives of leisure in Mérida. Do note that Isla Holbox is a considerable drive from Mérida, but it is included here since many expatriates now use Cancún as the gateway airport for coming to and leaving Mérida. As for Campeche and Izamal, these are not-to-be-missed destinations worthy of several "day" trips in the course of the year. What follows is a quick summary that does not do justice to any of these three locations—but we hope it is enough to entice you to gas up your car and hit road.

Campeche

Campeche

It sounds far away, but it isn't that far. Campeche, with its fortresses and walls, is a city filled with the lore of pirates. It's a terrific getaway from Mérida and a delightful surprise for visitors who probably have never heard of it. Many expatriates eventually find that they will go Campeche, both to enjoy the colonial beauty of this exquisite city as well as the perfect place in which to relax. The historic fortified walls—"baluartes" in Spanish—once protected the entire city. Today only a few sections remain, but they are brilliantly illuminated at night.

Campeche State government has a great website with all kinds of useful information: www.campeche.travel/en/.

Many expatriates comment on the city's broad seaside boulevard, known as the *malecón*: Well developed, clean and broad. Others say they go to Campeche to continue on to the beaches of Champotón, and the Restaurante Bahíia de Tortugas is a popular place to enjoy a fine meal.

If you spend the night, a popular hotel among Mérida residents is the Hotel Plaza Campeche:

Hotel Plaza Campeche
Website: *www.hotelplazacampeche.com*

Whatever you decide to do, remember this: If you have a car, you don't have an excuse not to visit Campeche.

Izamal

It's only about 50 miles east of Mérida and it is one of the most important places for Christian pilgrims from all over Mexico. Izamal, which is described as one of Mexico's most vivid examples of Three Cultures: ancient Maya pyramids surround one of the largest monasteries the Spanish ever built in Mexico, while contemporary Maya artisans do a brisk trade in their traditional crafts. The entire city center glows with brilliant ochre-yellow paint. The city is the center for artisanal handicrafts under the auspices of the Banamex Cultural Foundation. The massive Franciscan convent of **San Antonio de Padua** is a fortress commanding stunning views of the entire city and environs. The porticoed atrium, second in size only to the Vatican's, is a peaceful courtyard. Frescoes recently uncovered depict the apparition of Satan in Izamal and Bishop Fray Diego de Landa's presence, which became notorious for his brutal *auto-da-fé* at Maní, lingers. **The Centro Cultural y Artesanal**, housed in a colonial building across the square from the convent, offers an excellent introduction to Izamal's abundance of quality handicrafts. The shops offer top-quality hammocks, clothing, and other works crafted by local artists. There is also has a spa and a café in the interior courtyard.

118

Izamal, compared to the urban buzz of Mérida, is a wonderful day trip, a treasure for those who live in Mérida and want to take a break "to the country." The place exudes such calm that many want to spend the night. Two favorite places are:

Macan Ché Bed & Breakfast
Address: Calle 22 no. 305 between Calle 33 and 35th Street
Telephone: (988) 954-0287
Website: *www.macanche.com*

Hotel Rancho Santo Domingo
Telephone: (988) 967-6137
Website: *www.izamalhotel.com*

Isla Holbox

In the section on "getting to" Mérida, it is noted that air travel from the U.S. and Canada is expensive—and limited. In consequence, many expatriates prefer to fly into and out of Cancún's airport, where there are virtually nonstop flights to all the major hubs in the U.S. as well as many large Canadian cities and important European capitals. This, however, requires a long ride across the peninsula and that's before one sets out to board a flight leaving Cancún, or just arrived from a long flight into Cancún.

Either way, it makes for a dreary travel day. It's not surprising that many choose to travel in a more leisurely fashion. Some opt to arrive in Cancún and "acclimate" one day before embarking to Mérida. Others choose to drive to Cancún the day before their departure, and enjoy one last evening in the Yucatán before departing.

Isla Holbox is one of the favored places among Mérida expatriates, whichever way they are headed. Many delight in spending a final evening on this peaceful island before returning to the homes outside Mexico. Others enjoy being re-introduced to the Yucatán by spending their first night with the soothing sound of the breeze blowing through palm fronds. Whichever you prefer, here are two hotels on Isla Holbox that continue to receive rave reviews.

Casa Maya
Website: *www.casamayadejoselimaholbox.com/en/*

Villas Delfines
Website: *www.villasdelfines.com*

119

'ho want to end, or begin, their time in the Yucatán on an adventurous note,
_ report excellent things about two adventure outfits:

Dive Trip
Website: *www.divetrip.com/playa/holbox.htm*

Holbox Whale Shark Tours
Website: *http://holboxwhalesharktours.com/*

Coming or going, see you soon!

AirBNB in Mérida

Compared to other cities throughout Mexico, Mérida has been slow to AirBNB. Whereas there are thousands of listings in cities, from Havana to Miami, Mexico City to New York, there are only a few hundred in Mérida. Here are the best. Prices listed are the average for a room and are listed in U.S. dollars. Of course, check with AirBNB.com to book.

Cuarto Azul, Calle 37 #543-Bix, between Calle 74 and 74-A Street, Colonia García Ginerés. Price per night: $20.

Lovely House, Calle 23, on the corner of Calle 12, Colonia Centro. Price per night: $20.

Habitaciones Amuebladas, Calle 72, Reforma #411-B, between Calle 41 and 43 Street. Price per night: $22.

Habitaciones, Calle 24 #208-A, on the corner of Calle 31, Colonia García Ginerés. Price per night: $22.

Casa Turix, Calle 19 #197-A, between Calle 18 and 20 Street, Colonia García Ginerés. Price per night: $32.

Casa Colonial, Calle 72 #403-C, between Calle 39 and 41 Street, Colonia Centro. Price per night: $44.

Casa del Cantante, Calle 62-A, on the corner of Calle 37, Colonia Centro. Price per night: $49.

Casa Colorful Azul, Calle 62 #374, by Calle 43, Colonia Centro. Price per night: $49.

Casa Lorenzo, Calle 41 #516-A, by Calle 62, Colonia Centro. Price per night: $79.

Casa Carola, Calle 6 #90, Reparto Dolores. Price per night: $146.

Casa Five 8, Calle 58 #419, corner of Calle 43. Price per night: $275.

5 MUSEUMS & GALLERIES

Gran Museo de la Civilización Maya

This is the largest museum dedicated to the Maya civilization in Mexico. Adjacent to the Siglo XXI Convention Center, it attracts more visitors than all the other museums in the city combined. It is also a work in progress—barely a year since it opened to the public, it is still assembling its collections and exhibitions. But what a bold and grand architectural statement it is! And it has world-class facilities that will serve generations of visitors to come. Its Gift Shop has an interesting collection of gift items as well.

Address: Call 60 Norte, Unidad Revolución, ExCordemex (Adjacent to the Siglo XXI Convention Center)
Hours: Wednesday-Monday, 8 AM to 5 PM; closed on Tuesday
Website: *www.granmuseodelmundomaya.com*
Admission: $37 pesos for adults, children under 13, senior citizens over 60, students with valid IDs and teachers with valid credentials are admitted free.

Museum of Anthropology & History

An extensive exhibition of archaeological, anthropological and ethnographic materials related to the Maya civilization and the history of archaeology in the peninsula.

Address: Palacio Cantón, Paseo Montejo and 43rd Street
Hours: Tuesday-Saturday, 8 AM to 8 PM; Sunday, 8 AM to 2 PM; closed on Monday
Website: *www.inah.gob.mx*
Admission: $37 pesos for adults, children under 13, senior citizens over 60, students with valid IDs and teachers with valid credentials are admitted free.

Museum of Contemporary Art of Yucatán (MACAY) Museum

The MACAY has a permanent exhibition of work by Yucatecan artists.

Address: Calle 60, entrance in the corridor flanking the south side of the Cathedral
Hours: Monday, 10 AM to 6 PM; Wednesday-Thursday, 10 AM to 6 PM; Friday-Saturday, 10 AM to 8 PM; Sunday 10 AM to 6 PM; closed on Tuesday
Website: *www.macay.org*
Admission: Free

Centro Cultural La Cúpula

The newest addition to Mérida's cultural scene, La Cúpula has caused a sensation. Under the direction of Leila Godet Voight, La Cúpula has launched an ambitious program to bring contemporary cultural events to Mérida. Diana Castillo Castro, a capable and hardworking professional, runs a tight ship and the center has garnered a sophisticated following in a very short time. The center holds workshops, classes, and has "Jueves Culturales," or "Cultural Thursdays," when events, open to the public, are held. More than seven years in the planning, the center opened in December 2015. "Because of Merida's cultural life, the quality of the light and other reasons, we chose this ciety to open the center," Voight told reporters. "We have worked with many arts groups, as well as state and local cultural organizations, to create this space."

Address: Calle 43 #407, between Calle 41 and 43 Street
Telephone: (999) 688-9479
Website: *www.lacupulamerida.org*

Casa Frederick Catherwood

This gallery and gift store houses a permanent exhibition of Frederick Catherwood's lithographs of 1844, "Views of Ancient Monuments in Central America, Chiapas & Yucatán," in a beautifully restored Belle Epoque manse. This is the only gallery in town that has won critical acclaim from the international community and been profiled internationally in United Airlines' magazine *Hemisphere*. A "Fair Trade" gift shop on the first level has an extensive selection of silver by National Geographic Society sponsored Mexican silversmiths and jewelry designers.

Address: Calle 59 #572 between Calle 72 and 74 Street
Hours: Monday-Saturday, 9 AM to 2 PM and 5 PM to 9 PM; Closed on Sunday
Website: *casa-catherwood.com*
Admission: $50 pesos for adults, children under 12 are admitted free.

Casa Museo Montés Molina

The only mansion in Mérida that retains its original Victorian and Edwardian eras splendor, including its lavish furnishings, which coincide with the "Golden Age" of the Yucatán's sisal/henequen wealth. This is one of the homes that gave Mérida the moniker, "Paris of the West," in the 1900s and 1910s.

Address: Paseo de Montejo #469 between Calle 33 and 35 Street

123

Hours: English language house tours, Monday-Friday at 9 AM, 11 AM and 3 PM; closed to the public on Saturday and Sunday
Website: *www.laquintamm.com*
Admission: $50 pesos for adults, $25 pesos for children

Fundación de Artistas

Founded by Nicólas Malleville and Francesca Bonato, a husband and wife couple of artists and designers, the Fundación showcases up-and-rising artists from Mexico and abroad.
The Fundación conducts workshops and holds musical recitals. It also has a well-received café that features artisan dishes sourced from local farmers.

Address: Calle 55 #520, between Calle 62 and 64Street
Telephone: (999) 923-5905
Hours: Tuesday-Sunday, 11 AM to 7 PM; closed Monday
Website: *www.fundaciondeartistas.org*
Admission: Free

Museum of the City

Housed in the former Main Post & Telegraph offices, built in 1910 to commemorate Mexico's Centennial, the museum houses a curious selection of historical documents, artifacts, and material related to the origins and development of Mérida. Some of the items on view date back to when Mérida was T-hó, the original Maya city before the arrival of the Spanish.

Address: Calle 65 between Calle 56 and 56-A Street
Hours: Tuesday-Friday, 8 AM to 8 PM; Saturday-Sunday, 8 AM to 2 PM; closed Monday
Admission: Free

Tataya Gallery

Galería Tataya specializes in contemporary and mid-career Mexican and Cuban painters. They have a constant flow of new works and hold 6 to 8 exhibitions a year. In addition, they sell the highest quality Mexican *"artesanías"* (handcrafts) from Chiapas, Oaxaca, Michoacán, Sinaloa, Chihuahua, etc., most pieces being "one of a kind." It has the city's best collection of contemporary Cuban and Mexican paintings and prints, selected handicrafts from renowned Mexican artisans

Address: Calle 60 #409, between Calle 45 and 47 Street
Hours: Monday-Friday: 10 AM to 2 PM and 5 PM to 8 PM; Saturday: 10 AM to 2 PM. Closed Sunday
Telephone: (999) 928-2962
Website: *www.tataya.com.mx*
Admission: Free

Museum of the Yucatecan Song (Museo de la Canción Yucateca)

The museum has a permanent exhibition of photographs, recordings, musical instruments, and other artifacts that made Yucatecan music and musicians famous throughout the world. You may not recognize the names of Armando Manzanero, Pastor Cervera, Guty Cárdenas or Ricardo Palmerin, but when you hear their music, you will immediately recognize it from the radio programs and Hollywood films of yesteryear.

Address: Calle 47 #464-A, on the corner of 48 Street
Hours: Tuesday-Sunday, 9 AM to 5 PM; closed on Monday
Website: *www.enjoymexico.net/mexico/Merida-museos-mexico.php*
Admission: $15 pesos, except on Sundays when admission is free

"Juan Gamboa Guzmán Pinacotea" Museum

The museum showcases a permanent exhibition of paintings and sculptures housed in an adjunct entrance to the Church of the Three Orders, whose architecture is of equal historical as the works displayed.

Address: Calle 59, side entrance to the church, between Calle 58 and 60 Street
Hours: Tuesday-Saturday, 8 AM to 8 PM; Sunday, 8 AM to 2 PM; closed on Monday
Website: *www.enjoymexico.net/mexico/merida-museos-mexico.php*
Admission: Free

Mérida Gallery

This gallery focuses on emerging Yucatecan artists with a wide following and has rotating exhibitions approximately 10 times a year.

Address: Calle 59 #452 between Calle 52 and 54 Street
Hours: Wednesday-Monday, 9:30 AM to 6:30 PM; closed on Tuesday
Website: *www.galeriamerida.com/index.htm*
Admission: Free

Museum of Popular Folk Art

The museum offers a charming exhibition of folk art from the Yucatán and central Mexico.

Address: Calle 50-A #487 by 57 Street
Hours: Tuesday-Saturday, 9:30 AM to 6:30 PM; Sunday, 9 AM to 2 PM; closed on Monday
Website: *www.enjoymexico.net/mexico/merida-museos-mexico.php*
Admission: $20 pesos

City Art Museum (GAMM)

This museum showcases a populist exhibition of local artists, specializing in naïve and outsider works of art.

Address: Calle 65, between Calle 56 and 56-A Street
Hours: Tuesday-Friday, 9 AM to 8 PM; Saturday-Sunday, 9 AM to 2 PM; closed on Monday
Website: *www.merida.gob.mx/capitalcultural/galeria_arte/inicio.htm*
Admission: Free

In La'Kech Gallery

An innovative art space evoking a certain counter-culture perspective, this small gallery features work by some of Mérida's cutting edge emerging artists.

Address: Calle 60 #595-A, between Calle 73 and 75 Street
Hours: Hours not yet set, so please call (999) 242-3948, or if you drop by and ring the bell.
Website: *www.galeriainlakech.com/index_en.php*
Admission: Free

La Eskalera Gallery

A cutting-edge gallery that showcases Mexican and foreign artists La Eskalera strives to bring contemporary art and photography to a hipster level.

Address: Calle 70 #474-B, between Calle 57 and 59th Street
Hours: Visit their website for current hours.
Telephone: (999) 947-1218
Website: *www.artgandi.com*
Admission: Free

FrontGround Galería Manolo Rivero

If there was ever a cooperative in the spirit of nurturing state-of-the-art creativity, then this is it. Visitors continue to remark that this loose association of artists could very well be in Brooklyn, New York; Paris, France; London, England; or Tokyo, Japan. The installations and spirit of the energy—and life—in these works is truly astounding. One visit to their website is compelling. A visit to this gallery will open your eyes and dazzle your imagination.

Address: Calle 51, between Calle 58 and 60 Street
Hours: Visit their website for current hours.
Email: *frontground.ac@gmail.com*
Website: *www.frontground.net*
Admission: Free

In addition, a slew of new galleries are opening up in the Santiago area … which will be covered in greater detail in the 2017 edition. For now, here are three new galleries.

La Bodega Galería

Centro Cultural y Artístico "La Bodega" recently opened. It showcases collective exhibitions of artists represented by Humberto Suaste.

Address: Calle 70 #470, Corner of Calle 55
Admission: Free

Agustín Galería

This is a gallery specializing in Regional Primitive art of Yucatán, the building also houses a private club. It relocated from Centro to Itzimná in the last year.

Address: 58-A #483-A, between Calle 25 and 25-A Street, Colonia Itzimná
Telephone: (999) 926-9797
Website: *http://agustinart.com/*
Admission: Free

Galería Anónimo

This gallery, housed in a former Bed & Breakfast, is a new addition to the gallery scene in Santiago.

Address: Calle 57 #552, between Calle 66 and 68 Street
Admission: Free

Choco-Story México

Although Choco-Story is located across from the ruins of Uxmal, it is such an exceptional place that it merits mention—and is a "must see" destination. A museum, gallery, and educational center amid groves of cacao trees, Choco-Story tells the history of chocolate. The brainchild of Eddy van Belle and in partnership with Fernando Barbachano and Mathieu Brees, Choco-Story Uxmal is larger and more ambitious than its other locations in Paris, Prague and Bruges.

Address: Uxmal
Hours: 9 AM to 7:30 PM, every day except December 24, December 25, Decembr 31 and January 1.
Admission: $120 pesos
Website: *www.choco-storymexico.com*

6 RESTAURANTS IN MÉRIDA & ENVIRONS

Mérida is a city of foodies, but not of great restaurants.

People who love food have long known that. Jeremiah Tower, who along with Alice Waters made Chez Panisse the culinary tour de force that it is, lives here. Martha Stewart swings in to take a cooking class; *New York Magazine* critic Gael Greene spends a month sampling the peninsula's food offerings and restaurants. Gilbert Le Coze, of Le Bernardin, was fascinated by Maya marinades using Seville oranges when he was here. Jacques Pepin has been in town on several occasions. He has a home in Playa del Carmen. The private chef for Buckingham Palace spent a week not too long ago, anxious to learn about techniques for "enlivening" the offerings for Her Majesty. Years back Julia Child ventured here in search of the "perfect" free range turkey.

Recipes from the Yucatán find their way in the "Slow Food" cookbook and our region's cuisine caused a sensation in San Francisco in the summer of 2008 when "Tamales Yucatecos" were served at the Slow Food Nation convention, the first time ever, in the United States. That said, we can also say with confidence that international fast food restaurants are consistent around the world. McDonald's, Burger King, KFC, Pizza Hut, Chili's, etc. in Mérida are the same as what you find anywhere else. The same can be said of the kinds of restaurant choices one finds at international hotel chains, from the Marriott to the Hyatt, the Fiesta Americana to the Intercontinental. We are neither reviewing nor listing these restaurants in this section, since they are found in most guidebooks and online resources.

Now, a word about why Yucatecos don't frequent great restaurants. For a variety of reasons, cultural norms encourage home cooking. Many families boast tremendous culinary talents in their families. That is different from having a society, like in Buenos Aires, Barcelona, Tokyo or Paris, where people go out for great meals, whether at a sidewalk café, neighborhood bistro or full-service restaurant. The same can be said of the United States and Canada, where even in New York, the city that pretends to be the city that "never" sleeps, almost all kitchens take their last orders at 10:30 PM. If it's 1 AM and you want a meal, you're likely to end up at 24-hour fast-food place.

If you notice that our listing differs from what you find in your guidebooks, remember: *Travel writers are seldom restaurant critics, and many concentrate on the familiar* paths tourists

128

take while in town. This is not a criticism; it is reality. Not one guidebook, for example, lists Restaurant Byblos, probably because none is prepared to venture to the Lebanese Social & Sports Club, thinking that it is a private club.

With this background, here is a comprehensive listing of restaurants that we have been to, or guests have enjoyed, or that friends and colleagues have recommended. They have been arranged by neighborhood. So go out there and have a great meal somewhere in town!

An Appreciation: Alberto's Continental

Alberto's Continental, housed in the mansion located on the corner of Calle 64 and Calle 57, served Mérida and her visitors for more than half a century. Operated by Alberto Salum and his brother Pedro Salum, their Lebanese menu reflected the best of Mérida's international culinary offerings. From European royalty to Mérida's merry band of Alpha Delta Phi brothers, from National Geographic luminaries to Mexican presidents, from Jacqueline Kennedy to Jacques Pepin, Alberto's Continental served them all.

In 2013, after much reflection, the brothers decided to close their restaurant and retire.

"We are legends," Alberto Salum said, "and we want to conclude an era, rather than sell it and incur the risk of our reputation being diminished."

Thus, to avoid the fate of the Russian Room or Elaine's, they served their final meal in style and grace in the summer of 2013.

Thank you, Alberto! Thank you, Pedro! Thanks for the meals—and the memories.

Centro (Downtown) - Restaurants

2012 Espacios mayas
Cuisine: Yucatecan and Vegetarian
Telephone: (999) 155-6539
Address: Calle 62 #468-A, between Calle 55 and 57 Street
Parking: No (in public parking lots nearby)
Air Conditioned: No
Outdoors: Yes
Drinks: Coffees, Teas, Juices
Hours: 8 AM to 11 PM, Closed Monday

Amaro
Cuisine: Yucatecan and Vegetarian
Telephone: (999) 928-2451
Address: Calle 59 #507, between Calle 60 and 62 Street
Parking: No (in public parking lots nearby)
Air Conditioned: No
Outdoors: Yes
Drinks: Full bar
Hours: Daily, 11 AM to 2 AM
Website: *www.restauranteamaro.com*

Apoala
Cuisine: Mexican cuisine
Telephone: (999) 923-1979
Address: Calle 60 #471, between 53 60 and 55 Street

129

Parking: Yes
Air Conditioned: Yes
Outdoors: Yes
Drinks: Full bar
Hours: Daily, 11 AM to 2 AM
Website: *www.apoala.mx*

Bella Epoca

Cuisine: Yucatecan
Telephone: (999) 928-1928
Address: Calle 60 #497, between Calle 57 and 59 Street
Parking: 2 doors north of the restaurant is a parking lot
Air Conditioned: No
Outdoors: Yes
Drinks: Full bar
Hours: Daily, 5 PM to 1 AM

Bengala Kaffeehaus

Cuisine: Coffeeshop
Telephone: (999) 928-1246
Address: Calle 60 between Calle 55 and 53 Street
Parking: No
Air Conditioned: Yes
Outdoors: No
Drinks: Coffees, teas and light fare
Hours: Daily, 7AM to 11 PM
Facebook:
https://www.facebook.com/La-Cubanita-1535067146773215/?fref=ts

Bistro Cultural

Cuisine: Café and breakfasts
Telephone: (999) 217-9240
Address: Calle 66 #377, between Calle 41 and 43 Street
Parking: Street Parking
Air Conditioned: No
Outdoors: Covered patio
Drinks: Coffees and French breakfasts

Hours: Monday to Friday, 9 AM to 6 PM; Saturday, 9 AM to 2 PM; Closed Sundays

Bryan's Burger & Bar

Cuisine: Burgers and bar food
Telephone: (999) 923-3787
Address: Calle 60 and Calle 55, interior of Santa Lucia
Parking: Yes
Air Conditioned: Yes
Outdoors: Covered patio
Drinks: Full bar
Hours: Daily, Noon to 11 PM
Website: *www.trottersmerida.com*

Café Alameda

Cuisine: Lebanese
Telephone: (999) 928 3635
Address: Intersection of Calle 58 and Calle 55
Parking: Next door in a public lot
Air Conditioned: No
Drinks: Beer and soft drinks
Hours: Daily, 8:00 AM to 5:00 PM

Café la Blanca Mérida

Cuisine: Coffee Shop and Cafeteria
Telephone: (999) 928-4715
Address: Intersection of Calle 59 Calle 62
Parking: No
Air Conditioned: No
Outdoors: No
Drinks: Coffees, juices and sodas
Hours: Daily, 7 AM to 10 PM

Café Chocolate

Cuisine: Coffee Shop
Telephone: (999) 928-5113
Address: Intersection of Calle 60 Calle 49

Parking: Yes
Air Conditioned: No
Outdoors: Yes
Drinks: No alcohol is served
Hours: Daily, 7 AM to 12 AM
Website: *www.cafe-chocolate.com.mx*

Café Club Manushan
Cuisine: Café
Telephone: (999) 923-1592
Address: Intersection of Calle 55 and Calle 58
Parking: Next door in the public lot
Air Conditioned: One room is sometimes air conditioned
Outdoors: Yes
Drinks: Beer and soft drinks
Hours: Monday-Saturday from 7:00 AM to 5:00 PM

Café Creme
Cuisine: Café
Telephone: (999) 278-5073
Address: Calle 41 # 386-B, corner of Calle 60
Parking: Street
Air Conditioned: No
Outdoors: Yes
Drinks: Coffees and soft drinks
Hours: Monday-Saturday from 9:00 AM to 5:00 PM

Café El Hoyo
Cuisine: Café
Telephone: (999) 928-1531
Address: Calle 62 #487, between Calle 59 and 57 Street
Parking: No
Air Conditioned: No
Outdoors: Yes

Drinks: Lattes, soft drinks, non-alcoholic beverages
Hours: Monday- Saturday from 9 AM to 11 PM
Facebook: *www.facebook.com/pages/cafe-el-hoyo/103219969831#!/pages/cafe-el-hoyo/103219969831?v=wall*

Café La Habana
Cuisine: Coffee shop, Yucatán-style breakfasts
Telephone: (999) 928-0608
Address: Intersection of Calle 59 and 62 Street
Parking: Across the street in city parking lot
Air Conditioned: Yes
Outdoors: No
Drinks: Full bar
Hours: 24 hours

Café Creme
Cuisine: Coffee shop, specializing in French pastries, cakes, salads and cheese plates
Address: Calle 41 #386, between Calle 60 and 58th Street
Parking: No
Air Conditioned: No
Outdoors: Yes
Hours: 8 AM to 7 PM

Café Peón Contreras
Cuisine: International
Telephone: (999) 924-7003
Address: Calle 60, between Calle 57 and 59 Street
Parking: No
Air Conditioned: Yes
Outdoors: Yes

Drinks: Full bar
Hours: Daily, 7 AM to 1 AM

Café Pop

Cuisine: Coffee, breakfasts and light lunches
Telephone: (999) 928-6163
Address: Calle 57, between Calle 60 and 62 Street
Parking: Street parking
Air Conditioned: Yes
Outdoors: No
Drinks: Coffees, teas and breakfasts
Hours: Daily, 7AM to 12 AM

Café Punta del Cielo

Cuisine: Café
Telephone: (999) 923-1134
Address: Calle 63 #508, between Calle 60 and 62nd Street
Parking: No
Air Conditioned: Yes
Outdoors: No
Drinks: Lattes, soft drinks, non-alcoholic beverages
Hours: Monday- Saturday from 9 AM to 11 PM; Sundays from Noon to 7 PM
Second Location: Yes, at City Center Shopping Mall, Locals 71 and 72: Telephone: (999) 913-9090

Casa Catherwood

Cuisine: Contemporary Mexcian
Telephone: (999) 908-6802
Address: Calle 59 #573 between Calle 72 and 74 Street
Parking: No
Air Conditioned: Yes
OUTDOORS: Yes
Drinks: Non-alcoholic beverages
Drinks: Daily, 8 AM to 8 PM

Website: https://www.facebook.com/pages/Casa-Catherwood-Spa-boutique-Restaurante/653407858081298

Casa Lucía

Cuisine: International, mostly Italian
Telephone: (999) 928 2863
Address: Calle 60 #474 A between Calle 53 and 55 Street
Parking: No
Air Conditioned: Yes
OUTDOORS: Yes
Drinks: Full bar
Drinks: Daily, 7:30 AM to 11:00 PM
Website: www.casalucia.com.mx

El Gallito

Cuisine: Yucatecan
Telephone: (999) 928-6495
Address: Calle 45 between Calle 60 and 62 Street
Parking: Yes, across the street
Air Conditioned: No
Outdoors: Yes
Drinks: Soft drinks, beer and hard liquors
Hours: Daily, 11 AM to 7 PM
Website: cantinasdemerida.blogspot.com/2006/10/el-gallito.html

El Trapiche

Cuisine: Tacos and Yucatecan food
Telephone: (999) 928 1231
Address: Calle 62 #491 between Calle 59 and 61 Street
Parking: No
Air Conditioned: No
Outdoors: Yes
Drinks: Beer and soft drinks
Hours: Daily, 7:00 AM to 11:00 PM

El Pez Gordo

Cuisine: Seafood
Telephone: (999) 923-3009
Address: Calle 60, between Calle 53 and 55 Street
Parking: Yes
Air Conditioned: Yes
Outdoors: Yes
Drinks: Beer and soft drinks
Hours: Daily, Noon to 10:00 PM
Facebook:
https://www.facebook.com/PezGordo
Centro

El Venadito Azul

Cuisine: Mexican Bistro (Vegetarian)
Telephone: (999) 218-3946
Address: Calle 60 #429-II, between Calle 49 and 51 Street
Parking: No
Air Conditioned: No
Outdoors: Yes
Drinks: Beer and soft drinks
Hours: Daily, 5 PM to 2 AM
Email: elvenaditoazul@gmail.com

Hotel Casa del Balam

Cuisine: Yucatecan and International
Telephone: (999) 924-8844
Address: Calle 60 #488 by 57 Street
Parking: Yes
Air Conditioned: Yes
Outdoors: Yes
Drinks: Full bar
Hours: Daily, 7 AM to 12 PM
Website: *www.casadelbalam.com*

Ki'Hanah

Cuisine: Yucatecan Restaurant
Telephone: (999) 923-3987

Address: Calle 62 #502, by Calle 63
Parking: No
Air Conditioned: Yes
Outdoors: Yes
Drinks: Yes
Hours: Daily, 8 AM to 10 PM

La Blanca Mérida

Cuisine: Yucatecan
Address: Calle 62 and 59 Street
Parking: No
Air Conditioned: Yes
Outdoors: No
Drinks: Soft drinks and beers
Hours: Daily, 7AM to 2 AM

La Casa de Frida

Cuisine: Mexican
Telephone: (999) 928-2311
Address: Calle 61 #526-A between Calle 66 and 68 Street
Parking: No
Air Conditioned: No
Outdoors: Yes
Drinks: Full bar
Hours: Monday-Friday: 6 PM to 10 PM; Saturday: 12 AM to 5 PM and 6 PM to 10 PM; Sunday: 12 AM to 5 PM
Website: *www.lacasadefrida.com.mx*

La Casa de Te

Cuisine: Tea/Coffee House with salads and crepes
Address: Calle 62 between Calle 55 and 57 Street
Parking: No
Air Conditioned: No
Outdoors: Yes
Drinks: Soft drinks, coffees and teas
Hours: Monday—Saturday, 3:00 PM to 11:00 PM

133

La Casona della Nonna

Cuisine: Italian, handmade pastas
Address: Calle 43 #496 between Calle 58 and 60 Street
Parking: No
Air Conditioned: No
Outdoors: No
Drinks: Soft drinks, coffees and teas
Hours: Tuesday—Saturday, 6:00 PM to 11:00 PM

La Chaya Maya

Cuisine: Yucatecan
Telephone: (999) 928 4780
Address: Calle 62 and 57 Street
Parking: In adjacent city parking lot
Air Conditioned: Yes
Outdoors: No
Drinks: Beer and soft drinks
Hours: 7 AM to 11 PM Every Day

La Chaya Maya

Cuisine: Yucatecan
Telephone: (999) 928 4780
Address: Calle 55 #510, between Calle 60 and 62 Street
Parking: In adjacent city parking lot
Air Conditioned: Yes
Outdoors: Yes
Drinks: Beer and soft drinks
Hours: 7 AM to 11 PM Every Day

La Choperia

Cuisine: Brazilian and Mexican fusion
Telephone: (999) 924-4488
Address: Calle 56 #456 between Calle 51 and 53 Street
Parking: Yes
Air Conditioned: Yes
Outdoors: Yes
Drinks: Full bar

Hours: Tuesday to Saturday: 1 PM to 2 AM; Sunday 1 PM to 7 PM.

La Cubanita

Cuisine: Cuban
Telephone: (999) 923-4446
Address: Calle 51 #502, between Calle 60 and Calle 62
Parking: No
Air Conditioned: Yes
Outdoors: No
Drinks: Coffees, teas, soft drinks and beer
Hours: Daily, 8 AM to 4 PM

La Flor de Santiago

Cuisine: Coffee and breakfast/lunch diner
Telephone: (999) 928-5591
Address: Calle 70 between Calle 57 and 59 Street
Parking: No
Air Conditioned: Yes
Outdoors: Yes
Drinks: Coffees, teas, soft drinks and beer
Hours: Daily, 7AM to 2 AM

La Sabia Virtud

Cuisine: Mexican
Telephone: (999) 252-0380
Address: Calle 55 #504 between Calle 60 and 62 Street
Parking: No
Air Conditioned: Yes
Outdoors: No
Drinks: Soft drinks
Hours: Monday-Wednesday: 7:30 AM to 6 PM; Thursday- Saturday: 7:30 AM to 10 PM; Sunday: 8 AM to 6 PM
Websites: *www.lasabiavirtud.com*

La Recova (Santa Lucia)

Cuisine: Argentine
Telephone: (999) 944-0215
Address: Call 60 and Calle 55, Santa Lucia Park
Parking: Yes
Air Conditioned: Yes
Outdoors: Yes
Drinks: Full bar
Hours: Monday-Saturday: 1 PM to 2 AM; Sunday: 1 PM to 12 AM
Website: *www.larecovamerida.com*

La Tradición (Centro)

Cuisine: Yucatecan
Telephone: (999) 925-2526
Address: Calle 60 #462 between Calle 53 and 55th Street
Parking: Yes
Air Conditioned: Yes
Drinks: Full bar
Hours: Daily, 11:30 AM to 6:30 PM
Website: *www.facebook.com/latradicion*

Lo Que Hay

Cuisine: Vegetarian, Vegan, and International
Telephone: (999) 924-5472
Address: Inside the Medio Mundo Hotel, Calle 55 #533, between Calle 64 and 66 Street
Parking: No
Air Conditioned: Yes
Drinks: Full bar
Hours: Daily, 7 PM to 10 PM
Website: https://www.facebook.com/loquehay.mediomundo?fref=ts

Los Almendros

Cuisine: Yucatecan
Telephone: (999) 923-8135
Address: Calle 57 #468 by 52 Street
Parking: Yes
Air Conditioned: Yes
Outdoors: No
Drinks: Full bar
Hours: Daily, 12 AM to 6 PM

La Tratto

Cuisine: Italian
Telephone: (999) 927-0434
Address: Calle 60, between Calle 53 and 55 Street
Parking: Yes
Air Conditioned: Yes
Outdoors: Yes
Drinks: Full bar
Hours: Daily, 6 PM to 2 AM
Website: *www.trottersmerida.com*

Los Henequenes

Cuisine: Yucatecan
Telephone: (999) 923-6220
Address: Calle 57 #479 by 56 Street
Parking: Street parking available
Air Conditioned: Yes
Outdoors: No
Drinks: Full bar
Hours: Daily, 11 AM to 7 PM
Website: *www.loshenequenes.com*

Main Street

Cuisine: Mexican and Regional Cuisine
Telephone: (999) 923-6850
Address: Calle 60, between Calle 59 and 61 Sreet
Parking: No
Air Conditioned: Yes
Outdoors: No

Drinks: Full bar
Hours: Tuesday-Saturday: Noon to 10 AM; Sunday: 1PM to 6 PM, Closed on Monday

Pan E Vino

Cuisine: Italian
Address: Calle 59 and 64 Street
Parking: No
Air Conditioned: Yes
Outdoors: No
Drinks: Full bar
Hours: Tuesday-Saturday: 7 PM to 2 AM; Sunday: 1PM to 2 AM, Closed on Monday

Pancho's

Cuisine: Mexican &Yucatecan
Telephone: (999) 923-0942
Address: Calle 59, between Calle 60 and 52 Street
Parking: City parking on the corner of Calle 62 and 59 Street
Air Conditioned: No
Outdoors: Yes
Drinks: Full bar
Hours: Daily, 6PM to 2 AM
Website: *www.trottersmerida.com*

Pita

Cuisine: Mediterranean
Telephone: (999) 923-1592
Address: Calle 55 #496, between Calle 58 and 60 Street
Parking: No
Air Conditioned: Yes
Outdoors: Yes
Drinks: Soft drinks, teas, coffees, beers, wine
Hours: Daily, Noon to 11 PM

Pizzas Raffaelo

Cuisine: Pizza
Neighborhood: Centro
Telephone: (999) 924-9943
Address: Calle 60 by 49 Street
Parking: No
Air Conditioned: Yes
Outdoors: No
Drinks: Soft drinks
Hours: Monday-Friday, 12 PM to 4 PM and 5:30 PM to 11:30 PM; Saturday-Sunday, 5 PM to 12 AM

Portico del Peregrino

Cuisine: Yucatecan with some international cuisine
Telephone: (999) 928-6163
Address: Calle 57 by 60 Street
Parking: City parking on the corner of Calle 62 and 57 Street
Air Conditioned: Yes
Outdoors: Yes
Drinks: Full bar
Hours: 24 hours

Restaurant San José

Cuisine: Yucatecan
Telephone: (999) 928-6657
Address: Calle 63, between Calle 62 and 64 Street
Parking: No
Air Conditioned: No
Outdoors: Yes
Drinks: Beer and Soft Drinks
Hours: Daily, 7:00 AM to 10:30 PM

Rosa Sur 32

Cuisine: International
Telephone: (999) 924-2992
Address: Calle 60 and Calle 55, interior of Santa Lucia
Parking: No

Air Conditioned: No
Outdoors: Yes
Drinks: Full Bar
Hours: Daily, Noon to 11 PM
Facebook:
  https://www.facebook.com/rosasur32/timeline

Siqueff
Cuisine: Lebanese and International

Telephone: (999) 925-5027
Address: Calle 60 #350, between Calle 35 and 37 Street
Parking: Yes
Air Conditioned: Yes
Outdoors: Yes
Drinks: Full bar
Hours: Daily, 8 AM to 6 PM

Colonia Alcalá- Restaurants

La Tradición
Cuisine: Yucatecan
Telephone: (999) 925-2526
Address: Calle 60 #293 by 25 Street
Parking: Yes
Air Conditioned: Yes
Outdoors: No
Drinks: Full bar
Hours: Daily, 11:30 AM to 6:30 PM

Pimienta
Cuisine: Yucatecan, but only breakfast and lunch
Telephone: (999) 920-2953
Address: Calle 60 #326, between Calle 23 and 25 Street
Parking: Street parking
Air Conditioned: Yes
Outdoors: No
Drinks: Full bar
Hours: Daily at 8 AM to 6 PM

Colonia Benito Juárez Norte (Prolongación Montejo Norte) - Restaurants

Buda Wok
Cuisine: Chinese/International
Telephone: (999) 948-3088
Address: Prolongación Montejo #367, between Calle 47 and 49 Street
Parking: Yes
Air Conditioned: Yes
Outdoors: Yes
Drinks: Full bar
Hours: Monday-Saturday: 1 PM to 2 AM and Sunday: 1 PM a 6 PM

Konsushi
Cuisine: Japanese
Telephone: (999) 948-1377
Address: Calle 46-A #485, on the corner of Calle 33
Parking: Yes
Air Conditioned: Yes
Outdoors: Yes
Drinks: Domestic and International beers
Hours: Daily, 1 PM to 12 AM

La Recova

Cuisine: Argentinian steakhouse
Telephone: (999) 944-0215
Address: Prolongación Montejo #382 between Calle 33 and 35 Street
Parking: Yes (Valet)
Air Conditioned: Yes
Outdoors: No
Drinks: Full bar
Hours: Monday-Saturday: 1 PM to 2 AM; Sunday: 1 PM to 12 AM
Website: *www.larecovamerida.com*

Colonia Buenavista - Restaurants

El Santo Pez

Cuisine: Seafood
Telephone: (999) 926-4587
Address: Circuito Colonia, between Calle 36 and 38 Street
Parking: Yes
Air Conditioned: Yes
Outdoors: Yes
Drinks: Full bar
Hours: Daily, 12 PM to 7 AM

Muelle 8

Cuisine: Seafood
Telephone: (999) 944-5343
Address: Calle 21 #142 between Calle 30 and 32 Street
Parking: Street parking
Air Conditioned: Yes
Outdoors: No
Drinks: Full bar
Hours: Daily, 12 PM to 6 PM

Rincón Oaxaqueño

Cuisine: Oaxacan

Telephone: (999) 286-9492
Address: Circuito Colonias #151 between Calle 40 and 60 Street
Parking: Yes
Air Conditioned: Yes
Drinks: Soft drinks
Hours: Tuesday to Saturday: 12 AM to 11 PM; Sunday: 9 pm to 5 PM

Trotter's

Cuisine: Steak, Fish, Salads, Tapas
Telephone: (999) 927-2310
Address: Circuito Colonias, between Prolongación Montejo and Calle 60 Norte, adjacent to the Renault dealer
Parking: Yes
Air Conditioned: Yes
Outdoors: Yes
Drinks: Full bar
Hours: Monday-Saturday: 1 PM to 2 AM, Sunday: 1PM to 6 PM
Website: *www.trottersmerida.com*

Colonia Campestre - Restaurants

Café La Habana

Cuisine: Coffee shop, Yucatán-style breakfasts
Telephone: (999) 928-0608
Address: Prolongación Montejo #260, across from Club Campestre
Parking: Street parking
Air Conditioned: Yes
Outdoors: No

Drinks: Full bar
Hours: 24 hours

One Burger
Cuisine: Hamburgers and fries
Telephone: (999) 948-2626
Address: Prolongación Montejo #250, across from Club Campestre
Parking: Street parking
Air Conditioned: Yes
Outdoors: Yes
Drinks: Shakes and sodas
Hours: Sunday—Wednesday, 12 PM - 11 PM; Thursday—Saturday, 12 PM t- 2 AM

Pamplona Steak House
Cuisine: Steak house
Telephone: (999) 944-1413
Address: Prolongación Montejo #248-C and Calle 36
Parking: Street parking
Air Conditioned: Yes
Outdoors: Yes
Drinks: Full Bar
Hours: Sunday, 1 PM – PM; Monday-Saturday, Noon to 11 PM
Facebook:
https://www.facebook.com/Pamplona-Steak-House-tel9441413-448712515261765/timeline

Colonia Díaz Ordaz (Most near Paseo de Montejos at Monumento a la Patria) - Restaurants

Café Impala
Cuisine: International
Telephone: (999) 923-8196
Address: At the beginning of Paseo de Montejo and Calle 47
Parking: Parking along the side streets
Air Conditioned: No
Outdoors: Yes
Drinks: Coffee, sodas, waters, beer
Hours: Daily, 5 PM to 2 AM
Twitter: *https://twitter.com/cafeimpala*
Email: *cafeteriaimpala@gmail.com*

Cubaro
Cuisine: International
Telephone: (999) 926-6587
Address: Monumento a la Patria and Paseo de Montejo

Parking: Valet or on along the side streets
Air Conditioned: No
Outdoors: Yes
Drinks: Full bar
Hours: Daily, 1PM to 2 AM

Ku'uk
Cuisine: Yucatecan Gourmet
Telephone: (999) 944-3377
Address: Avenida Romulo Rozo #488 by Calle 27-A (Monumento a la Patria)
Parking: Yes
Air Conditioned: Yes
Drinks: Full Bar
Hours: Daily, 9 AM to Midnight
Website: *http://kuukrestaurant.com*

La Musa
Cuisine: Coffee Shop and Internet

139

Telephone: (999) 246-8944
Address: Paseo de Montejo between Calle 43 and 45 Street
Parking: Parking along the side streets
Air Conditioned: Yes
Outdoors: Yes
Drinks: Coffee Shop and Internet Cafe
Hours: Daily, 9 AM to 6 PM

Meson del Conde

Cuisine: Spanish
Telephone: (999) 943-2828
Address: Avenida Correa Rancho #370
Parking: Yes
Air Conditioned: Yes
Outdoors: Yes
Drinks: Full bar
Hours: Daily, 11 AM to 7 PM

Nectar

Cuisine: International
Telephone: (999) 938-0838
Address: Avenida 21 #413 between Calle 6-A and 8 Street
Parking: Yes
Air Conditioned: Yes
Outdoors: No
Drinks: Full bar

Hours: Tuesday-Saturday: 7 PM to 2 AM; Sunday: 1 PM to 2 AM, Closed on Monday
Website: *www.nectarmerida.com.mx*

Slavia

Cuisine: Tapas and International Entrees
Telephone: (999) 926-6587
Address: Monumento a la Patria and Paseo de Montejo
Parking: Yes, valet parking and some limited parking on the street
Air Conditioned: Yes
Outdoors: No
Drinks: Full bar
Hours: Daily, 6 PM to 2 AM

Tobago

Cuisine: Coffees, teas and desserts
Telephone: (999) 926-6587
Address: Monumento a la Patria and Paseo de Montejo
Parking: Valet parking at Slavia
Air Conditioned: No
Outdoors: Yes
Drinks: Full bar
Hours: Every Day: 6 PM to 2 AM

Colonia Emilio Zapata Norte (Prolongación Montejo Norte) - Restaurants

El Argentino

Cuisine: Steak House
Telephone: (999) 926-5444
Address: Prolongación Montejo #116, by Calle 25
Parking: Ample street parking
Air Conditioned: Yes
Outdoors: No
Drinks: Full bar

Hours: Monday- Saturday: 1 PM to 12 AM, Sunday 1 PM to 8 PM

La Rueda

Cuisine: Steak House
Telephone: (999) 912-2387
Address: Calle 37 #352-A by 67-B Street
Parking: Yes
Air Conditioned: Yes

Outdoors: No
Drinks: Full bar
Hours: Daily, 12 PM to 2 AM

Miyabi

Cuisine: Japanese
Telephone: (999) 948-9896
Address: Prolongación Montejo and Calle 34, inside the shopping center
Parking: Yes
Air Conditioned: Yes
Outdoors: No
Drinks: Non-alcoholic beverages, but customers can bring their own liquor.
Hours: Tuesday to Sunday: 1 PM to 11 PM

Tapioca Joe

Cuisine: Teas and smoothies
Address: Calle 34 #396, between Calle 39 and 41 Street
Parking: Yes
Air Conditioned: Yes
Outdoors: Yes

Drinks: Beverages
Hours: Monday - Thursday, 12 PM to 9 PM; Friday—Saturday, 12 PM to 10:30 PM; Sunday, 12:30 PM to 7 PM.
Website: *www.tapiocajoe.com*
Facebook: *www.facebook.com/people/Tapioca-Joe/100000638496040*

Colonia García Ginerés - Restaurants

El Tío Ricardo

Cuisine: Steak House
Telephone: (999) 925-2967
Address: Calle 8 #201 and 23 Street
Parking: Street parking
Air Conditioned: Yes
Outdoors: No
Drinks: Full bar
Hours: 24 hours

Los Platos Rotos

Cuisine: Central Mexican
Telephone: (999) 925-3097
Address: Calle 33-D #498, Suite 3, by Reforma
Parking: Street parking
Air Conditioned: No
Outdoors: Yes
Drinks: Soft Drinks and fruit juices
Hours: Monday—Friday, 8 AM to about 3 PM

Colonia Itzimná - Restaurants

Due Torri

Cuisine: Italian
Telephone: (999) 926-2505
Address: Calle 27 #349 between Calle 10 and 12 Street
Parking: Ample street parking
Air Conditioned: Yes
Outdoors: Yes
Drinks: Full bar

Hours: Daily, 1 PM to 11:15 PM

Entre Tangos

Cuisine: Steak House
Telephone: (999) 938-1838
Address: Ave. Pérez Ponce 118, between Calle 21 and 23 Street
Parking: Yes
Air Conditioned: Yes

Outdoors: No
Drinks: Full bar
Hours: Tuesday -Saturday: 1 PM to 12 AM; Sunday: 1 PM to 6 PM

Meyer's

Cuisine: German Deli
Telephone: (999) 926-0117
Address: Calle 18 #91-F, corner of Calle 13
Parking: Ample street parking
Air Conditioned: Yes
Outdoors: Yes
Drinks: Full bar
Hours: Daily, 7AM to 11 PM

Wine House International

Cuisine: International
Telephone: (999) 286-8029
Address: Calle 20 #91-A, between Calle 15 and 17 Street
Parking: Yes
Air Conditioned: Yes
Outdoors: Yes
Drinks: Full bar, specializing in rums
Hours: Tuesday—Sunday, 1:30 PM to 12 AM; Closed Mondays

Colonia Jesús Carranza - Restaurants

Hacienda San Antonio

Cuisine: Steak and Tacos
Neighborhood: Colonia Jesús Carranza
Telephone: (999) 926-0480
Address: Calle 27 by 44 Street

Parking: Yes
Air Conditioned: Yes
Outdoors: Yes
Drinks: Soft Drinks and beer
Hours: Daily, 12 PM to 7 PM

Colonia Málaga - Restaurants

SOMA

Cuisine: Modern American and Southeastern Cuisine
Neighborhood: Fraccionamiento Málaga
Telephone: (999) 195-6474

Address: Calle 21 #375 by Calle 60 and 12 Street
Parking: Yes
Air Conditioned: Yes
Outdoors: Yes
Drinks: Soft Drinks and beer
Hours: Monday-Thursday, 9 AM to 6 PM

Colonia Mejorada - Restaurants

El Café

Cuisine: Breakfast and Lunch
Telephone: (999) 924-0117
Address: Calle 59 #452-A between Calle 52 and 54 Street

Parking: Public parking across the street
Air Conditioned: No
Outdoors: Yes
Drinks: Coffees, teas and soft Drinks
Hours: Daily, 7:30 AM to 4 PM

Colonia Mexico - Restaurants

Acitrón

Cuisine: International, but with a Yucatecan twist
Telephone: (999) 926-0707
Address: Calle 30 #122-A, between Calle 27 and 29 Street, Plaza la Avenida (along Prolongación Montejo)
Parking: Street parking
Air Conditioned: Yes
Outdoors: Yes
Drinks: Full bar
Hours: Tuesday through Saturday, 1 PM to 2 AM; Sunday 1 PM to 6 PM
Facebook: *www.facebook.com/pages/merida-Mexico/ACITRON/75112500828*

Acqua

Cuisine: International
Telephone: (999) 926-8211
Address: Calle 21 #73, between Calle 12 and 14 Street
Parking: Yes
Air Conditioned: Yes
Outdoors: Yes
Drinks: Full bar
Hours: Monday-Saturday: 1.30 PM to 2 AM; Sunday: 1PM to 5 PM and Monday: 6 PM to 1 AM

BBT Wings

Cuisine: American
Telephone: (999) 254-0909
Address: Calle 27 #98, between Calle 20 and 18 Street
Parking: Yes
Air Conditioned: Yes
Outdoors: Yes

Drinks: Full bar
Hours: Daily, from 6 PM to 2 AM

Bennigan's

Cuisine: American
Telephone: (999) 927-2731
Address: Intersection of Prolongación Montejo and Calle 27
Parking: Yes
Air Conditioned: Yes
Outdoors: Yes
Drinks: Full bar
Hours: Sunday-Tuesday: 1 PM-12 AM; Wednesday-Thursday: 12 PM - 1 AM; Friday-Saturday: 1 PM—2 AM
Website: *www.bennigans.com*

Buenos Aires City

Cuisine: Steak House
Telephone: (999) 927-9090
Address: Circuito Colonias corner of Calle 12
Parking: Yes
Air Conditioned: Yes
Outdoors: Yes
Drinks: Full bar
Hours: Daily, 1 PM to 12 AM
Website: *www.buenosairescity.com.mx*

Campay

Cuisine: Japanese
Telephone: (999) 948-0385
Address: Calle 19 #106 on the corner of 22 Street
Parking: Street parking
Air Conditioned: Yes
Outdoors: No
Drinks: Full bar

143

Hours: Daily, 1 PM to 11 PM

Go Green
Cuisine: Salad Bar
Address: Prolongación Montejo and 19 Street
Parking: Yes
Air Conditioned: Yes
Outdoors: Yes
Drinks: Soft Drinks
Hours: 24 hours

Guru
Cuisine: Lebanese
Telephone: (999) 252-8400
Address: Calle 20 S/N (in Mexico, "S/N" means "without a number," meaning it's a short street with only one or two buildings, or a sliver of land dissected by major roads; this restaurant is across from the Pemex gas station on Calle 20)
Parking: Yes
Air Conditioned: Yes
Outdoors: Yes
Drinks: Full bar
Hours: Tuesday- Saturday: 1 PM to 2 AM; Sunday 1 PM to 6 PM
Facebook: *www.facebook.com/group.php?gid=42910880447*

La Nao de China
Cuisine: Chinese
Telephone: (999) 926-1441
Address: Circuito Colonias #13, between Prolongación Paseo Montejo and Chapur Department Store
Parking: Yes
Air Conditioned: Yes
Outdoors: No

Drinks: Soft drinks and beers
Hours: Daily, 11 AM to 9 PM

La Parrilla
Cuisine: Mexican
Telephone: (999) 944-3999
Address: Calle 30 #87 by 17 Street
Parking: Yes
Air Conditioned: Yes
Outdoors: Yes
Drinks: Full bar
Hours: Daily, 12 PM to 2 AM
Website: *www.laparrilla.com.mx*

Sushi Itto
Cuisine: Sushi
Telephone: (999) 944-3232
Address: Prolongación Montejo #348, between Calle 29 and 31 Street
Parking: Yes
Air Conditioned: Yes
Outdoors: Yes
Drinks: National and imported beers
Hours: Monday-Tuesday: 1 PM to 11 PM; Wednesday-Saturday: 1 PM to 12 AM; Sunday: 1 PM to 10 PM
Website: *www.sushi-itto.com.mx*

Taquitos PM
Cuisine: Mexican (tacos)
Telephone: (999) 944-0342
Address: Prolongación Montejo #382 on the corner of Calle 35
Parking: No
Air Conditioned: No
Outdoors: Yes
Drinks: Full bar
Hours: Monday-Thursday, 7 PM to 2 AM; Friday-Sunday, 12 PM to 2 AM
Facebook: *www.facebook.com/pages/Mérida-Mexico/Los-Taquitos-de-PM/30715198715*

Todo Latino

Cuisine: Pan-Latin American
Telephone: (999) 926-8090
Address: Avenida 31 #109, between Calle 22 and 24 Street
Parking: Yes
Air Conditioned: Yes

Outdoors: Yes, a rooftop area with seating
Drinks: Full bar
Hours: Wednesday to Monday, 12:30 PM to 2 AM; Sunday, 12:30 PM to 6 PM

Colonia Mexico Norte - Restaurants

Byblos

Cuisine: Lebanese
Telephone: (999) 899-0141
Address: Calle 1-G #101, between Calle 14-A and 16 Street
Parking: Yes
Air Conditioned: Yes
Outdoors: No
Drinks: Full bar
Hours: Daily, 1 PM to 7 PM

El Postrecito

Cuisine: Desserts and coffee
Telephone: (999) 927-2479
Address: Calle 21 #111 between Calle 22 and 24 Street
Parking: Yes
Air Conditioned: Yes
Outdoors: Yes
Drinks: Soft Drinks

Hours: Monday- Saturday: 12 PM to 11 PM; Sunday from 12 PM to 10 PM
Website: *www.elpostrecito.com*
Facebook:
www.facebook.com/pages/Mérida-Mexico/El-Postrecito/114905387216

Sazón Gourmet

Cuisine: Upscale Mexican dishes, breakfast and lunch
Telephone: (999) 927-8776
Address: Calle 21 #80, between Calle 14 and 16 Street
Parking: Street parking
Air Conditioned: Yes
Outdoors: Yes
Drinks: Full bar
Hours: Monday—Saturday, 8 AM to 4:30 PM

Colonia Mexico Oriente - Restaurants

Rue 21

Cuisine: French
Telephone: (999) 926-3626
Address: Calle 21 #416 by 8 Street
Parking: Yes
Air Conditioned: Yes

Outdoors: Yes
Drinks: Full bar
Hours: Daily, 12 PM to 12 AM
Website:
www.lahabichuela.com/merida/merida.htm

145

Colonia Misne - Restaurants

Hacienda Misne

Cuisine: Yucatecan and International
Telephone: (999) 940-7150
Address: Calle 19 #172
Parking: Yes

Air Conditioned: Yes
Outdoors: Yes
Drinks: Full bar
Hours: Daily, 7AM to 11 PM
Website: *www.haciendamisne.com.mx*

Colonia Montecristo - Restaurants

Ichi Sushi

Cuisine: Japanese
Neighborhood: Colonia Montecristo
Telephone: (999) 948-0203
Address: Calle 1 #105, between Calle 8 and 10 Street
Parking: Yes
Air Conditioned: Yes
Outdoors: Yes
Drinks: No
Hours: Daily, 1:30 PM to 11 PM

Bryan's

Cuisine: New York Steakhouse
Telephone: (999) 948-2034
Address: Avenida Cámara de Comercio between Boxito and Instituto Cumbres
Parking: Yes
Air Conditioned: Yes
Outdoors: Yes
Drinks: Full bar
Hours: Daily, 1 PM to 3 AM
Website: *www.trottersmerida.com*

Colonia Monterreal - Restaurants

Sensei
Cuisine: Sushi Bar
Telephone: (999) 944-0202
Address: Calle 37 #202, between Calle 18 and 22 Street
Parking: Yes
Air Conditioned: Yes
Outdoors: Yes
Drinks: Full bar
Hours: Daily, 1 PM to 12 AM
Website: *www.sensei.com.mx*

Silver Fish
Cuisine: Seafood
Telephone: (999) 948-2466
Address: Glorieta el Centrico
Parking: Yes
Air Conditioned: Yes
Outdoors: No
Drinks: Full bar
Hours: Daily, 11:30 AM to 6:30 PM

Colonia San Antonio Curul—Restaurants

Vibora de la Mar
Cuisine: Seafood
Telephone: (999) 944-9332
Address: Calle 32 #55, between Calle 55 and 57 Street
Parking: Yes
Air Conditioned: Yes
Outdoors: No

Drinks: Full bar
Hours: Tuesday to Sunday, 1 PM to 11 PM
Facebook: *www.facebook.com/group.php?gid=16781836654*

Colonia San Ramón—Restaurants

Merci
Cuisine: Health Food and Bakery
Telephone: (999) 941-6885
Address: Calle 25 # 218
Parking: Yes
Air Conditioned: Yes
Outdoors: No
Drinks: Coffees and waters
Hours: Daily, 1 PM to 11 PM
Website: *www.facebook.com/group.php?gid=16781836654*

Kii'wik Restaurant
Cuisine: Breakfast and Brunch
Telephone: (999) 944-0522
Address: Avenida García Lavín #313, on the corner of Calle 37-B
Parking: Yes
Air Conditioned: Yes
Outdoors: No
Drinks: Coffees and full bar
Hours: Daily, 8 PM to 2 PM
Website: *www.kuukrestaurant.com/*

Colonia Santa Ana—Restaurants

Bistro Cultural
Cuisine: French Bistro
Telephone: (999) 217-9240
Address: Calle 66 #377, between Calle 41 and 43 Street
Parking: Street
Air Conditioned: Ceiling fans
Outdoors: Yes
Drinks: Coffee and bistro fare
Hours: Monday-Friday, 9 AM to 6 AM; Saturday: 9 AM to 2 PM; Closed on Sunday

El Gran Café
Cuisine: Coffee and Yucatecan
Telephone: (999) 923 5356
Address: Remate de Paseo de Montejo and Calle 47
Parking: Yes
Air Conditioned: Yes
Outdoors: Yes
Drinks: Coffee
Hours: Daily, 7 AM to 2 AM

Hotel San Angel
Cuisine: Coffee and snacks, breakfasts and lunch service
Telephone: (999) 928-1800
Address: Remate de Montejo #1
Parking: Yes
Air Conditioned: Yes
Outdoors: Yes
Drinks: No
Hours: Daily, 7 AM to 10 PM
Website: *www.hotelcasasanangel.com*

La Boheme Café Shop
Cuisine: Coffees and desserts
Telephone: (999) 926-6039

Address: Paseo de Montejo #470-B, between Calle 37 and 39 Street
Parking: Street parking
Air Conditioned: No
Outdoors: Yes
Drinks: Coffees, teas and juices
Hours: Monday-Friday 8:30 AM to 8 PM; Saturday: 8:30 AM to 4 PM
PLEASE NOTE: *As this goes to press the shop is closed due to death of the owner. It is not clear if it will reopen.*

Oliva
Cuisine: Italian
Telephone: (999) 923-2248
Address: Corner of Calle 49 and Calle 56
Parking: Street
Air Conditioned: Yes
Outdoors: No
Drinks: Coffee, Beer and Wine

Rescoldos Mediterranean Bistro
Cuisine: Mediterranean
Telephone: (999) 286-1028
Address: Calle 62 #366, between Calle 41 and 43 Street
Parking: No
Air Conditioned: No
Outdoors: Yes
Drinks: Soft drinks
Hours: Tuesday-Friday 1 PM to 10 PM; Saturday 6 PM to 11 PM

Rosas y Xocolate
Cuisine: International
Telephone: (999) 924-4304
Address: Paseo Montejo #480, by 41 Street

Parking: Street parking, and Valet service
Air Conditioned: Yes
Outdoors: Yes
Drinks: Full bar

Hours: Daily, 7:30 AM to 12 PM, and 1:30 PM to 12 AM
Website: *www.rosasandxocolate.com*

Gran Plaza Shopping Mall

100% Natural

Cuisine: Vegetarian
Telephone: (999) 948-4590
Address: Calle 8 #306, between Calle 1 and 1-A Street
Parking: Yes
Air Conditioned: Yes
Outdoors: Yes
Drinks: Beer and soft drinks
Hours: Daily, 7 AM to 11 PM
Website: *www.100natural.com.mx*

Boston's

Cuisine: American
Telephone: (999) 948-3333
Address: Prolongación Montejo #482
Parking: Yes
Air Conditioned: Yes
Outdoors: No
Drinks: Full bar
Hours: Daily, 11 AM to 2 AM
Website: *www.bostonsmerida.com*

Italianni's

Cuisine: Italian
Telephone: (999) 948-4597
Address: In the Gran Plaza shopping mall
Parking: Yes
Air Conditioned: Yes
Outdoors: No
Drinks: Full bar
Hours: Daily, 8 AM to 2 AM
Website: *www.italiannis.com*

Lapa Lapa

Cuisine: American
Telephone: (999) 948-0102
Address: In the Gran Plaza shopping mall
Parking: Yes
Air Conditioned: Yes
Outdoors: No
Drinks: Full bar
Hours: Daily, 1 PM to 3 AM

Hotel Zone
(Paseo de Montejo & Avenida Colón)—Restaurants

Chili's

Cuisine: American
Telephone: (999) 925-6346
Address: Hotel Fiesta Americana
Parking: Yes, underground parking at the Fiesta Americana
Air Conditioned: Yes
Outdoors: No

Drinks: Full bar
Hours: Daily, 8 AM to 12 AM
Website: *www.chilis.com*

Fiesta Americana Restaurant

Cuisine: Buffet and International Menu
Telephone: (999) 942-1111
Address: Fiesta Americana

149

Parking: Yes
Air Conditioned: Yes
Outdoors: No
Drinks: Full bar
Hours: Daily, 8 AM to 1 PM

Katun

Cuisine: Yucatecan Regional
Telephone: (999) 920-1482
Address: Calle 60 #319-B between
  Avenida Colón and Avenida Cupules
Parking: Yes
Air Conditioned: Yes
Outdoors: No
Drinks: Full bar
Hours: Daily: Noon to 1 PM

La Pigua

Cuisine: Seafood
Telephone: (999) 920-3605
Address: Avenida Cupules and 32 Street
Parking: Yes (Valet)
Air Conditioned: Yes
Outdoors: No
Drinks: Full bar
Hours: Sunday-Tuesday: 12AM to 6 PM;
  Wednesday-Saturday:12 AM to 10:30
  PM
Website: *www.lapiguamerida.com*

Los Almendros (Fiesta America)

Cuisine: Yucatecan Cuisine
Telephone: (999) 942-1111
Address: Fiesta Americana Hotel
Parking: Yes
Air Conditioned: Yes
Outdoors: No
Drinks: Full bar
Hours: Daily, 12:30 AM to 10:30 PM

Peregrina Bistro (Hyatt Hotel)

Cuisine: International
Telephone: (999) 942-1234
Address: Hyatt Hotel
Parking: Yes
Air Conditioned: Yes
Outdoors: No
Drinks: Full bar
Hours: Daily, 6:30 AM to 6 PM

Spasso

Cuisine: Italian
Telephone: (999) 942-1228
Address: Inside the Hyatt Hotel
Parking: Yes
Air Conditioned: Yes
Outdoors: No
Drinks: Full bar
Hours: Daily, 6 PM to 2 AM
Website:
  *merida.regency.hyatt.com/hyatt/hotels/e
  ntertainment/restaurants/index.jsp*

Mexican Restaurants with various locations

There are a good number of Mexican chains with multiple locations. These are some that are found in several neighborhoods and are worth a try. Many have a presence in Centro and along Paseo Montejo—and most also have websites, so you can look up their locations in other neighborhoods.

El Fogoncito

Cuisine: Tacos and Mexican traditional foods
Telephone: (999) 944-0315
Locations include: Centro (Calle 62 and 61 Street); Prolongación Montejo; and Altabrisa Mall
Parking: Varies with location
Air Conditioned: Yes
Outdoors: Only at Fogoncito on Prolongación Montejo
Drinks: Full bar
Hours: Daily, 12 PM to 2 AM
Website:
www.gruponicxa.com.mx/rest/fog/index.html

Eladios

Cuisine: Yucatecan snack and bar foods
Neighborhood: Various locations
Telephone: (999) 984-0057
Locations include: Colonia Itzimná, Centro, Avenida Itzáes, Colonia Pensiones
Parking: Yes, at all locations
Air Conditioned: Yes
Outdoors: Yes
Drinks: Beer and Cocktails
Hours: Daily, 12 PM to 7 PM
Website: *www.eladios.com.mx*

Italian Coffee Company

Cuisine: Coffee and sandwiches
Neighborhood: Centro (Calle 62 between Calle 59 and 61 Street) and other locations
Air Conditioned: Yes
Outdoors: No in Centro, Yes for other locations
Drinks: Coffee

Hours: Sunday-Friday: 7:30 AM to 11 PM Saturdays: 7:30 AM to 12 PM
Website: *www.italiancoffee.com*

Las Jirafas

Cuisine: Tacos
Telephone: (999) 926-4391
Locations include: Paseo Montejo, at Calle 56-A #494
Parking: Street parking
Air Conditioned: Varies with location
Outdoors: Yes
Drinks: Beer and cocktails
Hours: Daily, 7 PM to 2 AM

Los Trompos

Cuisine: Tacos and pizzas
Telephone: (999) 988-4444
Locations include: There are currently 15 locations, so see website
Parking: Some locations
Air Conditioned: Some locations
Outdoors: Some locations
Drinks: Beers and cocktails
Hours: For those located in shopping centers, daily: 11 AM to 10 PM; other restaurants, daily: 6 PM to 2 AM
Website: *www.lostrompos.com.mx*

Messina's

Cuisine: Pizza
Locations include: Centro
Telephone: (999) 924-9899, or (999) 924-0011
Address: Calle 57 #514-A by 64 Street
Parking: No
Air Conditioned: No
Outdoors: Yes
Drinks: Soft drinks
Hours: Daily, 11 AM to 12 PM, depending on location

151

Website:
*www.buscatan.com/directorio/pizza-
messinas-pizzerias-Merida-yucatan-505-
203.html*

P. F. Chang's

Cuisine: Contemporary Chinese
Locations include: Altabrisa
Telephone: (999) 245-3675
Address: Altabrisa Shopping Center
Parking: Yes
Air Conditioned: Yes
Outdoors: Yes
Drinks: Soft drinks, beer and wine
Hours: Daily, 11 AM to 12 PM
Website:
http://www.pfchangsmexico.com.mx/

Wok to Walk

Cuisine: Asian
Telephone: (999) 944-5866
Address: Various locations, including
Prolongación Montejo, Plaza Altabrisa
and Plaza Senderos. Check their
website.
Parking: Yes
Air Conditioned: Yes
Outdoors: Only at Plaza Mayor
Drinks: No
Hours: Daily, 12 PM to 10 PM
Website:
www.woktowalk.com/en/find/index.php

The Best Tacos

New to Mérida? That's great. It's an opportunity to make up your mind about which place has the best tacos. Here are five places that keep the debate going on which has the best tacos. Once you sample each one, you'll be able to join in the debate.

La Lupita

Cuisine: Tacos and Yucatecan Food
Neighborhood: Santiago
The cochinita pibil tacos are the best in
town. Or are they? Jeremiah Tower
had them once a week. Located inside
the market on Calle 57 between Calle
70 and 72 Street.

El Cazito de Michoacan

Cuisine: Tacos
Neighborhood: Fracc. De Montejo
Opened only Wednesday to Sunday,
this taquería has exquisite sauces to
accompany their tacos. Calle 50 #111
between Calle 39 and 39-C Street.

Wayan'e

Cuisine: Tacos
Neighborhood: Itzimná
The tacos from pork belly, with no fat,
are reputed to be the best in the
world. What is certain is that this
place sells out every day by 2 PM. On
the corner of Calle 20 and Calle 15, call
if you get lost: (999) 927-4160.

El Fabuloso Pez

Cuisine: Fish Tacos
Neighborhood: Colonia Mexico
Fish tacos are all the rage in California,
but some of the best fish tacos are
here in the Yucatán—made from the
fantastic seafood caught along the

Gulf. And with that, are the tacos here the best in town? You decide. Calle 30 #370, Local 1, Colonia Mexico.

Taco Árabe

Cuisine: Tacos
Neighborhood: Colonia Montecristo

With so much of an Arab presence in the Yucatán, it's natural that there are exceptional Arab-influenced tacos. But are these the best? Mushrooms, bacon, and thick flour tortillas are tempting reasons to say yes. On Calle 35, steps from the Glorieta Brisas. If you get lost, call: (999) 134-6334.

Yucatecan Dishes that Will Become Part of Your Life

As you settle into your life in Mérida, there are five dishes that form part of the culinary menu of everyday life. The sooner you set out to try these various dishes, the quicker you'll become acclimated to the community. Of course there's always a debate about which are the top five, or even top ten restaurants, but the truth is that the culinary landscape is always changing—and for the better. So be adventurous and have fun!

Cochinita:Pibil

It's hard to believe that the dish—pork marinated in sour orange and annatto spice, wrapped in banana leaves, and baked in an earth pit over with hot stones on the bottom—that is so linked with the Maya culinary tradition has two ingredients introduced by the Spanish: Pork and citruses. That said, the cochinita pibil is the best-loved Maya dish. Any restaurant that serves Yucatecan cuisine will have it. Favorites? Try the cochinita pibil at La Chaya, La Tradición, Hacienda Teya, or even market stands, such as La Lupita in Santiago market.

Huevos Motuleños (Motul Style Eggs)

Huevos Motuleños originated at the "La Sin Rival" restaurant in the town of Motul when governor Felipe Carrillo Puerto (1922-1924) unexpectedly showed up with an entourage. The restaurant owner, Jorge Siqueff Febles, on the spot, had to come up with a dish that would serve everyone: A Toast with refried beans, a fried egg, diced ham, peas, and tomato sauce—topped with cheese. The combination proved so surprising that it became the signature breakfast dish of the town—and a culinary legend followed.

Panuchos and Salbutes

Panuchos and salbutes are a traditional Yucatecan corn tortilla dishes served in the evening or at parties. A panucho is made with a refried corn tortilla and is stuffed with refried black beans and topped with chopped cabbage, pulled chicken or turkey, tomato, pickled red onion, avocado, and pickled jalapeño pepper. A salbute is a puffed deep fried corn tortilla and is topped with chopped cabbage, pulled chicken or turkey, tomato, pickled red onion, avocado, and pickled jalapeño pepper. These are offered at almost every restaurant that serves Yucatecan cuisine. El Kanasín, with several locations in Merida, is reputed to have among the best.

153

Sopa de Lima

Lime soup in Yucatán is a light, refreshing meal served with sliced limes floating in the broth. It is, however, an entire meal, since it has chicken, tomato, bell pepper, cilantro, deep fried corn tortilla chips, and habanero pepper. The best sopa de lima is one where the broth is clear and you can see all the ingredients.

The "Queso Relleno"

Queso Relleno, or "Stuffed Cheese," represents the height of culinary art in Yucatán. Legend has it that Dutch Edam cheese, brought over from British Honduras, now known as Belize, became the basis of this dish. The Stuffed Cheese features ground pork prepared inside of a carved Edam cheese ball served with tomato sauce and gravy.

The Top Five Restaurants in Mérida You Must Try

As you settle in Mérida there will be five dining experiences that will shape your perception of this city and the people who live here. These are the five top restaurants that you must try in order to understand more profoundly the culinary traditions of this magnificent city.

Ku'uk

The recipient of the Best New Restaurant in 2013, Ku'uk won this prestigious Gourmet Award presented by Travel + Leisure México to the surprise of no one. This, however, is the first time a restaurant in Mérida wins this award. The fare, a molecular menu created by Chef Pedro Evia, reflects a reinterpretation of local Maya ingredients, each course presented as a work of art. The meal is similar to Per Se or Gramercy Tavern in New York, or the tasting menu at Macéo in Paris. Website: *http://kuukrestaurant.com*

Nectar

Roberto Solís has been credited with pioneering nouvelle Yucatecan cuisine, a passion shaped by his culinary travels around the world. It was Roberto Solís who invited René Redzepi, the mastermind behind Noma, one of the world's top-ranked restaurants, to travel to Mexico in search of the perfect taco. It warranted an article in the *New York Times* by Jeff Gordinier: "In Search of the Perfect Taco." And many believe that Nectar is the perfect meal in Mérida. Website: *http://nectarmerida.com.mx/*

Apoala

The chef-proprietor Sara Arnaud and her brother, Carlos, are credited with bringing the authentic flavors of the Mexican highlands to Yucatán—known as the northern Maya lowlands. The flavors of Oaxaca suffuse this restaurant that has taken Santa Lucia by storm and changed the standards for dining in the Historic Center. This is one restaurant that has local expants coming back often, and for good reason. Website: *http://www.apoala.mx/*

154

Casa de Piedra at Hacienda Xcanatún

A short distance from Mérida, Casa de Piedra at the Hacienda Xcanatún is the labor of Cristina Baker who, with Executive Chef Alexander Martínez, have created an exceptional dining experience against the backdrop of a beautiful hacienda. The fare exceeds expectations, given that the restaurant is located in a retreat with a spa. But the simple presentation of exceptional ingredients properly prepared continues to win fans, both among the expats in Mérida, Mexicans from other parts of Mexico, and locals. Website: *http://www.xcanatun.com/restaurante.html*

Acqua

The owners Maricela Chaia and Ernesto Casares have created a loyal following amont locals and expats alike. The Tarta Gorgonzola and Boqinette Fish in Xcatic sauce garner rave reviews. It is not a pretentious place, but the service and creative menu keeps this place buzzing. This is definitely one place that will have you wondering about excellence in Mérida's dining experience. Website: *https://www.facebook.com/AcquaMerida*

As 2016 unfolds, these are the five restaurants that set the bar for the culinary scene in Mérida. Enjoy as you try them out and make up your own mind as to which one you think is the best.

Day Trips from Mérida - Restaurants

Izamal

Hotel Macanche
Cuisine: Yucatecan and International
Telephone: (998) 954-0287
Address: Calle 22 #305 between Calle 33 and 35 Street
Parking: Yes
Air Conditioned: No
Outdoors: Yes
Drinks: Wine or beer
Hours: Daily, but call for reservations
Website: *www.macanche.com*

Sabor de Izamal
Cuisine: Traditional Yucatecan
Telephone: (990) 954-0489
Address: Calle 27 #299, between Calle 28 and 30 Street
Parking: Yes

Air Conditioned: Yes
Outdoors: Yes
Drinks: Full bar
Hours: Daily, 11 AM to 6 PM
Website: *www.sabordeizamal.com*

Progreso/Celestun

La Palapa
Cuisine: Seafood
Telephone: (998) 916-2063
Address: On the beach
Parking: Yes
Air Conditioned: No
Outdoors: Yes
Drinks: Full bar
Hours: Daily, 11 AM to 6 PM

San Bruno Beach Grill
Cuisine: International
Telephone: (999) 122-5021

155

Address: On the beach, Km 27.5 on the Carretera Progreso-Telchac
Parking: Yes
Air Conditioned: No
Outdoors: Yes
Drinks: Full bar
Hours: Every Day: 1 PM to 10 PM

Taco Maya

Cuisine: Mexican and American
Telephone: (999) 145-0623
Address: In front of the baseball park in Chelem
Parking: Yes
Air Conditioned: No
Outdoors: Yes
Drinks: Beer and soft drinks
Hours: Saturday—Wednesday, 10 AM to 2.30 PM; Closed Thursday & Friday

Thai Flash

Cuisine: Thai
Telephone: (999) 101-7330
Address: Calle 27-B, between Calle 32 and 30 Street
Parking: Street parking
Air Conditioned: No
Outdoors: Yes
Drinks: Thai Mojitos, beers and teas
Hours: Thursday - Saturday, 6 AM to 12 AM; Sunday: 1 PM to 11 PM

Motul

Casa Vainilla

Town/Village: Motul
Cuisine: Coffee and Pastry Shop
Address: Calle 26 #255 between Calle 17 and 19 Street
Parking: Yes (Street)
Air Conditioned: No
Outdoors: Yes

Drinks: Coffee shop
Hours: Friday-Saturday, 6 PM—11:30 PM; Sunday, 4 PM-9 PM

Haciendas Near Mérida

Hacienda de Chunkanan

Town/Village: Cuzamá
Cuisine: Yucatecan
Address: In town (where the horse-drawn carriages are hitched)
Parking: Yes
Air Conditioned: No
Outdoors: Yes
Drinks: Not sure, probably beer
Hours: Daily, 10 AM—6 PM

Hacienda Ochil

Town/Village: On highway towards Uxmal
Cuisine: Yucatecan
Telephone: (999) 924-7465
Address: Km. 27 Uman-Uxmal highway, near Abala
Parking: Yes
Air Conditioned: No
Outdoors: Yes
Drinks: Full bar
Hours: Daily, 10 AM to 6 PM
Website: *www.haciendaochil.com*

Hacienda San José

Town/Village: East of Mérida, just past Tixkokob
Cuisine: Yucatecan
Telephone: (999) 924-1313
Parking: Yes
Air Conditioned: No
Outdoors: Yes
Drinks: Full bar
Hours: Daily, 7 AM to 12 PM

Website: *www.thehaciendas.com*

Hacienda Santa Cruz

Town/Village: Santa Cruz Palomeque, south of the Superhighway Periférico, road to Dzununcan
Cuisine: French and Yucatecan Fusion
Neighborhood: Santa Cruz Palomeque
Telephone: (999) 254-0541
Address: Santa Cruz Palomeque Main Street
Parking: Yes
Air Conditioned: No
Outdoors: Yes
Drinks: Full bar
Hours: Daily, 7 AM to 12 AM
Website: *www.haciendasantacruz.com*

Hacienda Santa Rosa

Town/Village: Maxcanú, on the road to Campeche
Cuisine: Yucatecan
Telephone: (999) 910-0174
Address: In the pueblo of Santa Rosa
Parking: Yes
Air Conditioned: No
Outdoors: Yes
Drinks: Full bar
Hours: Daily, 7 AM to 12 AM
Website: *www.thehaciendas.com*

Hacienda Temozón

Town/Village: Temozón Sur, on the road to Uxmal, near Temozón village
Cuisine: Yucatecan
Telephone: (999) 923-8089

Parking: Yes
Air Conditioned: No
Outdoors: Yes
Drinks: Full bar
Hours: Daily, 7 AM to 12 PM
Website: *www.thehaciendas.com*

Hacienda Teya

Town/Village: East of Mérida, on the road to Cancún
Cuisine: Yucatecan
Telephone: (999) 988-0800
Parking: Yes
Air Conditioned: Yes
Outdoors: Yes
Drinks: Full bar
Hours: Daily, 12 AM to 6 PM
Website: *haciendateya.com*

Hacienda Xcantún

Town/Village: On the road to Progreso, village of Xcantún
Cuisine: International, with Yucatecan flair
Telephone: (999) 930-2140
Address: Mérida—Progreso Highway, Km. 12
Parking: Parking lot on hacienda grounds
Air Conditioned: Yes
Outdoors: Yes
Drinks: Full bar
Hours: Daily, 8 AM to 11:30 AM and 1:30 PM to 11 PM
Website: *www.xcantun.com*

A Recognition: Paul Trotter & Wayne Trotter

The tradition of exceptional restauranteurs continues in Mérida. Paul and Wayne Trotter are the owners of Pancho's, La Tratto (two locations), Trotter's, and Bryan's. These four restaurants have added much to the city's life. Since 1972 the Trotters have been dedicated to

157

their craft and Mérida's restaurant scene is the more vibrant for it. In some ways, the culinary tradition started by Alberto and Pedro Salum is now carried forward by Paul and Wayne Trotter.

Cheers!

Part III

The Fundamentals of Moving to Mérida

7 GETTING HERE! IMMIGRATION FIRST, THEN TO DRIVE, OR NOT TO DRIVE!

Mexico's new immigration laws are now being implemented. These laws were enacted on May 25, 2011 and began to be implemented on November 9, 2012.

These changes have gradually unfolded throughout 2013. Foreigners who had various types of visas (FM2 or FM3) are "grandfathered" in to the previous rules and regulations. As a result, all immigration applications are handled on a case-by-case determination by immigration officials. For new immigrants, here is an overview of these changes.

Please note that all the information presented here is general. This information may vary depending on each individual case. Immigration officials are the only ones who can provide definite information on any individual's specific circumstances. With this in mind, as a public service, following is an overview of the new Immigration Law, known as the "Ley de Migración."

There are three broad categories of the new INM immigration laws. These changes now apply to foreign full- and part-time residents and visitors alike:

Visitante (Tourist) permits are valid for a maximum stay of 180 days. During this period the holder (tourist) is allowed to open a bank account, make investments, purchase real property or get married in Mexico without other permission or requirements.

Once that time expires, most tourists or visitors must leave the country. Applications for a new type of permit must be submitted to the nearest Mexican consular offices in their home country.

Foreigners who have married or established family ties to Mexican citizens are exempt and can request a change in status through INM. If he foreigner becomes the parent of a child born in Mexico, or is a Mexican citizen, status changes can be expedited through INM.

Residente Temporal (Temporary Resident) permits are valid for up to four years. All persons living in Mexico under no-inmigrante or inmigrante status granted before the law changed now automatically fall into that category. The status now expires 12 months after the holder obtains the third renewal permitted under the new law, or a fourth renewal as allowed under the prior rules in place.

During the 30 days before the permit lapses, there is an opportunity to apply for permanent status without proving investments or pension income levels that were increased considerably as of last November 2012.

Otherwise, foreigners are required to leave the country, with options to apply for a new four-year permit through a Mexican Consulate in their home country, or to return to Mexico under 180-day tourist/visitor status.

Those who already are in possession of a temporary resident permit are not required to meet the new financial solvency threshold when filing for their remaining renewals. However, be advised that it is taken into account if they decide to start over as retirees or pensioners in the same category once their 4 years expire. When that occurs, the 2013 requirement is an average monthly balance of $12,000 USD in investment holdings over the last 12 months, or bank statements proving a monthly income of $3,000 USD.

The new regulations do, indeed, lay out alternative paths that may be followed in lieu of the retiree qualification route, such as job offers, investment in a Mexican enterprise or investments (such a monkey market or stock market), or proof of family ties in Mexico.

Residente Permanente (Permanent Resident) takes into account the growing trend towards permanent foreigners requesting resident status.

Residents with Temporary status may apply for Permanent status at the local INM office at any time, located on Avenida Colón in Mérida. Those who choose to wait out the full 4 years of their permits automatically qualify for the change in status at that time. Those who apply for the change beforehand are subject to satisfying the new investment or income standards as outlined above.

Couples can circumvent the income and investment guidelines for each party if one obtains permanent status first and the spouse subsequently applies under the family ties pathway.

162

Those who previously obtained Inmigrado status automatically rank as permanent residents under the new laws. For the time being INM booklets and ID cards issued prior to November 2012 do remain valid, although notifications requiring exchange of those documents for new cards may be issued at a later date.

Here is a summary of the changes:

If you have an FM3 or FM2, these will become Non-Immigrant or Immigrant, and in turn these are eligible for Temporary Resident. If you have a Permanent Immigrant ("Inmigrado") this will become Permanent Resident.

Furthermore:

Tourists on visitor permits or visas will not be able to change their stay condition within Mexico and will require to exit the country upon expiration of their authorized time of stay.

The only exception applies to those who are kin of Mexican citizens or for humanitarian reasons.

New Stay Terms:
Visitors: up to 180 days
Temporary Resident: up to 4 years
Permanent Resident: Does not expire, except for minors.

Temporary Resident:
Can apply for a card with a validity of 1, 2, 3 or 4 years
Has the possibility of a work permit
Unlimited entries and exits
Right to family unity

Required to report, within ninety days, changes in:
Address
Employer
Civil status
Change in citizenship

Permanent Resident:

Unlimited stay
Work permitted
Unlimited entries and exits
Right to family unity

Required to report, within ninety days, changes in:
Address
Employer
Civil status
Change in citizenship

Who qualifies for permanent residence?
By next-of-kin to preserve family unit
Retirees ($3,000 USD in monthly income or $12,000 USD in investments)
4 years of uninterrupted and regular status as temporary resident
2 years as temporary resident and legal spouse of a permanent resident or Mexican citizen
Humanitarian reasons

Official overviews are available online at:

http://mesoamerica-foundation.org/newimmigrationlaw.html

Expats Who Want to Work in Mexico

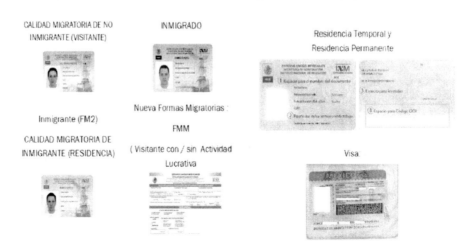

Expats who wish to work in Mexico must be aware of the new Mexican Immigration rules. If you own a business and want to hire foreigners or if you are a foreigner and wish to work in

Mexico, it is important that you get familiar with the Mexican Immigration rules currently in force. Hiring foreigners in Mexico is entirely legal under the Migration Act.

The 2012 General Population Act (*Ley General de Migración*) allowed foreigners to change their immigration status, allowing them to work in Mexico. Since November 2012, in consequence, the new Immigration Law established the different rules for hiring foreigners in Mexico.

Following is an overview of the new immigration rules:

1. Every employer who wants to hire a foreigner must request a *"Constancia de Inscripción de Empleador"* (Certificate of Employer Registration) from the National Migration Institute.

2. The employer, either in person or through his or her legal representative, must request a *"Visa por Oferta de Empleo"* (Visa for Job Offering), from the National Migration Institute. This visa is independent from the foreigner's visa required for entering to Mexico. The visa to offer a job must be granted by the National Migration Institute, but is issued by a Mexican consulate overseas.

3. If the contract period exceeds 180 days, the foreigner must apply for the replacement of the FMM form provided on arrival to Mexico, for a *"Temporary Resident Card,"* within 30 calendar days of entry into Mexico. This procedure can be handled at any office of the National Migration Institute in the state where he or she has established residence.

A visa is not required for a job offer in the following cases:

a) For business persons who are not employed directly by a company incorporated in Mexico and who travel to Mexico to attend work meetings, perform supervisory duties on behalf of a foreign company, or provide technical services under agreements to transfer technology or train staff on behalf of a foreign company. (In such cases the arrival into Mexico from abroad is authorized with the FMM form, which will be stamped by the immigration authorities as visitor status without permission to perform gainful activity, designating the option "business" as purpose of stay.)

b) For a temporary visitor, there is a maximum stay of 180 days. Business persons may enter Mexico without a visa if there is no visa requirement for their nationality. If a visa is required, it must be requested at any Mexican consulate overseas.

For information on immigration procedures and a list of the countries that require visa to enter Mexico, please refer to the page: *www.inm.gob.mx*

By Mónica López Medina

Instituto Nacional de Migración

Becoming a Mexican Citizen?

Becoming a Mexican citizen?

Why not?

As James Fields and Ellen Fields said, once their dream home had been finished in Mérida and they planned to remain in Mexico for the rests of their lives, "If one passport is good, two are better. And being a citizen means we don't have to do the visa renewal thing every year."

That said, consider this:

Mexican naturalization offers several benefits to foreigners. Among them (in no particular order of importance): you can vote, change address or jobs without having to inform the National Institute of Immigration (INM) of your every move, wait less time in immigration lines at airports, and avoid having to pay to change your immigration status and/or renew your visa each year to extend you stay in Mexico.

The procedures which lead to Mexican naturalization demand a number of requirements for qualification. These depend upon an assortment of factors such as your links to Mexico, whether you are of Latin American descent, whether you are married to a Mexican, your current immigration status, and how long you have resided in Mexico. A good immigration lawyer can help you establish your eligibility.

Once you file the application, the procedures take up to one year to complete, and perhaps even longer. Toward the end of the process you will get tested on your knowledge of Mexico in a "multiple choice" type examination consisting of some fifteen questions. It's not hard, but you will need to have a basic grasp of the Spanish language to pass it.

At the completion of the journey that leads to your Mexican naturalization, you will get a handshake from one of the SRE officials and a certificate with your photo on it.

—Source: Mexperience.com

Do note, however, that Mexico has strict "morality" regulations in place and foreigners who have engaged in "immoral" activities—which can range from operating a night club of ill-repute, or creating websites that promote the sexual exploitation of minors, or being associates in a gambling operation—may be deemed ineligible for Mexican citizenship.

By Air

Mérida has nonstop flights to Cancún, Havana, Houston, Mexico City and Miami. Connections around the world are possible from these gateway cities. Mérida is served by a modern, world-class international airport located a short drive south from the Historic Center. The Manuel Crescencio Rejón International Airport's IATA Code is MID.

Here are the routes served by Mérida's airport:

Airline	Destinations
Aeromar	Villahermosa
Aeroméxico	Mexico City
Aeroméxico Connect	Mexico City, Miami, Monterrey, Veracruz, Villahermosa
Aeroméxico Express	Monterrey, Tampico, Veracruz, Villahermosa
American Airlines	Dallas/Fort Worth
Blue Panorama Airlines	Rome-Fiumicino
Interjet	Mexico City
Magni	Mexico City
MAYAir	Cancún, Cozumel, Veracruz, Villahermosa
TAR Tampico	Toluca/Mexico City, Tuxtla Gutiérrez, Veracruz, Villahermosa

Tropic Air	Belize City
United Airlines	Houston-Intercontinental
Volaris	Guadalajara, Mexico City, Monterrey
VivaAerobus	Guadalajara, Mexico City, Monterrey
WestJet Seasonal:	Toronto-Pearson

In addition, nonstop service to Havana, Cuba is expected to begin in the summer of 2016.

Finally, Interjet chose Mérida for its second hub, the first one being in Mexico City. This new hub, which began to unfold last year, will expand air service domestically at first—and internationally by the end of the year. Initially there will be additional flights to Mexico City and new service to Tuxtla Gutiérrez. Planned international service includes nonstop flights to Miami, Houston, and Havana. There are plans for weekly service to Orlando and reestablishment of the former Eastern Airlines flight: Mérida-New Orleans-New York (LGA) and back. Stay tuned as announcements are made as the hub is established.

That said, the truth is that flying into Mérida has been relatively expensive and schedules are limited. That American is now competing with United, however, has resulted that—for now—prices are much more reasonable. That said, many avoid flying to MID. Why? Because over the past quarter century Cancún has emerged as a major tourist destination and it has almost as many flights as Mexico City. Many Yucatecans miss the days when there were two daily nonstop flights to Miami and regular nonstop flights to Atlanta, New Orleans, and Guatemala City.

The good news, of course, is that Mérida is "off the beaten path," a place that is an adventure, a destination that is purposeful. The bad news is that, if you fly from the U.S. or Canada, it can cost around $300 USD more to fly into Mérida than it would to fly to Cancún. One suggestion: find the cheapest flight to Cancún and connect with the ADO first-class bus to Mérida. It may sound counterintuitive, but the three and half hour bus ride from Cancún to Mérida can save you both time and money. Why? Many flights via Houston or Mexico City have layovers that last a few hours. If you are coming from the Eastern Seaboard, flying to Mexico City means you are flying about 700 miles west of Mérida, so your connection will simply fly you back 700 miles east to Mérida.

Savings can be substantial. Comparing recent flights from New York to Mérida; and San Francisco to Mérida turned up that flying New York to Cancún was $400 USD cheaper than New

168

York to Mérida, and flying San Francisco to Cancún was $425 USD cheaper than flying San Francisco to Mérida. So it might just be worthwhile to fly to Cancún and then take the bus. It may also be worth the effort to see if you fly into Cancún, take the bus to Mérida, and fly home from Mérida, or the other way around. The preferred websites for finding deals online are Kayak.com, Orbitz.com, and Travelocity.com.

Be patient, shop around for a deal online, and consider various options. Once you get there, however, you will be glad you came!

Listed below are the websites for all the airlines that serve Mérida:

Aeroméxico
www.aeromexico.com

American Airlines
www.aa.com

Blue Panorama
www.blue-panoram.it

Interjet
www.interjet.com.mx

Magni
www.magnicharters.com.mx

Maya Air
www.mayair.com.mx

TAR Regional Airline
www.tarmexico.com

Tropic Air
www.tropicair.com

United
www.united.com

Viva Aerobus
www.vivaaerobus.com

Volaris
www.volaris.com.mx

WestJet
www.westjet.com

Business Travel to Mexico: Advice from the State Department

Business Travel: Upon arrival in Mexico, business travelers must complete and submit a form (Form FMM) authorizing the conduct of business, but not employment, for a 30-day period. Travelers entering Mexico for purposes other than tourism or business or for stays of longer than 180 days require a visa and must carry a valid U.S. passport. U.S. citizens planning to work or live in Mexico should apply for the appropriate Mexican visa at the Mexican Embassy in Washington, DC, or at the nearest Mexican consulate in the United States.

Getting to Mérida by Bus

Mérida by bus from Cancún is easy: ADO operates convenient schedules and has good fares. They even have a shuttle bus from Cancún's airport ($55 pesos, or about $4.50 USD) that takes you directly from the airport parking lot to their bus terminal downton. Depending on the time of day and the class of service ("Servicio de Lujo" on many Mexican bus lines have seats as wide and comfortable as Business Class on most U.S. airlines; movies, videos and complimentary coffee and teas are included!). One-way tickets to Mérida range from $14—31 USD.

Our recommendation? Find the best fare to Cancún. Then give yourself a couple of hours between arrival time and the departing Express Bus to Mérida. The ADO bus line has an English-language website (*www.adogl.com.mx/en/index.htm*). Remember, if you are staying in the Historic Center, you will want to go to Mérida Terminal (CAME) station, which is downtown Mérida. There are two daily buses that leave the Fiesta Americana Hotel and Altabrisa ADO station and travel directly for Cancún Airport.

For traveling to other locations from Mérida by Bus

Once you are here, you'll find that ADO operates convenient schedules and at good prices. Unless you are on a tight budget or simply want to travel in a more adventurous way, go Primera Clase (First Class). There are fewer stops, the seats are more comfortable and the service a bit more attentive. ADO is great if you want to travel to Campeche City, Palenque, Villahermosa, Chetumal, or even venture all the way to Mexico City. ADO also has Express buses to Cancún and Playa del Carmen. ADO operates from the main terminal station downtown as well as from the Fiesta Americana Hotel (Calle 60 and Avenida Cupules).

The Second Class Bus

Terminal Station (Terminal de Autobuses de 2a. Clase) is located at Calle 50 #531 by Calle 67. If you are traveling to the smaller communities throughout the Yucatán, these are the buses that you might want to consider:

Lineas Unidas del Sur Bus Line

Telephone: (999) 924-7565
Service to: Kanasín, Tepich, Tecoh, Telchaquillo, Maní, Oxkutzcab, Sotuta, Cholul, Peto, Homún, Tekit and villages en route to these towns.

Autobuses de Oriente Bus Line

Telephone: (999) 928-6230
Service to: Cancún, Valladolid, Chichén Itzá, Playa del Carmen, Coba and Tulum.

Autobuses de Occidente Bus Line

Telephone: (999) 928-6230
Service to: Izamal, Tizimín, Celestún, Seye, Sotuta, Cenotillo, Dzitas, Cantemaya, Espita, Hunucmá and villages en route to these towns.

Autobuses del Noreste Bus Line

Telephone: (999) 924-6355
Service to: Tizimín, Ría Lagartos, San Felipe, Chicxulub Pueblo, Temax, Cancún, Valladolid, Cholul, Conkal, Motul, Baca, Dzemul, Telchac, San Cristiano, Chabihau and villages en route to these towns.

New Bus Service to Belize on ADO

Telephone: Telephone: (999) 928-6230
Service to: Caracol, Belize and Belize City, Belize. ADO has inaugurated a new non-stop bus service from Mérida to Belize. The bus leaves at 9 PM daily, and arrives at 7 AM in Caracol, Belize, before continuing on to Belize City. Price, one-way, is $430 pesos.

By Car

If you are driving to Mérida from the United States, it is necessary to point out that currently there are concerns about safety. The continuing conflicts between the Mexican Government and drug cartels have led to some dangerous conditions, particularly at night. It is recommended that you arrive to your point of entry on the U.S. side the evening before, get a good night's sleep and bright and early the following day you enter Mexico and drive as far away from the border as you can reasonably do so. It is recommended that by evening, you arrive at the city where you will be spending the night, get a good night's sleep, and continue your journey bright and early the next morning. It has been the experience of many drivers that it is best to enter Mexico at Nuevo Laredo and drive around the Gulf of Mexico.

Here is general advice on bringing your private car into Mexico provided by the State Department:

Entry of private vehicles into Mexico

"Tourists traveling to Mexico by car must have a valid driver's license and a certificate of title or vehicle registration. In the case of a rented vehicle, it is necessary to show a rental agreement in the name of the person driving the vehicle. In the case of a company car, a notarized document proving that the vehicle was assigned to the driver and a proof of employment.

Current government regulations also require you to fill a Temporary Import Permit, a Vehicle Return Promise and to post a vehicle bond to ensure that the vehicle is returned to its country of origin. There are three options for posting a vehicle bond: a credit card, a vehicle value bond, or a cash deposit. All these procedures must be fulfilled at the border before entering the country. When you leave the country you must return the documents that were issued when entering. Sanctions will be imposed to persons who fail to do so.

Requirements for the entry of vehicles into Mexico: On April 1, 1992, the Government of Mexico revised its requirements for the temporary entry (less than six months) of personal vehicles into Mexico. The purpose of these measures is to ensure that illegally imported vehicles do not remain in Mexico. These regulations pertain only to those vehicles which will be driven beyond the approximate 20 kilometer "free zone" south of the U.S.-Mexican border. The Government of Mexico's Ministry of Finance has indicated that these regulations do not affect vehicles which will remain within the "free zone" (note: all of Baja California is considered a "free zone").

Owners of personal vehicles traveling beyond the "free zone" must present the importer's immigration document (tourist card or visa), the original and a copy of the importer's driver's license and vehicle title in the name of the importer. If the operator of the vehicle is other than the importer, the operator must have the same immigration status as the importer and the importer of the vehicle must be present at all times it is being operated in Mexico. If the above documents are in order, the temporary importer of the vehicle has two options for bringing the vehicle into Mexico:

- **Post a bond** based on the value of the vehicle as determined by local customs officials. However, there is no need to pay a bond on the total value of the vehicle. Instead, licensed Mexican bonding agencies on both sides of the U.S.-Mexican border provide this service for a fee of up to 1 or 2 percent of the value of the vehicle.

- **Make a sworn statement** at the Mexican Army and Air Force Bank (Banco Nacional del Ejercito Fuerza Aerea y Armada S.N.C.). A fee of $10 is required and can only be paid with a credit card (Visa and Mastercard) issued by a bank in the importer's country of foreign residence (e.g., the United States for U.S. citizens). American Express and Diners Club cards are not considered to be bank issues cards and therefore cannot be used to pay the fee (payment may not be made in cash). Offices of the Banco Nacional del Ejercito are located in all customs offices at ports of entry and their hours are reportedly the same as those of the customs offices. The bank will provide the appropriate forms for this service. All vehicle importation documents should be in the vehicle when it is operated. When leaving Mexico, these documents should be returned to the Mexican customs office at the border.

When vehicle importation documentation is lost or stolen, replacement documents can be issued by regional Mexican customs offices to the importer after he or she obtains a certified document from the U.S. Embassy or one of its consulates attesting to the loss.

In the "free zone," foreign vehicles can only be operated by the owner or (if the owner is present but not driving the vehicle) by a citizen or permanent legal resident (LPR) of the vehicle's place of registration.

For additional information, individuals traveling to Mexico by personal vehicle should (prior to their travel) contact the Mexican Embassy in Washington, DC, or the Mexican Consulate nearest their residence.

Thousands of U.S. citizens travel throughout Mexico each year using both privately owned and rental vehicles. U.S. citizens planning to drive in Mexico may do so on a current U.S. driver's license but should confirm that their current U.S. insurance will cover driving in Mexico or purchase additional insurance to cover the period of their travel in Mexico. While Mexico has an extensive primary and secondary road system, driving conditions are crowded and often hazardous to the uninitiated driver. Drivers in Mexico should exercise particular care and should not drive after nightfall outside urban areas. Night time driving can be particularly hazardous because of slow moving unlighted vehicles even on primary roads. In addition, some Mexican roads, particularly in isolated regions, have at times been targets for robbery by bandits who operate primarily after dark.

Driving restrictions in Mexico City: In an effort to reduce air pollution in Mexico City, Mexican authorities restrict all vehicular traffic including vehicles of tourists in Mexico City. For vehicles of non-Mexican registration, the restriction is based on the last digit of the license plates. The schedule is as follows:

> **Monday** - no driving of vehicles with license plates with final digit of 5 or 6.
> **Tuesday** - no driving of vehicles with license plates with final digit of 7 or 8.
> **Wednesday** - no driving of vehicles with license plates with final digit of 3 or 4.
> **Thursday** - no driving of vehicles with license plates with final digit of 1 or 2.
> **Friday** - no driving of vehicles with license plated with final digit of 9 or 0.

Also, no driving of vehicles with temporary license plates or any other plate that does not conform with the above.

Saturday and Sunday—all vehicles may be driven.

Failure to comply with Mexican laws governing temporarily imported vehicles can result in vehicle confiscation and/or fines.

A publication entitled "Tips for Travelers to Mexico" with additional useful information is available through the Office of Mexico's Flash Facts system at (202) 482-4464 by requesting document #8112. The nearest Mexican Consulate can also provide current information on safety and recommendations."

There are certain procedures for the "temporary" importing of your U.S.-purchased vehicle into Mexico. The process normally takes about an hour to complete at the border, and it can be considerably less if the paperwork has been completed beforehand, either online or by going to the nearest Mexican Consulate in your area. Following is an explanation of the process provided by MexConnect.com:

Regulations for Bringing Your Car into Mexico

"Here are a couple of steps you need to take when you decide to drive across the border into Mexico. If you abide by these rules, you'll be making sure you can legally take your trip to Mexico by car.

If your travel is within the **Border Zone** (usually up to 20 kilometers south of the U.S.-Mexico Border) or the **Free Trade Zone** (including the *Baja California Peninsula* and the *Sonora Free Trade Zone*) there are no procedures to comply with. However, if you wish to pass these zones, the following procedures will apply. You must secure a permit by following the next few steps.

174

Applying for a permit at the Mexico Border

Step One

To acquire a permit, simply drive your vehicle (including RVs) to a Mexican customs office at the border and present an original plus two (2) copies of the following documents:

Valid proof of citizenship (passport or birth certificate)

In the case of dual citizenship, the solicitant must present his or her Mexican passport or proof of Mexican nationality

The appropiate immigration form (FMT or "tourist card")

The valid vehicle registration certificate, or a document, such as the original title that certifies the legal ownership of the vehicle. It must be in the driver's name.

The leasing contract (if the vehicle is leased or rented), which must be in the name of the person importing the car. If the vehicle belongs to a company, present the document that certifies the employee works for the company.

A valid driver's license, issued outside Mexico.

If the documentation shows the vehicle is registered in the name of the spouse, the importation can be done as long as the marriage certificate (and one copy) is presented.

An international credit or debit card, also issued outside Mexico (American Express, Mastercard or Visa), in the name of the driver of the vehicle.

Note: If you do not possess an international credit card, you will be asked to post a bond, payable to the **Federal Treasury,** *issued by an authorized bonding company in Mexico.*

As an alternative to posting a bond, you may make a cash deposit at Banco del Ejército in an amount equal to the value of your vehicle according to the "Table of Vehicle Values for Bonding Companies" (see table on the next page for an idea of the cost).

Banco del Ejército now has a website (see on next page) wherein you can obtain the most recent rates and regulations. In addition, you may now apply in advance via Internet, but you will still need to have all the copies (as above) when you arrive at the border.

Step Two

Once you have the originals and a set of photocopies of these documents, present them to the Vehicular Control Module located in Customs to process the importation permit.

All documents and the credit card must be in the name of the owner, who must also be in the vehicle when crossing the border.

Step Three

Your international credit card will be charged an amount in national currency equivalent to $27.00 USD at the Banco del Ejército.

If you do not have an international credit card or debit card, Banco del Ejército will accept a cash deposit in an amount equal to the value of your vehicle (see table). Your deposit plus any interest it may earn will be returned to you when you leave Mexico. Or, you may choose to obtain a bond through an authorized Mexican bonding company located at all the border crossings. The authorized bonding companies will require a refundable deposit equal to the value of the vehicle, according to the table below. The bonding company will also assess taxes and processing costs for this service.

Step Four

Upon your departure from Mexico, and if the vehicle is not going to be driven back into Mexico, the permit for temporary importation must be cancelled at Customs. That's all there is to it. Follow these simple steps and you shouldn't have any problems. **However, please remember, if your car is found in Mexico beyond the authorized time limit, or without the appropiate documents, it will be immediately confiscated.**

Amount of Bond in U.S. Dollars

2001-2010 $400.00	1996-2000 $300.00	1996 and older models $200.00

The car permit can be requested at the following border crossing points

Arizona Border Points
Agua Prieta
Naco
Nogales
San Luis Río Colorado
Sonoyta

California Border Points
Mexicali
Otay Mesa
Tecate
Tijuana

Texas Border Points
Ciudad Acuña
Ciudad Juárez

Ciudad Miguel Alemán
Columbia
General Rodrigo M. Quevedo
Matamoros
Nuevo Laredo
Ojinaga
Piedras Negras
Reynosa

Requesting Car Import Permits in Advance and Via Internet

If you wish, you can apply for the import permits up to six months before the vehicle enters Mexico. This can be done through any of the following Mexican consulates in the United States:

Chicago, Illinois; Austin, Dallas, Fort Worth and Houston, Texas; Los Angeles, San Bernardino and Sacramento, California; Albuquerque, New Mexico; Denver, Colorado; and Phoenix, Arizona

By presenting all the documentation and requesting the import permit from Banjercito you will then be charged the equivalent of $36.00 USD plus tax (I.V.A. 15%), and this will need to be billed to an international credit/debit card issued inside the U.S.

Applying for a Car Permit Online

You may now apply for a car permit in advance, online. The request can be made between 20 and 60 days prior to the vehicle crossing the border. By using the Internet service, your temporary permit will be sent to you by mail. This service is to help speed up the permit process. If you would like to apply online, the English-language website is:

www.banjercito.com.mx/site/imagenes/iitv/instruccionesIITV_ing.html.

177

- You must electronically accept the terms agreement
- You then register all your personal information
- You must input the vehicle data as well
- Your credit/debit card will be charged an amount in national currency equivalent to $45.00 USD plus taxes (I.V.A. 15%)

You will then receive confirmation electronically as well as a limit date by when you must have sent copies of all the required documents. There are three ways this documentation can be sent:

Electronically via email to:
CIITEVAduanaMexico@sat.gob.mx.
The subject must include the applicant's name and the folio

Via certified mail to:
Avenida Industria Militar #1055 Colonia Lomas de Sotelo
Delegación Miguel Hidalgo
11200, México, D.F.
The remittent must be the applicant and the folio.

You can also personally deliver the copies at any of the CITEV modules in the customs offices at any border.
Upon electronic confirmation, Banjercito will send the import permit to the address requested on the application in less than 20 days.

When you arrive at the border crossing, you will need to provide the Folio number assigned to you during the on-line process, and there is a charge of 27.00 USD at the border modules (or $39.60 USD at the consulate modules).

In addition, the same documentation must be presented, the original and two photocopies:

Valid proof of citizenship (passport or birth certificate) In the case of dual citizenship, the solicitant must present his or her Mexican passport or proof of Mexican nationality.

The appropiate immigration form (FMT or "tourist card")

The valid vehicle registration certificate, or a document, such as the original title that certifies the legal ownership of the vehicle. It must be in the driver's name.

178

The leasing contract (if the vehicle is leased or rented), which must be in the name of the person importing the car. If the vehicle belongs to a company, present the document that certifies the employee works for the company.

A valid driver's license, issued outside Mexico.
If the documentation shows the vehicle is registered in the name of the spouse, the importation can be done as long as the marriage certificate (and a copy) is presented.

An international credit or debit card, also issued outside Mexico (American Express, Mastercard or Visa), in the name of the driver of the vehicle.

Importing Your Car into Mexico

Mexican Customs is now allowing for the importation of foreign-licensed vehicles. If you want to import your car, motorcycle or motorhome it is now, under most circumstances, possible. To learn more, please be aware that the new regulations fall under the Legal Framework:

Article 95 of the Mexican Customs Law, Rule 3.5.1, 3.5.6 and 3.5.7 of the Regulations of Foreign Trade for 2012.

General information is provided as a public service here (PowerPoint slides 26, 27,28 and 29):

http://mesoamerica-foundation.org/images/Immigration_Reform.pdf:

A list of Authorized Customs Agents is found at either of these sites:

www.claa.org.mx or *www.caaarem.org.mx*

Or you can call: 01 (55) 1107-8515 or 01 (55) 3300-7500.

Insurance

U.S. and Canadian auto insurance is <u>NOT</u> valid in Mexico. Mexican auto insurance is mandatory in many states and cities and you should <u>NOT</u> drive without it. If you are in an accident or other vehicle-related problems and you do not have insurance, you may be arrested and your vehicle impounded until the authorities can figure out the situation. A list of insurance companies that can provide the coverage you need appears later in this chapter. Most allow you to buy insurance over the phone, fax or Internet.

Gas: Filling Up at Pemex

Mexico's state-owned oil monopoly is Pemex, which operates or franchises all the gas stations throughout the country. The price of gas is set by the government. As such, there is no need to drive around looking for the cheapest gas: it is the same everywhere. But because gas stations are Pemex franchises, there are fewer than in the U.S. and Canada. Make sure you fill up before heading for a long trip! Please note that Mexico's gas stations are staffed with attendants who pump the gas, wipe your windshields, and check your oil upon request. These attendants should be tipped. The best way to handle yourself is to say, "*$195 pesos, por favor*," while holding a $200 peso note in your hand. (Pronounciation: "See-Ehn-Tow-Noh-Ven-Tah-Seen-Coh".)

Answers to Commonly Asked Questions

1) The temporary authorization for the importation of vehicles is valid for any type of vehicle weighing less than three tons for periods up to six months (180 days).

2) The temporarily imported vehicle may be driven across the border multiple times during the authorized period.

3) Always carry with you the importation permit when driving your car in Mexico. Do not leave this document in the vehicle; it is indispensible in the case of damage, theft, or accident.

4) The sale, abandonment, or use of the vehicle for financial gain will result in its confiscation.

5) The vehicle temporarily imported by the owner may be driven in Mexico by the spouse or adult children, as long as they have the same immigration status. Other persons may drive the vehicle as long as the owner is in the vehicle."

On the road to Mérida!

Once you are well on your way, take time to enjoy the ride. Most of the highways are modern, and some have tolls, so be prepared. It is best to drive carefully and cautiously, taking time to rest at the Pemex gas stations, stretch your legs, be hydrated. Never drive if you are tired or sleepy. Try to avoid driving with the sun in your face. As you approach the Yucatán peninsula, the geography changes quickly and you soon realize you are entering a tropical environment.

Military Checkpoints:

It is probably not news to you, but there's a drug problem in the world out there, and it just so happens that, geographically, Mexico is in the middle of it. What you probably don't know, however, is that the U.S. doesn't control the export of firearms. As a result, as you drive around the peninsula, you may encounter military checkpoints. There is nothing to fear. If they wave you to stop, simply comply. If you are traveling away from the U.S. (east or south) they are probably looking for firearms. If you are traveling towards the U.S. (west or north) they are probably looking for drugs. In either case, the young soldiers are polite and we know of no one who has found them to be anything other than respectful and courteous while doing their jobs. No matter what you have seen in Hollywood films, nothing untoward is going to happen, and they are there for your protection, since you are a guest in this country.

Free Highway Assistance: Green Angels

The Secretariat of Tourism (a federal agency) operates "Angeles Verdes," or "Green Angels." This is a public service that helps motorists who are distressed along the road. As you drive the highways, you probably will see their helping motorists in distress. They are there to help you with flat tires, drivers who ran out of gas, motorists experiencing general car problems (overheated radiators, dead batteries), and they will even tow you to the nearest gas station or town. There is no charge for their help, but the young men and women who work for them won't turn down a tip if offered ($50 or $100 pesos, depending on how much they helped). If you are in trouble, you can contact them by dialing 078 983-1184.

The Yucatán's One and Only Toll Road:

When you arrive in the Yucatán, you will find that there is only one toll road between Mérida and Cancún (*Autopista de Cuota*) is fast and safe, but not cheap. The toll between Mérida and Cancún is $407 pesos, one way. (The toll between Mérida to Chichén Itzá (Kantunil exit) is $86 pesos. The toll between Mérida to Valladolid (Kantunil exit) is $149 pesos). The toll between Valladolid and Cancún is $258 and the toll between Chichén Itzá (Pisté exit) and Valladolid is $63. There is only one gas station and rest area, about halfway between Mérida and Cancún. Take a break, stretch your legs, go to the restroom, or buy a soda or water. If you are hesitant to pay the hefty toll, you may want to consider that the Toll Road avoids 43 towns and villages, so that's a lot of school crossings and 146 speed bumps ("topes") along the way. (Yes, we have counted them!) If you are making a roundtrip, you might want to consider using the Toll Road one way, and the take the secondary road (marked "Libre," meaning "Free"), which will add about an hour to your travel time, but then again, it meanders through scenic Maya villages.

Recommendations from the U.S. State Department on Driving in Mexico

Driving and Vehicle Regulations

U.S. driver's licenses are valid in Mexico. Mexican law requires that only owners drive their vehicles, or that the owner be inside the vehicle. If not, the vehicle may be seized by Mexican customs and will not be returned under any circumstances. The Government of Mexico strictly regulates the entry of vehicles into Mexico.

Insurance

Mexican insurance is required for all vehicles, including rental vehicles. Mexican auto insurance is sold in most cities and towns on both sides of the border. U.S. automobile liability insurance is not valid in Mexico, nor is most collision and comprehensive coverage issued by U.S. companies. Motor vehicle insurance is considered invalid in Mexico if the driver is found to be under the influence of alcohol or drugs.

Road Emergencies and Automobile Accidents

Motor vehicle accidents are the leading cause of death of U.S. citizens in Mexico. Motorists should exercise special caution on the heavily-traveled expressway south of Cancún, particularly the two stretches between Cancún/Playa Del Carmen and Playa del Carmen/Tulum.

If you have an emergency while driving, the equivalent of "911" in Mexico is "066", but this number is not always answered. If you are driving on a toll highway (or "cuota") or any other major highway, you may contact the Green Angels (Angeles Verdes), a fleet of trucks with bilingual crews. The Green Angels may be reached directly at (01) (55) 5250-8221. If you are unable to call them, pull off to the side of the road and lift the hood of your car; chances are that they will find you.

If you are involved in an automobile accident, you will be taken into police custody until it can be determined who is liable and whether you have the ability to pay any penalty. If you do not have Mexican liability insurance, you may be prevented from departing the country even if you require life-saving medical care, and you are almost certain to spend some time in jail until all parties are satisfied that responsibility has been assigned and adequate financial satisfaction received. Drivers may face criminal charges if injuries or damages are serious.

Road Safety

Avoid driving on Mexican highways at night. Even multi-lane expressways in Mexico often have narrow lanes and steep shoulders. Single-vehicle rollover accidents involving U.S. citizens are common, often resulting in death or serious injury to vehicle occupants. Use extreme caution when approaching towns, driving on curves, and passing large trucks. All vehicle occupants should use seatbelts at all times. Please refer to *Road Safety Overseas* for more information.

The website is: *www.travel.state.gov/travel/tips/safety/safety_1179.html*

For additional information in English concerning Mexican driver's permits, vehicle inspection, road tax, mandatory insurance, etc., please telephone the Mexican Secretariat of Tourism (SECTUR) at 1-800-44-MEXICO (639-426).

For detailed information in Spanish only, visit Mexican Customs' website *Importación Temporal de Vehículos* ("Temporary Importation of Vehicles"). The website is: *www.aduanas.sat.gob.mx/aduana_mexico/2007/A_Body_Vehiculos.htm*

Travelers are advised to consult with the Mexican Embassy or the nearest Mexican consulate in the United States for additional, detailed information prior to entering Mexico.

In recent years, moped rentals have become very widespread in Cancún and Cozumel, and the number of serious moped accidents has risen accordingly. Most operators carry no insurance and do not conduct safety checks. The U.S. Embassy recommends avoiding operators who do not provide a helmet with the rental. Some operators have been known to demand fees many times in excess of damages caused to the vehicles, even if renters have purchased insurance in advance. Vacationers at other beach resorts have encountered similar problems after accidents involving rented jet-skis."

State Department Advice on Bringing U.S. cars into Mexico:

Vehicle Permits: Tourists wishing to travel beyond the border zone with their vehicle must obtain a temporary import permit or risk having their vehicle confiscated by Mexican customs officials. At present the only exceptions to the requirement are for vehicles entering through the Nogales port of entry and traveling in the Baja Peninsula and in most of the state of Sonora. To acquire a permit, one must submit evidence of citizenship, title for the vehicle, a vehicle registration certificate, a driver's license, and a processing fee to either a Banjercito (Mexican Army Bank) branch located at a Mexican Customs (Aduanas) office at the port of entry, or at one of the Mexican consulates located in the U.S. Mexican law also requires the posting of a bond at a Banjercito office to guarantee the export of the car from Mexico within a time period determined at the time of the application. For this purpose, American Express, Visa or MasterCard credit card holders will be asked to provide credit card information; others will need to make a cash deposit of between $200 and $400, depending on the make/model/year of the vehicle. In order to recover this bond or avoid credit card charges, travelers must go to any Mexican Customs office immediately prior to departing Mexico. Regardless of any official or unofficial advice to the contrary, vehicle permits cannot be obtained at checkpoints in the interior of Mexico.

Travelers should avoid individuals who wait outside vehicle permit offices and offer to obtain the permits without waiting in line, even if they appear to be government officials. There have been reports of fraudulent or counterfeit permits being issued adjacent to the vehicle import permit office in Nuevo Laredo, Cuidad Juárez and other border areas. If the proper permit is not obtained before entering Mexico and cannot be obtained at the Banjercito branch at the port of entry, do not proceed to the interior. Travelers without the proper permit may be incarcerated, fined and/or have their vehicle seized at immigration/customs checkpoints. For further information, contact Mexican Customs about appropriate vehicle permits. Motorists should exercise special caution on the heavily-traveled expressway south of Cancún, particularly the two stretches between Cancún/Playa Del Carmen and Playa del Carmen/Tulum.

State Department Advice on Travel Medical Insurance in Mexico

What's the difference between Travel Insurance and Travel Medical Insurance?

- Travel Insurance insures your financial investment in your trip. Typically it covers such things as the cost of lost baggage and cancelled flights, but it may or may not cover costs of medical attention you may need while abroad.

- Travel Medical Insurance covers costs of medical attention you may need while abroad.

State Department Advice: Know Before You Go

Before you take your car into Mexico, we recommend that you check the State Department Travel Advisories in effect concerning driving conditions in Mexico. International Travel information is available at: http://www.travel.state.gov/travel/cis_pa_tw/tw/tw_1764.html

Mexican Automobile Insurance

The following companies specialize in providing comprehensive automobilie insurance for those driving from the U.S. to Mexico.

ADA-VIS Global

Full service insurance agency by phone or fax.
Website: *www.mexicoinsurance.com*

Adventure Mexican Insurance

Complete insurance services.
Website: *www.mexadventure.com*

Baja Bound

Mexican insurance online.
Website*: www.bajabound.com*

DriveMex

Purchase and print online policy.
Website: *www.drivemex.com*

Instant Mexico Insurance

Complete auto/car insurance.
Website: *www.instant-mex-auto-insur.com*

Lewis and Lewis Insurance Agency

Mexican auto insurance, Mexican home insurance, international boat insurance, international medical insurance
Website: *www.mexicanautoinsurance.com*

MexBound.com

Purchase and print online policy.
Website: *www.mexbound.com*

MexicanInsurance.com

Purchase and print online policy.
Website: *www.mexicaninsurance.com*

Mexico Insurance Professionals

Serving all of Mexico.
Website: *www.mexicanautoinsurance.com*

Sanborns Mexico Auto Insurance

Full coverage auto insurance in Mexico.
Website: *www.sanbornsinsurance.com*

West Coast Insurance Services

Standard and special lines auto insurance for your vehicles in Mexico.
Website: *www.westcoastri.com*

Vehicle Registration, or *Tenencia* and *Referendo*

Once you move to Mérida, at some point, you'll end up buying a car (or legally importing the car you drove from the U.S.) When you do buy a car in Mexico, here's how the annual vehicle registration works. Remember, if you are delinquent in paying your vehicle registration fees, your car can be seized by the police. That's never a pleasant experience, in Mexico or anywhere else in the world.

Vehicle registration fees are comprised of two categories. The first is the *Derecho Vehicular*, simply referred to as *referendo*. This is a fixed amount, regardless of the value of your vehicle.

Now to the peculiar tax: *Tenencia*. The *tenencia* applies to motor vehicles that are less than 10 years old. What's the *tenencia* all about, many people ask. Well, the *tenencia* is a lot like the

185

toll on the Florida Turnpike. And it's a lot like what governments around the world are accustomed to doing: once they see a source of revenue, it's hard to shut it off.

So, here's the story. In Florida, the toll on the turnpike was supposed to be a *temporary* fee to pay for the construction of the toll road. But it generates so much income for the State of Florida that, although tolls collected have paid in full for the turnpike (back in 1989), the tolls continue to this day—ostensibly to have a fund for road improvements! (Doesn't the State of Florida impose a $2.50 a day tax on all car rentals to defray highway maintenance expenses?)

Here in Mexico, the *tenencia* was enacted in 1962, when Adolfo López Mateo was president, for the purposes of paying for the 1968 Summer Olympic Games! Eleven years later, when the law was due to expire, Congress reauthorized it, giving 30% of all funds raised to the respective states for general funding purposes. And so it has gone forth.

Regardless of its history, its important simply to note that the *tenencia* is levied on cars less than 10 years old, and it is based on the value of the car. If you have an inexpensive vehicle, you pay considerably less than if you have Rolls Royce.

It's possible to pay for your dues online, but most people prefer to go in person to the *Módulos de Vialidad y Padron Vehícular*. There are two convenient locations. The least crowded one is located across from Gran Plaza, in the parking garage where Chedrahui Supermarket. The other, in the *Centro Histórico*, is adjacent to the Military Hospital, on the south side of the *Parque de la Paz*, which fronts the Centenario on Avenida Itzáes and Calle 59.

To expedite matters, here is what you will need to pay your vehicle fees and get your new license plates:

- *Comprobante domiciliario*: This is a utility bill, such as electric (CFE) or water (JAPAY). It must be in your name, and you have to show the original and a copy, which they will keep
- Photo identification, again the original and a copy to leave behind. If you are a foreign citizen, you will need to show your passport and FM3, along with copies of each, including the section listing your current status and renewals (*prorrogas*)
- The old license plates
- Money, preferably cash, to pay the corresponding fees (and outstanding fines) on the vehicle
- To find out what the current *tenencia* and *referendo* on your vehicle is, there is a website that, with your plate number and car serial number, will calculate what is due.

The address is: *https://srvshyweb.yucatan.gob.mx/reemplacamiento/solpagreem.htm*

If you are sending someone on your behalf, in addition to the above, you will have to provide a *Carta de Poder*, or Power of Attorney, with your signature and the signature of the designated person acting on your behalf. The letter has to be in Spanish, and you will need to show the original and have a copy to leave behind.

A simple Power of Attorney consists of:

A quién corresponda:

Por medio de la presente se autoriza a (name of the person you acting on your behalf) *quien ampara su personalidad moral con su* (list identification used, a IFE card, a driver's license, a passport), *para tramitar el pago de la tenencia, el referendo y cambio de placas, del vehículo* (list car manufacture and make of vehicle, such as a Volkswagen GTI), *número de serie* (vehicle ID number), *y número de placas* (license plate number).

Atentamente,

(*Your name*)

Make sure you sign the letter—exactly as your signature appears in your passport and FM3—and that you print your name below.

You will need the original, and a copy. The person you are sending on your behalf will need to produce his or her official identification, and have a copy to leave behind. The person will also have to show official identification, and have a copy to leave behind.

As with everything else, the sooner you do this, the shorter the lines since it is human nature to procrastinate!

In 2011, Yucatán State announced that it would end the tenencia tax for vehicles valued at $300,000 pesos (about $24,000 USD) or less. Vehicles valued at more than $300,000 pesos will still have to pay the tenencia, and vehicles used for commercial purposes, regardless of their value, are still subject to the tenencia.

Oh, yes, one more detail: The *tenencia* ceases to exist as a federal tax on December 31, 2011. What's the bad news, you ask? On January 1, 2012 it was up to each state to decide whether or not to enact its own version of the tax! This, of course, makes as much sense as the State of

187

Florida "ending" the toll tax on the Florida Turnpike, only to say that it's now up to each individual county to decide whether to continue imposing the toll ... what do you think the answer to that little question would be? So get ready for a whole new set of rules and procedures for the state-imposed *tenencia* come January 2017!

Car Insurance

Now that you have a car, you need insurance. Here are reputable insurance agencies that can provide all kinds of automobile coverage.

GNP
Calle 16 #97, between Calle 17 and 19 Street, Colonia Mexico
Telephone: (999) 944-6333

Inbursa
Paseo de Montejo #497, between Calle 45 and 47 Street, Colonia Santa Ana
Telephone: (999) 928-0629

ING Insurance
Calle 21 #117-D, between Calle 24 and 24-A Street, Centro
Telephone: (999) 926-3343

Interacciones
Calle 31 #170, between Calle 20 and 22 Street, Colonia Alemán
Telephone: (999) 938-2218

Seguros La Peninsular
Calle 47-A #501, between Calle 66 and 64 Street, Centro
Telephone: (999) 928-1187

Moving Your Possessions

It's one thing to drive or fly to Mérida ... but if you're moving here, how do you get your stuff into town?

If you are driving across the border, you will have to do all the shipping and Customs work at that time. If, as most people end up deciding, you will have your household goods shipped to Mexico, then this will be done through the Port of Progreso. The most reliable company is Linea Peninsular, Inc., which ships from the Port of Panama City, Florida to the Port of Progreso, Yucatán. The cost of shipping, of course, depends on the amount of furniture being shipped, and the distance from your home in the U.S. to Panama City, Florida.

Once it arrives at the Port of Progreso, you will need a Customs Broker to handle the paperwork to import legally your furnishings and household goods. There are two Customs Brokers that are extraordinary: María Luisa Uc Varguez of Agencia Aduanal Del Valle Sureste, and

188

Hiram Cervera of Agencia Aduanal Cervera. Each continues to win praise for their selfless, thorough, and professional work. Each has vast experience helping expatriates get their household goods safely and quickly through Mexican Customs.

Here is the contact information to ship to Yucatán and clear Mexican Customs:

Shipping company

Linea Peninsular, Inc.

US Address:
5323 W. Highway 98, Suite 215
Panama City, FL 32401
Telephone: (800) 858-4280 or (850) 522-4500
Email: *usoffice@lineaships.com*
Website: *www.lineaships.com*
Mexico Address:
Calle 25 #151-A, between Calle 80 and 82 Street, Centro, Progreso, Yucatán
Telephone: (969) 935-5519
Website: *www.lineaships.com*
Email: *mexicooffice@lineaships.com*

Customs Brokers

Agencia Aduanal Del Valle Sureste

Lic. María Luisa Uc Varguez
Calle 27 #168-A, between Calle 84
and 86 Street, Centro
Progreso, Yucatán
Telephone: (969) 934-30-55, Ext.127
Email: *malu@aadelvalle.com.mx*
Website: *www.aadelvalle.com.mx*

Agencia Aduanal Cervera

Hiram Cervera
Calle 84 #127, between Calle 27 and
29 Street, Centro
Progreso, Yucatán
Telephone: (969) 935-3535
Email: *Agencia@cervera.com.mx*
Website: *www.cervera.com.mx*

Going somewhere?

We are a sparsely populated peninsula, with long stretches of road between towns. Before you head out, head to a gas station. Fill up the tank, have the attendant check the tires, the oil and clean your windshield. Make sure you have water, sunscreen and a hat. Taking a map is a good idea. Here are the distances:

Distance from Mérida to:

Destination	Miles	Kilometers
Campeche City	158	253
Cancún	199	318
Ceiba Club de Golf	9	14
Celestún	58	93
Chetumal	285	456
Chichén Itzá	75	120
Cobá	145	232
Dzibilchaltún	10	16
Ek Balam	111	179
Holbox Island	218	350
Isla Mujeres	206	330
Izamal	44	72
Kabah	63	102
Labná	74	118
Lol-Tún Caves	70	113
Mexico City	969	1550
Motul	28	45
Ochil, Hacienda	16	26
Oxkutzcab	60	100
Petac, Hacienda	13	20
Playa del Carmen	240	386
Progreso	22	35
Ría Lagartos	165	263
Sayil	79	126
Sisal	33	53
Telchac Puerto	39	62
Temozón, Hacienda	21	34

Destination	Miles	Kilometers
Teya, Hacienda	8	12
Ticul	53	84
Tizimin	132	212
Tulum (via Coba)	171	274
Uxmal	50	80
Valladolid	100	160
Xcanatún, Hacienda	8	12
Yaxcopoil	14	22

Conversion Chart

Kilometer-Mile Conversion

1 kilometer = 0.60 miles

So if you multiply kilometers by 0.6, you'll end up with miles.

Example: 10 kilometers (10 x 0.6) is equivalent to 6 miles.

And if you multiply miles by 1.6, you'll end up with kilometers.

Example: 10 miles (10 x 1.6) is equivalent to 16 kilometers

8 THE EXPAT LIFE, OR WHAT THE MEXICANS CALL "GRINGOLANDIA"

Americans call it "Gringo Gulch," and Yucatecans and Mexicans refer to it as "Gringolandia." These are the Colonias of Santiago and Santa Ana in the heart of Mérida's Historic Center. But what does this mean?

The self-effacing ways of thinking about the American (and Canadian) presence in Mérida speaks to the nature of our presence: at all times, foreigners are *guests* of Mexico. Until you become a Mexican citizen, or marry a Mexican citizen and have a child born in Mexico, your presence is that of a *guest*. It's possible to own entire city blocks of buildings, or have millions of dollars invested in businesses, but that does not detract from the tenuous nature of every foreigner's presence in Mexico.

This is important to remember: Mexico's hospitality is generously extended, but it can also be withdrawn.

Why are so few permanent rights extended to foreigners? Because history has taught Mexico that it must be cautious of others' intentions. Mexico, throughout its history, has been besieged. It was the target of an unprovoked war by the United States, it has been occupied by Napoleon III (who sent over Maximilian I to serve as "Emperor"). It has been the subject of intrigue during World War I with the notorious and infamous Zimmerman Telegram.

As a result, Mexico is wary of the political influence of foreigners in Mexico and imposes significant restrictions on the right of foreign citizens residing in Mexico to engage in the political process. Foreigners are forbidden to join political parties, attend political rallies, make political statements in public, or engage in public debate on all political issues. This is both *liberating* and *humbling*.

Liberating: It is liberating because you can forget any ideas about attending political rallies, becoming involved in one or another candidate's campaign, or even walking door-to-door gathering signatures on any petition.

Humbling: It is humbling because it makes you realize that, in the political life of the Mexican nation, foreigners have no power whatsoever. In a city like Mérida, with almost a million people, the American expat community, comprised of about 3,500 permanent residents, is small.

Indeed, consider this: Of the hundreds of thousands of Americans who have resided in Mérida over the past 200 years, only *four* have entered the consciousness of Yucatecan society! Who are they? John Lloyd Stephens, an attorney and diplomat, who came down here in the 1830s and 1840s and produced two bestselling books, *Incidents of Travel*, which brought to the attention of the world the magnificent architectural and archaeological accomplishments of the Maya. Edward Thompson, the American Consul in Mérida who supervised the archaeological excavations at the Sacred Cenote at Chichén Itzá—and who remains notorious for having shipped untold treasure to Harvard's Peabody Museum. Alma Reed, who was invited to Mexico by President Alvaro Obregón, hailed a "Hero of Mexico" for saving the life of a Mexican teenager sentenced to death by the State of California, and who carried out a tawdry, impossible affair with Felipe Carrillo Puerto, Governor of Yucatán. And Joann Andrews, who has dedicated decades of her life to building and nurturing an environmental consciousness on the Yucatán Peninsula, and is cherished by generations of Yucatecans as one of their own—"una joya del Mayab," meaning, "a jewel of the land of the Maya."

There are, of course, other expatriates who have become legends. Antonio Menéndez who, along with his wife, Angela González, arrived in the Yucatán in the 1860s from Cuba, fought for social justice and established schools for women and the Maya, both believing that education for women and the less privileged was necessary for progress. (Their son, Carlos R. Menéndez went on to found the *Diario de Yucatán*.) Joaquin García Ginerés, a native of Catalonia and who worked to modernize Mérida along the lines that the great cities of Europe were expanding during the Edwardian age. He was so instrumental in the growth of Mérida that the Colonia García Ginerés is named after him by official proclamation to honor his memory. In our time, Miguel A. Bretos, another Cuban, who has had a distinguished career as a historian, scholar and was the first director of the Hispanic department at the Smithsonian in Washington, D.C. is much beloved. His intellectual contributions to Mérida continue to astonish, from the first history of the colonial churches of the Yucatán (*Iglesias de Yucatán*, 1992), to the most comprehensive history of Mérida's cathedral (*Mérida: Biografía de una Catedral*, 2011).

And how political sensitive is Mexico to foreigners interfering in the political process of the Mexican nation? Consider this: Article XXXIII of the Mexican Constitution empowers the president to expel, immediately and without recourse, any foreigner deemed "inconvenient." The last time this was used widely was by president Ernesto Zedillo who expelled hundreds of foreigners who supported the Zapatistas in Chiapas. Felipe Calderon has used it sparingly, primarily against foreigners involved in drug trafficking and money laundering activities. Current president Peña Nieto has only used it on a few occasions—thus far.

What does this "political insignificance" mean? It means that you are absolutely free to come here and enjoy yourself, delight in this beautiful city, make lifelong friends with other expats, Mexicans and Yucatecans, build a wonderful life for yourself without any political or civic questions entering your life. It also means that you can forget about bringing down a clipboard and to collect signatures for a petition in front of City Hall!

The moral of the story is that only if you think otherwise—that you can become an active agent in a country that really doesn't want your input about anything unless you are working for an accredited international agency on official business –you will be disappointed.

There is wisdom to this advice, since Mérida's recent history is littered with well-meaning and well-intentioned foreigners who arrive here, think they can contribute significantly to the city's life, who then find out that, although they are received politely, their overtures are ignored, and they are, if not turned away, then at least relegated to the sidelines.

After all, if you are an entrepreneur and start a business, that's great. But no one forgets that business ventures exist to make the entrepreneurs money. And if you come here thinking you can donate your time and skills to a worthy cause, just go to Chapter 18 and you will see an overwhelming list of bona fide nonprofit organizations duly authorized to work in fields from helping children with autism to saving endangered sea turtles, from protecting women in abusive relationships to improving the city's urban planning. In addition, there are hundreds of "civil associations"—"asociaciones civiles"—that are involved in all manner of things, from rescuing abandoned pets to providing support groups for caregivers of people with Alzheimer's.

Many Americans, unfamiliar with how Mexican society is organized, embark independently and start initiatives that are doomed to failure, as they are seen as working *outside* established norms. Why create a parallel organization to duplicate work that is already being carried out by Mexicans? Why insult the people of Mérida by coming across as thinking you are better qualified to do this or carry out that?

It's a curious place, this "Gringolandia," this "Gringo Gulch."

But it is a welcoming place.

194

The "Expat Life" is one of measured leisure, and careful overtures to the community at large. The Cubans and Lebanese have been very successful at integrating themselves into the fabric of Yucatecan life. For information on the expatriate community in Mexico, you may want to learn about the International Community Foundation:

International Community Foundation
Website: *www.icfdn.org*
Email: *info@icfdn.org*

Expats in Yucatán State

Nationality	Number
Cubans	7,298
Lebanese	6,879
Americans	4,322*
Spaniards	1,489
Chinese**	1,097
Canadian	1,214***
South American	756
Italian	478
Korean	475
Argentine	298
German	296
Guatemalan	243
Other European	1,785
Other Asia	296
Africa	136
Total	**27,062**

Please note that this excludes Cuban-Mexicans and Lebanese-Mexicans, which number in the scores of thousands.

*American fulltime residents are 3,500 and 1,500 additional part-time residents

**Chinese from Taiwan, not mainland China

***Canadian fulltime residents are 395 and 615 are part-time residents

These figures are compiled from various sources, including foreign embassies in Mexico City and data from INEGI (Instituto Nacional de Estadística Geografía e Informática), as of November 2011.

Restrictions on Foreigners and Political Activites

Advice from the State Department:

"The Mexican Constitution prohibits political activities by foreigners; such actions may result in detention and/or deportation. Travelers should avoid political demonstrations and other activities that might be deemed political by the Mexican authorities. Even demonstrations intended to be peaceful can turn confrontational and escalate into violence. U.S. citizens are urged to avoid areas of demonstrations, and to exercise caution if in the vicinity of any protests."

Expatriate Sex-Tourism Scandals in Mérida

In 2011 Mérida was shaken by two sex-tourism scandals operated by foreigners. In one, an expatriate who went by the name of La Madame was operating a sex-tourism operation in which she lured young women from other countries with the promise of glamorous jobs along the Maya Riviera. Once in Mérida, these women were held against their will and forced into prostitution. "La Madame" was arrested and prosecuted for sex-tourism, operating a prostitution ring, and human trafficking. The other sex-tourism scandal centered on another expatriate who went by the name of John the Match Maker Truax, who, using a charity as a front, brought foreigners to Mérida for sex tourism. John the Match Maker Truax and his associates fled Mérida after abruptly shutting down their clandestine guest house before they could be formally charged. Mexico, as a signatory nation to international treaties on sex tourism, the exploitation of children and human trafficking, takes a strong stand against these kinds of activities; the FBI's Houston office launched an investigation into the participation of U.S. citizens in sex tourism activites in Mérida.

Here is an excerpt from an American expatriate who offers his own perspective on being a newcomer to Mérida.

> *When I moved here a few years ago, which I did not to retire but to study (I myself am not quite thirty years old yet,) I curiously perused Google to see what the gay scene was like. As I said, I'm partnered and monogamous, but I had always been involved in the respective communities I was a part of prior to my move south of the border, usually volunteering for AIDS organizations and homeless youth outreach.*

The first page I came across was a guide for gay tourists coming to Merida, written in English, that hosted such valuable tidbits as which pereferico bars had the best male strippers, which parks to cruise for public sex in Cancún, and even an advertisement for a Rent-a-Boy service. This page has since been taken down after it was exposed on another blog, though I still have screenshots of it.

And the more research I did the quicker I realized that Merida's English-speaking gay community was more or less a cadre of retired sex tourists, and I got the impression that I wasn't the only "normal" gay expat living here who just wanted to make friends and wasn't here to cruise for foreign tail.

I also got the impression that these other "normal" men avoided the gringo gay scene, probably because, like me, they had been humiliated in public by other gay gringos' bad behavior.

Edward V. Byrne

To read Mr. Byrne's complete statement on the matter, please see his article at: http://mexicogulfreporter.blogspot.mx/2012/05/word-from-very-wise-and-gay-reader.html

Be mindful of the repercussions these scandals have caused to the people of Mérida, especially when, in 2012, there were several high-profile murders of American pedophiles who part of this clandestine sex-tourism/pedophile community.

The Mérida English Language Library (MELL) has been at the center of a scandal involving sex tourism in town. As former Board Member Daniel Tyrrell admitted in writing, the use of MELL facilities by pedophiles "was [the activity of] a private 'entrepreneur' making use of a public gathering to run his sleazy business. The board of the day did put a quick end to it and appointed coordinators to attend each session and to be aware of this type of thing. I know for a fact there are at least one or two such coordinators at every Monday night session as I was the desk volunteer at those sessions for the past year or so."

In other words, instead of reporting these activites to law enforcement, MELL "covered it up" by availing itself to volunteers to "monitor" the activities of pedophiles on MELL premises.

Mr. Tyrrell's communications were handed over to law enforcement in Mexico and the FBI offices in Houston, Texas which monitor sex tourism activites by American citizens in Yucatán. Also, the murder of Sam Woodruff, a pedophile slain by the teenage boy he had preyed upon for years, provided much information when law enforcement examined Mr. Woodruff's computer and email accounts. If you have any information on sex tourism involving expats and Mexican minors, you are urged to contact Carol Smolenski (in the U.S.) or Guillermo Alonso (in Mérida).

Carol Smolenski
Executive Director
End Child Prostitution and Trafficking USA (ECPAT-USA)
30 Third Avenue
Suite 800A
Brooklyn, NY 11217
www.ecpatusa.org

Guillermo Alonso
Investigación y Educación Popular Autogestiva, A.C.
Calle 27 No. 199-C, between Calle 18 and 20 Street
Col. García Gineres
97070, Mérida, Yucatán, México
Tel :(999) 920-6405
www.iepaac.org

If you have any information concerning the sexual exploitation of minors in Yucatán by American citizens, please note that the FBI's Houston office has ongoing investigations. You can report such activities by contacting the U.S Consulate in Mérida, or by writing:

Perrye K. Turner
Special Agent in Charge
Federal Bureau of Investigation
1 Justice Park Drive
Houston, TX 77092

The Enigma of Arrival

In the spirit of learning what it means to be an expatriate, here are Hugo de Naranja's recommendations for becoming a Good Expat!

The Ten Must-Read Works of Fiction for Anyone Living Abroad
By Hugo de Naranja

Lonely Planet and *Rough Guides* and the CIA's *World Factbook* may give you extremely useful practical information, but the project of long-term displacement, the demands of living outside your country of origin for extended periods of time, often requires a different order of *know-how* and an approach that hard facts alone can't explain.

Fiction is invaluable for learning to see yourself and what you're up to more clearly, and understanding how other people see themselves and what they're up to. The very finest fiction also takes you where you didn't know you wanted to go. What follows is a list of ten books, in alphabetical order, who we consider among the best for taking you there:

Democracy, by Joan Didion

Inez Victor gets around.

The Vietnam War nears its disastrous end. Post-colonial discontent convulses Southeast Asia. Inez travels a lot with her pompous husband Harry, a senator aspiring to the presidency, and takes some side-trips with Jack, her tight-lipped intermittent soul mate who shares her uncanny knack for "interesting times."

Saigon falls to the North Vietnamese. The American evacuation dissolves into anarchy. Inez loses patience with her countrymen's faith in their specialness — an insight that ushers her story toward its ineffably sad, almost hopeful, conclusion.

This is perhaps the funniest work in all of American 20th century literary fiction, and after turning its last page, you'll forever miss Inez, Janet, Harry, Jack, Billy, Dwight, Ruthie, and, yes, even Frances.

Geography III, by Elizabeth Bishop

Bishop's father died eight months after she was born. Her mother lost her mind a few years later. Bishop spent her life wandering — Europe, North Africa, Latin America — staying the longest, twenty-six years, in Brazil.

She was never ambitious about her career as a poet. She spent years, sometimes decades, reworking a single poem. Her humility was uncompromising: she refused to use her work for confession or self-disclosure. She took a dim view of poets who thought they were prophets and of poems that smacked of oracular self-importance. Bishop wrote about what she'd directly observed in the world outside herself, and referred to her personal life, her emotions, only rarely, and with a diamond cutter's precision.

Small, witty, a frequent hostage to asthma and alcohol, Bishop wondered what travel meant and why she never felt at home in the world. And she was always dazzled by nature's ability, through its beauty and oddness, to lift her above the loneliness that followed her everywhere. She's now regarded as one of America's greatest poets, and *Geography III* represents her finest work.

The Good Terrorist, by Dorris Lessing

Lessing seems to be coolly examining a group of politically minded misfits who coalesce long enough in London to dream up and execute a fatal plan.

But she's less interested in politics than in the specific deficiencies that make a person so despise and reject his own country's liberal democracy that he'd do it harm.

Ticking away at the heart of this novel is an ingenious technique so covert and subversive in its cunning that you may never quite figure out just why *The Good Terrorist* haunts and unsettles you long after you've read it.

Guerrillas, by VS Naipaul

The English-speaking world's most famously merciless writer fixes his eye on moth-to-the-flame characters drawn to a revolutionary movement on a Caribbean island.

Dread, doom, and folly are as thick in the air as the bauxite dust covering the island's roads. Something sinister announces its approach with flashes of surprising violence.

Pay close attention to the game Harry introduces to his guests after brunch at his beachfront home. It's a booby-trap Naipaul has set for his characters, but you, the reader, are an intended target, too.

How German Is It?, by Walter Abish

The past is a slow-acting venom that causes dreamy stupor leading to moral paralysis.

Abish had never visited Germany before writing *How German Is It?*, but readers and critics agreed that he captured the essential essence of post-war Germanness better than any native-born German.

His characters, including the son of a German officer involved in the 1944 plot to assassinate Hitler, can't wake themselves from the nightmare of history. Terrorism and its origins flicker throughout the story until the unforeseeable revelation at its end.

In a Free State, by VS Naipaul

The novella's pretext is a road-trip through troubled East Africa.

But Bobby and Linda aren't just hapless characters Naipaul has set up to take a fall. With a light touch and singular economy, Naipaul makes the two live and breathe as much as Flaubert does Emma Bovary.

And just as Flaubert set out to describe and indict mid-19th century France, Naipaul, with far fewer words, makes the entirety of Western colonialism his target and, with a ruthlessness and speed that will leave you gasping, pulls the trigger.

Life: A User's Manual, by Georges Perec

To live abroad successfully, you ought to be able to pay close attention to the fine details of how other people live their lives — their habits, customs, histories, pretensions, and vulnerabilities. But this attention must also be the sort that can be focused quickly and remain acute despite frequent, and arbitrary, interruption.

Life: A User's Manual moves forward and backward in time, in fits and starts, in 99 chapters, as it obsessively scrutinizes the fascinating inhabitants of a fictional Parisian apartment block.

Since the novel's clever puzzle-like structure doesn't march orderly from beginning to middle to end, you can open to any random chapter, or read them all in their given sequence, with equal pleasure. Which makes *Life: A User's Manual* perfectly suited for reading while traveling, and for the distractions and disruptions of living abroad.

The Sailor From Gibraltar, by Marguerite Duras

The French often think of travel as pure escape, and find whatever's exotic in the foreign to be elegant, as opposed to alienating.

In *The Sailor From Gibraltar*, Marguerite Duras gives us a sun-struck narrator who, while on vacation in Italy, abandons everything to follow Anna, a seductive American who plies the Mediterranean in her gorgeous yacht, perpetually searching for her lost great love, a sailor from Gibraltar. The sunshine. The sea. Life at sea. Pleasure. All the necessary romantic elements appear to be in place. Yet Duras isn't handing you romance, but mystery.

The Sheltering Sky, by Paul Bowles

A friend once described *Without Stopping*, Bowles' globe-trotting name-dropping memoir, as a "very meaty *People* article." You wish there was more to it, but what you have is satisfying enough that you're willing to accept it on its own terms.

Bowles makes a similar demand of his readers in *The Sheltering Sky,* the story of a well-heeled intellectual couple, Port and Kit, who wander into North Africa, incautiously looking for answers to some unstated questions they have about their lives.

Yes, of course, self-absorption can be addictive and dangerous. Had Kit been less distracted, however, she'd have never drifted away in the amazing "vision quest" that makes up the final third of the book.

Speak, Memory, by Vladimir Nabokov

Nabokov said he never wanted to return to Russia because he'd kept everything worth keeping from his homeland in his memory and in his heart.

If you've ever wondered what you might take with you from the places and people who formed you, long after those places and people have vanished, *Speak, Memory* will show you how the world's greatest connoisseur of the irretrievable past guarded his treasures against the predations of time.

His pretty mother returning home after a morning of mushroom hunting. His handsome father returning home after a close-call with an assassin. Biarritz in the summer. A lovely little girl rolling a hoop through a Parisian park. It's all there. All of it. Luminous, distinct, and eternal.

9 THE COST OF LIVING IN MÉRIDA

How much does it cost to live in Mérida? What do you need to know in order to come up with a realistic budget? What are "unexpected" expenses that you can "expect" to encounter once you make the move?

The answer, of course, is that it depends on your lifestyle. If you are accustomed to drinking champagne every evening with dinner and you have a lavish home that requires a full-time staff, then that's a far different budget than if you are retired, living on a fixed income, and are more frugal in your ways.

Consider that most people in Mérida manage to live decent, honorable, and comfortable lives on about $325 USD a month, excluding rent or mortgage. But also consider that most Yucatecans do not own cars, have air conditioners or expect to make one or two trips back to the States every year. On the other hand, there is at least one residence in Mérida that is equipped with a heliport and has a household staff of 37 full-time employees, so you can imagine the expenses in maintaining that lifestyle.

In Mérida, as in the world over, the sky's the limit!

But to get down to the matter of figuring out a realistic budget, let's start at the beginning. Every year UBS in Switzerland surveys the most important cities in the world and then ranks the cost of living in them, using New York City as the benchmark. Out of the 70 cities surveyed, Mexico City ranked 64th *least expensive*. That means that when, 122 goods and services (including housing) were taken into account, what costs $1 USD in New York, costs only $0.40 USD in Mexico City! That means that Mexico City is about 60% cheaper than New York.

That's step one, because it gives you an idea of where Mexico ranks relative to other cities, from Miami to Los Angeles, Tokyo to Dubai. The second step, of course, is figuring out how cheaper or more expensive it is to live in Mérida than in the nation's capital. Fortunately, the Mexican government does a great job of analyzing and monitoring costs of living throughout the country. Most people don't know this, but Mexico classifies the country into three economic zones, "A," "B," and "C." Zone A, which includes Mexico City is the most expensive area. Zone C, which includes Mérida, (and the entire Yucatán peninsula) is the least expensive area to live.

The National Commission on Minimum Wages, CONASAMI, for "Comision Nacional de Salarios Minimos," and INEGI, Mexico's Census Bureau, estimate that it is about 25% less expensive to live in Mérida than it is in Mexico City for everything, excluding energy (the prices for gasoline and electricity these products are set at the federal level and are the same for the entire country). [2]

That means that when you discount the cost of living from Mexico City's UBS ranking, Mérida is one of the more affordable places to live in Mexico. (It's about one third of what one would expect to pay for a comparable lifestyle in New York City.) This, of course, gives you a perspective with which you can start to set a budget for living in Mérida.

There are two other factors to consider. First is your housing. If you own your place (as most expatriates do), then you don't have a mortgage. The annual Predial tax is rather insignificant, usually the cost of an elaborate birthday dinner at one of the fancier restaurants or hotels in town. If you rent, then you have to consider whether you are "renting like an expat" or "renting like a Yucatecan."

The difference is considerable and well worth pondering. In the chapter on Real Estate, we discuss the "artificial" real estate market that has emerged around the Historic Center and the questionable role that American expatriates working in the real estate business have played in making this once-affordable part of town into an almost unbearable place in which to rent. Colonial houses that have been refurbished, remodeled, and upgraded have been "dollarized"— priced to fetch prices as if this were exclusive neighborhoods of Miami, Ft. Lauderdale or Boca Raton.

Many American and Canadian expatriates are told to "expect" to pay ridiculous prices. "For approximately $900 to $1,600 USD per month, furnished homes with swimming pools, in desirable neighborhoods, are available," Jane McCarthy and Bruce Kelley advise would-be expatriates. For those prices you can rent a wonderful, two story home with three or four bedrooms, as many bathrooms, a two-car garage, with staff in residential neighborhoods where Yucatecan professional live with their families! To pay that much for anything in the Historic Center—where there probably isn't parking, the "pool" is so small one would be challenged to swim a lap, and the décor is, in all likelihood, what was on-sale at some discounted "rustic Mexican" operation, defies reason.

---

[2] For information on Mexico's Commission on Minimum Wages, see: *www.conasami.gob.mx/*. For information on Mexico's Census Bureau, see: *www.inegi.org.mx/*.

To find value in renting an apartment or house, you have to go "native"—use the "Avisos Económicos" of the *Diario de Yucatán* to understand what the fair market price is for renting in various neighborhoods. Here's a benchmark: the average rent for a two-bedroom, one-bathroom dwelling (apartment of single-family house) in an average neighborhood in Mérida, unfurnished (except for stove and refrigerator) is $3,000 pesos, or about $240 USD. That's what Mexicans pay, and that's what you can also pay.

The other factor to consider is that energy is as expensive in Mexico as it is in the rest of the world. Depending on where you moving from in the U.S., electricity can be a bit more expensive than what you are used to paying. Mexico's state-owned oil monopoly, Petroleos Mexicanos, or Pemex, sets the price for gasoline (unleaded, super unleaded) and diesel. The prices are uniform throughout the country, and the only gas stations are operated by, or franchises of, Pemex. For almost the entire country, the electric power company is the Comision Federal de Electricidad, known as CFE. The CFE sets the price of electricity, through complicated formulas, for the various economic "zones," and then depending on whether it is residential, government, industry and other categories (hospitals, etc.). If further allow for subsidies applied during various times of year, and there are formulas that increase rates for "above-average" residential use. The bottom line is that no matter how you look at it, electricity is one of the most expensive commodities in Mexico. People really try their best to conserve power, and it is almost unheard of for a landlord to include the price of electricity in any rental agreement. This is one reason why there are more fans in Mérida than air-conditioners!

So, it's settled: housing will be very inexpensive, but energy costs require that you be more frugal than you are probably accustomed to back in the United States or Canada.

But how do you go about building a budget? Simple: item by item. This is how to go about it in a comprehensive way.

Building a Budget for Living in Mérida

The first step, of course, is to consider your current lifestyle. How much do you already spend? Whatever that figure is, you should expect to pay considerably less for basic staples and perhaps a bit more for luxuries.

Why? Because things like fresh fruit, utilities (except electricity), household help, and taxes are considerably lower in Mexico than in the U.S. or Canada. On the other hand, many luxuries in Mexico are subject to import taxes. For the most part, for instance, luxury goods, such as fine wines and high-end electronics are a bit more expensive. If you are accustomed to enjoying a case of French wine throughout the month, you may be better off finding some wines you enjoy from countries (such as Chile and Spain) that enjoy preferential trade agreements with Mexico.

It's also important to keep in mind that items you find at familiar places, such as Costco, Sam's Club and Home Depot can be a bit more expensive: Mexico has a 16% sales tax, called IVA, for Impuesto al Valor Agregado, which is familiar to Canadians and Europeans as the "Value-Added Tax"). It's possible to rationalize this consumption tax by realizing that Mexico has, for all intents and purposes, no real income tax—unless you make a considerable income. Most expatriates in Mérida are retired, and not working, and very few have permission from Immigration authorities to be engaged in income-generating activies, whether it comes from either working as an employee or from money from renting homes.

Housing

If you own your home in Mérida, the only expenses are the Predial tax, which, as discussed in Chapter 11, is a nominal fee. It is hardly the equivalent of the onerous property taxes levied in the United States. On the other hand, since almost all of Mérida and its environs are within the Restricted Zone, you own your property through a Fideicomiso, usually administered by a bank.

These trusts levy an annual fee, which run into several hundred dollars. An average Fideicomiso tax for foreigners in Mérida is about $5,000 to $7,500 pesos, or between $400 USD to $600 USD. When the Predial tax is added, the costs of maintaining your home in Mérida is well under $750 USD for most people.

If, on the other hand, you are renting, then you know outright how much your housing expenses will be. For most expatriates, the average cost of renting a 2 bedroom, 1 bathroom house is about $42,000 pesos a year, or $3,360 USD. Of course, there are privileged individuals who live in lavish homes that cost them upwards of $750,000 USD, and there are residences that rent for about $2,750 USD a month, but considering the options, housing is a very reasonable expense, far less than homeowners' association fees, or monthly maintenances on condominiums or co-ops in the U.S. and a mere fraction of the property taxes levied by local governments.

Utilities: Electricity, Gas, Water and Garbage

These are the basics of life, and in Mérida they are, except for electric power, more than economical. In the next chapter, how to set up service for basic utilities is addressed. For now, however, as you go about creating a budget for yourself, keep these guidelines in mind.

Electricity

The state-owned Comision Federal de Electricidad, or CFE, provides electric power to Mérida. Energy throughout Mexico is owned by the government, both electric and petroleum. Electric power is supplied in 110V, 60 cycle which is consistent with the U.S. and Canada; whatever appliances anyone brings from the U.S. or Canada will work in Mexican outlets. Mexico's economic growth, however, has outpaced the ability of the CFE to build new plants and expand service as necessary. Electric rates are high, and there is a great civic effort to conserve as much electricity as possible. In fact, on a globalized basis, Mexico's electric bill is about 20% higher than the median electric bill in the U.S.

Electricity will be the most expensive utility on your budget without a doubt, and yet, it is not a deal breaker. The CFE has a bimonthly billing cycle, and you will receive a bill every other month. The rate you pay, however, reflects prior usage, over the previous six billing periods (an entire year). If your consumption falls in relation to what you consumed around the same time the previous bill and this is a consistent trend, your rate will decline. If, on the other hand, your consumption rises over the same period and this is a trend, your rate will increase—this is a bureaucratic attempt to get you to conserve.

The average residential bill for a home where there are two air-conditioners in use is about $3,500 pesos, or about $280 USD. This may sound high, but the billing cycle is for two months, so the monthly bill for the average home in Mérida is about $140 USD. For Yucatecans and Mexicans, this is an extravagant expenditure. For most Americans and Canadians, it is steep, but not unreasonable. Many expatriates (and Yucatecans and Mexicans) become compulsive about conservation—preferring ceiling fans and turning on their air-conditioners only at night. Did we mention that rates at night are lower than during day-time hours? Yes, it is a complicated system.

Overall, frugal expatriates can expect to pay about $80 USD a month for electricity. Those who have a swimming pool and run air-conditioners habitually can expect to pay about twice that much or more.

Gas

There is no natural gas in Mérida. Propane tanks are used. Most residences can fill their gas tanks for about $2,000 pesos, or about $160 USD. This should last about six months. The annual expenditure that the normal expatriate household can expect to spend is about $320 USD a year, or just under $27.00 a month. Unless you're taking hot baths every day, or doing laundry daily, or are cooking for an army, there's no reason to use more than this in propane gas.

207

Water

At the beginning of this book it was mentioned that Mérida is built over what is believed to be one of the largest underground river systems in the world. Water is plentiful and very, very inexpensive. Water is provided by the Junta de Agua Potable y Alcantarillado de Yucatán, known as JAPAY, and pronounced, "Hah-Pie." How cheap is cheap? Consider this: few people pay more than the minimum and this is determined by neighborhood. In most of Mérida's Colonias, the bill is $72 pesos or less than $6 USD—for two months! Unless you are filling an Olympic-size pool every week or running the washing machine every day, average Yucatecan household budgets the equivalent of $35-40 USD for water for an entire year.

Garbage Collection

Here again, expect to pay a minimal amount. In the older Colonias in poor neighborhoods, the garbage collection fee is $20 pesos a month—less than $1.70 USD. In the more affluent neighborhoods, the fee is an average of $50 pesos—or under $3.85 USD. This means that the Christmas tip you give the garbage man will probably amount to most of the annual cost of garbage collection. And let's face it: you do have to give the garbage man a Christmas bonus, right?

Internet

Apart from utilities, there are other "essentials" of modern life: Internet, cable television, and telephone service. Here again, given the global nature of the world and the fact that Carlos Slim, who is, according to *Forbes* magazine, the richest man in the world, he made his fortune in telecommunications. That means there are no bargains to be found. There are, happily, no major rip-offs, either!

Cable television is now so intertwined with the Internet that it's almost impossible to separate the two. The two largest cable television companies serving Mérida are CableMAS and CableRED. Each offers competitive packages that allow unlimited Internet along with a broad selection of cable channels for about $1,200 pesos a month, or about $96 USD. If you are a fan of certain programming channels, such as HBO, CNN, Bloomberg, Showtime, Cinemax, TLC, Discovery, E! and Fox, you can get them in Mérida. SKY offers a comprehensive package for about $650 pesos a month, which is about $52 USD. (SKY offers a less comprehensive selection for about $450 pesos, or $36 USD, but you have to check with them to see if the channels you want are or are not included.) As you can see, however, CableMAS, CableRED and SKY offer packages that are somewhat less expensive than in the U.S.

208

Telephone

If there's one area where "globalization" is evident, it has to been in the sheer number of telephone calling plans and options available. It would fill a small book. You can choose between Telmex, Telcel, Iusacell, Telefónica and Axtel. You can choose calling cards, or almost-disposable cell phones that can be recharged at any convenience store. You can use Skype or Magic Jack, or you can even try two Dixie cups and a string. OK, perhaps the last option is not really an option. The bottom line is that for standard land lines, a regular telephone that you plug into the wall, the basic rate is about $200 pesos a month, and that includes 100 free local telephone calls. After that, there's a $5 peso charge for additional calls. There are plans that include all manner of options, but be mindful that for about $1,100 pesos per month, which is about $88 USD. Telmex has a "Telmex Sin Limites," or "Telmex Without Limit" which allows you to enjoy all the local and domestic long distance service you can use, and it includes 2 MB of broadband Internet connection with wireless router. Bottom line, telephone could cost you as little as $200 pesos a month ($16 USD) or as much as $1,100 pesos ($88 USD), Internet included, unless you're doing something wrong.

Food

What kind of diet do you have? If you eat locally, then your groceries in Mérida can be reasonable. A diet that consists of seasonal fruits bought at the local market, along with standard vegetables (from onions to carrots, potatoes to celery) will run you about a third of what you can expect to pay in the U.S. Seasonal fruits are an even better deal. In Mérida it's possible to pull up to a street vendor and purchase 100 oranges for $50 pesos, which comes out to four cents of a US dollar per orange! By the same token, if you eat local meats—chicken, turkey and pork—you will be surprised at how far your money goes. On the other hand, if you insist on having kiwis from New Zealand, grapes from Chile and apples from Vermont, you can expect to pay a premium. If you insist on beef (hardly a head of cattle is found in the Yucatán!) or other meats like lamb, then it will be a bit more expensive. Many expatriates insist on shopping at Costco and Sam's Club, while forgetting that if you go local—Aurrera, Chedraui, Comercial Mexicana and AKI—you are likely to get deals. The same applies to beverages: tequila and rum drinkers save more money than those who insist on whiskeys and European vodka. Wines from Chile and Spain are a bargain, whereas wines from France and Italy can be a bit pricey. California and Oregon wines are no bargains, but they are not unreasonable either. If you cultivate a taste for Mexico's excellent beers, you will be better off than if you insist on American brands, such as Budweiser and Miller. Soft drinks are a bargain, as are the basic staples which are price-controlled by the government through a series of subsidies and ceilings: eggs, flour, and cornmeal. Most expatriates find that their average grocery bill is about 25% less than it is in the U.S., and a full 45% less if they go local—and shop for produce, poultry, fish and pork at local markets.

Transportation

What do you include in transportation? The cost of maintaining your car? The amount you spend on taxis? Bus fare? Round-trip airfare back home two or three times a year to visit friends and family? It's all up to you. But getting around town should cost no more than $30 or $40 pesos per taxi ride, which comes out to somewhere between $2 or $3 USD per ride. Bus fare in Mérida is $7 pesos, or about half a US dollar. If you own your car, then how much do you budget for car maintenance, gas and insurance? It all depends on the state of your vehicle, its value (which affects the insurance premium), and how much you drive. In other words, these are all variables that more or less duplicate your expenses back home—with the exception of taxis and public transportation, which are considerably lower in Mexico. The price of gasoline you ask? Once upon a time gas in Mexico was very cheap; today it approximates prices in the least expensive markets in the U.S. Many expatriates, who live in the Historic Center, walk, take taxis or will rent a car only when they need to drive somewhere. (Roundtrip cab fare from downtown Mérida to Costco, or Sam's Club or Home Depot runs under $150 pesos, or $11 USD, so doing a biweekly run for staples fits easily into anyone's budget.)

So now you can build a budget. There are some expatriates who own their own homes and can live comfortably just on the Social Security checks. There are others who are more privileged and spend money with abandon. It's possible to live very comfortably in Mérida on $1,000 USD per person per month, and comfortable enough on about $850 USD a month.

What does the average expatriate couple in Mérida spends? According to educated guesses from city officials and the U.S. consular personnel, a typical American retired couple in Mérida lives on a budget of $1,925 USD a month. This is seen as extravagant by Mexican standards, but reflects what it costs to live in a very comfortable manner, enjoying meals out, seeing movies, having drinks with friends, and not counting every *centavo*.

And speaking of extravagance, let's talk a little about household help.

Household Help

One reason many Americans retire outside the U.S. is because getting household help is much cheaper than in the U.S. Unless you are very privileged, almost no one in the U.S. or Canada has full-time servants. Yes, there are professional maid services in the U.S.—Merry Maids, Maid Services of America, Maid Brigade and so on—but these are by-the-hour services that are not inexpensive, and the scope of services they provide are very limited, and dictated by the agencies for which they work.

By comparison, in Mexico, there are vast numbers of middle-aged women who, because they are raising their children alone, or need to supplement their families' income for a variety of reasons, are available to work a few hours a day, or a few days a week. A quarter century ago it was not uncommon for middle class families in Mérida to drive to a nearby village, find a young woman to work for them for the entire week or longer, and then return to their families for a few days off. That's one reason so many homes in the Centro Histórico have a "maid's quarter," usually a small bedroom with a utilitarian bathroom. That's seldom the case nowadays, simply because the government does a better job of making sure that young people stay in school longer, and there are other opportunities for employment in nearby villages. (Is it necessary to comment on the thousands of employees that the resorts of Cancún, Playa del Carmen, and Isla Mujeres require to keep tourism industry churning away?)

It's odd to find a *young* woman working as a full-time maid in anyone's house nowadays. But habits die hard and many still think of "maids" as "young" women from villages. In the same way that it has taken Americans an entire generation to resist the derogatory and demeaning practice of calling black men "boys," in the Yucatán there are still some Yucatecan families that use the degrading term "muchachas" to refer to women in their 30s, 40s and 50s who help around the house. What's worse, of course, is when some expats arrive and, with an inexplicable sense of entitlement and arrogance, think that it's appropriate to refer to a grown woman as a "girl." How would an American or Canadian woman react if a fellow expat walked up and said, "Hey babe, nice tits!"

Well, that's how Mexican women feel when they are referred to as "muchachas" by their employers—so please refrain from using this derogatory term. And if you find yourself in the company of *anyone* who refers to domestic workers as "muchachas," "muchachos" or "mozos," you'd be well advised to find yourself a better class of acquaintances, unless you came to Mexico to surround yourself with American low-lifes as seen on "The Jerry Springer Show"!

The same applies for handimen who work for you. The term "mozo" is a carryover from Victorian times, when households consisted of several full-time live-in help. The "mozo" was the man who, unlike the gardener or watchman, was allowed inside the house, usually to carry out more difficult work, moving furniture, scrubbing terraces, handling the dogs, cleaning windows and chandeliers, and doing basic repairs, from fixing toilets and sinks, to replacing doorknobs and broken tiles.

In 2014, the correct way of referring to people who are employed as household help is by their given name, and to establish the relationship to you, by their job. "Elena, the lady who helps around the house," or "Juan, the man who helps us with chores" will suffice. (In Spanish, "Elena, la señora que nos ayuda en la casa" or "Juan, el señor que nos ayuda con las diligencias.") Now that it's clear there are no "muchachas" or "mozos" and that the only person who calls household help their "muchacha" or their "mozo," is, in one word, an idiot, how do you go about getting help around the house?

Domestic Workers

Daily wages

Domestic workers are usually contracted by the day. They are expected to work no more than 10 hours in a day, have their duties spelled out, and have all the supplies they will need provided for them. They are not expected to bring supplies with them, unless one of their responsibilities is to do the shopping, they have a list of items to buy, and they are given money beforehand.

The wage depends on the level of work, the hours expected and the price negotiated. It depends on many factors, including the size of your house and the duties involved. A person who has a one-bedroom house and needs someone to come dust has a different requirement than someone with a four-bedroom house, two terraces, a swimming pool and throws dinner parties every night for friends, family, and hangers-on. A family with children is a different client than a mostly sedentary retired couple. In 2014 for a full day's work, it is common to pay between $250-$450 pesos.

Transportation and Meals

Roundtrip bus fare is expected to be provided. Lunch is to be provided. The bus fare should reflect the cost of your worker's round trip cost from their home to yours and back to theirs. Lunch is handled one of two ways: they can be served a ration of the same lunch that you yourself will be having, or you can give them enough money $35-$50 pesos to buy lunch at the nearest Cocina Económica. It's not acceptable for you to have a lunch of lobster bisque and serve your employee soda crackers and a glass of water.

Live-In Workers

The employer-worker situation changes dramatically if you have live-in help. If you are privileged enough to have a maid or a handyman live in your home full-time, then you are privileged enough to formalize the business relationship so that each employee enjoys the

212

benefits of health insurance, vacation time, and all the other amenities that full-time workers are entitled to expect.

When to Pay

For live-in help, they are expected normally to work Monday through Saturday morning. They are to be paid for the week in full, including bus fare to return home. They are expected to return on Monday. It is always a good idea to have them sign a receipt for the wages they received, which is almost always in cash. Remember that in December it is customary to pay the Christmas bonus, known as the *Aguinaldo*, which is an extra two weeks' salary or an entire month if someone has been working for you for five years or more. Of course, this is to be paid no later than December 15, since most people in Mexico use this money for Christmas expenses.

Room and Board

It is expected that you provide room and board for live-in domestic help. This means a room of their own, preferably with their own bathroom, and they are to be fed three meals a day. In Mexico, it is expected that this includes two soft drinks a day, but alcohol is strictly forbidden. Many employers provide a small television set as well.

Health Insurance

The easiest way to fulfil the expectation that you provide health insurance for live-in domestic help is to have each person sign up with the Instituto Mexicano del Seguro Social (IMSS), which has a *Seguro Voluntario* program for individuals who are not employed by formal employers. (Your home is a residence, not a place of business.) The monthly premium varies, depending on the person's age, health, and other details, but it usually runs $350 to $450 pesos a month. It is expected that you provide the money for their premium, thus making sure that if they become ill, you won't have to worry about their health, or their ability to pay their doctor's bills and medicines.

Sick Leave

It is expected that you are to accommodate medical requests. If a person has a doctor's note to justify days off, these are honored ordinarily. If a request is made to take care of ailing relative or a sick child, reasonable accommodation of such requests are expected.

Vacation Pay

As with everyone else who works in Mexico, domestic workers are entitled to federal holidays are days off, and you should negotiate a two-week paid vacation that accommodates their needs and your schedule as well.

Treating Domestic Workers with Respect and Fairness

Remember that even the rich and famous and powerful get into trouble if they treat their household staff poorly. Remember Caroline Kennedy? How could she have "forgotten" to pay her nanny's Social Security taxes for years? There's no doubt her mother Jackie Kennedy Onassis taught her better. And what happened to Caroline? When her ethical lapse became known, she had to withdraw from consideration for being appointed U.S. Senator from the State of New York. In Mérida, a number of prominent socialites have faced social scorn for how they treat their help. Among expats, some have been ostracized for their callous behavior, thinking that workers in Mexico can be treated like plantation workers in "Gone With the Wind." The last thing you want is to be whispered about behind your back by the proper Yucatecan ladies from the International Women's Club. Or worse yet, the last thing you want is to be served notice that you've been ordered to appear before the labor board!

Gardeners

Unlike maids and handymen, gardeners are a rare and coveted breed. Often equipped with their own tools, the lush, tropical environment in Mérida makes it a pleasure to have wonderful gardens. But they require much attention. Finding a reliable gardener is a difficult challenge. Why? Simple: There are more gardens than there are gardeners! And this is exacerbated by the fact that, believe it or not, friends *steal* gardeners from one another by enticing them with— higher pay! Friendships have ended over gardeners that changed clients and there is always a peculiar subtext to conversations about gardeners. Of course there are gardening care services, but these charge market rates comparable to the U.S. And a word of advice: once you find a gardener whose work you like, try to build a great relationship with him on a personal level. Why? If you don't, remember that there are many of others in need of gardening services! Expect to pay between $300 and $600 pesos for a gardener (for larger gardens, they often have an assistant or apprentice).

How to Find Domestic Help

Word of mouth and personal referrals are always the best, of course. And then there are the "Avisos Económicos" in the *Diario de Yucatán*. It's possible to post notices at places like the Mérida English Language Library and on the Main Square, City Hall has a "Jobs Available" listing.

Always check a person's references before you let them into your home and always exercise prudence with your cash and valuables. This applies in Mexico the same way it applies everywhere else on earth!

Mexican Labor Laws

Advice from the U.S. State Department on Mexican Labor Laws:

"U.S. citizen property owners should consult legal counsel or local authorities before hiring employees to serve in their homes or on their vessels moored in Mexico. Several U.S. citizen property owners have faced lengthy lawsuits for failure to comply with Mexican labor laws regarding severance pay and Mexican social security benefits."

Cash vs. Credit

Mexico's consumer protection agency encourages stores to pass along savings to consumers who choose to pay cash instead of credit cards for two reasons. Since merchants have to pay fees to the banks when they accept credit and debit cards, it's only fair that consumers who pay cash enjoy a 1-3% discount. Also, the government wants to discourage consumers from getting into credit card debt.

What this means is that many retailers—from Sam's Club to Comercial Mexicana—will offer a discount if you pay cash. Take advantage of this by going to an ATM before heading out to shop.

Planning a Budget

The Mexican Government provides assistance for those who need to set up a budget. The Comisión Nacional para la Protección y Defensa de los Usuarios de Servicios Financieros, known as CONDUSEF, has an online portal, albeit in Spanish, to help budget planning.

The website is: *www.condusef.gob.mx*

Mexico Cost of Living Report: Autumn 2011

The Autumn 2013 Mexico Cost of Living Report is published by MexExperience to help anyone who is considering a move to Mexico, whether to live here full time or part time, to work, study, take a sabatical or retire and who wants to better understand the cost of living in Mexico today.

The report will enable you to get a good understanding of current living costs in Mexico and create a financial budget tailored to your specific lifestyle choices and requirements.

This report offers readers a detailed analysis of the real costs of day-to-day living in Mexico. The report has been compiled from data gathered during October 2010 and is fully up-to-date with the latest prices and cost trends in Mexico.

The report highlights prices and costs across a range of products and services most foreign expatriates will seek when they live in Mexico. It also includes a number of overlooked costs which people forget to include when they compile their budgets, sometimes with significant consequences when the actual costs are compared with the estimates after having lived in Mexico for a while.

To order the report, go to: *www.mexperience.com/liveandwork/mexico-cost-of-living.php*

Cost of Living for a Retired Couple

Based on a U.S. dollar exchange rate of 17.50 pesos the cost of living in Mérida can be as little as $1,192 USD a month to as much as $3,270 USD. These figures are based on expenditure on housing, food, education, transportation, clothing, recreation, health, furniture, appliances and personal use.

For expatriates often the most important starting references upon arriving in a foreign country are expatriate clubs and associations. Some of the most important are the American Society along with the DAR, the International Friendship Club, and Rotary International. American Society acts as a large umbrella organization harboring smaller clubs and associations that are based on particular fields of interest.

Source: *SolutionsAbroad.com*

Sample Prices in Mérida, 2014

Renting a house or an apartment,
2 bedroom, 1 bathroom in an average neighborhood: **3,925 Pesos**

Renting a room in a private home: **1,600 Pesos**

Bus fare: **7 Pesos**

A cappuccino, café latte or espresso in a café: **25 Pesos**

216

Lunch at an average sit-down restaurant:	**60 Pesos**
Dinner at an average sit-down restaurant:	**120 Pesos**
A bottle of beer at a bar:	**25 Pesos**
A drink at a nightclub:	**70 Pesos**
A soft drink (from a vending machine):	**12 Pesos**
A newspaper:	**8 Pesos**
A cab ride, within Historic Center:	**40 Pesos**
Ticket to the movies (weekday performance):	**45 Pesos**
Roundtrip airfare to Mexico City:	**2,350 Pesos**

10   Settling In: Utilities, Telephone, Gas Stations & Other Necessities

The previous chapter covers most utilities in planning a budget. In Mexico, unlike the United States, electric power generation and the petroleum industry are state-owned and state-run, with prices set on a federal level through a complicated system. In Yucatán, state government provides potable water. Here is a general orientation into basic utilities and related services.

Electricity

The Comision Federal de Electricidad, known as CFE, is responsible for almost all of Mexico's electricity production. Their website is *www.cfe.gob.mx* and here is how they describe their Mission:

"The Federal Electricity Commission (CFE) is a company created and owned by the Mexican government. It generates, distributes and markets electric power for almost 34.2 million customers. This figure represents almost 100 million people. The CFE incorporates more than a million new customers every year.

The infrastructure to generate electric power is made up of 178 generating plants, having an installed capacity of 51,571 megawatts (MW). 23.09% of its installed capacity stems from 22 plants which were built using private capital by Productores Independientes de Energía (PIE).

The CFE creates electric power using various technologies and various primary energy sources. It has thermoelectric, hydroelectric, coal-fired, geothermal and wind powered plants and facilities, as well as one nuclear power plant.

In order to take the power from its generating plants to the household of each one of its customers, the CFE has more than 745,000 Km. of power lines that transmit and distribute electric power.

Electricity reaches almost 137,000 communities (of these, 133,390 are not cities, while 3,356 are). Also, 96.85 % of the population uses electricity.

218

During the last decade, 42,000 solar modules have been installed in small communities very distant from large population centers. In the future, this technology will be the most widely used in the villages that do not have access to conventional electric power.

As to total sales volume, 99 % and the remaining 1 % is for export purposes.

Even if the household sector makes up 88.23% of CFE's customers, sales in this area represent 26.69% of total sales to the general public. Inversely so, in the industrial sector, less than 1% of the customers make up more than half of the sales volume.

The CFE is also the government agency in charge of planning the national electrical system. Said plan is set forth in the Works and Investment Program of the Electrical Sector (POISE), which describes the evolution of the electrical market, as well as the expansion of the generation and transmission capacity, in order to satisfy the demand for electricity in the next ten years. This plan is annually updated.

CFE's commitment is to offer excellent service, and as it guarantees high quality standards in all its processes, it rivals the best electrical companies in the world."

If you're wondering what the CFE means by "exporting" electricity, it sells some to U.S. utilities across the border, and more importantly, it provides free electric power to northern Belize as part of Mexico's foreign aid program to that nation.

Water

Junta de Agua Potable y Alcantarillado de Yucatán, known as JAPAY, is responsible for potable water throughout Yucatán State. It is very reasonable, with the average bill being about $3 USD a month! Japay operates several offices around town to serve the public. All are open 8 AM to 3 PM, Monday-Friday. Most are open 8:30 AM to 1 PM on Saturdays. All are closed on Sundays.

These are located:

Centro

Calle 60 #526, between Calle 65 and 67 Street

Colón

Avenida Colón #503, by Avenida Reforma, Department 5

San Benito

Interior of the San Benito Market, Third Level, Department 9, Block C12

Plaza Dorada

Interior of Plaza Dorada, adjacent to Coppel

Colonia Miguel Alemán

Calle 27 s/n, between Calle 24 and 26 Street

Chedraui Norte

Calle 60 #301, Colonia Loma Bonita (Interior of Centro Comercial Chedraui, Department 1)

Chenkú

Calle 43 #229, between Calle 28 and 32 Street, Casco Hacienda Chenkú

Xoclan

Calle 71-B s/n, by Avenida 128, Colonia Bosques de Yucalpetén

Vergel

Avenida Universidad Pedagógica, by Calle 25 D, Fracc. Vergel II

Their website is: *www.japay.yucatan.gob.mx.*

Telephone

What can be said about telephone services around the world? What a plethora of choices—some dismal, others fantastic, but always complicated. In Mexico, suffice it to say that Teléfonos de Mexico, to Telmex, made Carlos Slim a billionaire! Basic service runs about $160 pesos (about $13 USD) a month for 100 telephone calls. Then there are the "disposable" cell phones which cost about $300 pesos ($24 USD) for the phone itself, and which you can buy air time from most convenience stores in increments of $20, $50, $100 or more pesos. Most cable companies also now provide telephone service.

In addition, many expatriates use SKYPE or Magic Jack or have "Mexico plans" for their iPhone or Blackberry service, usually on AT&T or Verizon.

With so many choices, knock yourself out finding out which plan works best for your needs and budget:

Alestra (ATT)

Call 800-288-000 and they will set you up with a plan that allows you to call the US for one monthly fee.
Website: *www.att.com.mx*

Axtel

Paseo de Monetejo #473, Colonia Santa Ana
Website: *www.axtel.com.mx*

Cablemas

Call (999) 942-7900, and they will set you up with cable TV, Internet and phone service
Website: *www.cablemas.com*

Skype

Skype has great plans that many expatriates find wonderful for their needs, especially those who have home offices and work on their computers.
Website: *www.skype.com*

Telmex

Call 800-123-000 and they will set you up.
Website: *www.telmex.com.mx*

Verizon

Verizon Wireless has plans that many expatriates find excellent for their needs in Mérida. They are found under the "Nationwide Plus Mexico Plans."
Website: *www.verizonwireless.com*

Vonage

This is another company that has great plans for expatriates. If you sign up during one of their on-going promotions, they will wave the initial set up fee (about $30 USD).
Website: *www.vonage.com*

Internet Service Providers

Telmex, Axtel and Cablemas are the leading Internet service providers in Mérida. They all have comprehensive and competitive plans, and you are sure to find one plan that meets all your needs. The standard plans will run you about $1200 pesos, just under $100 USD a month, and this should include a cable television plan.

Pemex Gas Stations

Petroleos de Mexico, known as Pemex, operates or franchises all the gas stations throughout the country. The price of gas and diesel is set by the government. There are no self-service stations in Mexico: all gasoline must be pumped by an attendant, who also will wipe your windshield, and if requested, check your oil and tires. A tip for these services, of course, is expected and $5 pesos, about forty-cents USD, is expected.

Be mindful that because the government operates retail gasoline service stations, there are far fewer gas stations in Mexico than there are in the U.S. or Canada. What does this mean? That you should always fill up whenever your tank is about one-quarter full!

Propane Gas

Gas Imperial

Telephone: (999) 982-2222

Delta Gas

Telephone: (999) 943-5050

Gas Peninsular Telephone

Telephone: (999) 946-1241

Gas de Yucatán, S.A.

Telephone: (999) 983-4232

Garbage

Servilimpia

Carretera Mérida-Susula, Tablaje
Catastral
Telephone: (999) 945-1213

Pamplona

Calle 66 #720, between Calle 99 and
101 Street
Telephone: (999) 984-479

11 BANKING & FINANCIAL AFFAIRS

As recently as the mid-1980s if you wanted to open an account at J. P. Morgan on Wall Street in New York, you were required to maintain a minimum of $5,000 USD. In today's money, that's the equivalent of just over $12,000 USD. That's a considerable sum of money to have in a non-interest bearing account, just to say your bank was J. P. Morgan.

We forget that until the era of deregulation ushered in by Ronald Reagan, most Americans were excluded from the formal banking system—and phrases such as "Bankers' Hours" referred to a business culture where banks opened at 9:30 AM and closed for the day at 1:30 PM. Few Americans understand that the "arbitrary" rule among banks that no wire transfers are executed after 1 PM isn't arbitrary at all. It is a legacy of the tradition that banks closed for business at 1:30 PM. It was considered "bad form" to do actual work a half hour before finishing business to the public for the day! (Of course, just because banks closed their doors at 1:30 PM, bankers kept working on behalf of institutional investors and clients, often late into the night.)

Reagan, however, wanted to democratize banking and financial services. He wanted to make checking accounts and bank loans accessible to virtually everyone. Today, with the advent of ATMs (introduced in the mid-1980s as well), there are banking services around the clock, and some banks, most notably TD Bank, even open on Sundays.

It's therefore not surprising that in 2010 Citibank was given an award for its pioneering work in helping Americans from all economic backgrounds open and maintain checking and savings accounts. "The award we are receiving is for fifteen years of work," Vikram Pandit, Chief Executive Officer of Citibank, told John Cassidy, a reporter for the *New Yorker*, at the awards ceremony. "It was work that was pioneered by Citi to get more financial inclusion. And it's part of a broader reform effort we are involved in under the heading of responsible banking."

Banking in Mexico, similarly, has long been seen as something for the privileged. Achieving greater "financial inclusion" remains one of the nation's top priorities in banking. Before Nafta, many banks required a minimum of the equivalent of $1,500 USD to open an account. Only a small number of Mexicans were able to have access to formal banking services. It was only after Nafta—and the 1994 devaluation of the peso—that Mexico's banking system embarked on an accelerated program of globalization and transnational integration. In 1994 the top ten Mexican banks were Mexican-owned; today nine of the top ten banks are owned by foreign banks. (Banorte is the last major Mexican-owned bank.)

As a result, there is a mixed legacy, and banking in Mexico, compared with banking in the U.S., remains a *more* formal activity. That means that banking in Mexico is accomplished in a more meticulous manner, characterized by ritualized procedures and has double-safeguard measures at every step.

In Mérida, banking culture is even more reverential to old traditions. Why? With the peninsula so far removed from Mexico City, it was up to wealthy families in the Yucatán to establish the first banks in town. José Castelló, whose Banco de Campeche, was a major force on the peninsula, merged his bank with the Banco Yucateco, owned by Eusebio Escalante, his son Nicolás Escalante Peón and his wife's brother Manuel Peón Contreras to form the Banco Peninsular de Yucatán, an institution where coffee on porcelain was served when one came to cash a check.

These Old World customs prevailed throughout the 20th century. It was only after World War II, when the Yucatán became more connected to Mexico City (think highways, civilian aviation) that "Mexican" banks came in and began to acquire independent Yucatecan banks. Established Yucatecan families, however, saw Bancomer and Banamex as interlopers that brought crass commercialism to banking. Many Yucatecan families switched to banks to those in Miami, Houston and New York. After Nafta, the arrival of Citibank (which acquired Banamex) and the Spanish banks (one of which, BBVA, acquired Bancomer) arrived on the scene the city's banking culture changed once again, effectively ending the traditions of Yucatecan banking completely.

Today, banking is far more "democratic" than it once was, but nonetheless, by American standards, banking is still too formal. Patience, in other words, is required.

Do You Need a Mexican Bank Account?

A Message on Banking from Glynna Prentice, editor of "Mexico Insider" magazine:

"Long-term, most expats end up opening a Mexican bank account. You can wire in much larger amounts, which you can then access with a local ATM card or by check. However, here are a few things to keep in mind:

- Like many other countries, Mexico requires you to show proof that you *need* an account in Mexico. Banks likely will require some evidence that you actually plan to live in Mexico, such as a residence visa, a property title, or at least a utility bill in your name, before they'll open an account for you. So keep in mind, when you buy property in Mexico, that you may not be allowed to open a peso-based account until *after* you've taken title — and make your payment arrangements accordingly.

- International wire transfers can be costly—at both ends. Be sure to ask what your home country bank charges to wire the money internationally *and* what the Mexican bank charges to receive it and convert it to pesos. For the home-country end, check if you can lower the fee by doing the transfer yourself over the Internet. (You may want to check into this anyway.) At the Mexico end, ask other expats in the area for their recommendations on banks and on transfer methods.

- Mexican bank fees are exorbitant, so be sure you check what they are. Overdraft fees, for instance, are a whopping $1000 per overdraft (about $85 USD plus tax).

And, of course, you can also use a home-country credit card. I know some expats who manage perfectly well in Mexico with just a home-country ATM card and credit cards (and never have to risk those high Mexican overdraft fees)."

Source: *www.MexicoInsider.com*

Checking Accounts

For a checking account, or *cuenta bancaria*, the paperwork is in Spanish, which means that if you are not fluent in Spanish, you should bring along a friend who can help with the translation and any questions you may have. Bring your passport, along with three copies, which will probably be needed to adhere to various forms. (If you plan on opening a business account, you will also need a copy of your FM2 and FM3 visas or the new immigration visas, along with four copies of these documents.) When you fill out the signature card, your signature must be signed exactly the same as it appears in your passport. Every check you sign must be signed as it appears on the signature cards as well. If there is a variation, the check will be refused.

Checkbooks

Checkbooks, or *chequeras*, are considered important legal documents and are treated as such. Each check has to be accounted for, so if you make a mistake, you can't simply write "void" across it, or rip it up. If this happens, you have to keep the check and report it as "cancelled" to invalidate it—which is different from stopping payment. Upon opening an account, you will receive temporary checks, usually three or five, until your regular checks are ordered. As in the United States, your checks will have your name printed on them. But in Mexico, when your checks are ready, you will have to pick them up at the bank. When you do, you will be asked to show the same identification that you did when you opened the account. You will have to sign receipt for it (and the banker will sign receipt of delivery for the branch manager).

Checkbook Activation

When you have your checkbook in hand, there's one additional security measure: the checks have to be *activated*. This can be done with at the bank when you pick-up the checks (each branch has to call the customer service office to initiate the process), or you can call the toll-free number when you are ready to use the checks. If you call the bank there are two security codes that will be requested of you to verify your identity over the telephone. First is the "key," or *clave*, which is a secret code given to everyone upon opening a bank account. The second is your PIN number, referred to as "NIP" in Spanish. When you activate your checkbook you can activate the entire series of checks, or just the one you plan to use. Why do the banks do this? This is simply an additional layer of protection against fraud. If you only plan to use the first five checks, you have the peace of mind of knowing that no one can use the subsequent ones until you call the bank to "activate" those checks.

How to Write a Check

Everyone knows how to write a check, which is why it's well worth reviewing how to write a check for the Mexican banking system!

1. Any error will render the check void. Nothing can be crossed out, nothing can be misspelled.
2. The name of the person must be correctly spelled out. The quantity must be clearly written in numbers and spelled out (in Spanish).
3. You must write out "pesos" and "centavos" after the written amount, and you must write out "M.N." after the written amount. ("M.N." stands for "Moneda nacional," or national currency).
4. Be careful to make sure that the month is written in Spanish, and remember that in Spanish, the names of the months are written in lower case! (If you write "Febrero" for "febrero," the check may be returned unpaid!)
5. Your signature must match exactly as it appears when you opened your account, which is why it is a good idea to sign your name exactly as it appears in your passport—you can refer to your passport to see if you are "John Smith," of "John A. Smith" or "John Anthony Smith." Many people sit at a desk, turn off all distractions, have their passports in hand and set about writing out their checks to make sure everything is correct.
6. Please remember that checks written over $100,000 pesos must be cleared through the Central Bank. Mexico is enacting a series of laws to combat money laundering and this is one necessary measure, even though it has become quite burdensome for business. Remember, anything that approximates more than $10,000 USD is checked and double-checked!

Accepting a Check

The lesson is that if this is what you are required to do when you *write* a check, then it follows that these are the details that you need to look for when you *receive* a check!

If there is *any* error or discrepancy, the bank will refuse to process the check. That's the bad news. The good news is that, unlike the U.S., Mexican banks operate throughout the entire country, and it is common for people simply to deposit funds into each other's account. Someone in Mexico City can deposit into your account cash rather than send you a check and you can verify the deposit online or by calling the toll-free number. Similarly, you may be asked to deposit money into someone else's account rather than giving him or her a check. This, of course, depends on the level of trust.

Another practice that is common is to write the check payable to "Al Portador." No, Al's not a person. It means "To the bearer," roughly the equivalent of writing a check payable to "Cash" in the U.S. and Canada.

Remember Glynna Prentice's advice: Banking fees are exorbitant in Mexico. Bounce a check, and you are in for a $100 USD penalty! Don't do it. And if you bounce a check to a merchant, you will be blacklisted for a minimum period of five years! Why? The merchant is also assessed a fee, and their own banking credit history is negatively impacted. Even if you offer to pay the penalty the merchant was assessed, they will still have a blemish on their record with the bank for having accepted a check that bounced!

Statements and Balances

Your bank statement will be sent to the address provided when you opened your account. If you move or want to change the mailing address, you cannot do it over the phone. It has to be done in person, face to face with an officer, and you have to provide proof of your new address, such as a utility bill (CFE or JAPAY), known as a *comprobante*, in your name with the new address listed. Note: the only exception is if you have someone go on your behalf who is a Power of Attorney, a *carta de poder*, along with his or her official identification (IFE card or passport) and three copies the identification. They will also need originals and copies of *your* utility bill.

Why so much security?

As mentioned when we discussed all the "papelitos" Mexican bureaucracy requires, we noted that Identity Theft is almost unheard of in Mexico, and the reason for that is the layer upon layer of safeguards enlisted every step of the way. Yes, it is tedious, but you can have peace of mind knowing that your banking account is safe!

227

List of Banks (most have English-language versions on their websites)

Banamex (Banco Nacional de Mexico)

www.banamex.com.mx

Banco Azteca

www.bancoazteca.com.mx

Banco del Bajio

www.bb.com.mx

Banco de Comercio Exterior

www.bancomext.com

Banco de Mexico (Central Bank of Mexico)

www.banxico.org.mx

Banco Nacional de Credito Rural (Banrural)

www.banrural.gob.mx

Banco Nacional de Obras y Servicios Públicos

www.banobras.gob.mx

Bank of America Mexico

www.bankofamerica.com.mx

BanRegio

*www.banregio.com*BBVA

Bancomer

www.bancomer.com.mx

Bansi

www.bansi.com.mx

Consultores Financieros (Confia)

www.comfia.com.mx

Grupo Financiero Banorte

www.banorte.com

HSBC Mexico

www.hsbc.com.mx

Nacional Financiera/Banco de Desarrollo

www.nafin.com

Santander Serfin

www.santander.com.mx

Scotiabank Inverlat

www.scotiabank.com.mx

National Associations and Regulators

Asociación de Bancos de Mexico

www.abm.org.mx

Comision Nacional Bancaria y de Valores

www.cnbv.gob.mx

Note on US/Peso Restrictions

Do note that there are certain banking restrictions that you may want to consider:

1) When wiring money to a Mexican bank account, it will be automatically converted to pesos. If you wire, for example, $10,000 USD to your account, upon arriving in Mexico, it will be converted to pesos at that moment's interbank exchange rate.
2) It is not possible to make a cash withdrawal from your Mexican bank account when you are out of Mexico. This means that Mexican pesos cannot be repatriated via any kind of electronic transfer.
3)

Financial Scam Warning

There is absolutely, positively no reason whatsoever why anyone in Mexico would request your Social Security number, with the exception of a bank officer opening a bank account. Mexican law now requires that bank accounts opened in Mexico by U.S. citizens and residents be reported to the IRS, which is part of efforts by the U.S. and Mexican governments to combat money laundering and tax evasion. This is the only legitimate reason for disclosing your Social Security number.

A number of Americans have set up companies in Mérida to provide "expatriate services" to other Americans moving to Mérida. In the process of providing these "services," individuals are being asked to disclose their Social Security numbers.

This is a scam that works one of two ways. First, they use your Social Security number to run a credit report on you with the U.S. credit agencies. Then they have an idea of your financial worth—and how much they can charge or bilk you for their services. Second, by compiling that much financial information about you, and knowing when you are in Mexico, you are exposed to identity theft. If you're out of the country, and they have so much confidential information, it can be used in ways that are unauthorized by you.

Never, ever give anyone in Mexico your Social Security number who is not a bank officer and then only at the time you are opening a bank account. The only other exception is for official business with the IRS at the American Consulate. **Be especially wary if one of these so-called "expatriate services" companies asks for your Social Security number!**

229

Part IV

Making a Home and Building a Life

12   REAL ESTATE

Assessing the Real Estate Market in Mérida in 2014

Good news!

Mérida's real estate market survived 2014, a year that saw the nation's conscious shaken by the massacre of forty-three students in the town of Iguala. Mexico's economy, with ample resources and astute planning, is weathering the fall in the price of oil much better than other countries, such as Russia or Venezuela. (Or even some U.S. states, where Texas and Alaska are now facing daunting state deficits.)

Better news!

In addition, the economic prospects in the U.S. and Canada are more promising and, despite recent reversals, Mexico remains one of the fastest-growing countries in Latin America. Europe is still struggling—some of the European Union member states slipped back into recession in 2014.

Best news!

Against this political and economic background of relative stability and continuity, the real estate market in Mérida recovered from the 2008-2012 Global Recession. The market is once again picking up, real estate prices have stabilized, and prime properties are increasing in value. Foreigners are moving in and the inventory of available housing is declining as sales increase across the board … and better yet …

Realistic News!

It has to be noted that the "boom" that characterized the market pre-2008 is a distant phenomenon that is not likely to be duplicated any time soon. Why? Because there have been two important legal and economic changes that have impacted the local real estate market. These changes are: 1) Mexico's new immigration laws are fast-transforming the economic profile of new expats arriving in Mérida; and 2) the Global Recession of 2008-2012 reshaped the local real estate industry.

Mexico's new immigration laws were designed for one purpose: to weed out immigrants who would otherwise subsist near the poverty line in their home countries. For more than a decade Mexican officials have noted with alarm at the growing number of expats who are in Mexico for only one reason: these are individuals who are poor, relying solely on their Social Security checks and becoming a significant burden on Mexico's free public health care system. American officials were also alarmed by the number of third-country expats using Mexico as a "trampoline" into the U.S. (A person from country X who was denied entry to the U.S. would "retire" to Mexico … and then clandestinely enter the U.S.) In consequence, Mexican and American officials worked together to revamp Mexican requirements for permanent residency.

This means that the expats now moving into Mexico—expats already in Mexico have, for the most part, been "grandfathered" accoding to the old laws—have more assets and retirement income. This bodes well for realtors offering more expensive—and expansive—properties. Critics of Mexico's new immigration laws point out that these changes have resulted in income disparities creating two distinct expat communities. One group of expats lives from Social Security check to Social Security check. The other is far wealthier, for whom Mérida is a second, or third, home—and these new residents are absent for months at a time when the weather is hottest.

Mérida, happily, continues to be considered a jewel to be treasured.

"Like Havana, for which the city doubled in the film *Before Night Falls*, the historical center known simply as Centro has had a Unesco makeover. It's not always easy to spot. While the cobbled streets are mostly swept, and the gardens of the Plaza Grande are manicured and in flower—its glossy-leaved trees sculpted into squat oblongs or perfect spheres—still the tangled wiring of telephones and electricity hangs low and wild, and local buses belch black fumes as they charge down the narrow streets," Joanna Weinberg, wrote of Mérida in *Condé Nast Traveller* magazine last year. "There are as many derelict buildings as there are restored ones. Here a newly painted white façade with Yves Klein-blue brickwork, there a faded terracotta one with peeling, paneled shutters. All are secured by old iron bars. Peer into a run-down house, with windows hanging off their hinges, and you'll see impressively proportioned rooms with intricately tiled floors just visible through the layers of dust, an overgrown tropical courtyard and, as an estate agent might phrase it, bags of potential."

If you contract the services of a professional realtor and follow the recommendations in this section then you are well on your way to finding a wonderful property in Mérida, its suburbs or the beach communities along the coast.

234

Rising Real Estate Superstar: Debora Whifield (Colyn)

A native of South Africa, Debora is one of the post-Global Recession stars of Mérida's real estate market. Debora has lived in Mérida for over eight years and is now a naturalized Mexican citizen. After working for Remax, S.A. for years, she still truly enjoys assisting her clients in fulfilling their needs and realizing their goals and has done so in Yucatán for a number of years as well. A colorful character, Debora has a zest for life and a flair for adventure. Her experience in real estate, business, and adventure; coupled with her boundless energy, open attitude and willingness to go the extra mile; make her a great real estate agent. Her friendly, inviting smile and exuberant confidence will set your mind at ease as she sets out on her mission to find or manage your dream home or investment property.

Telephone: (999) 241-4396
U.S. Cell Phone: (917) 832-8305
Website: *www.merida-properties.com*
Email: *dcolyn@me.com*
Languages: English, Spanish, Afrikaans

Rising Real Estate Superstar: Carlos Betancourt

Carlos is a native of Mérida. He's lived all his life in Centro making him an expert in the colonial homes. He knows all the rules and standards that protect the historical homes in Centro; he can help you find that perfect home that is suited for your personal needs. He also is the owner of Management 23, a property management company here in Mérida. Besides doing Real Estate he is eager to make your stay in Mérida smooth and stress-free as possible. Carlos has a wide knowledge in all aspects of life in Mérida. He's the man to use for any need you have including issue dealing with immigrations and getting your personal items shipped to your new home here in Mérida. Let Carlos help you find your dream home here in Mérida..

Telephone: (999) 289-3896
Website: *www.pm23yucatan.com*
Email: *contacto@pm23yucatan.com*
Languages: English and Spanish

Established Real Estate Superstar: Jim Mann

If Debora Whifield (Colyn) and Carlos Betancourt are "rising" stars, then Jim Mann is clearly the "established" star of the expat real estate market in Mérida. With decades of experience under his belt, Jim brings a breathtaking knowledge of the market, buyers, sellers and the stories behind the "why" of real estate in the Historic Center. Although considered the "elder statesman" of the real estate market for expat in Mérida, Jim has assembled an engaging team of younger real estate agents who are doing a remarkable job matching buyers and sellers through the ebbs and flows of the markets and economic changes that impact Mérida's real estate market.

Website: http://meridayucatanrealestate.com/
Email: *jim@meridayucatanproperties.com*
Languages: English, proficient Spanish

Established Real Estate Superstar: Delfina Guedimin

Delfina Guedimin, originally from Mexico City, but of Yucatecan parents, she has lived in Mexico City and Madrid. Now established in Mérida, she is one of the rising go-getters who has garnered lavish praise from expats who have complimented her professionalism and savvy understanding of the local marketplace. With associates throughout town—and with Canadian realtors as associates—she is well on her way of becoming one of the go-to professionals as the expat market in Mérida continues to grow and prosper. Indeed, she is a member of the Canadian Real Estate Association (CREA), the Ontario Real Estate Association (OREA) and the Real Estate Council of Ontario (RECO).—*Eduviges Montejo*

Website: *www.yucatanhomefinders.com*
Email: *dgb1602@gmail.com*
Languages: English and Spanish

Canadian Realtor: Roma Barss

If you are a Loonie who is more comfortable with a fellow Loonie … then you may want to consider Roma Barss, a Canadian realtor who is an established realtor in the Mérida and Yucatán real estate markets A sales representative at keller Williams and Yucatán Home Finders, she may just be the right realtor for you.

Linkedin Profile: http://www.linkedin.com/pub/roma-barss/29/327/318
Website: *www.romabarss.com*
Email: *rbwhistler@hotmail.com*
Languages: English, proficient Spanish

The Role of a Realtor: A Canadian Perspective

"The Real Estate Agent

As a long-time observer of this industry, it continues to be glaring to me that the real estate agent in North America is the focal point of a real estate purchase or sale. I have written this over and over in all the years that I have watched this business.

Spare me all the mean-spirited comments about Realtors self-promoting and marketing their own pictures and names in advertising. They are the business! They have to advertise themselves to get more business. What business do you know that does not advertise itself?

A Realtor in the process of selling a home creates business for others.

Home inspectors, mortgage brokers and agents, home stagers, lawyers, appraisers, loan officers at banks and trust companies, surveyors, legal clerks, movers, renovators, window blind makers and everybody you can think of is in the blast of business that is set off when a real estate agent pulls the trigger on the sale of a home.

I have even talked to automobile salespeople who have told me that cars are often purchased once a home is sold because that's when people tend to review their financial resources and decide this is also the time to get a new vehicle for the growing family or the empty nesters. They claim it is common that these purchases go hand in hand. I am told an astute car dealer watches the real estate market.

Everything begins with a Realtor who lists a home and gets maximum value for their client as they guide them through the process of selling or buying their property or both. It is a nonstarter for the do-it-yourselfers who do not know their way down this road.

I rarely hear real estate agents brag about the impact they have on the small army of people that they call upon and provide work for. They should. The fence builders, the painters, the roofers and the landscape people who are often called in to build up curb appeal as well as indoor improvement specialists who make a property shine inside and out before it is put up for sale. The same people are called by the same Realtor when new people buy a home and add the touches they want. Who do you think they ask for advice on who they should call for good service and renovation? They ask their real estate agent.

In over 30 years of working for this industry I have never once come upon a Realtor who claimed to be an expert on any of the work they create by marketing or buying a home. Every agent I have known talks about the importance of calling upon expertise for a particular service.

The great irony to me is that sometimes I hear people in the service field claim that they are more knowledgeable about buying and selling homes than the very Realtor who provided the

237

work they were hired to do. I am agog when I hear about a painter who will be well paid for his expert painting say to the homeowner; the next time she or he wants to sell or buy a home they should call on him instead of the Realtor. What gall!

In the hurly burly of buying or marketing a home, the swirl of activity spins around the real estate agent who efficiently organizes the steps, outlines the service needs and acts as a buffer for the shills that come out of the woodwork ready to take advantage of the home owner seller or buyer.

More often than not, Realtors provide their calm reassuring advice and direction to their customers in the evening hours when most of the service providers to a real estate deal are at home with their families.

How is it that some people in our communities whose work and expertise in their field are promoted by Realtors turn on the very Realtors who help them? Why do some people come to Realtors for advice on the market and guidance on how to buy or sell a home and then claim that this is all stuff they know when they repeat the very same advice to others?

Why do some people walk around clapping themselves on the back for the terrific marketing and wise decisions they made with no acknowledgement to the Realtor who guided them?

Think about it. I understand that Realtors guide more property sales and purchases in Canada by almost nine times more than private sellers. I think more people have made more money in real estate transactions working with Realtors than all other money making ventures in Canada combined.

So if you are buying or selling real estate without a Realtor, like, what are you thinking?"

By Heino Molls who is publisher of (Canadian) Real Estate Magazine

House Hunters International

The ability of Mérida to transcend the real estate "crisis" following the 2008-2012 Global Recession was, without a doubt, facilitated by the favorable episodes about the city featured on House Hunters International. The U.S. cable network has produced six episodes on expats moving to Mérida. Each time one of these episodes airs, social media activity concerning Mérida skyrockets—and generates more interest in the local real estate market. The only criticism? That the episodes focus disproportionately on same-sex couples when Mérida is for everyone, regardless of one's sexual orientation!

If you visit the website below, search "Mérida," you will be able to see some of the episodes.

Website: *http://www.hgtv.com*

The Curious Case of the Real Estate Market in Mérida's Historic Centro

Since the 1970s there has been a steady exodus of residents from Mérida's historic center. There are several reasons for this migration. The most important one has to do with the rise of Mexico's middle class. As educational opportunities grew for more Mexicans in the 1950s and 1960s, expectations changed. Whereas before, people in Mérida were unable to get college degrees, their financial independence was limited. Most were resigned to living with their parents in multi-generational households.

As Yucatecan families in Centro were able to send their kids to college, suddenly their adult children, once they started to form their own families, could aspire to their own homes and to different lifestyles. The rise of Mérida's middle class created demand for new suburbs that were built around the city on the periphery of the "Circuito Colonias." Whether it was the lower-middle class Colonia Pensiones or the more affluent middle class Colonia Miguel Alemán, suddenly two-story homes, with gardens and garages, others with swimming pools and basketball courts were accessible. American suburban life as seen on "Bewitched" and "I Dream of Jeannie" was possible. Through this process, Yucatecans have moved out of the Historic Center, leaving elderly grandparents, many of whom resisted leaving the homes in which they lived most of their lives, behind. When elder relatives were no longer able to live independently, they moved in with their adult children, and the houses were closed down, some virtually abandoned. As time passed, the heirs often bickered over what to do with their parents' former home, or didn't care enough to do anything about it, simply because the homes were deemed to have little value, and the legal fees for getting titles changed and paying overdue *predial* taxes offered even more disincentives to do anything about it.

In the 1980s, when American expatriates began to "discover" Mérida's center, a good number of the homes in downtown Mérida were occupied by senior citizens, and a surprising number were closed up, or just abandoned, by their owners. It was possible to buy a colonial home in the Historic Center for $12,000 USD to $25,000 USD. A good number did, and this was the beginning of a demand for something in which Mexicans saw little value: colonial buildings in a congested city center that had none of the modern conveniences. Again, up until the mid-1990s, the owners of those old homes are primarily occupied by elderly people whose adult children lived elsewhere in town, or were houses that had been closed up.

239

Mérida's experience was radically different from other Mexican cities. When people bemoan that other cities—Guanajuato, Puebla, San Miguel de Allende—boast vibrant colonial city centers, with European-style cafés and bars, lively restaurants and an exuberant night life, and wonder why Mérida's historic center becomes silent as cemetery come sundown, there's a reason.

The obvious one is flight to the suburbs, where most Yucatecans under the age of 50 live. But there is another one that is seldom mentioned: geography. Most of Mexico's colonial cities are in the highlands, surrounded by mountains or ravines. Mérida is flat as a pancake, with cheap land all around. If you wanted to build a golf course in Guanajuato, it simply cannot be done because there is no land for it. But in Mérida, there is the possibility of dreaming up an ambitious project, and carrying it out.

A new gated neighborhood with an enormous community center that boasts tennis courts and swimming pools? Why not?

A Jack Nicklaus-designed golf course with a Mark Spitzer swimming academy, with million dollar homes throughout? Why not?

A new division for working-class people that has easy access to highways? Why not?

An L.A.-style shopping center with lots of parking and American anchor stores? Why not?

A new university campus for 5,000 students? Why not?

A shopping mall that has an ice skating rink? Why not?

A private subdivision minutes from the golf practice range? Why not?

A state-of-the-art medical facility with its own hotel? Why not?

And the "Why not" scenarios continue, creating a vast city of breathtaking sprawl.

It is the abundant supply of choices—and cheap land—that fuels the growth of the city. Mexicans from other areas of the country—from Mexico City and Cancún—delight in the options open to them, from gated communities to U.S.-style suburban sprawl. Thousands of families continue to flock to the numerous developments that ring the northern and northeastern areas of the city. Few Mexicans have any interest whatsoever in the Historic Center as a place to live. Fewer still have the desire to live out a "tropical" version of Mexican colonial living.

240

The result is the very odd fact that, if you review the offerings on the websites for real estate companies, you will see that there are properties that have been listed there for *years*! This is a peculiar phenomenon that is relegated to Mérida's Historic Center—but no where else in Mérida.

Think about it. Proceed with eyes wide open.

Now, what does this mean for 2016?

Consider this report from the Mérida Historic Center Patrimony Office (Patronato del Centro Histórico de Mérida) which conducted a survey of the 455 city blocks, running clockwise from the Main Square, that constitute the city's historic zone. The neighborhoods this area encompasses include Santa Ana, Mejorada, San Cristóbal, San Sebastián, and Santiago.

This report found:

1,915 properties in the area.

909 of these were uninhabited;

43 are empty lots;

105 are under renovation;

344 are for rent; and

562 are for sale.

This indicates that, if you are ready to buy a fixer upper, then this is a buyer's market. This report was so shocking that it was posted on YouTube by MegaMedia, which publishes the *Diario de Yucatán*. You can watch it here: *https://www.youtube.com/watch?v=bNbxR8MXBA8.*

Before you let a real estate agent weave a fantastic tale, be informed and knowledgeable about the peculiar economic forces at work in Mérida's Historic Center.

Assessing a Local Real Estate Market: Days on the Market

Each area of any geographic location or subdivision in residential real estate has what is called an "average number of days on the market." This indication shows home sellers in any particular area how long most homes remain on the market prior to a sale. In some places, like Texas, certain areas average a very impressive 30 days on the market prior to the property being sold. In other areas, like Nevada, average time on market could peak at 542 days on the market prior to a successful sale.

Days on market and cumulative days on market can be a death sentence for most home sellers. The longer a home stays available, the more buyers will wonder what is wrong with it and why it hasn't sold. While in reality the home might be perfectly sound and in good condition, homes that have not sold quickly can earn a stigma that is less than desirable. It could kill a potential deal before an offer is ever even made.

Source: www.ehow.com/about_5347814_long-can-house-listed.html

Consider Mérida's Entire Real Estate Market

Average days on the market for a colonial home in the "Historic Center": **1,094**

Average days on the market for an existing home outside the Historic Center: **86***

Average days on the market for a new subdivision: **27**

Average days on the market for a home financed through Infonavit, Mexico's federal agency for residential real estate: **0****

*This figure excludes properties outside the Historic Center that are listed with American-owned real estate firms that are pricing in U.S. dollars and marketing primarily to foreigners.

**For homes financed by Infonavit, there's a waiting list!

Yucatán Country Club

The Yucatán Country Club is an exclusive gated community located on an extension of 815 acres northeast of Mérida. This residential development offers different residential models, built around a spectacular Jack Nicklaus Design golf course and a Clubhouse that features amenities beyond all expectations. With extensive greens, numerous lakes, a detailed landscaping where functionality and harmony reign, and a Town Center, this club offers recreational, shopping and educational alternatives to residents of the Yucatán Country Club as new construction is completed. All complement this imposing complex which invites you to select a serene lifestyle touched by elegance and sophistication in an environment of absolute security. It is surprising to see the growing popularity of the Yucatán Country Club among expats who want to enjoy a comfortable lifestyle without being relegated to the Historic Center.

Website: *http://www.yucatancountry.com*

Buying Real Estate in Mexico

By Inspiring Expatriatism

"If you set out to buy real estate in Mexico, you usually must deal with a real estate company, a buyer's lawyer, a bank and a public notary. Though there are legal regulations, keep in mind that Mexican real estate agents do not have to be licensed or certified; anyone can set up a real estate company.

Attorneys and Real Estate Agents

You should have a Mexican attorney involved in this process so they can draw up contracts, and review the conditions and terms of sale. An attorney can also perform background research on real estate agents. It is a good idea to have your own attorney, not one appointed by a real estate company. Attorneys must be licensed, and are the only ones who can give you real legal advice. Make sure your attorney can present you a "cédula professional." Attorneys can also take care of some bureaucratic procedures in their behalf, and save you money this way.

Notary publics are also important in this process. Unlike in other countries, being a notary public is highly regulated; one must be at least 35 years old, have a degree in law, at least 3 years of experience at a notary public office, and pass an exam. They are the ones who officialize all of your documentation and permits in this process. You are allowed to choose your own notary public. Most real estate deals in Mexico are done in cash, but financing is becoming more common.

Rules, Regulations and Restrictions

According to the law, the Mexican nation owns all land and water in Mexico, along with minerals, salts, ore deposits, natural gas and oil. That ownership can be assigned to individuals, however.

There are also restricted zones, which Mexico prohibits foreigners from legally owning. They include land within 100 kilometers of the Mexican border and 50 kilometers within a Mexican coastline. However, a foreigner can invest in such lands under a real estate trust, known as "fideicomiso." A Mexican bank is to be assigned as the trustee, has title to the property and owns the records. Foreigners can have unrestricted use of the lands under this loophole, but not officially own that land.

243

Real Estate Developments are companies that buy large quantities of land, and then develop it with creating a residential community, and putting in some facilities.

General Process

First, you should find a property that you like and agree a price verbally, and then set it up in a document, "Convenio de Compra/Venta." You must set up a trust if this property is within restricted zones. Then you must seek permission from the Foreign Secretary's office to buy land, followed by signing a "Calvo Clause." If you are buying property from a Real Estate Developer, have your notary public invesitage them.

Next, you should get a copy of the Land/Property Deeds from whoever is selling you your property, and have it investigated by your notary public. You must have the land appraised, which can also be organized by a notary public.

You must obtain a permit, and you'll have to submit the following documents:

- Passport
- Birth Certificate
- Marriage Cerificate (if necessary)
- Visa (could be a tourist visa)

Your notary public will probably assist you in this process. They must also get the following documents from the property seller:

- Original property deed
- Tax receipts
- Public utilities bills
- Details of land service fee

Your seller must pay a Capital Gains Tax. Then your payment of the property will take place when the deed is signed over to you, at the notary public's office. You must also pay any other fees and taxes."

For more information, see *www.expatify.com*.

What is a Fideicomiso?

"To own property in the restricted area which includes Mérida and some areas of the Yucatán, you engage a Mexican bank to execute and hold title to the property using a contract known as a fideicomiso. With this, you and the bank are both listed on the title papers.

The fideicomiso creates a trust contract for the benefit of the foreign buyer. The bank has a fiduciary obligation to the owner. The owner has all the benefits of ownership and retains the legal right to lease, sell, and/or will the property to his heirs. Fideicomisos are currently 50 years documents. They can be renewed at the end of the term for an additional 50 years. There is no limit to the number of times the fideicomiso can be renewed.

The renewal fee is currently about $900 USD.

The cost for initiating a fideicomiso is approximately $2,800 USD. There is an annual fee to the bank for maintaining the contract. The annual fee is based upon a percentage of the value of the home. An estimated figure for a home in the $100,000 range is about $600 USD a year. Current law does not allow a fideicomiso for properties larger than 2,000 square meters (approx. 21,520 square ft.)"

From: www.realestate-yucatan.net

Fideicomiso and the IRS

U.S. citizens and permanent residents should be aware that the IRS considers a Fideicomiso a trust and has strict reporting guidelines. Check the IRS website and search for "Foreign Trusts." The website is: *www.irs.gov*.

Before you consider buying Real Estate in Mérida, heed these "Lessons Well Learned"

It will come as no surprise to anyone that the world is still recovering from the real estate bubble that burst in 2008.

Not all countries, however, were affected in the same way. In Mexico, the government has programs administered through an agency known as INFONAVIT that regulates the majority of housing construction, mortgages, and real estate transactions. It is intended to make home ownership possible for Mexico's working and lower middle classes. This, which represents the majority of Mexico's housing market, was insulated from the excesses of the market excesses and speculation that led to the worldwide collapse in housing.

But when it comes to the *unregulated* real estate—which is where almost all expats buy and sell their homes in Mexico—Mérida was not immune to excesses.

One American Expat's Experience in Mérida's Real Estate Market

By Vince Gricus

When I arrived in Mérida for the first time, I came here as an ordinary tourist. I had recently retired from a long career working in the aviation industry, and one of my unfulfilled dreams was to own a Bed & Breakfast. I was staying at a Bed & Breakfast, and I mentioned this to my hosts. One of them indicated there was a suitable business for sale, and I inquired about the asking price. "It's $349,000 dollars," I was told, which seemed reasonable to me. My reference was the greater real estate market in St. Louis, Missouri. I mentioned that I had a partner, and I would have to discuss it with him. In my absence, the realtor met with my partner. My partner disclosed that he was an attorney with his own practice. In the morning, I asked for a confirmation of the asking price and I was told it was a "bargain" at $399,000 USD. The asking price shot up by $50,000 USD overnight, once they found out my partner's ability to pay!

Let me share with you my personal experience with Tierra Yucatán. Perhaps others have had different experiences, but I can only speak for myself. When I arrived in Mérida, I spoke no Spanish and I knew no one in town, and neither did my partner. As a result, we wanted a turnkey property, ready to move in. We explained this to the agent at Tierra Yucatán. Our tour of several properties began with an Agent and his Assistant. The Assistant looked displeased to be even driving around with us, as the Agent asked all kinds of questions. Our request was to be shown a property that was move-in ready, had three or four bedrooms which could be suitable for a Bed & Breakfast, with a swimming pool, and hopefully a garage as well. The first property we were shown was on the corner of Calle 57 and 72 Street, a very busy intersection. One of the rooms was being used as a TV repair shop. And when we walked inside, we could see the sky. Why? Because some of the rooms had no roof! It was in shambles. (That property, five years later was still for sale.) The next property was equally unsuitable, but for different reasons—it was next to "bath house," and we could imagine just the kind of people who would be knocking on the door at all hours of the night asking for a room! The third property was equally unsuitable, with all the bathrooms needing to be remodeled and updated.

It was clear that they were interested in showing you what they wanted to show you, and not what you asked to see.

We then went for lunch at a nearby restaurant. I was ready to scrap the whole project. The restaurant owner came by and we discussed the waste of a morning we'd had with the folks from Tierra Yucatán. Then he offered, "Why didn't they show you Tom's place? It's for sale." After lunch, we were off to see this place, right in the heart of Santiago. It was exactly what we asked for: up and running as a Bed & Breakfast, it had four bedrooms, a pool and parking. It was just a question of settling on a price, and the paperwork was handled by another real estate company, with minor delays or headaches!

As a general rule, the less informed you are about the local market and the options available to you, the more likely you are to run into trouble. There are untold horror stories of uninformed foreigners being bamboozled into make decisions they subsequently regret. "Had I know X, I would have done Y," is a familiar refrain among many expats. Over the past five years or so, there's been an explosion of "Buy Owner" signs ("Trato Directo" in Spanish) that have appeared around town. Many Yucatecans who do want to sell their houses are fed up with the empty promises of "dollars" made to them, and are happy to get "pesos" for their properties.

Lesson #1

It's a very fluid market and one of the curious things is that the realtors in question are expatriates!

One reason for it being such a fluid market is that there are no regulations for being a real estate agent. It's become quite easy for anyone to come to Mérida, learn the basics of buying and selling and set up shop—using their ability to speak English as a competitive advantage to sell to other expatriates! Forget that stereotype that Mexicans will take you for a ride. That has not been the case, at least in my experience. In fact, it's been the opposite: foreign expats in business down here are more likely to think in terms of dollars and not in pesos.

Lesson #2:

During the 2010s as more and more Americans have been discovering Mérida, the local market has been "dollarized"!

What do I mean by this? That during the height of the real estate frenzy that engulfed the world—think 2002 through 2008—here in Mérida, foreigners arrived, set up shop as "realtors" and went around knocking on every door that had a "Se Vende"—"For Sale"—sign and promised the owners that they could get *dólares* for their houses.

In no time, Yucatecans living in these glorious but often neglected and outdated homes in the *Centro Histórico* could only think in terms of dollars.

And it worked. For Americans, the real estate was "a bargain," even when they took into account the expense of remodeling and upgrading their homes. Some wanted all the modern conveniences, others wanted to transform their homes into a "Frida Kahlo Mexican Fantasy." Still others wanted a luxurious home with infinity pools and gracious terraces for outdoor living that they could never afford back in the States.

Is it any wonder that Mérida's Historic Center became "dollarized"? If you didn't offer to pay in dollars, local sellers were not impressed.

Consider this anecdote. A local friend tells me this story. His granduncle, who lived out of town, wanted his grandsons to study in Mérida, and to do so, they needed a local address. A colleague mentioned to him that a neighbor was selling his house. It was a small house, and it would need major renovations to bring it up to date, but it was structurally fine, and, while modest, would meet the needs of two teenage brothers who would be visited by their mother on the weekends. Best yet, the price was right: $600,000 pesos, or about $48,000 USD. A few months later, the granduncle was in Mérida, and went by to see the house. It still had a "Se Vende" sign on it, but now it was listed with a realtor. During that time, an American real estate agent, driving around town, saw the "Se Vende" sign and called up the seller. The American realtor convinced the Yucatecan owner that $48,000 USD was not enough to ask for. "We can get you $67,000 USD!" the American real estate agent promised, and that's the price it was listed for. The granduncle was somewhat discouraged when he heard that the price had jumped from $48,000 USD to $67,000 USD, but was willing to be patient. Time passed, and the house, listed for $67,000 USD languished on the market. Months later, the granduncle, back in town, went to see the seller.

"How much do you want for this property?" he asked.

"It's $67,000 American dollars," was the reply.

"This is Mexico! The currency is the *peso*! Don't talk to me about American *dollars*," the granduncle protested.

Pause.

248

"I think your house is worth $600,000 pesos, and that's what I'm willing to offer you right now."

The Yucatecan was silent, probably thinking that the house had been on the market for more than 10 months without a single offer, and that he was now being offered what he originally wanted for the house in the first place.

"That's what I can offer you, and the offer is good until I hear back from another seller where I made an offer earlier this morning," the granduncle added.

"It's yours," the seller said, extending his hand.

A property that had been "dollarized"—and remained unsold—was now brought back to the "real world" of Mexican pesos and Mexican prices.

The Global Recession of 2008 is taking care of a great deal of the "dollarized" properties in Mérida's Historic Center, although this is often news to the American real estate agents who contributed to dollarizing and inflating Mérida's real estate market! With these experiences under my belt, I cannot in good conscience recommend three of the most popular real estate agencies in town that have contributed much to creating a speculative bubble here in Mérida, and which have sold properties at far above their market value in recent years.

This is not to say that there are no American real estate companies in Mérida that I would recommend, or who have demonstrated their professionalism and integrity. Jim Mann of Mérida Yucatán Properties is one agent whose praise many people continue to sing. (For the sake of full disclosure, Jim Mann was not the agent who sold us our Bed & Breakfast, and neither I nor my partner have bought or sold real estate properties through Jim Mann's Mérida Yucatán Properties.) Of the real estate agencies in Mérida founded and run by Americans, Mérida Yucatán Properties is the one that, to my knowledge, has the highest customer satisfaction and it is the one that has tried to "rationalize" the market by pointing out that in 2011, the U.S. dollar continues to fluctuate against the Mexican peso in an unpredictable way, and that the market in Mérida is still recovering from the Global Recession. But remember, like Jim Mann there are scores of reputable, honest and ethical realtors in Mérida, American and Yucatecan alike, who will look out for you and your interests.

Lesson #3

There are lots of neighborhoods that offer wonderful values, and which are almost always ignored by expatriate real estate companies that are obsessed with the "Centro Histórico" or the beaches near Progreso.

The point to consider is that Mérida is blessed with many neighborhoods where there are exceptional values. For those on fixed incomes, there are lovely houses in Colonia Pensiones, which is close to the Historic Center, the highway to the beaches near Progreso, and which is often overlooked. For those who are more willing to live among "locals," Colonia Miguel Alemán, which was designed and built in the 1960s, has wonderful homes, in a solidly middle class neighborhood with wonderful amenities and a terrific "small town" feel. Consider that each afternoon it seems that all the families are out in the neighborhood park, with kids on their bicycles and multi-generational families enjoying the late afternoon and early evening sense of community by being out with neighbors.

These are just two neighborhoods that are often overlooked, and which a real estate agent who has your interest at heart, and is willing to do a little legwork will find suitable places for you to consider.

Keep these three lessons in mind, and you will be a smart buyer in Mérida's real estate market. This is the only advice that I can give a newcomer to Mérida.

 ## Is Mérida's Historic Center a Bargain?

What has happened to Mérida's Historic Center?

In 2006, Kate Murphy, writing in the *New York Times*, reported this: "Most of the plaster buildings in the historic district are from the early 19th century and have high ceilings, Moorish ironwork and colorful, patterned floor tiles called mosaico. They are also bargains, at around $40,000 for a four-bedroom, two-bathroom colonial home."*

This described a colonial home in downtown Mérida that would need an equal amount of "remodeling" and "upgrades." The total cost of a lovely, colonial home with all the modern conveniences would cost absolutely, positively no more than $80,000 USD, about the same price as a simple, one-bedroom retirement condo just about anywhere in Florida!

Now consider Mérida's Historic Center in 2016:

In December 2014, there were 32 properties listed on one real estate website catering primarily to other Americans. **The average price: $357,550 USD!**

That same month, a survey of the "**Renta y Ventas**" website, which is by Mexicans primarily for Mexicans, yielded an **average price of $86,382 USD** (or $1,252,550 pesos, at an exchange rate of 14.50 pesos to 1 dollar), for a 3-bedroom, 2.5 bathroom home, with a garage in any of the Colonias outside the Historic Center.

Have Americans become their own worst enemies in their relentless marketing and hype surrounding Mérida's Historic Center?

How did a retirement home that should cost no more than $80,000 USD in 2006 become an over-the-top extravagance of excess, now presented as a "deal" at an average price that is almost three times the average price of a residence in the U.S. in 2014? (The median price of a home in a metropolitan area in the U.S.: $199,500 USD as of December 2013.**)

Consider all your real estate options in Mérida, and there are plenty.

*Sources: *"Mérida: Finding a Home (Cheerios Included) in Mexico," by Kate Murphy, New York Times, March 12, 2006. **The price of a median home in a metropolitan area, for the fourth quarter 2013, is provided by* www.Realtor.org. *To verify the figure, go to Realtor.org and check under the "Research and Statistics" tab.*

Resort Communities and Condominiums

"Those looking to make a quick transition without worrying about remodeling, refitting, or building a new place can buy into a development. In many beach towns, as well as in colonial cities, there are large residential communities that are built and overseen by a single company. Many offer diverse living arrangements (with similar design), and some even provide furnishings in the total cost -- a good pick for those who don't want to go through the hassle of moving their household items. Many developments offer the opportunity to invest in a condo before the development is complete. The rates for pre-purchased houses may be significantly lower. These places may also have finance plans."—*Julie Doherty Meade*

The Seven Realities for the Real Estate Market in Mérida's Centro Histórico

1. This is an area where there is little demand for residential real estate by the people who are from Mérida.

251

2. Mexicans moving in from other areas of Mexico have also shown little interest in this district as a place to live.

3. Yucatecan owners are seldom in a hurry to sell these properties since they were mostly inherited from their parents or grandparents, meaning there is little interest in lowering asking prices once an asking price is set. This makes the real estate market price inelastic.

4. Demand for these properties is generated primarily by foreigners moving to Mérida.

5. Demand is cultivated principally by foreigners who are working in the real estate business in Mérida and sell almost exclusively to other foreigners.

6. Mérida's real estate market in the Historic Center operates like a localized market bubble, with little, if any, relation to the forces of supply and demand that shape the real estate market in other areas of Mérida.

7. Given the peculiar circumstances of local demand, or lack thereof, the principal market for homes in the Historic Center are other expatriates, meaning that once you buy a property in Mérida' Historic Center you are almost exclusively limited to selling to other foreigners.

Recommended Real Estate Companies

Jim Mann

www.Meridayucatanproperties.com

Gabriela Cornelio

www.casayucatanrealestate.com

Debora Whifield (Colyn)

www.merida-properties.com

Rupert Millautz

www.buenavidarealtors.com

Does Your Realtor Have a Certificate from INFONAVIT?

If your real estate agent cannot produce a copy of his or her Certificado from INFONAVIT, ask yourself this: Does this person know the rules and regulations governing real estate in Mexico, or is this a con artist? Protect yourself: **Always use a real estate agent who has been certified by INFONAVIT!**

Source: Asociación Mexicana de Profesionales Inmobiliarios (AMPI)

Where Can You Search for "Non-Dollarized" Real Estate?

If there is one mantra about Mérida in this book, is that to get a "fair market value" for just about anything, it is best to search the "Avisos Económicos," or the Classified Section, of the *Diario de Yucatán*. From guitars to bookshelves, hammocks to rental houses, if it's out there, it's probably listed in the *Diario*'s classified section. This will give you a basic understanding of what people in Mérida expect to pay for just about anything.

So how do you shop for real estate as if you were a Mexican citizen?

When it comes to real estate, there are ample offerings, from two-bedroom houses in the Historic Center, to four-bedroom homes in the outlying Colonias. Once you peruse the "Avisos Económicos," then you are in a position to search for real estate as if you were a Mexican! And fortunately, there are Spanish-language sites that cater to Mexicans looking for real estate in Mérida. The advantage, of course, is that everything is priced in pesos, and that the entire market has not been distorted by expatriate realtors selling real estate in Mexico.

The disadvantage, on the other hand, is that almost everything on these websites is in Spanish. But then again, there lies the "authenticity" of the offerings—these are companies that are designed *by* Mexicans *for* Mexicans. There are other websites, of course, but these seven, listed alphabetically, will give you an idea of what's out there, what's available, and what's reasonable.

Here are a Rising Real Estate Companies

These real estate companies are quickly establishing themselves as the premier real estate companies for expats moving to Mérida.

Yucatán Premier

www.yucatanpremier.com.mx

Inmobiliere Bienes & Raíces (Spanish speaking)

www.inmobiliere.com

Yucatán Properties (Spanish speaking)

www.yucatanproperties.com.mx

Yucatán Home Finders

www.yucatanhomefinders.com

Here is a list of Mexican Real Estate Companies, by Mexicans for Mexicans

Some of these are national companies, meaning that they have classified listings for the entire country, and you should be confident in your Spanish, at least confident enough to make the initial inquiry.

Enormo

www.enormo.com.mx

InmoMexico

www.inmomexico.com

Quality Yucatán

www.qualityyucatan.com

Rentas y Ventas

www.rentasyventas.com

Semerena Properties

www.semerena.com

Trovit Mexico

www.asas.trovitmexico.com.mx

2 Casa Realty

www.2casarealty.com

Real Estate Companies Specializing in Progreso and Beach Homes

Kab Yucatán

www.kab-yucatan.com

Mayan Living

www.mayanliving.com

Two Real Estate Companies to Consider with Caution

It is important to point out several expatriate realtors who have contributed to the "hyping" of Mérida and who have skewed their offerings towards properties that exceed the price of a median home in the U.S. If you are in a position to have your bank execute a wire transfer for about half a million dollars, simply because you have that much money, or all you want to do is be handed the keys to a property that's move-in ready, there's nothing wrong with that. As editor of this book, however, I would not recommend these two real estate outfits to anyone thinking of purchasing a retirement home on a budget, or who is interested in getting value for his or her money, but this is my own opinion and advice.

www.MexIntl.com

www.tierrayucatan.com

Is Mérida really right for you?

Mérida is a great place to visit, but do you truly, madly, deeply want to live here?

Only you can answer that question! That's why, in all fairness to you, it is important for you to consider that question thoroughly and thoughtfully. Yes, Mérida is a tropical paradise, but it is not paradise. The greatest obstacles are the summer heat and the mosquitoes. Everyone who lives here full-time has to cope with both.

It's not difficult to understand why: Look at the globe. Yucatán lies along the same parallels as does the Arabian peninsula! And the median temperature in Yucatán is hotter! Why? Because the Arabian peninsula is desert, so at night, it cools down. Yucatán is covered by forests, which keep the sun's warmth during nighttime. The result? The average temperature is higher here than it is in Mecca!

That is the reason you are advised to spend some time here, before you decide this is where you want to live. Mind you, there are thousands of expatriates from the world over living here, and there are thousands more who spend a portion of the year here. It is a wonderful place, but it isn't for everyone.

The best way to find out for yourself, one way or the other, is to spend a few weeks here. Beryl Gorbman, who lived been here for over a quarter century, recommends spending the months of May or August here. Then again, bear in mind that the city, like Rome, Italy, is virtually abandoned in August—everyone it seems is at the beach towns that spread east and west of

Progreso! But her point is well taken, even if Mérida seems like a ghost town in August. If you are only going to come here between Christmas and Easter, you won't have a problem with the heat. But if you plan on being down here year-round, take note of the weather patterns that exacerbate summer's heat.

Take into Account Mérida's Hot Weather

Mérida, the Schvitzing Capital of the World

By Beryl Gorbman

The yenta does not understand why so many foreigners move to Mérida. Sometimes she doesn't understand why she herself moved to Mérida. It is so awfully hot most of the time. In May, we had nearly a month of consecutive days over 105 degrees F and humid. You couldn't leave your house, except to run to the a/c car and drive to the a/c store and return to your a/c house. That is, IF you can afford a/c.

Sweating is a constant state of the human body here. Schvitzing, as it's called in the Yiddish vernacular. You can be sitting perfectly quietly watching TV and the sweat will roll down your face and neck.

Schvitzing is okay once in a while, but when there's an extended period of days of 100 degrees F and high humidity, it makes me crazy (er). I rebel and keep the a/c on starting at around 4 PM and then all through the night. I worship the god of a/c. Electricity costs more here the more you use, so our bill in the hot months is a major expense.

We have at least three groups of house-guests coming in the next few months and they will think this place is just fabulous. Lots of North Americans come in the winter and have a great time. They fall in love with the place because it is so gorgeous and gracious and then immediately buy houses because "the houses are so cheap." Many of these buyers sell the following year, or retreat back up north from late April until October. That's most of the year.

So if you're thinking of moving here, try visiting in May or August.

Contemporary Urban Developments

It's no secret that the Yucatán Country Club is the premier residential development in Yucatán State, with a Jack Nicklaus-designed championship golf course and the Mark Spitzer Swimming Academy. (Website: *www.yucatancountry.com*.) This is just one of scores of development recently completed, well underway or in the development phase. Here are the "top

256

four" developments—in terms of the number of foreign buyers moving into them. The editor is not endorsing any of them, but they are listed here for informational purposes, since it demonstrates the tremendous variety available now and available to you.

Yucatán Country Club
www.yucatancountry.com

Villa Harmonia at Yucatán Country Club
www.yucatancountry.com

Jardines de Conkal
www.jardinesdeconkalcom

Manantiales de Cocoyloes
www.manantialesdecocoyoles.com

Playa Chacá
www.playachaca.com

A Note about Shorter Stays

Renting an apartment or house is, as is common in the United States and Canada, usually done through a year-long contract. But what if you want to explore Mérida and check out the city for several weeks, or several months, without signing a year-long contract?

One solution is negotiating a long-term stay at one of the better Bed & Breakfasts in town. It's possible to get a deal for a two-week, three-week or month-long stays. Many visitors, who are in Mérida on "medical tourism"— and require several visits to doctors, dentists or other health professionals, rent by the week, or month. A good number of would-be expatriates, likewise, rent for a month to decide if, indeed, Mérida is the right place for them. Others enjoy having a comfortable "base of operations" while they search for the ideal property.

Here is a list of Bed & Breakfasts, in alphabetical order, that are among Mérida's finest

Angeles de Mérida
Calle 74-A #494-A, between Calle 57 and 59 Street
Centro

Website:
www.angelesdemerida.com

257

La Casa Lorenzo
Calle 41 #516-A between Calle 62 and 64 Street
Centro
Website: *www.lacasalorenzo.com*

Casa Mexilio
Calle 68 #495, between Calle 57 and 59 street
Centro
Website: *www.casamexilio.com*

Casa Santiago
Calle 63 #562, between Calle 70 and 72 street
Centro
Website: *www.casasantiago.net*

"In Ka'an"
Calle 15 #527 between Calle 24 and 26 Street
Colonia Maya
Website: *www.inkaan.com*

Los Arcos
Calle 66 #448-B, between Calle 49 and 53 Street
Centro
Website: *www.losarcosmerida.com*

In addition, there are two splendid boutique hotels, one run by a gracious husband-and-wife team from the United Kingdom and the other by a refined Yucatecan gentleman. Both hotels accommodate stays for individuals checking out the real estate market in Mérida.

Hotel Zamná
Calle 53 #547, between Calle 70 and 72 Street
Centro
Telephone: (999) 924-0103
Email:
zamna.merida.centro@gmail.com
Website: *www.casazamna.webs.com*

Hotel Casa Nobel
Calle 72 #403-C, between Calle 39 and 41 Street
Centro (Avenida Reforma)
Telephone: (999) 920-0369
Email:
reservaciones@hotelcasanobel.com
Website: *www.hotelcasanobel.com*

A Note about Renting an Apartment or House

Many expatriates find it prudent to rent while remodeling a home. This, of course, makes perfect sense. As with realtors, be forewarned, there are currently no licensing requirements for "property management" in Mexico. Anyone can set up a rental and property management company. Furthermore, if you purchased a "fixer-upper" it might make sense to live down here for the 6, 9 or 12 months that a renovation, reconstruction, and building takes place. It's difficult to deal with architects, contractors and designers about a house in Mérida if you happen to be thousands of miles away!

Renting a house or an apartment is much the same as it is in other countries with the exception of the attorney fees and the contract. You will be responsible for the fee to prepare the contract, which is one month's rent. The attorney will prepare a lease contract and 12 promissory notes. The rest is standard with first and last month's rent. Often you can avoid a security deposit if you have a Mexican citizen sponsor (co-sign) you. This is often difficult to do with casual acquaintances, since the Mexican citizen will be legally responsible to pay the rent should you default on the rental agreement.

It is also important to remember that, once again, the rental market has been "dollarized." If someone quotes you rent in dollars, what's the matter with them? This is Mexico!

Your best bet is to check out the "Avisos Económicos" in the *Diario de Yucatán* to know what the fair market value of a rental apartment or rental house goes for in the different Colonias around town. And of course you can rent a comfortable, but modest home in the Historic Center (2 bedroom, 1 bathroom for about $2,800 pesos, or $220 USD per month), or you can rent a more contemporary and comfortable home (a 3 bedroom, 2.5 bathroom, split level house with a garage in Colonia Buenavista goes for $5,000 pesos, or $400 USD per month).

Furnished, luxury rentals can go much higher, whether priced in pesos or dollars, but as a general rule, the same Mexican real estate companies that cater to Mexicans have the best deals. For a reference point, check out Rentas y Ventas (*www.rentasyventas.com*) simply because they have hundreds of listings, ranging from $1,800 pesos to $25,000 pesos per month.

Rental Procedures in Yucatán State

Home and apartment rental conventions vary from state to state in Mexico. In Yucatán, because tenant eviction is difficult for landlords to obtain through the courts of law, rental requirements often include the following:

1) An "Aval" or guarantee secured by real estate property

2) The signing of financial obligations such as "Pagarés" (IOUs) in lieu of a rental contract, and/or

3) A security deposit in the amount of one month's rent or more.

Furthermore, the renter must pay the landlord's attorney the equivalent of one month's rent for preparing and legalizing the various documents. In reality, the process is less onerous than it sounds, but renters should be aware in case they opt for renting from Mexican landlords. Often certain requirements are waived or modified. For example, instead of the "aval," an additional amount towards the security deposit can be requested. Renters who speak little or no Spanish: We recommend using their own local attorney to represent them in the negotiations, as the landlord's attorney represents only the landlord's interests. A list of attorneys is provided in Chapter 20.

If you rent, protect yourself!

Another necessary warning: If you rent from a Mexican citizen, every adult Mexican has two numbers, one is the IFE (Instituto Federal Electoral), which is issued as a national identification number. The other is an RFC, or Registro Federal de Causante, which is used for tax purposes. Renting from a Mexican citizen requires no other tax formalities on your part.

But if you are renting from a foreign national—an American or Canadian or European citizen in Mérida—please protect yourself by asking for a "Recibo Fiscal." This means that the person renting you the apartment or house is authorized to be a foreigner engaged in the business of renting properties in Mexico.

In recent years, some Americans and Canadians have been deported for renting out apartments and houses without authorization. (This is a form of tax evasion.) And as a consequence, renters—that could be you!—have been forced to find other housing. **Always ask for a Recibo Fiscal if your landlord is not a Mexican citizen!**

> **Please note**: Many Spanish websites list prices with an "MN" at the end of a price, such as $5,000 MN. "MN" stands for "Moneda Nacional," or "National Currency." It means pesos. $5,000 MN is read as "Five thousand, national currency."

A Final Guide on Rental Prices in 2014

Be an informed renter. Heed these price guidelines:

- A 2 bedroom, 1 bath house or apartment in a perfectly decent, safe Mexican neighborhood (unfurnished, possibly no appliances): $250 USD to 300 USD

- Want to go more upscale? The rental of a 2 bedroom, 2 bathroom house or apartment, with a yard, in a professional, middle-class neighborhoods north of Centro: $500 USD to $600 USD

Need luxury living? Upper-class homes and apartments in newer, north of Mérida neighborhoods from with two-car garages, an ample garden and many with small pools, and even a maid/guest quarters: $850 USD and higher.

New Regulations on the Horizon for 2014?

If it seems that the Historic Center's real estate market appears to be in disarray, there's comfort in knowing that Mexican officials have taken notice. Miguel Ángel Aguayo de Pau, president of the Asociación Mexicana de Profesionales Inmobiliarios, or Mexican Association of Professional Realtors, who took office in early 2011, has gone the record for establishing regulations on realtors and how real estate companies operate in Yucatán State. Noting that there are "around 100" foreigners acting as real estate agents—and only about 300 properties in the Historic Center or Progreso beach are registered in the names of foreigners. Mr. Aguayo de Pau, wants tighter regulation. He pointed out that although real estate companies are not currently regulated by the state, real estate agents are expected to have certifications issued by INFONAVIT to prove that they meet the minimum standards of training in order to be considered bona fide real estate agents. Mr. Aguayo de Pau expressed his concern that under current conditions, it is too easy for real estate agents who have not been certified by INFONAVIT are more likely to commit fraudulent real estate transactions, or be themselves defrauded because of their ignorance of real estate norms. He has expressed concern that members of his industry organization are becoming alarmed at the trends in pricing—and lack of sales—in the city's Historic Center, creating an unsustainable situation for both buyers and sellers in this area.

Bottom line: If your realtor cannot show you his or her Certificate from INFONAVIT, find yourself another agent!

Property Taxes, or *Predial*

Finally, once you have purchased a home in Mérida, there's the matter of the annual "property tax," which is really not a property tax, but a jurisdiction fee. It is a nominal fee.

Known as the *predial*, this annual tax is assessed on all real property. The word *predial*—which is pronounced, PREH-dyahl—is the equivalent of the property tax assessed in the United States, but with an enormous difference: it is almost inconsequential.

To understand the difference, it's necessary to review its origins. *Predial* is an adjective for *predio*, and *predio* is a parcel of land. Mexican law is derived from the Napoleonic Code, which in turn is based on Roman law. Throughout Latin America, Roman law forms the basis of the legal institutions. Where property is concerned, the biggest difference between Roman law and Common law (which is the basis of English law and American legal principles) concerns subsoil resources. Under Roman law everything under the ground belongs to the state (Caesar). And under U.S. law, everything under the ground belongs to the property owner. That's why if you have a ranch in Mexico and, in the course of digging a well you strike oil, well, that's not your oil. It belongs to the federal government, which reserves the right to exercise eminent domain. In the U.S., on the other hand, John D. Rockefeller was able to keep the oil he discovered on his property in Texas and went on to become the world's richest man.

This idea, that you own the property (and everything on it, but nothing beneath it), gave rise to the question of government authority and state jurisdiction. Do you acquiesce to the idea that your property is located within the jurisdiction of the government?

The *predial*, or tax on terrains, is based on the principle that by paying a nominal tax you are acknowledging that you are subject to the jurisdiction of the government that imposes this fee. This idea is so engrained in the legal system inherited from Spain that, for instance, the Constitution of Ecuador explicitly states that any communal property held by a recognized community of First Peoples (indigenous populations) is automatically exempt from any *predial*. The rationale behind this is that, symbolically, the sovereignty of the First Nations is recognized and they are not, technically, required to acquiesce to the authority of the modern nation-state under whose jurisdiction their communities reside.

Over the years, the concept has evolved, simply out of fairness. If you own a piece of land that has a high rise hotel on it, you should pay more than someone who owns a parcel of land where they have a simple one-bedroom home. On the other hand, the *predial* has never been viewed as a source of "substantial" income, but merely a formal mechanism of establishing jurisdiction and validating the social contract between the government and those governed. This is the reason, relative to U.S. property taxes, which are used to fund an array of government services, in Mexico the *predial* is a nominal fee, one that seldom creates financial hardship on property owners. In contrast, it's no uncommon to hear stories of Americans who decide to sell their homes in the U.S. because they can no longer bear the burden of property taxes!

Now comes two important factors. First, because Mexico is loath to create homelessness, failure to pay the *predial* is never used to seize a property, or evict people from their homes. Unlike the United States where governments are empowered to put liens on properties, or seize a property for back taxes owed, that simply doesn't happen in Mexico. Second, it's easy to see why, since there are no real, immediate sanctions for failing to pay the *predial*, there is a very high incidence of noncompliance. Folks just don't pay, and as a result, government offers incentives to pay the tax. If you pay in January, you will probably receive a 10%-15% discount, depending on what city government approved for the year in question. If you pay within the first trimester of the year, you're automatically entered to win a prize, like a house or a car.

Incentives aside, you can imagine what happens where there is no real penalty for failing to comply with paying a tax. That's right! Many people go years, or even *decades*, without paying it. But, of course, in the end government finds a way to get its due. For the *predial*, there is an enforcement mechanism at the end of the day: The law prohibits the sale of a property or changing the name on a property title if there are unpaid *predial* taxes that are outstanding.

When it comes time to sell a property, or you inherited a property and you want the title in your name, the Notario Público is required to square all pending taxes with the Catastro. This is one of the important tasks that real estate agents are supposed to provide and it is one that is often burdensome to individuals who, upon inheriting a property, realize that their beloved old grand-aunt had been a scofflaw for years!

With this in mind, remember that because the city continues to grow so rapidly, the *predial* is now a significant source of discretionary income for the city of Mérida, and that it is used for funding general functions of the city government services, from school lunch programs to repairing the dilapitaded facades throughout the Centro Histórico. And, unless you plan to be in your home until you die and are content to let your heirs deal with back taxes, interest, and penalties, it's best just to do the right thing, and enjoy the generous discount offered if you pay your *predial* in January—and you might even win a lovely gift, such as a brand new car!

Deferred Maintenance on your Home

By Cenote Sally

It's a fact of life: Mother Nature conspires against humanity in the tropics. Life flourishes all around us in Mérida. Nature wants to reclaim everything that humanity builds. That's one reason the Maya ruins are, well, in ruins! Don't let your home suffer the same fate.

Whether you've been away for a few months, or just bought a home that was "renovated" and been sitting on the market for a year, the moment you return to a house that has not been lived in, there will be things to take of *immediately*.

Consider these the necessary deferred maintenance required of every homeowner in Mérida.

Clean the Roof & Repair Leaks

It's an annual rite of passage: checking for leaks once the rain arrives. But if you arrive before the rains do, the first order of business is to check your roof for debris.

Even if you don't have trees on your property, the winds—and there are mighty strong winds during rainstorms—blow leaves everywhere. In a matter of days, enough leaves can accumulate in a corner of your roof for things to start to sprout, or at least moisture to start to work its havoc.

Immediately upon arrival, climb on the roof—or get a gardener or handyman to do it for you—to make sure that it is clear of any debris.

Also be mindful that regardless of the sealant applied to your roof, you will have to reapply sealant every two or three years. There is no product on the market that was designed for the intense heat and powerful downpours throughout the peninsula. Expect leaks every now and then, and always, always, always wait for the dry season (winter time) to reapply sealant to the entire roof, otherwise, you are wasting your money.

But check for debris on your roof within 24 hours of arriving.

Activate the Bacteria in Your Septic Tank

If no one's been living in your home, then no one has been feeding the bacteria in your septic tank. That's right, for better or for worse, it's an ecosystem in there, and it needs nourishment.

If a house has been closed up for years—and most of the properties on the market in the historic center have been unoccupied for at least a year—then there may be little, if any, bacteria left alive in your septic tank.

First order of business with the first flush: introduce bacteria and enzymes that will regenerate a healthy ecosystem in your tank capable of breaking down waste products.

The easiest thing to do is to bring some Rid-X with you from the States of Canada. If you forgot, there are only two places in town where you can get these products: Home Depot and Casa Catherwood.

Surge Protectors are a Must!

Every electrical storm brings fluctuations in the electric current. It's a fact of life: Mérida is growing so quickly that the Comisión Federal de Electricidad (CFE) is having trouble keeping up with demand for electrical power. In the older areas—and the historic center is as old as it gets—there are power outages, fluctuations, and brownouts often enough.

In fact, the federal consumer protection agency has a division set up to help consumers file claims against the CFE for their fried electronics.

That's the good news. The bad news is that it takes anywhere from 6 to 12 months to get the CFE to respond. The smart thing is an ounce of prevention …

And that means: *Surge Protectors.*

Under no circumstances should you ever, ever, ever have your computer, television or stereo equipment plugged directly into an outlet. In my home, there is even a surge protector on the kitchen counter just for the blender, toaster, microwave, and the cell phone chargers.

If you forgot to get a deal on them at Staples or Costco before coming down, then get yourself over to Sam's Club, Costco, Home Depot, Boxito, Office Depot or Wal-Mart and get surge protectors.

And be smart: if there's a storm, turn everything off and unplug the surge protector. This is especially true if the lights begin to flicker, or if they go out. The last thing you want to do is have the power come back on with an electrical surge—and fry everything that's plugged into the wall.

Let the Sun Shine In!

In the tropic, stagnant air means one thing: MOLD!

Yes, mold spores will settle and start to grow! It's horrible, but it's true. That's a lesson learned he hard way.

The remedy? Let the sun shine in. Open the shutters, draw the curtains, let the air flow, flow, flow! And do it again. Let the sun shine in, and if you need to spray with Lysol and turn on fans, do that. You have to get the air circulating for the first 48 hours upon returning to your house. Air it out, and it will make a big difference.

And while you're at it, gently clean all leather furniture, since these are were the mold spores hide and breed—and they can really make you sick.

If you don't have Lysol spray on hand, get some!

Banish Mosquitoes

Not quite paradise! The most annoying thing about living in Mérida are the mosquitoes. And givent the global health warning about the Zika virus, it is important that you take steps to protect yourself from these annoying insects. Truth is, there's nothing that can be done about it, since it's their planet as much as it is ours, and they love the tropics. Every year health officials warn about them and report on outbreaks of dengue fever in poorer neighborhoods. It is a perennial concern. But there is a solution! A natural, organic and sustainable solution: **Colibri incense**.

Imported from Auroville, India this is the only all-natural incense made of scents that scare them away. Ideal for indoor and outdoor use, many Hacienda resorts and local restaurants and bars use them for patio and terrace seating. In town, only Casa Catherwood sells them, although if you are in Celestún or near Uxmal there are resorts that have them in their gift shops. You can't have a gracious home if you have mosquitoes buzzing around! More information at: *www.casa-catherwood.com/colibri.html*, or just drop by and stock up.

After you take these steps, you are ready to enjoy being back!

My Easy, Breezy Tips!

Let's face it! After more than half a century living in Yucatán, I have assembled hundreds of tips that have saved me thousands of dollars over the years. These tips have been assembled in my new book, *CENOTE SALLY'S EASY, BREEZY TROPICAL LIVING*.

Here are my tips for everyday household uses for lemons!

Brighten Kitchen Sinks
Dissolve salt in lime juice and use a damp cloth to wipe down stainless steel and aluminum surfaces. They will shine like new!

Scorpions Away!
In tropical climes . . . there are scorpions! One secret I've found that helps is simple: one cup lemon or lime juice and one cup water, and mix in spray bottle. Spray in your shower floor and terrace areas. Scorpions hate the scent and will not venture forth!

Freshen Garbage Disposal
Cut up a few lemons, grinds and all, and run through the garbage disposal. This will deodorize the disposal, while killing bacteria.

Cleaning Shower Curtains

If you have shower curtains—and there's really no reason you should—one way of preventing mildew from appearing is to soak the curtains in soap and water. Then sponge one cup lime juice and let it dry in the sun. That's the secret to minimizing mildew!

Extend the Life of Shower Curtains

All you have to do is spray your shower curtain with a combination of one cup hydrogen peroxide and water once a week. If you want it to work faster, let the shower curtains dry out in direct sunlight! Works wonders!

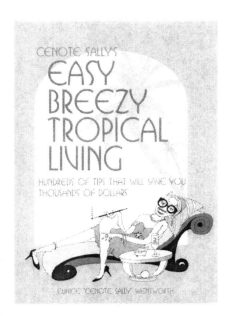

Cleaning Copper Cookware

Make a paste with table salt and lime juice. Rub it (with glove on!) over any copper item in your kitchen. Scrub using a sponge, then rinse and dry.

Clean Coffee Pots, Decanters and Glass Pitchers

If you use a solution of ¾ cup lime juice and ¼ cup white vinegar, you can make your coffee pot, decanter or glass pitcher sparkle like new!

Polish Wood Surfaces

For varnished wood surfaces, add three or four drops of lime juice to ½ cup warm water. Spray on a damp cloth and wipe furniture. For unvarnished wood surfaces, mix two teaspoons lime juice and two teaspoons olive oil. Using a cotton cloth polish wood, making sure you distribute the solution evenly.

Freshen Up Wilting Vegetables

If your veggies start to wilt, or go soft, because they've been in the refrigerator too long, here's an Easy, Breezy remedy. Pour ¼ cup lemon or lime juice in a bowl of cool water (a couple of ice cubes helps!). Then soak your carrots, spinach, lettuce, radishes or celery for about 10 or 15 minutes!

Freshen Rooms

An economical way of freshening any room—especially guests rooms—is using a portable humidifier. Pour ¼ cup lime juice into the water and the scent of mustiness will dissipate in a few hours!

Remove Scratches from Wood

A few drops of lime juice and olive oil will, using a soft cloth, do wonders in eliminating light scratches from wood furniture and surfaces.

Reduce Dust

A simple way of minimizing dust is simple enough: mix 10 drops lemon or lime just with a few drops olive oil. Shake vigorously and, using a spray bottle, "dust" surfaces in your kitchen—ceiling fan, top of microwave, refrigerator or any other surface. The lemon will repel dust particles!

Keep Painted Surface Insect-Free

For so many years whenever we did patch-up painting, insects would get stuck on the wet paint! Then a Maya friend shared with me her secret: add a few drops of lime juice to the paint, and the bugs will stay away while the paint dries!

Keep Paint Brushes Looking Like New

You can save a small fortune if you bring to boil a cup of lemon juice and then dip hardened paintbrushes. Remove from heat and 15 minutes later wash the brush in soapy water!

Keep Apples from Turning Brown

A few drops of lime juice on a cut apple will also prevent oxidation and your apple slices won't turn brown.

Cleaning Brass

Cut a lemon wedge, dip in baking soda and use this to clean brass. Rub it into the brass surface, let sit for 10 minutes. Rinse and buff dry. Next problem!

Cutting Board Stains

Oh, no! Beet juice staining your cutting board? Quick, reach for a lime. Rub the lime into the stain and let rest for about 15 minutes. Then rinse under cool water!

Removing Carpet Stains

Baking soda and a few drops of lime juice rubbed into a carpet stain is one solution—provided the carpet is colorfast. If it is, then you can easily remove any organic stain—from wine to fruit juice. Let sit for a few minutes, then wipe with a damp cloth.

Clean Ivory

Dissolve enough salt in a ¼ cup lemon juice to make a paste. Gently rub—even piano keys—and then wipe clean with a damp cloth.

Fluffier Rice

One tablespoon of lime juice added to water will make rice fluffier—and taste better.

Extend the Life of Guacamole

A few lime drops on guacamole will prevent them from oxidizing—and turning brown!

Cleaner Toilet

Yes, it's true. Pour a cup of lime juice in your toilet tank, and then flush . . . and this will reduce hard water and clean your toilet from the inside out!

Cleaner Glass Windows!

A ¼ cup of lemon juice, and a sponge is all you need to clean glass, whether it is a kitchen window, a sliding glass door or in the shower. Wipe the glass with lemon juice, then use a soft cloth (or newspaper) to rub dry!

Disinfect Cutting Boards

Bacteria certainly breed! A quick way of disinfecting any cutting board, or other cutting surface, is to pour salt and then use half a lime as a scouring pad. The salt and acidity in the lime will kill off the bacteria.

Eliminate Odors

If someone you spilled an alkaline onto your skin, such as those found in bleaches, then rub lemon. Lemon is acidic and counteracts alkaline! The odor is gone almost instantly. Then wash your hands in cool water.

Brighten Tennis Shoes

Here's an Easy, Breezy secret: spray lemon juice on your white tennis shoes and leave in the sun. They will whiten—and smell fresh!

Freshen Microwaves

Too dependent on your microwave? If you are, then you might have odors or stains. A simple solution? Here it is: place a small bowl with tepid water and slices of lemons or limes floating. Microwave for four or five minutes. Remove and then you will be surprised how easily the stains are wiped away with a damp cloth—and your microwave will smell fresh!

Extracting Juice

Speaking of microwaves, did you know that if you place a lime or lemon in the microwave and heat for just 10 or 12 seconds you will then be able to extract that much more juice?

Kitchen Counter Cleaned and Bacteria Free

One quarter cup lemon juice, ¼ cup white vinegar and ½ cup water is all you need—and a spray bottle. Spray and wipe counters to clean and disinfect surfaces in your kitchen! (Also works great in your bathroom!)

Natural Insect Repellent!

Before heading out to the terrace or patio for the evening, spray lightly your blouse with a solution of water and lemon juice—the scent of the lemon will keep mosquitoes far away from you!

Upset Stomach? No more!

Did you know that if you suck on a lemon you can settle an upset stomach? Now you do!

Not only will I enchant you with my real-life adventures and misadventures over the decades, but I will provide time-tested and time-proven solutions for all kinds of challenges and problems we encounter as we live in a tropical paradise. Trust me when I say my book will save you thousands of dollars as you enjoy an easy, breezy life in this wonderful place!

And this is the advice that I, Cenote Sally, can confer on you!

13 CONTRACTORS, ARCHITECTS AND DESIGNERS

One of the great things about living in Mérida is that you get to live in a great city, filled with wonderful architecture and a rich history. Mérida's Cathedral, for instance, celebrated its 450th anniversary in 2011—and it was the first Cathedral built on the mainland of the Americas! With a history so rich, it is difficult to decide where one will be inspired when it comes to architecture and design.

To get your creativity going, here are 15 great books that everyone should check out from the library (or better yet, buy) that will offer inspiration on what can be done, and how it should be done. The descriptions for each book are from Amazon.com and there are links provided to two iBookstore pages have been set up to allow you to read more about each book, and to get whatever discount Amazon.com offers should you decide to purchase any of these books.

After these brief descriptions of these books, there's a discussion on the Contractors, Architects and Designers who can help you make your home everything you want it to be. Look over these books, and then we'll get on to making recommendations on who can make your dream home in Mérida a reality!

Books to Inspire

Here is a list of our recommended books. Please note: The description of each book is provided by the publisher.

Casa Yucatán

By Karen Witynski and Joe P. Carr

A dazzling photographic journey, *Casa Yucatán* focuses on architectural elements, water spaces, and open-air living in houses both colonial and contemporary, including haciendas and coastal retreats. The Yucatán has undergone a remarkable restoration renaissance of late: ancient pyramids now share the dense jungle landscape with revived haciendas, and colonial homes boasting high-beamed ceilings and cool tile floors posture amidst elegant plazas and renovated nineteenth-century mansions.

Hacienda Style
By Karen Witynski and Joe P. Carr

Invite the rich colors, natural textures, and romantic beauty of Mexico into your home.

Hacienda Courtyards
By Karen Witynski and Joe P. Carr

Explore the architectural elements and water havens that will inspire your own courtyard paradise.

Traditional Mexican Style Interiors
By Donna McMenamin and Richard Loper

There is charm and character in a Mexican home like no other architectural style. It is a classic, timeless style that remains in constant demand. All who enjoy looking at beautiful interiors and want new ideas for their own home will find this book irresistible. Over 280 color photographs of some of the most beautiful new, old, and remodeled Mexican-style homes are compiled here. Color is everywhere vibrantly painted walls offer a rainbow of hues, hand painted talavera tiles cover every available surface, and traditional Mexican folk arts adorn walls and furnishings. Twelve chapters illustrate beautiful entryways, living rooms, kitchens, dining rooms, bedrooms, bathrooms, ceilings and floors, stairways, niches, fireplaces, lighting, and arts. Having specific rooms and architectural details divided into separate chapters is a format sure to please decorators, designers, architects, builders, and homeowners looking for new and exciting ideas.

Casa Mexicana Style
By Annie Kelly and Tim Street-Porter

Acclaimed architectural photographer Tim Street-Porter vividly captures this enduring passion for design in *Casa Mexicana Style*, the follow-up to his best-selling *Casa Mexicana* (more than 100,000 copies sold). In this gorgeous new book featuring more than 250 photographs, Street-Porter takes us on an insider's tour of 30 stunning homes, from urbane city apartments and modernist beach houses to stately rural haciendas and lovingly restored colonial townhouses.

Mexican Country Style

By Karen Witynski and Joe P. Carr

Now in paperback, *Mexican Country Style* is the classic that helped launch the popular Mexican design revival. Authors Karen Witynski and Joe P. Carr navigated coastal villages and old colonial mining towns by bus and burro, bumping down narrow cobblestone streets in search of simple and utilitarian elements like country tables, workbenches, storage trunks, corral gates, and heavy old doors. Intrigued by the diversity they encountered, the authors documented the wide variety in style, design, and shape of each object they encountered. Weathered coffee mortars, milking stools shaped like animals, and sculptured sugar molds reflect a rich local history as well as the ingenuity of the hands that crafted them. *Mexican Country Style* is the result of those fascinating journeys and boundless discoveries, a celebration of a rugged, romantic beauty and magical antiquity that continues to make its way into the contemporary interiors, gardens, and commercial settings across the country.

In A Mexican Garden: Courtyards, Pools, and Open-Air Living Rooms

By Gina Hyams and Melba Levick

The team behind the best-selling *Mexicolor* and *Mexicasa* has unlocked the gates to Mexico's patios, courtyards, and walled gardens. From private homes to luxurious resorts, *In A Mexican Garden* celebrates Mexico's hidden oasis where lovers meet for margaritas at sunset and families gather for spirited fiestas. The dazzling array of featured properties includes rustic coastal hideaways, elegant Spanish Colonial mansions, rural haciendas, and Modernist architectural masterpieces. Melba Levick's stunning photographs capture page after vibrant page of bold Mexican design elements: swirling mosaic floors, elaborate frescoes, hand-carved stone fountains, and lush native plants. Gina Hyams' informative text explains the historic roots of these uniquely Mexican outdoor spaces. Garden design enthusiasts, fans of Mexico, and anyone who appreciates a siesta in the sun need only open this book to hear the quiet babble of fountains and glasses clinking to toast another beautiful sunset.

Adobe Details

By Karen Witynski and Joe P. Carr

In their fourth book, authors/designers Karen Witynski and Joe Carr forage through the American Southwest and mountains of Mexico in search of the furnishings, accents and architectural elements that reveal its time-honored beauty and character.

The New Hacienda

By Karen Witynski and Joe P. Carr

The New Hacienda looks at the ways in which designers and architects have integrated the visual culture of the hacienda and blended Mexican elements in new homes on both sides of the border. From ancient stone walls and arcaded portals to cobbled courtyards and grand salons, hacienda style comes alive with a spirited mix of once-forgotten objects and contemporary furniture.

Mexicocina: The Spirit and Style of the Mexican Kitchen

By Betsy McNair and Melba Levick

In the tradition of the popular *Mexicolor*, photographer Melba Levick captures the bright colors and bold shapes of the kitchens of Mexico, this time touring private historic homes, resorts, and cooking schools. Here, priceless collections of indigenous pottery sit side-by-side with sleek appliances, Frida Kahlo's wooden spoons are right where she left them, and San Pasqual Bailón, the patron saint of cooks and kitchens, blesses every last handmade copper kettle, Talavera tile, and neon sign. *Mexicocina* tantalizes more than just the eyes, featuring mouthwatering recipes for innovative Mexican dishes at the end of each chapter, from appetizers to dessert. Inspiration abounds in these Mexican kitchens, whether the reader is redecorating, making travel reservations, or just dreaming of the scent of café de ollas.

Mexicolor: The Spirit of Mexican Design

By Tony Cohan, Masako Takahashi and Melba Levick

Basking in sunlight and coursing with energy, Mexico enjoys a unique relationship with color-inspired, intrinsic, inseparable from life itself. This vibrance sings forth in the pages of *Mexicolor*, the collaborative project of an artist, a photographer, and a writer all in love with the brilliant displays of color seen everywhere in Mexico. Walls washed flamingo pink on top, deep matte blue on the bottom. A green flatbed truck heaped with orange marigolds. A sea of colorful skeletons at a Day of the Dead fiesta. The radiant reds, yellows, purples, and greens of the fruits and vegetables at *el mercado*. *Mexicolor* explores Mexico high and low, from colonial towns to dazzling beaches, from traditional workshops to contemporary interiors, from open markets to extraordinary homes and inns, uncovering the colorful artistry that permeates everyday life across this vast nation. *Mexicolor* is an ideal resource for anyone looking to brighten a home, and a beautiful picture book brimming with imagination, creative ideas, and pure pleasure.

Casa San Miguel: Inspired Design and Decorations

By Annie Kelly, Tim Street-Porter and Jorge Almada

San Miguel de Allende, one of the prettiest destinations in Mexico, has become a fabulous source for stylish decorating ideas as many international designers are flocking to this artistic mecca. Acclaimed architectural photographer Tim Street-Porter and style writer Annie Kelly take us on an insider's tour, from stately rural haciendas and villas to renovated colonial townhouses. Featured are more than 250 glorious photographs of residences that show a blending of local crafts and handiwork with antiques and contemporary furnishings. Beautiful outdoor entertaining and garden areas enliven many of the houses. With a foreword by Jorge Almada of Casamidy, a design company based in San Miguel, *Casa San Miguel* is a unique inspirational design resource. It provides a vicarious look at daily life in this picturesque Mexican town that is attracting many international trendsetters.

Traditional Mexican Style Exteriors

By Donna McMenamin and Richard Loper

Beautiful, classic, and timeless architectural details of Mexican style are shown in over 300 color photographs of new, old, and remodeled traditional homes and gardens. From Spanish Colonial facades in San Miguel de Allende, Guanajuato, Mexico, to the best of the Mission and Spanish Eclectic homes, this volume is a must for everyone interested in Mexican architecture and outdoor charm. This book excites the readers imagination through nine chapters, including facades, doors, gates, portales & patios, columns, fountains, pools, cantera stonework, and gardens. Sparkling pools and spouting fountains bring tranquility to flower-filled gardens and courtyards. The pictures will inspire decorators, designers, architects, builders, and homeowners looking for traditional and exciting ideas.

Santa Barbara Style

By Kathryn Masson and James Chen

This book showcases Southern California's most historically significant and beautifully preserved Spanish-revival houses of this century. Twenty-one private homes built between 1922 and 1991 are featured in stunning color photography that captures exterior and interior architectural details, Spanish and Mexican antique furnishings and folk art, and lush landscaping and tiled fountains. Among these are the Adamson House in Malibu, with its extraordinary collection of custom tile from Malibu Potteries; the contemporary Greenberg House in Brentwood, by Ricardo Legorreta; The Andalusia Courtyard Apartments in Hollywood; and Casa

Pacifica. Brief narratives highlight the history of each building and its design influences on the Spanish-revival movement in California.

 ## Mexicasa: The Enchanting Inns and Haciendas of Mexico

By Gina Hyams and Melba Levick

Perched on a rugged coastline, set in verdant ranch land, or tucked away in a picturesque colonial town, the magnificent inns and haciendas of Mexico spring to life in the pages of *Mexicasa*. Historically and culturally important, these living museums contain wondrous collections of Mexican arts and crafts as well as enchanting gardens and courtyards. Acclaimed photographer Melba Levick captures the stunning architecture and colorful folk art that draws admirers from all over the world, while author Gina Hyams reveals the tradition and unique story behind each retreat. An extensive directory listing the contact information for each of the 21 featured inns makes this an indispensible resource book as well as a celebration of the spirit of Mexico.

Getting it done

By Vince Gricus

Now that you have settled on a house, or at least have whittled down the multitude of options to a few, it's time to think about what you want to do. The wonderful books featured in this section should inspire anyone, and the great thing about Mérida is that a good number of the architects whose work is featured in these books happen to live in town. There are also excellent contractors, some of whom have worked on restoration projects of the most important buildings in Mérida.

Construction Practices

Construction Managers in Mexico are responsible for all the employees who work for them. The client is responsible to pay the Construction Manager. The Construction Manager pays wages and taxes (health insurance, payroll deductions, etc.) that are applicable. Construction Managers are also expected to carry personal liability insurance. Construction Managers normally procure all the materials needed for the project and hire subcontractors who will do specialized work, such as pool design or solar panel installation.

As the Client, however, your responsibility is to make sure that the Construction Manager is complying with the law. This is rather easy to do by simply requesting to see, for instance, proof

276

of insurance, receipts for health insurance payment, and payroll signed by the employees. (Most employees in Mexico are paid in cash. They are required to sign receipt of their cash wages every time they are paid.) As the Client, you are entitled to the receipts for all the materials purchased and for copies of all the payroll sheets indicating that the workers were paid.

As is the case in the U.S., it is customary to follow the "30" percent rule—have a reserve of about 30% because unforeseen problems are bound to arise, causing original budgets to increase, and expect such delays to add about a third of the initial projected time. A $30,000 USD renovation that should take three months, might end up costing $40,000 USD and take four months. That's well within the norm, in Mexico as it is in the U.S.!

Where things are a bit different in Mexico than in the U.S. is one very important—and fortuitous aspect: architectural firms enlist a staff of contractors and designers who can marshal resources to complete the entire project. In the U.S., by contrast, an architect will design a building and that's that. The rest is up to the Client. In Mexico, the architect also has a contractor, or works with contractors, to make the design a reality. What's better is that the entire project is seen as an organic endeavor. This means that architects often work with a number of designers who can flesh out the vision in its entirety.

This is a blessing for expatriates, since working with an architect one has available an entire team of contractors and designers at his or her disposal. There have been many instances when, for instance, a specific dining room set was designed to match the vision for the kitche, and the wrought iron used throughout was then used to inspire bathroom fixtures and bedroom furniture. In other words, architects more than design: they carry out the project until completion.

A final caveat: If you are purchasing a historic building, the National Institute of Anthropology and History (INAH) has jurisdiction over what can and cannot be demolished. The integrity of the original design has to be respected, plans have to be submitted for approval to INAH, and permits have to be issued. If you think that a "gratuity" will solve any lingering questions about whether a room can be knocked down to build a luxurious bathroom, think again. Many a homeowner has been forced to restore rooms and walls that were modified in violation of approved plans. This is one reason so many architects recommend that Clients purchase houses with ample—and they mean ample—backyards. Why? If you must restore the original structure with little modifications, remember, there's no limit to the fantasy kitchen, extravagant bathrooms and luxurious bedrooms that can be added on from where the *back terrace opens onto the backyard.* Yes, there are master bedroom suites that open onto swimming pools.

Americans Scamming Americans

"In reflecting on our experience [building our dream home], we are chagrined to find that it wasn't the locals that misrepresented themselves or took advantage of us, as many *norteamericanos* might fear when undertaking a project like this. It was [David Sterling] a fellow expatriate. Do we think he did it on purpose? We hope not. Giving him the benefit of the doubt, we think he bit off more than he could chew and couldn't admit it," James and Ellen Fields.

Source: "Building Our House IV," in "Yucatán Living"

Recommended Architects

Here is a list, although it is not comprehensive, of professionals who continue to win praise from expatriates. The person ultimately responsible for looking out for your best interests is, of course, you. All these architects, however, have relationships with contractors and designers. Two additional contractors are listed, simply because they are the crème de la crème when it comes to expertise, skills and reputations in Mérida.

Architects

Salvador Reyes

The Reyes Rios + Larrain Studio of Architecture and Design.

Located in Mérida, Yucatán, Mexico, this firm was founded by Architect Salvador Reyes Rios and Josefina Larrain Lagos. Their award-winning work has established the standard for colonial remodeling and hacienda restoration in Mexico. Many of the former colonial mansions and haciendas in the state of Yucatán and elsewhere in Mexico have been converted to luxury hotels and private homes under their supervision.

Email: *info@reyesrioslarrain.com*
Website: *www.reyesrioslarrain.com*

Alvaro Ponce

Alvaro Ponce Arquitectos
An award-winning architect, Alvaro Ponce's work has been featured in *Casa Yucatán*, which is reason enough to consult him if you are engaged in major undertaking. His work on the haciendas in the area, as well as important *casonas*—mansions—in Mérida harks back to a time when excellence was demanded and expected.

278

Calle 45 #172, between Calle 38 and 40 Street
Colonia Benito Juárez Norte
Telephone: (999) 943-3075
Website: *www.aponce.com.mx*

Victor Cruz

ESTILO Arquitectura
Telephone: (999) 738-9089
Website: *www.estiloyucatan.com*

Arturo Campos

Campos Architects
Telephone: (999) 926-9080
Website: *www.camposarquitecto.com*

Mercedes Sánchez & Alvaro Cervera

Cervera & Sánchez Arquitectos
Telephone: (999) 958-0961
Website: *www.architectsinyucatan.com*

Rubén Portela Rodríguez

Ambientes Diseño Arquitectónico
Telephone: (999) 928-7488
Email: *ambientesda@prodigy.net.mx*

Miguel Rojanes

Miguel Rojanes Arquitectos
Telephone: (999) 101-0060
Website: *www.miguelrojano.com*
Email: *m_rojano@yahoo.com*

A + A Arquitectos

Fernando Ancona T. and Fernando Ancona G
A father-and-son architectural firm working with Alberto Rodríguez.
Calle 28 #98-A between Calle 15 and 17 Street
Colonia Itzimná
Telephone: (999) 902-0349 and (999) 927-2613
Website: *www.anconayancona.com*

279

Email: *contacto@anconayancona.com*

A Note on Two of these Architects: Salvador Reyes and Álvaro Ponce are the "superstars" of architects in Mérida.

Why?

The answer is simple: many of their projects end up being photographed and showcased in design books and architectural magazines. But there are other architects who work on more modest scale, and whose work is exceptional. Some of the works of the architects listed below have appeared in the pages of the most prestigious magazines, including *Architectural Digest*.

Contractors

José Luis Cáceres

The Cáceres family is synonymous with executing masterful renovations and restorations. Much of the work done at Palacio Cantón and the Teatro Peón Contreras was supervised by this family, which has been in Yucatán for generations. At present, apart from world-class contractors, the firm has arguably the best carpentry services in Mérida. Many of the woodwork projects in galleries and museums around town were done by this firm. The same applies for upscale resorts and hotels in Cancún, which are regular clients for custom work.

Construcción de la Penínsual, S.A. de C.V.
Calle 59 #572 by Calle 72
Centro
Cell Phone: (984) 113-2088
Facebook: *https://www.facebook.com/joseluis.caceresnovelo*
Email: *caceres@construcciondelapeninsula.com*

G. Fernando González

Fernando González spent years working in the United States, and is both fluent in English and he is with the expectations of American clients. His no-nonsense professionalism exudes confidence, and his authoritative familiarity with labor norms in Mérida proves exceptional. In recent years, Fernando González has become the "go to" resource for English-speaking expatriates who want a reputable, honest and conscientious firm for their projects.

Sistemas a Mano, S.A. de C.V.

Calle 15 #80, between Calle 23 and 25 Street
Dzitya, Yucatán
Telephone: (999) 176-2154 and (999) 101-0878
Email: *ggonz98294@aol.com*

Recommended Reference Books:

If you are engaged in a hands-on manner in the design, construction or rehabilitation of your property, it might a good thing to get a copy of either of these reference books:

Construction Spanish (en inglés y español), by A. P. Scott.

Over 1,000 words and terms both English/Spanish and Spanish/English make this book a real help on any construction project. The right term for the tools and equipment make a safer and more efficient jobsite. The book saves time and money and it will also help teach English or Spanish. Tools, equipment, safety, landscaping and more are covered in this pocket sized, 116 page book.

Constructionary, Second Edition: English-Spanish by the ICC

The International Code Council Constructionary is a handy, on-the-job English-Spanish, Spanish-English dictionary containing more than 1,000 construction terms, as well as pronunciations, useful phrases, and conversion tables. This resource will help you improve communications, creating a safer and more efficient job site. The International Code Council (Whittier, CA) is the organization that produces the International Building Code — the most widely adopted building code in the world. They offer unmatched technical, educational, and informational products and services, including code application assistance, educational and certification programs, plan reviews, monthly magazines and newsletters, and training and informational videos. They have more than 16 locations throughout the U.S. and Latin America.

Water Treatment Solutions

In recent years more ambitious projects have been undertaken by expats. Some of these projects require state-of-the-art water treatment and water solutions. Watch Water, a German company with offices in Mérida, is up to the task of these projects:

Zero Sarro/Watch Water

Martin Nizet
Sales Manager
Calle 27 #101, between Calle 20 and 22 Street
Colonia Loma Bonita Xcumpich

Mérida, Yucatán
Telephone: (999) 920-1972
Cell phone: (999) 192-5385
Email: *martin.nizet@watchwater.mx*
Website: *www.watchwater.mx*

14   FURNITURE, FURNISHINGS & ANTIQUES

Furniture

If you are making the move to Mérida, many people take advantage of the one-time opportunity to ship your household goods from abroad into Mexico. This provision in the law is designed to let people bring their furniture, kitchen wares, household items, art, books, and whatever one normally finds in a home without having to pay taxes. There are, of course, shipping fees, but that depends on the shipping line or moving company, and there are fees that are charged by the Customs Brokers who take care of all the paperwork.

Of course, there are restrictions: whatever you find in a pantry or a medicine cabinet is not allowed. (What's the point in bringing a half-used bottle of ketchup, or an open tube of toothpaste?) And the items have to be used—if you want to import six ceiling fans in their unopened boxes that you got for a bargain off the Internet, you're going to have to pay a duty on that, since the fans, obviously, weren't in use in the home you're vacating.

Some people want a fresh start, and sell their furniture before moving to Mexico. Others find that their furniture, at some point, will need to be replaced. That old sofa from the 1980s? The dining room set that really doesn't fit in with your Mérida home? Those bookcases that you forgot to treat for termites and are falling apart?

You get the idea. Chances are you will be buying furniture at some point. If you want to find a few antiques, that subject is discussed later in this chapter. Bear in mind that the best Mexican antiques are in Mexico City and Guadalajara, and that Mérida is better known for having antiques from Spain, France and Italy, although most of these remain in private homes, and seldom come on the market.

Two things to consider as you choose furniture for your Mérida home. First of all, make sure that the wood is treated for termites and think about choosing light colors. Yes, there is tremendous beauty in the dark, rich mahogany, but as a matter of maintenance, it's important to be able to spot evidence of termites, or other bugs, and there are a lot of critters in the Yucatán!

Second, be mindful of the balmy evening air—as charming as it is, the breezes carry mold, which grows on leather, especially in rooms where the air doesn't circulate. Leather furniture needs to be cleaned regularly. Always follow the manufacturer's instructions. As a general rule, most leather furniture can be cleaned with lukewarm water and a very mild soap. (Never use alcohol, cleaning solvents, oils, varnishes or polishes on leather. Always avoid extreme temperatures. For more information, see *www.ehow.com/how_2086289_care-leather-furniture.html*.) If you will be leaving for more than a couple of weeks, you will have to cover all your leather furniture with cotton sheets.

The following furniture stores are listed in alphabetical order, not in any preference. It is recommended that you visit a variety of stores to comparison shop, and to get a better understanding of the options around town. Following are a listing of furniture stores.

Furniture Stores

Actual Decoración

Prolongicación Montejo, corner of Calle 25, Colonia Mexico
Telephone: (999) 289-7888
www.actualdecoracion.com

This is an upscale, contemporary furniture store with three locations. Two are in Cancún and one is in Mérida. Providing a line of full services—from consultation to designing custom-made pieces for your home, this is a team of young of professionals that offers a wide variety of cutting edge products, services in decoration, and design. More inclined to serve a "clientele from the North" of Mérida, their purpose is to redefine a style of tropical life, which satisfies the expectations of quality and uniqueness of our customers, backed by a great network of brands and contacts, always seeking to create value for customers, society and environment. Some of the more well-appointed homes in the Yucatán Country Club have been furnished by Actual Decoración.

Casa Italia

Prolongacion Montejo #99, between Calle 19 and 21 Street
Telephone: (999) 948-0551

This store primarily sells from a catalog, since the furniture takes about three months to deliver. It has to first be made in Italy, then shipped to Progreso, and then trucked to you. It operates much the same way that Luminare, in Coral Gables, Florida and Chicago, Illinois sells high-end Italian design furnishings (*www.luminaire.com*). But there are a few pieces on hand, which is a great way to appreciate the design, quality and workmanship of the pieces. If you are wondering where all those mansions being built in the Yucatán Country Club are going to get their exquisite furniture, well, now you know.

Colomer

Calle 20 #99, between Calle 19 and 21 Street, Colonia Itzimná
Telephone: (999) 926-9977
www.colomermuebles.com

This is another company that specializes in furniture for institutions—hotels, resorts, government offices—and does a great job of it. Its residential line is very much in keeping with contemporary Mexican aesthetics and the needs of the modern family. Their dining room sets are very comfortable, and make great use of combining woods, fabrics that complement the paste tiles of Mérida. They also excel at bookcases and cabinets, almost like a high-end version of Restoration Hardware in the U.S. Best yet? Yes, they can reproduce whatever piece of furniture you saw in a magazine and ripped out the page!

D'Europe Muebles

Calle 60 #370, between Calle 39 and 37 Street, Centro
Telephone: (999) 925-3086
www.deurope.com.mx

The furniture store for the Europhile! Fast approaching the half-century mark, this furniture store (founded in Mexico City and with locations in Puebla, Hidaldo, Morelos and Mexico State as well as Yucatán), offers a vast selection of contemporary European design. They operate two locations (the other is on Calle 21 #321, adjacent to Plaza de las Américas), and their staff is knowledgable about finding pieces that fit your own individual aesthetics. With prices in the mid-range of what is available in town, this is a terrific resource, especially for dining room and bedroom sets. They have built a reputation for customer service, and when they have a sale, some sets are reduced as much as half off.

Gringo Furniture

Calle 20 #99, between Calle 19 and 21 Street, Colonia Itzimná
Telephone: (999) 926-9977
www.gringofurniture.com

285

What do you get when enterprising Americans set up shop to cater to the Mexican fantasies of other Americans? Gringo Furniture. And that's a good thing. It takes special skill to be able to channel the aesthetics of the Founding Fathers, Mexican colonial aesthetics, Frank Lloyd Wright and a certain neo-Colonialism, but it works. While one can question the political sensibilities of a "Plantation Dining Set," there are no arguments to be made with a "Safari Sectional with Wood Arm Rests." No one gets it 100% right all the time, but Gringo Furniture has some homeruns with their Rattan, Designer and Rustic Contemporary series.

Luna del Oriente (antique Asian imports)

Calle 65 #541-A, between Calle 66 and 68 Street
Telephone: (999) 247-2953
www.lunadeloriente.com

This store, run by an American husband-and-wife team, carries the best Chinese and Indian antiques and architectural elements anywhere outside Mexico City! Really, they do. The taste, selection and aesthetics are exquisite, and it is one of the few shops in Mexico that carry Mongolian furniture, and Chinese antiques from the Gansu region. If Asian furnishings capture your imagination, and didn't bring some with you, an appointment to this store will give you a vast selection of extraordinary pieces from which to choose.

Marbol

Factory Showroom: Umán Town
Telephone: (999) 948-3048
www.marbol.com.mx

Marbol specializes in a resort aesthetic. If you see any of those alluring brochures for the fancy hotels and resorts from Cancún to Playa del Carmen which boast furniture that is slightly colonial in nature and definitely laid-back resort in feel, then you already know the spirit of their offerings. It is certainly a favorite among Mexicans living in Mérida who hail from the Valley of Mexico and futher north (think of the triangle formed by Monterrey, Guadalajara, and Mexico City). Their principal clients are resorts, and that means you are sure to find tasteful designs in dark wood and fine rattan.

Mérida Tradicional

Paseo de Montejo #498, by Calle 47
Telephone: (999) 923-8560
www.meridatradicional.com

Email: contacto@meridatradicional.com

Mérida Tradicional offers traditional Mexican design that reflects a traditional Mexican highland style. What does this mean? This means that the designers favor a more traditional, colonial approach to furnishings. It's easy to see how their time in San Miguel de Allende shaped their design philosophy and outlook. Their focus is traditional furniture in wood and iron with a great selection of patio and garden furnishings. They also provide furniture design and cabinetry services. Their aesthetics are geared for mature, old school tastes, which mean that this is not the place for "modern" or "contemporary" design. For Mérida Tradicional, think of British Colonial furniture from the Caribbean—very Ralph Lauren in their approach to furnishing homes in the lush tropical environment of the Yucatán peninsula.

MID Muebles

Calle 18 #66 between Calle 5 and 7 Street, Colonia San Antonio Cinta
Telephone: (999) 286-4477
www.midmuebles.com

A bit off the beaten path, this is one of the most innovative furniture stores around. They offer contemporary and sleek designs, excellent craftsmanship, and exceptional value. Aimed at Mérida's middle class families, the prices are quite something—and because they are also manufacturers, they can custom built to your specifications. They have an extensive selection for all rooms in their online catalog. One of the wonderful services they offer is re-upholstery, which can save you a significant amount, especially for pieces that have sentimental value and just need to be refreshened up. And if you have a home office, they offer one of the most extensive selections of furniture for home offices anywhere on the peninsula.

Nasström

Calle 31 #104, between Calle 20 and 24 Street, Colonia Mexico
Telephone: (999) 927-2354
www.nasstrom.com.mx

This company is a manufacturer for Ikea. As a result, you have a line of Scandanavian-inspired furniture that is manufactured just south of the airport in the town of Uman. Who would have thought? But there it is! You can select from an overwhelming selection of styles and fabrics, and it will be made-to-order in Uman. The prices are reasonable (think of the higher end items at an Ikea store). When they have their sales, you can get sofas and club-style chairs at an exceptional value. The staff is bilingual and although they don't offer designer services. They are quite knowledgeable about appointing colonial homes that have been recently remodeled.

Paladium

Calle 30 #76-B between Calle 11 and 13 Street, Prolongación Montejo
Telephone: (999) 944-9782

This is a one-stop furniture and furnishings store. It carries living room sets, dining room sets, bedroom sets, and every imaginable accessory, from side tables to lamps. The designs are contemporary, with slick lines and lots of glass. There is a small design staff on hand that can assist in designing a room or selecting individual pieces to complement what you have. The staff is pleasant and helpful. It merits a visit to see what's out there on the market.

Triunfo

Paseo de Montejo at Calle 39

What can be said about this place? It's a madhouse. This is a Mexican company that buys containers full merchandise that has been seized by Mexican Customs, auctioned off by U.S. Customs and sold, often as discontinued merchandise, primarily by Indian and Chinese companies. It is a bazaar of the bizarre. It's certainly worth a look, especially if you are in the market for utilitarian tableware, eclectic outdoor, and garden furniture. It's great if you want to have some items in your home that are camp or kitsch, or a bit of both. The only thing that's missing is popcorn, since this place is such a carnival.

Sol y Sombra

Calle 55 #464, Centro
Telephone: (999) 923-2797
Website: *www.solysombra.mx*
Facebook: *https://www.facebook.com/SolYSombraEcotropicalFurniture*

One has to admit that Cuau Solis is a great designer. Having left a legal career, he has embarked on creating the most sublime line of furniture that speak both to the Mid-Century lines but also to today's lifestyle. His home furnishing lines, including his reimainged Adirondack chair, are real finds. Customs designs are his speciality. This is really one place you have to check out.

Yucatán Custom Furniture

Telephone: (999) 286-3427

www.yucatancustomfurniture.com

The husband-and-wife team (she is Yucatecan and he is Canadian) behind Yucatán Custom Furniture strive to provide a one-stop online resource, with one exception: they offer the ability to customize woods, colors and tones, finishes at various price ranges. Their collections reflect both the physical requirements of the Yucatecan climate with the aesthetics of the local architecture. Their line of platform beds, modern canopy bed frames, and colonial bed frames continue to win lavish praise, as does their customer service.

An Alternative to Furniture Stores: Mom-and-Pop Shops

Along Calle 67, between Calle 58 and 64 Street

Many of the furniture stores found along this street have "Rustic" lines, meaning furniture that resembles very utilitarian pieces found in many Mexican homes. That's great, and there's something to be said for having a few pieces of "authentic" Mexican furniture, and along Calle 67 you will see a good number of stores selling dressers, beds, cabinets, shelves, and wardrobes that are found in many homes of working and middle class Yucatecans. These are terrific values, and with sandpaper you can distress the paint, or select several shades of stain. Not only will you have a unique piece, but it certainly will have the cachet of authenticity—at bargain prices.

Caoba/Tropical Mahogany Furnishings

In recent decades tropical mahogany furniture (caoba) that is made from sustainable forests from Campeche has been in much demand. One of the most successful manufacturers and distributors is based in Spain. **Rustic Ross** has developed several lines that are so favored by Europeans—whose aesthetics differ strikingly from those of Americans and Canadians—that various models of furniture (Queen Anne cabinets, Holland display case, Ortega cabinets, Jonker wine racks) are now made in Mexico for export to Europe and South America. For more information, just contact them at: *Ross_Systems@terra.es*

Mexican Antiques

No matter what your style, it's always wonderful to have a few old pieces in your home. Let's face it, you're getting better every day, and there's something about a piece of furniture, architectural piece or artwork that's been around for a while and, like you, has been getting better every day. Even if you live in a house inspired by the modern minimalism of Philippe Starck, it's always a good idea to have one vintage or antique object to provide a focal point to a room in a way that reflects your personality.

In the section above on furniture we noted the wonderful shops, Luna del Oriente. This foreign-owned company, however, specializes in objects from India, the Subcontinent and Far East. In this section, we provide a list of local companies that offer antiques from Mexico, the United States and Europe. This means that now is a great time to look through those design books we recommended and to get inspired!

But first, of course, a digression to explain the unique character of the antiques found in Mérida. The Yucatán's historic isolation from the rest of Mexico is a constant theme that has shaped the peninsula's culture, society and tastes. When it comes to antiques, Yucatecans usually brought furniture from Havana and from Europe. During the height of the henequen wealth a century ago, Yucatecans imported the finest antiques from Europe, the United States and central Mexico. To give you an idea of the sheer variety that was prevalent one, consider the following anectdotes.

It's a little known fact that many of the antiques found at the Napoleonic Museum in Havana, Cuba have a Mérida connection. Housing one of the most important collections in the world of Napoleonic and French Revolutionary memorabilia outside France, this museum is located in a mansion named the *Dolce Dimora*, a structure designed in the style of a Florentine Renaissance villa. It was built by the Italian-Cuban politician Orestes Ferrara in 1928. The current museum opened in 1961 and it features thousands of items from the personal collections of Cuban tycoon Julio Lobo, who had shipped several important pieces to Mérida, as they made their way to Cuba. Bought over a period of almost two decades at auctions and from antiques dealers around the globe, Lobo had a number of representatives and buyers search the world for pieces connected to Napoleon. The collection on exhibit—Lobo fled the Cuban Revolution—includes paintings, engravings, and a library with over 5,000 books, hand-written notes, glassware, porcelains, and weapons. One of the most riveting pieces is the Emperor's death mask. Francesco Antommarchi, Napoleon's personal physician, made it in order to have the sculptor Antonio Canovas cast several copies in bronze. Other notable pieces include Napoleon's pistol used at the Battle of Borodino and the spyglasses he used while in exile at St. Helena. This, of course, is an extraordinary story, and the Mérida connection is both superfluous to this great collection, but intriguing nevertheless.

The point is that in the same way that wonderful antiques have landed in Mérida and been sent elsewhere, the reverse has happened. Important collections of Cuban antiques were surreptitiously shipped to Mérida in the 1960s. The Pantaleon family sent what would be a container of furnishings in the early days of the Cuban Revolution for safekeeping in Mérida.

Similarly, important pieces of American memorabilia from the Civil War have found their way to Mérida. Several carte-de-visite photographs of General Robert E. Lee are in Mérida, which range in price from $12,000 to $17,000 USD! American collectors over the years have acquired several Audubon drawings—which today fetch astronomical prices. A cachet of letters from Louis C. Tiffany caused quite a stir a decade or so ago when they were found in an old trunk of an established family.

Mérida's own history is also found in antique shops. When the legendary Hotel Itzá, on the intersection of 59 and 58 Streets, closed downtown, the Arts & Crafts furniture in the lobby was sold at a bargain price. If you venture to Centro del Paseo, on Paseo de Montejo and Avenida Pérez Ponce, enter from the main entrance of the original house. Where the utilitarian (read: ugly) stairs go to the second floor, there used to be a magnificent stained glass window depicting a pastoral scene in an hacienda. When the building was remodeled, the glass was carefully removed, and stacked, and then removed by the original owners. That stained glass window was designed by Tiffany in New York!

Treasures are everywhere. Indeed, the most important pieces today remain with local families, or have been bought and sold among Yucatecans directly. Only after the economic crisis of 1982 and then the peso devaluation of 1994 have some families sold objects through "antique shops" in town. Those with significant holdings prefer to deal with Mexico City dealers, and Mexicans moving to Mérida often prefer to deal with reputable dealers with whom they are familiar—in Mexico City or Guadalajara or wherever they came from. One rare exception are the contemporary Virgin of Guadalupe images of Enrique Salazar which remain in great demand, particularly since John F. Kennedy, Jr. had one in the loft in Tribeca he shared with his wife, Carolyn Bissette. If you see them in a gallery around town, buy one—and hoard it!

What does this history mean? Well, it means that while Mérida is awash in antiques and antiquities, there are few dealers who have generations-old traditions of being in the antique business. This doesn't mean that you can't find hidden treasures, but it means that you have to be diligent about it. And if you have not been able to befriend Yucatecan families of a certain level, chances are that the best bet is to avail yourself to one of the shops listed alphabeticlly below, which just might help you find something extraordinary.

Antique shops

Antiguedades Jorge

Calle 21, Local 4-Bis, between Calle 38 and 38-A Street,
Colonia San Pedro Uxmal Chuburná
Mérida, Yucatán
Cell Telephone: (999) 163-6596

Jorge Vázquez, who speaks a little English, owns this delightful business. The "shop" is actually two adjacent warehouses packed with all manner of stuff located behind his home. He spends most of the morning running errands and seeing clients. If you want to catch him, the best bet is to show up at Santa Lucía Park downtown on Sundays, where there is an open-air flea market. The varied selection of objects he offers gives you a glimpse into what he specializes in: old photographs; lots of various kinds of bottles and glasses; 19th and early 20th century cast irons; religious objects and artifacts; ceramic tiles; and personal objects from lives long past. If anything catches your eye, do make an appointment to visit him, and there you will see the furnishings where these objects were kept: tables, drawers, wardrobes, dressers, with chairs and tables and fancier table settings and mirrors. It's a place to find something special and unique that speaks to you, and will bring Yucatecan history into your home.

Candiles & Decoración

Calle 59 #530, between Calle 64 and 66 Street
Mérida, Yucatán
Telephone: (999) 928-6321
Website: *www.candilesydecoracion.com*

Mario Cáceres, who is bilingual, is the manager of this family-owned business. It is, technically, a chandelier and lighting fixture company, but they are antiquarians and they carry an extensive selection of antiques. The company was founded by Mario Cáceres Bernés, and he was one of the leading voices in Mérida for reclaiming the historic center. In the 1970s, the Peón Contreras Theater on the corner of Calle 60 and 57 Street was in such a state of disrepair that authorities feared it was on the verge of collapsing. It was only after the government bought it that repairs began, and it was Mario Cáceres Bernés who spearheaded the interior restoration. That grand chandelier in the theater, you ask? Yes, it was restored by Candiles & Decoracion, and so have the chandeliers in scores of homes along Paseo de Montejo, Avenida Colón and Calle 59. In Yucatecan society, the Cáceres are the go-to family for restoration work, and they are also the go-to family for specific, hard-to-find colonial furniture and furnishings. An advantage that Mario

Cáceres has is that, by virtue of being part of Mérida's social scene, he is familiar with the families, family histories and family holdings behind many of the mansions in town. Chances are that if you are interested in, say, a portrait of a pope painted in the 17th century, they know who has such an object. Interested in some religious artifacts from a cathedral in Havana that somehow made its way to Mérida? They probably can direct you in the right direction. At present, they are remodeling their location to include a showroom with antiques, but this is one resource that can answer your questions, and work with you to find what you are looking for. And when you need your antique Swarovski crystal chandelier cleaned, this is the place up to the task.

El Bazar

Calle 19 #201-D, between Calle 22 and 24 Street, Colonia García Ginerés
Mérida, Yucatán
Cell Telephone: (999) 157-6636

Roberto Guzmán, who is bilingual, is the proprietor of this shop. A physician by profession—he grew tired of seeing sick people all day, he says. So he changed professions. It seems like every foreigner meanders through this shop, and often times, Guzmán will be sitting, smoking a cigarette and sipping a soft drink in the company of another Yucatecan. (Yes, doctors smoke.) The folks he entertains are usually the owners of the objects for sale. Most of the inventory is on consignment from Yucatecan families who want to discreetly liquidate a few items. Sometimes you will find an exceptional piece at a terrific value, and at other times it's obvious that now that both dear great-grandmothers have passed away, it is no longer necessary to have so many wardrobes or dining room tables, especially since most homes now have closets, and everyone is either eating in the kitchen, or the family room. There are also several tables overflowing with the detritus of privileged lives: souvenirs from trips to Tokyo, ashtrays from France, knick-knacks from Africa, tschostskes from Disney World, Niagra Falls and a charming souvenir Statue of Liberty from the 1950s. Guzmán is often authorized to offer a discount, so if you see something you like for $2,000 pesos but think it's worth $1,600 pesos, make an offer. He might be authorized to grant it, or will call the owner and get back to you.

Julio Alfaro

Calle 75, at the intersection of 72 Street, Centro
Mérida, Yucatán
Cell Telephone: (999) 151-9030

Julio Alfaro, who is not very familiar with English, has quite a set-up. The actual building is jam-packed with all kinds of furniture—mostly dining rooms, bedroom furnishings and hallway closets and stands. There are a good number of mirrors. The outside terrace and yard, on the other hand, are different creatures. Doors and chairs in all states of repair and disrepair are stacked on top of each other, or leaning against the wall. The yard is strewn with all manner of carved stones, fountains, wrought iron doors, distressed doors, mechanical engines. It is a mess! And tucked in the northwest corner of the compound, well, there's a workshop where restoration takes place. When it comes to a vast selection of objects that are truly authentic in their history, this is the place! It's easy to envision seeing several doors being refurbished and be transformed into glass-topped tables, and there is a great selection of carved stones or artifacts that will enhance any garden. Alfaro is hard to reach at times, and it's unfortunate that his kids mind the shop when he's not there. They are not very helpful: they are more engaged watching television or playing games on their cell phones than they are in answering questions, or even know the asking price on anything. You might as well drop by, and if anything catches your eye, then call to see when you can see Alfaro directly.

Decorative Motifs

There will come a time when you realize you might need a decorative object here or there, or need to find something for a friend—a fellow expat, another foreigner, a Yucatecan or a Mexican—as a housewarming gift.

These are stores that offer a wide selection of decorative objects for the indoors and Babu Xixim, which has an excellent line of bamboo products.

Bambu Xixim

Pen Xixim Km. 4, 190 Carretera Muna Opichen
Muna, Yucatán
Telephone: (999) 971-0245
http://www.yucatanbamboo.com/

AJ Arte Objeto

Calle 30, Plaza 333 Local 1, San Ramón Norte
Mérida, Yucatán
Telephone: (999) 948-4563

Arte di Firenze

Calle 26 #115-A, between Calle 13 and 15 Street, Colonia San Antonio Cinta
Mérida, Yucatán
Cell Telephone: (999) 129-5114

Decoración Inn

Calle 7 #186-A, Colonia García Ginerés
Mérida, Yucatán
Telephone: (999) 925-0302
https://www.facebook.com/DecoracionInn

Inex

Calle 10 #321, between Calle 27 and 29 Street, Colonia San Esteban
Mérida, Yucatán
Cell Telephone: (999) 183-5052

RC Arte & Decoración

Calle 42 #365, Colonia Monte Albán
Mérida, Yucatán
Telephone: (999) 988-4777

Trailer Park Kitsch: El Estudio

If "Triunfo" is a triumph of bad taste, it's also appropriate to point out that El Estudio a short stroll away is the best place for kitsch in Mérida. True, Mérida doesn't have a trailer park, but if it did, here's the place to furbish a white trash residence. So awful, it's a fun place to visit.

El Estudio
Paseo de Montejo #486 between Calle 41 and 43 Street
Mérida, Yucatán
Telephone: (999) 239-0401

Mosaícos La Peninsular

Nothing makes a statement as much as paste tiles. Whether it is an entire room, or a few select pieces to highlight colors, designs, and light ceramics are a must in Mérida. Mosaícos La Peninsular manufactures paste tiles and they can reproduce any design. There are scores of traditional designs from which to choose—and they will produce an exclusive line for you as well.

Mosaícos La Peninsular
Calle 62 #619, between Calle 81 and 85 Street
Colonia Centro
Mérida, Yucatán
Telephone: (999) 923-1196

295

Email: *ventas@mosaicoslapeninsular.com*
Website: *www.mosaicoslapeninsular.com*

A Warning on Pre-Columbian Artifacts

You may have noticed that in discussing "antiques" we have stayed away from mentioning "antiquities."

There's a reason for that and here is a very important note: **All pre-Columbian art and antiquities belong to the Mexican State.** If you have any pre-Columbian art, it must be registered with the National Institute of Anthropology and History (Insituto Nacional de Antropología e Historia, or INAH). Buying and selling pre-Columbian art without a license is a **federal offense.** Be aware that many Yucatecan families own stunning pre-Columbian ceramics, engravings and sculptures that have been inherited over several generations, which should have been registered with officials.

Furthermore, U.S. federal law makes it a crime to import or export Mexican pre-Columbian artifacts without a license from INAH. **Go for reproductions instead!**

15 Handicrafts, Artists, Bookstores & Foreign-Language Libraries

Handicrafts

Visitors and new residents alike often express disappointment in the lack of handicrafts in Yucatán. This is a valid complaint and there is a reason. Historically, the traditional crafts of the Maya people in Yucatán have centered on red and black coral, and tortoise shell. Since the 1970s, consistent with concern for protecting our planet, strict laws have transformed contemporary practices. Coral reefs are protected habitats and marine sea turtles are endangered species under federal protection. Coral and tortoise shell handicrafts are illegal, and it takes generations for new traditions to emerge.

Nevertheless, there are other products that are in abundance: honey, chocolate, anise liqueur, henequen (sisal) goods, silver (filigree) jewelry, men's *guayabera* shirts and women's embroidered sun dresses *(huipiles)*, and fine Panama hats *(jipis)*.

But that doesn't mean that there are not wonderful handicrafts from *other* regions of Mexico!

Whether you are visiting or establishing a residence in Mérida, one of the pleasures is acquiring Mexican handicrafts. Nelson Rockefeller and Frida Kahlo are largely credited with bringing to the world's attention the vitality, integrity, and beauty of Mexican handicrafts.

And good news! Mérida has three authorities with breathtaking knowledge, refined tastes and sweeping resources that can help you appreciate—and acquire—handicrafts that are museum quality. The Mexican government recognizes that the artisanal arts are part of the world's cultural heritage, and it nurtures its development. Through the Fondo Nacional para el Fomento de las Artesanías, or National Fund for the Development of Arts and Crafts, and every ethnic group is represented in its program.

297

Why is this important? Because in Mérida there is only one place where you can find handicrafts from each of Mexico's 32 states and the Federal District. It's 100% Mexico, located in the lobby of the Casa San Angel Hotel, where Paseo de Montejo begins. Its proprietor is Homa Abhari, a Persian immigrant to Mexico, who is a true connoisseur with refined taste and she can guide you. For instance, the great Sonoran desert is home to many Native Americans on both sides of the U.S.-Mexico border, and some of the pottery from Chihuahua is as exquisite as the finest Hopi pottery found in the U.S. Homa Abhari is one of Mérida's living treasures, a resource where visiting dignitaries and celebrities shop. Her shop also has an extensive selection of silk scarves, blouses, and purses from Pineda Covalin, one of Mexico's leading designers.

There are two other connoisseurs in town. These are Francois Valcke, from Belgium and his partner Gerardo Martínez, from Venezuela. They own Tataya Gallery. After decades on the Continent and London, they settled in Mérida, where they showcase exquisite handicrafts that they source from around the country. Each year they close shop and embark on pilgrimages of discovery, often tracking down the very artisans that contributed to the famed Nelson Rockefeller Collection of Mexican arts and crafts. Their Gallery—with two locations, one in Santiago downtown, and the other on Calle 60 across the street from Santa Ana church—reflects their connoisseurship of pottery from Oaxaca, Chiapas and Puebla, along with sculpture. Tataya Gallery also represents established Cuban artists, which are coveted primarily by European collectors, and long-established Mérida families.

Whether you want to spend $25 USD or $2,500 USD, between Homa Abhari, Francois Valcke and Gerardo Martínez you are sure to find something exceptional.

100% Mexico
Homa Abhari
Paseo de Montejo #1, Remate
Centro
Mérida, Yucatán
Telephone: (999) 928-1800
Hours: Monday—Saturday 10 AM to 1 PM and 4 PM to 7 PM; Closed Sundays

Galeria Tataya (Santiago)
Gerardo Martínez
Calle 72 #478, between 53 and 55 Streets
Centro
Mérida, Yucatán
Telephone: (999) 928-2962

This location is By Appointment Only.

Galería Tataya (Santa Ana)

Francois Valcke
Calle 60 #409, between 45 and 47 Streets
Colonia Santa Ana
Mérida, Yucatán
Telephone: (999) 287-0685
Hours: Monday—Friday: 10 AM—2 PM and 5 PM—8 PM; Saturday: 10 AM to 2 PM.
Closed Sunday

Casa de las Artesanías

Yucatán State government operates Casa de las Artesanías, a handicraft and artisan market that provides the infrastructure to Maya craftsmen and craftswomen to practice their arts. It's an extraordinary effort, one that is paralleled by all other state governments throughout Mexico. There are four stores where one can purchase local crafts are remarkable prices. Although the skill and taste level reflects the entire panorama of crafts traditions, there is something for everyone to enjoy and want to bring home.

The website, run by Yucatán State government, is: http://www.artesanias.yucatan.gob.mx/

Flagship Shop (Monjas)
Address: Calle 63 between Calle 64 and 66 Street, Centro
Hours:
    Monday-Saturday: 9:30 AM to 10 PM
    Sunday: 10 AM to 5 PM
Telephone: 01 (999) 928-6676

Airport Shop
Address: Airport, Second Level Departure Gates
Hours:
    Monday-Sunday: 6:30 AM to 7 PM
Telephone: 01 (999) 946-3294

Paseo de Montejo Shop
Address: Paseo de Montejo, between Calle 41 and 43 Street
Hours:
    Monday-Saturday: 9:30 AM to 10 PM
    Sunday: 10 AM to 5 PM

Telephone: 01 (999) 924-2890

Shop at Uxmal (Ruins)
Address: Parador Turístico at Uxmal
Hours:
    Monday-Saturday: 9 AM to 8:30 PM
    Sunday: 9 AM to 5 PM
Telephone: 01 (999) 976-2100

Artists

In addition, there are a few living artists who are in town whose work is exceptional, both as fine artists and outsider artists. If you have the chance to purchase something from any of these artists, by all means do so. One, Karen Clarke, spends considerable time in Mérida and has a studio here, but she is represented by Mercury Gallery in Boston. The others are gracious and can accommodate your request to see their work—Ariel Guzmán, whose work is often on view at the MACAY, and Marcela Díaz, whose beautiful henequen sculptures are in the lobby of Rosas & Xocolate. Katrin Schikora has a wonderful studio in Cholul, and Enrique Salazar, whose work became highly sought after when John F. Kennedy, Jr. purchased one of his "Virgin of Guadalupe" paintings for his loft in Tribeca, has a studio in town. No sophisticated residence in the Yucatán is complete without the work of these artists!

Karen Clarke

Website: *http://www.mercurygallery.com/*

Marcela Díaz

Email: *marceladiazmdeoca@hotmail.com*

Ariel Guzmán

Email: *arielguzman@cablered.net.mx*

Enrique Salazar

Website: *www.casa-catherwood.com/salazar*

Katrin Schikora

Website: *www.takto.mx*

Outsider Artists

There are also a number of talented Outsider Artists in town whose work you might consider for your home.

Juan Pablo Bavio

Website: *www.juanpablobavio.com*

Mark Callaghan

Email: *markca@prodigy.net.mx*

Bárbara Lobatón

Email: *artelobaton@gmail.com*

José Pool

Email: *mashkaayd@hotmail.com*

Emerging Artists

The State's cultural institute maintains a listing of Mérida-based artists whose works might be of interest. A directory can be found at:

Website: *http://artesvisualesyucatan.com.mx/ListaArtistas.htm*

Art Scene

Over the past two years Mérida's profile on the international scene has enjoyed a tremendous revival. Mérida's artists have participated in international events, have mounted impressive shows overseas, and have received important commissions. A glimpse into the work of these talented artists is seen in the work of two artists: José Luis Loria and Ramón González.

If you have any interest in the contemporary art scene, here are two wonderful resources.

José Luis Loria

Long renowned as an illustrator of nature in the best tradition of John James Audubon, his work has been showcased around the world, from Mérida's MACAY to the Americas Society in Washington, D.C. At present José Luis Loria received a commission from China for a series of monumental illustrations of cats. This project has received such acclaim that he has received private commissions from individuals who also want to immortalize their feline companions through portraiture. To contact him, use the email provided below.

Email: *canaris_jll@hotmail.com*

Ramón González

Ramón González's energy know no bound and his blogspot showcases a stunning array of the activity and work of emerging young men and women artists in Mérida. A visit to his blogspot quickly becomes hours-long since there is such a treasure trove of art, artists, and interviews with the members of this creative community.

Website: *http://ex-grafica.blogspot.com/*

Books

Yes, there are two great places to buy English-language books. One is Amate Books and the other is Casa Catherwood. Amate Books, which is based in Oaxaca City, is the brain child of Henry and Rosa Wangeman. They are a splendid couple who have long championed books and artisans. That means that Amate Books not only has an extensive collection of books, but also handicrafts and weavings from Oaxaca. The other, much smaller and specialized, book store is Casa Catherwood. Originally started by Rosa Raquel Romero in 1991, it is now housed on the first level of a restored manse, which also houses a collection of lithographs drawn by Frederick Catherwood when he accompanied John Lloyd Stephens in the first half of the 19th century. What makes this book store exceptional is that it will bring down any book or DVD you purchase on Amazon.com in the U.S. for a small fee. This is quite a service, since shipping books and DVDs from the U.S. to Mexico remains an expensive proposition. The shop also has a lovely collection of handicrafts created by women's cooperatives from Mexico, Tanzania (formerly known as Zanzibar), Cambodia, Thailand and Kenya, reflecting Mrs. Romero's commitment to helping women in the developing world—and the countries she adored.

Casa Catherwood

Alberto Huchim
Calle 59 #572, between 70 and 72 Streets
Centro
Telephone: (999) 154-5565
Email: *info@casa-catherwood.com*
Website: *www.casa-catherwood.com*

Amazon.com shipping service information:
http://casa-catherwood.com/amazoncom.html

Must Have Books on the Yucatán

Anyone who makes a home in Mérida needs to have a few books about this magnificent place. There are two kinds of books: the "must have" books, and the "recommended" books. The Must-Have books are the books that define this place and they are

Incidents of Travel in Yucatán. 2 vols., Stephens, John Lloyd. New York: Dover Publications, 1963.

Incidents of Travel in Central America, Chiapas, and Yucatán. 2 vols., by Stephens, John Lloyd. New York: Dover Publications, 1969.

Yucatán: Recipes from a Culinary Expedition, David Sterling. University of Texas Press, Austin: 2014.

Yucatán at the Time of the Spanish Encounter, Landa, Diego de, translated by Louis E.V. Nevaer. Coral Gables: 2013.

The Ghosts of Mérida. By Nevaer, Louis E.V. Coral Gables, FL: Hispanic Economics, 2012.

The Yucatán Peninsula. By Lockwood, C.C. New Orleans: Louis State University Press, 1989.

Cenote Sally's Easy Breazy Tropical Living, Wentworth, Eunice "Cenote Sally." Coral Gables, FL: Hispanic Economics, 2013.

Mexico: The Cookbook, Carrillo Arronte, Margarita. Phaidon Press, New York: 2014.

The "recommended" books are exceptional books that explore the archaeology and history of the peoples who have lived here. At your leisure, over the next several years, make it a point to read these books—and build up a solid library while you're at it!

Bourbon, Fabio. **The Lost Cities of the Mayas**: The Life, Art, and Discoveries of Frederick Catherwood. New York: Abbeville Press, 2000.

Coe, Michael D., and Rex Koontz. **Mexico: From the Olmecs to the Aztecs**. Fifth Edition. New York: Thames and Hudson, 2002.

Coe, Michael D. and Mark Van Stone. **Reading the Maya Glyphs**. New York: Thames and Hudson, 2001.

Coe, Sophie D. **America's First Cuisines**. Austin: University of Texas Press, 1994

Demarest, Arthur. **Ancient Maya: The Rise and Fall of a Rainforest Civilization**. Cambridge: Cambridge University Press, 2004

Díaz Del Castillo, Bernal. **The Conquest of New Spain**. New York: Viking Press,1963.

Freidel, David, Linda Schele, and Joy Parker. **Maya Cosmos: Three Thousand Years on the Shaman's Path**. New York: William Morrow, 1993.

Kelly, Joyce. **An Archaeological Guide to Mexico's Yucatán Peninsula**. Norman: University of Oklahoma Press, 1993; and **An Archaeological Guide to Northern Central America: Belize, Guatemala, Honduras and El Salvador**. Norman: University of Oklahoma Press, 1996.

Milbrath, Susan. **Star Gods of the Maya: Astronomy in Art**, Folklore, and Calendars. Austin: University of Texas Press, 1999.

Miller, Mary Ellen. **Maya Art and Architecture**. London: Thames and Hudson, 1999

Miller, Mary and Simon Martin. **Courtly Art of the Ancient Maya**. New York: Thames and Hudson, 2004.

Reents-Budet, Dorie. **Painting the Maya Universe: Royal Ceramics of the Classic Period**. Durham, North Carolina: Duke University Press, 1994.

Schele, Linda and David Freidel. **A Forest of Kings: The Untold Story of the Ancient Maya**. New York: William Morrow and Company, Inc., 1990.

Schele, Linda and Mary Miller. **The Blood of Kings**. New York: George Braziller, Inc., 1986.

Schele, L. and P. Mathews. **The Code of Kings**. Touchstone, New York, 1998.

Sharer, Robert J. with Loa P. Traxler. **The Ancient Maya**. Sixth Edition. Stanford, California: Stanford University Press, 2006.

Tedlock, Dennis. **Popul Vuh**. Revised edition. New York: Touchstone, 1996.

With so many foreigners living in Mérida, it's not surprising to find that there are several foreign-language libraries, most of which are open to the public. There is an extensive library of Arabic-language books, but this is a private collection and normally available by appointment. The same is true of the large English-language research library on Maya studies housed at Quinta M.A.R.I. in Colonia García Ginerés. These listed below are open to the public.

Catalan

Biblioteca L'Alba de Ferran de Ral
Calle 14 #187, between Calle 23 and 25 Street
Colonia García Ginerés
There is an extensive selection of Catalan language books and periodicals. The society also provides for travel to Catalonia for those who want to improve their language skills.
Telephone: (999) 925-1155
Email: *casaldeyucatan@yahoo.com.mx*
Website: *www.casaldeyucatan.cat*

English: Instituto Benjamin Franklin de Yucatán

Guillermo Vales Duarte
Director General
Instituto Benjamin Franklin
Calle 57 #474-A, between Calle 52 and 54 Street
Centro
The Instituto Benjamin Franklin de Yucatán has been operating as a Mexican-North American Binational Center for Cultural Relations for almost half a century. The center is a non-profit organization promotes cultural and educational exchanges between Yucatán and the rest of the world. Their Spanish-as-a-second language program teaches students from all over the world. The Institute offers intensive Spanish courses from as little as a week to as long as a year. Courses begin every Monday the entire year, regardless of the course length. Intensive courses are available for students who have little or no knowledge of Spanish. Intermediate and advanced students may enroll in six or eight-week Spanish classes. Courses feature grammar and conversation classes as well as guided tours to places of historic and cultural interest in the city. Students will be given placement exams upon arrival to determine their appropriate level. The Conversation Classes offered are designed jointly by the teacher and students. In lieu of textbooks, students are giving handouts on various topics and current issues they will receive a certificate of program completion. Academic credits can be arranged at student's request.

For Yucatecan and Mexican students, the Institute provides courses for TOEFL (English as a second language), GRE, GMAT and SAT exams. The Institute is certified to administer tests from the College Board (*www.collegeboard.com*).

Telephones: (999) 928-0097 and (999) 928-6005
Fax: (999) 928-0097
Website: *www.benjaminfranklin.com.mx*
Email: *franklin@benjaminfranklin.com.mx*

English: Mérida English Library

Mérida English Library (MEL)
Calle 53 #524, between Calle 66 and 68 Street
Centro
Silly resources on the Internet make such flippant declarations as, "When visitors ask us where they can find the heart of the expat community in Mérida, we tell them it's the Mérida English Language Library, of course!" There are about 3,500 fulltime Americans, Canadians and other English-speaking residents in Mérida, and only about 250 are members of the Library. That means that MEL serves less than 10 percent of the English-speaking expat community. Furthermore, MEL claims to be a member of the American Library Association, which, as of December 2013 it was not. It claims to be a "Mexican nonprofit institution," implying that it is authorized to solicit donations from the public, or to issue tax-deductible receipts that are recognized as legitimate by Mexico's federal taxing authority, known as SHCP, when this is not true. It is a "civil association," or an "asociacion civil," which is different from being a bona fide nonprofit organization authorized to solicit donations from the public and issue tax-deductible receipts. In the summer of 2011, MEL was the victim of a major financial scandal when then-president José Martínez embezzled their monies. Because the library is a scofflaw organization operating in violation of Mexican laws, MEL was unable to avail itself to the District Attorney to file charges. **In addition, MEL was sued for fraud and theft of services in early 2016.**

NOTE: The situation has been exacerbated when a former Board Member, Daniel Tyrrell admitted that MELL's premises had been used to promote sexual tourism and these sexual encounters included Mexican minors.

Telephone: (999) 924-8401
Website: *www.MeridaEnglishLibrary.com*

French

L'Alliance Francaise
Calle 23 #117 by Calle 24

Colonia Mexico

L'Alliance Francaise has an extensive French-language instruction program, along with materials to become fluent in French.

Telephone: (999) 927-2403

Francophile Website: *www.quoideneuf-merida.com*

Part V

Going Native: The Essence of Mexican and Yucatecan Culture

16 THE BEST OF MÉRIDA ... AND ABOUT THE YUCATECANS ... *HUACHES* ... AND *GRINGOS!*

At this point you might be wondering why sometimes the word "Mexican" is used and on other occasions the word "Yucatecan" is used. Well, there's a reason ... and it is a very interesting reason that has its origins about a thousand years ago ... during the time when the Classic Maya civilization began to collapse!

Before we get to Classic Maya, let's consider more recent events. For most of its history, the Yucatán peninsula has been isolated. Distant from Mexico City, the overland voyage between Campeche and Tabasco was treacherous. And if you set sail for Veracruz, it still was an arduous journey from there to Mexico City. If you were in Mérida, it was, believe it or not, easier to board a vessel to Havana than it was to embark on a journey to Mexico City. In consequence, Yucatecans gravitated towards Havana—and from there to Spain. Its isolation was such that the Yucatán has declared its independence from Mexico on two different occasions, without success. Proper Yucatecan families still smart at the reminder that it was the hated dicator Porfirio Díaz who ordered the "Chac Mool" be removed from the Yucatán to Mexico City.

To Yucatecans, "Mexicans" are foreigners. And the sentiment is returned: Mexicans joke that the Yucatán is the reluctant "Sister Republic."

For the Maya, the animosities run deeper—and are more heartfelt. As the Classic Maya civilization collapsed, the "northern Maya lowlands"—the technical name for the Yucatán peninsula proper—was occupied by peoples from Central Mexico, most famously the Itzas. This "occupation" resulted in the subjugation of the Maya by the peoples of the hated Valley of Mexico. The Maya resented these interlopers (which is one reason they enthusiastically supported Hernán Cortés and his quest to conquer the Aztecs). But there was one word that the Maya used to denote the hated occupiers: *Huach.*

The word is curt and terse:

Huach.

Pronounced as "watch," it is often heard among the Maya and Yucatecans of European-descent alike to express their displeasure at the presence of "Mexicans" in the "land of the Mayab."

"*Los huaches nos han invadidos*," meaning "the huaches have invaded us," is one way of describing the arrival of "Mexicans"—people from outside the Yucatán peninsula, be it Mexico City or Guadalajara, Puebla or Monterrey.

So "Yucatecan" is a person from the Yucatán. "Mexican" is a person from outside the Yucatán (but a region that is part of the "República Mexicana"). A *huach*, in essence, is a Mexican who is not from the Yucatán peninsula.

What makes this more curious is that since the Mexico City earthquake of 1985, many middle class and professional class Mexican families have left central Mexico and settled elsewhere. Many chose Mérida for its excellent schools, First World medical facilities, low crime rate, virtually no pollution and its short flight time back to Mexico City. The influx of "Mexicans" in such unprecedented number has unnerved established Yucatecan families, and frightened the Maya. One reason former Governor Ivonne Ortega insisted on wearing traditional Maya dresses in public is because this becomes a bold, political affirmation of Maya pride—and a reminder to "las familias del interior del país"—families from other areas of Mexico—that they must acculturate to Yucatecan culture and society if they are to be successful here.

The result is one in which you'll hear things like, "*Ese Juan, es* huach, *pero buena persona.*" ("That Juan, he's *huach*, but a good person." In other words, "He may be an outsider, but you can do business with him.") Or the Maya might say something like, "Huach, *pero criatura de dios.*" ("He's a *huach*, but a child of God." In other words, "We can't make him go back to Mexico, so you might as well come to peace at his being here.") Shrug your shoulders, as if to say, "What can be done?"

The Mexicans, for their part, have a tendency of looking down on the Yucatecans as being "provincials," slow and stupid. The Yucatecans, in turn, think the "huaches" are crass, obnoxious, and arrogant. For either group, the Maya don't register as people of consequence in their world views, since this is very much a class-conscious society.

For comparison, consider how the handicapped are invisible in the U.S. People who are in wheelchairs or blind are routinely ignored. Or consider how anyone speaking with a Southern accent in the U.S. is automatically considered "slow" and "stupid." This is the underlying social tension in Mérida, and one reason why City Government has its "Noche Mexicana" in the Remate de Paseo de Montejo once a week: it's an olive branch to the Mexicans living here. It's a way of making them feel more welcome—and less "homesick."

It's such a Yucatecan thing to offer an olive branch to a lifelong enemy!

Then there are the *estadounidenses*, or norteamericanos, or gringos—"*estadounidense*" means, literally, "United-Stater." That is to say, it is someone from the United States. "Norteamericano" means "North American"—which is not satisfying, since Canadians *and* Mexicans are also from North America! And "gringos" has become a term of endearment, half mocking, half not, for people from the United States.

The Loonies (Canadians), the Brits, Aussies and Kiwis, technically, are *never* gringos, so watch it! But Yucatecans affectionately call all English-speaking expatriates "gringos." They find it "charming" and "quaint" that Americans willingly choose to live in centuries-old buildings in a part of town that is filled with narrow streets, traffic congestion, and none of the modern conveniences conducive to a "contemporary" life. They also have a great deal of respect for Americans who are doing something that the Yucatecans themselves are not: **Restoring and preserving the wreckage of the city's Historic Center!**

There's the irony, for there you can sense the ambivalence felt by our hosts: On the one hand, they admire what we are doing, saving their cultural heritage, but on the other hand, they don't quite know what to make of us. They welcome us, but find us distant, and curious. This is all the more reason to reach out to the people of Mérida and reciprocate their kindness, friendliness and willingness to welcome us to their city.

Warning: Los Muertos de Hambre de la Casta Divina

At the beginning of this book, the French generalization about other Frenchmen overseas was brought up as a cautionary tale. It was a gentle way of pointing out that a disproportionate number of American expatriates you will encounter anywhere in the world are never-do-wells who have left the U.S. to reinvent themselves, or to carry out scams of one sort or another, either on naïve locals or trusting fellow Americans—or both.

That point has already been made. It is only fair to warn you of local leeches and scoundrels that are native to the Yucatán! Yes, there are Mexicans and Yucatecans who will look at you, as an American or Canadian, and see a gullible and trusting fool who can be deceived. **Yes, there are**

Mexicans and Yucatecans who will see you as nothing more than a Walking ATM that, once the right buttons are pushed, will spit out cash.

So what in the world does "los muertos de hambre de la Casta Divina" mean? "Muertos de hambre," is a dramatic Spanish expression that means, "Those dying of hunger," and it means "destitute" or "desperate." It's used as a derogatory phrase to describe someone who is "penniless." In American vernacular, it's roughly the equivalent of dismissing someone who "doesn't have a pot to piss in." "Casta Divina" means "Divine Caste," and refers to Yucatecans of impeccable pedigree, those who can trace their family's arrival to the Yucatán several centuries back in time.

As you can imagine, not everyone in the world is as successful as their parents or grandparents. The classic examples in the United States are the descendants of Commodore Cornelius Vanderbilt, the Gilded Age Robber Baron. Leaving an unimaginable fortune, a century later, none of his descendents had built on that fortune, and few were millionaires in their own right. In Mérida, one peculiar thing you may have noticed is that if the founder was Francisco Montejo and the main boulevard is Paseo de Montejo, and everyone knows that the Casa de Montejo is one of the most important landmarks in the city, but, well, where are all the Montejos? The truth of the matter is that through an odd happenstance of life, the name "Montejo" disappeared through daughters being born to the family and a few Montejos returning to Spain centuries ago. (*Note: the editor of this present volume is a Montejo, but of Cuban origin, not from the founding family of Mérida.*)

But it is in this odd fact that you see the names that dominate the social and political life of the city. When Montejo died, everything was left to his son, Francisco Montejo "El Mozo." Upon his death, it is his widow, Andrea del Castillo, who inherited everything. Upon her death, the properties passed on to her son, Juan Montejo Castillo, and then to his son, Juan Montejo Maldonado. And so it goes until 1832, when the Montejos disappear as a family name, and seven years later, the Casa de Montejo is purchased by Simón Peón Peón, who made a vast fortune as an hacienda owner during the height of the sisal trade, and as a cruel slaveowner. When he died in 1869, the house passed on to his widow, then his son, José María Peón Losa. In 1914, it is inherited by Eduviges Peón Peón, who was married to Manuel Arrigunaga Gutiérrez. So there you have the names that feature prominently on the social scene: Arrigunaga, Castillo, Gutiérrez, Peón; along with other distinguished families: Barbachano, Cantón, Carrillo, Castellanos, Contreras, Molina, Moreno, Palomeque, Pino, Puerto, Sierra, Sobrino, Suárez. You could also add a few names that are associated with the dominance of certain families in the State's politics, such as Cervera, Pacheco, Sauri.

314

Since the 1970s, Arab names have appeared as important actors on the scene, but they are seen as arrivistes, since they cannot trace their families' presence in the Yucatán by more than a century.

So what is the point?

The point is that not every one of these families has been as successful as their ancestors. There are many Yucatecans who have bright ancestors in their pasts, but a dim future ahead of them. There are many who struggle to get by, disdaining work, but having little to live from, especially if they aspire to a certain standard of living. There are many Yucatecan families who see the influx of foreigners as a way of finding a way to make a quick buck. These are the Yucatecans who lurk around in places where foreigners hang out—the U.S. Consulate, the International Women's Club, the real estate companies that cater to American and Canadian expatriates, the foreign language schools and libraries—and affect false friendships to ensnare victims and see what you have, and how best they can swindle you.

How can you recognize them?

That's easy enough: The same way you recognize players and grifters the world over. You should ask yourself these basic questions when you encounter someone:

- o   Are they being too friendly?
- o   Are they moving too quickly to become a confidant?
- o   Are they bringing up investments in casual conversation?
- o   Are they offering to "help" me identify opportunities to make money?
- o   Are they always talking about their pedigree and the achievements of their ancestors, but never of their own accomplishments?
- o   Are they tring to sell you something—whether it is a membership to a private club, or some atrocious painting by a well-known nobody?

Then you should look at how they carry themselves. Anyone can inherit a diamond necklace or a gold watch from dead relatives (or borrow them from well-off relations), but:

- o   What kind of shoes is the man wearing?
- o   What kind of purse is the woman sporting?
- o   Do their clothes look fashionable and current—or is it two seasons old, that could have been bought from the "Clearance" rack at a fine department store?
- o   What kind of car are they driving?

315

And when it comes to the question of money, investments or business opportunities enters the conversation, never be the one who is putting up all the money:

- o Are they prepared to write a check for the same amount as you are?
- o Do they reciprocate by picking up the bill at a bar or restaurant when meeting to discuss this "opportunity"?
- o How many other locals do they have investing in this venture?
- o Why are they bringing this wonderful business opportunity to you—a stranger in a strange land—and not to their life-long best friend or other relative?

There are many Yucatecans who have, on paper, impeccable pedigrees, but whose bank statements reveal people who are one ATM withdrawal from having nothing.

In other words, be aware that you may be the target of a swindle, and as is the case everywhere around the world, *If a deal sounds too good to be true, it probably is!*

Expat Scams

It is a sad commentary when so many grifters and con artists from other countries arrive in Mérida prepared to swindle other expats—and locals—with one scam or another.

Beware!

House & Garden Tour *versus* House & Garden Tour

How many "House & Garden Tours" and one town take?

House & Garden Tour: Billing itself as the "original" Mérida English Library House & Garden Tour, this scam is the result of a falling out between Judy Abbott and friends (see above) and the current library administration over how to divide the plunder secured from unsuspecting tourists who actually believed the $200 peso donation is a donation. Unable to settle the matter—the library demanded half the proceeds—they are now conducting their own tours on Tuesdays, beginning at 9 AM, October through March. Again, there is some compensation for participating homeowners, although the lack of transparency on the part of the library continues to undermine its credibility. (A former Board Member, Daniel Tyrrell, admitted in 2013 that the library's premises had been used to promote sex tourism, opening a criminal investigation into the activities of the organization.) The library is located at Calle 53 #524 between Calle 66 and 68 Street.

Finally: As a point of information, to protect yourself—and any donation you make to a charitable organization in Mexico—under Mexican law, bonafide nonprofits are required by law to give donors OFFICIAL receipts, which have a government seal and are known as a RECIBO FISCAL (Fiscal Receipt). If any organization is not able to provide you with a RECIBO FISCAL, then it is not authorized to be soliciting donations from the public. There are no exceptions.

The Best of Mérida

With the warnings about scams out of the way, on the showcase the very best of Mérida.

17   Social Expectations and Customs: Being a Good Neighbor

Over the centuries, the conduct of U.S. citizens—individuals, corporations, government representatives—in Latin America has been so outrageous that a word has evolved to describe any dirty trick: "Gringada."[3]

The same way that most U.S. citizens make unkind assumptions about Mexico, people in Mexico have a nagging suspicion about the motives of Americans, and about how, in the relentless pursuit of material things, Americans have lost their moral compass.

What does this mean?

It means that as an expatriate living in Mérida, you have, to be blunt, something to prove, or to disprove, depending on how you want to look at it. And the best way of doing that, is by being a good neighbor.

There are, of course, many ways to be a good neighbor. Learn a few words of Spanish. This is a country where people say good morning to each other on the streets, even if you don't know each other. This is a society where children are valued, and it is expected that you open doors for mothers with children, step aside for strollers, and never snap impatiently if children are running circles in the park. This is a society where the elderly are respected, and not shunned or ignored.

This is a society where people are greatly flattered if you express more than a casual interest in history, or customs and traditions. It's quite possible to score many, many points by simply learning about some of the wonderful "fun facts" about Mexico. Not only will this make you much more interesting at cocktail parties and get-togethers, but it will convey that you are different: a cultured, educated stranger making a life for yourself in the Yucatán.

With the kind cooperation of Tony Burton, what follows in this chapter are a series of essays that will edify you—and make you more cultured and smarter than the average expatriate walking around town.

---

[3] See: diccionario.reverso.net/espanol-ingles/gringada

Did you know?

The Green Revolution began in Mexico

by Tony Burton

Most people probably have a vague idea that the Green Revolution was something to do with improving crops in the developing world, but how many realize that it began in Mexico? In fact, the Green Revolution continues in Mexico through the pioneering work of CIMMYT, the International Wheat and Maize Improvement Center based in Texcoco, near Mexico City.

The Green Revolution refers to the application of science and technology to increase crop yields and agricultural productivity which began in Mexico in the 1940s. In the Green Revolution, special high yield varieties (HYVs) of several cereals were developed. To grow most effectively, these needed carefully calibrated applications of fertilizers, pesticides and water. The Green Revolution allowed countries to expand their cereal production to more than keep pace with the growing demands of their rapidly rising populations.

The initial stimulus for the Green Revolution was Mexico's desire to become self-sufficient in wheat production. Rockefeller Foundation funding helped establish the Mexican Agricultural Program in 1943, an institution which became later became CIMMYT.

Led by Dr. Norman Borlaug, a plant breeding program was begun to develop new hybrid varieties of wheat and maize. These had higher yields and more resistance to common diseases. Successful strains were then crossed with dwarf or semi-dwarf varieties to reduce the height of the plants, preventing them from collapsing under the strain of the heavier ears of grain.

By 1963, 95% of Mexico's wheat fields were growing the new seeds. Yields were much higher. The 1964 harvest was six times larger than in 1944. Whereas Mexico had imported half its wheat in 1943, by 1964 it was exporting 500,000 tons a year. (Since that time, the combined effects of growing population and farmers changing to other crops have returned Mexico to its previous status of being a net importer of wheat).

The success of the program was repeated elsewhere in the developing world. India's wheat production increased more than 400% between 1965 and 1986, turning India into the world's third largest producer. Pakistan became self-sufficient in wheat within three years of adopting the high yielding hybrids.

A similar breeding program in the Philippines produced IR8 Miracle Rice, which was quickly adopted with spectacular increases in yield throughout Asia. In the first eleven countries where farmers adopted the new rice varieties, the average yields for rice increased by 52% between 1965 and 1983. In countries where the new varieties were not adopted, rice yields declined 4% during the same period.

The Green Revolution also boosted agriculture in developed nations. Corn yields in the USA, for example, quadrupled in 60 years. In recognition of his pioneering work, Borlaug was awarded the 1970 Nobel Peace Prize.

In recent years, CIMYTT has developed strains of wheat that are resistant to the deadly Ug99 strain of stem rust fungus, first identified in Uganda in 1999, which threatens world wheat supplies. Existing wheat hybrids had resistance to several other forms of wheat rust, but not Ug99, which quickly spread to wheat fields in Iran and looked set to enter southern Asia. A new CIMYTT-developed wheat variety, immune to Ug99, has been planted in Bangladesh, Nepal, Pakistan and other countries in an effort to halt its spread.

CIMMYT is part of the Consultative Group for International Agricultural Research (CGIAR), a network of agricultural research centers around the world sponsored by the Food and Agriculture Organization, the United Nations Development Programme and the World Bank.

A review of the Green Revolution published in Science and quoted on the CIMMYT website claims that without the work of CIMMYT and its CGIAR partners, crop yields in developing countries would have been about one-fifth lower; prices for food crops would have been between one-third and two-thirds higher; imports would have been a third higher; calorie intake would have been an eighth lower; and between 32 and 42 million more children would have been malnourished.

Here's hoping that the next developments in the Green Revolution are at least as successful as the first.

For further reading:

R. E. Evenson and D. Gollin. Assessing the Impact of the Green Revolution, 1960 to 2000. Science vol 300, pp 758-62, 2003.

Debora MacKenzie. Wheat in shining armor arives. New Scientist. Volume 201, No 2700, 21 March 2009.

To learn more about the vitally important work being undertaken at CIMMYT (Centro Internacional de Mejoramiento de Maíz y Trigo), visit its website: *www.cimmyt.org*

Blacks outnumbered Spaniards until after 1810

by Tony Burton

By common consent, the history of blacks in Mexico is a long one. The first black slave to set foot in Mexico is thought to have been Juan Cortés. He accompanied the conquistadors in 1519. It has been claimed that some natives thought he must be a god, since they had never seen a black man before.

A few years later, six blacks are believed to have taken part in the successful siege of the Aztec capital Tenochtitlan. Several hundred other blacks formed part of the wandering, fighting forces employed in the name of the Spanish crown to secure other parts of New Spain.(1)

The indigenous population crashed in the first hundred years following the conquest, largely as a result of smallpox and other European diseases. Estimates of the native population prior to the conquest range from 4 to 30 million. A century later, there were just 1.6 million.

New Spain had been conquered by a ludicrously small number of Spaniards. To retain control and in order to begin exploiting the potential riches of the virgin territory they had won, a good supply of laborers was essential. There were not enough locals, so imports of slaves became a high priority.

By 1570, almost 35% of all the mine workers in the largest mines of Zacatecas and neighboring locations were African slaves.(2) Large numbers of slaves were also imported for the sugar plantations and factories in areas along the Gulf coast, such as Veracruz. By the mid-seventeenth century, some 8,000-10,000 blacks were Gulf coast residents. After this time, the slave trade to Mexico gradually diminished.

Miguel Hidalgo, the Independence leader, first demanded an end to slavery in 1810 (the same year that Upper Canada freed all slaves). Slavery was abolished by President Vicente Guerrero on September 15, 1829.

During the succeeding 36 years, prior to the abolition of slavery in the U.S. (1865), some U.S. slaves seized their chance and headed south in search of freedom and opportunity. Recognizing the potential, in 1831, one Mexican senator, Sánchez de Tagle, a signatory of the Act of Independence, called for assistance to be given to any blacks wanting to move south on the grounds that this movement would possibly prevent Mexico being invaded by white Americans.(3) Sánchez de Tagle's point was that black immigrants would be strong supporters of Mexico since they wouldn't want to be returned to slavery, and would be preferable to white Americans, who might be seeking an opportunity to annex parts of Mexico for their homeland. Sánchez de Tagle's fears came to pass. One year after the U.S. annexed the slave-holding Republic of Texas in 1845, it invaded Mexico.

Perhaps as many as 4,000 blacks entered Mexico between 1840 and 1860. At the beginning of 1850, several states enacted a series of land concessions for black immigrants, in order that undeveloped areas with agricultural potential might be settled and farmed.

Even after the abolition of slavery in the U.S., small waves of blacks continued to arrive periodically in Mexico. Many came from the Caribbean after 1870 to help build the growing national railway network. In 1882, some 300 Jamaicans arrived to help build the San Luis Potosí-Tampico line; another 300 Jamaicans made the trip in 1905 to take jobs in mines in the state of Durango.(4) Partially as a response to their own independence struggles, thousands of Cubans came after 1895. They favored the tropical coastal lowlands such as Veracruz, Yucatán and parts of Oaxaca, where the climate and landscapes were more familiar to them than the high interior plateaux of central Mexico.

Mexican historians have largely ignored the in-migration of blacks and their gradual intermarriage and assimilation into Mexican society. For a variety of reasons, they chose to focus instead on either the indigenous peoples, or the mestizos who form the majority of Mexicans today. The pendulum is finally beginning to swing back, as researchers like Charles Henry Rowell, Ben Vinson III and Bobby Vaughn re-evaluate the original sources, and examine the life and culture of the communities where many blacks settled.

Most work about the influence of blacks on modern-day Mexico has focused on the Veracruz area, in particular on the settlements of Coyolillo, Alvarado, Mandinga and Tlacotalpan.(5) On the opposite coast, Bobby Vaughn has spent more than a decade studying the Costa Chica of Oaxaca and Guerrero.(6)

Analysts of Mexican population history emphasize the poor reliability of early estimates and censuses, as well as the complex mixing of races which occurred with time. While the precise figures and dates may vary, most demographers appear to agree with Bobby Vaughn that the black population, which rose rapidly to around 20,000 shortly after the conquest, continued to exceed the Spanish population in New Spain until around 1810.

322

It is estimated that more than 110,000 black slaves (perhaps even as many as 200,000) were brought to New Spain during colonial times. Happily, their legacy is still with us, and lives on in the language, customs and culture of all these areas.

Sources / Further Reading:

1. Matthew Restall. Seven Myths of the Spanish Conquest. (Oxford University Press) 2003

2. Peter J. Bakewell. Silver Mining and Society in Colonial Mexico: Zacatecas, 1546-1700, cited in Afroméxico.

3. Vinson III, Ben & Vaughn, Bobby. Afroméxico. (in Spanish; translation by Clara García Ayluardo) Mexico: CIDE/CFE. 2004. The main source for this column, divided into three parts. Following a joint introduction, Ben Vinson III, Professor of Latin American History at Penn State University, provides a detailed overview of studies connected to blacks in Mexico. Then Bobby Vaughn, who has a doctorate in anthropology from Stanford University, adopts an ethnographic perspective in writing about the Costa Chica of Oaxaca and Guerrero; his short essay includes discussion of the Black Mexico movement. The work concludes with an extensive bibliography of sources relating to Afroméxico.

4. Vinson III, Ben & Vaughn, Bobby. Afroméxico. Mexico: CIDE/CFE. 2004

5. See, for example, the Winter 2004 and Spring 2006 issues of Callaloo (A Journal of African Diaspora Arts and Letters). The Spring 2006 issue, vol 29, #2, pp 397-543, has a series of articles under the general heading of "Africa in Mexico", including transcriptions of fascinating interviews with such characters as Rodolfo Figueroa Martínez, who relates the history of how several local towns, including San Lorenzo de los Negros (now Yanga) were founded by blacks, and of how a black identity gradually emerged. Other interviewees discuss how they view their color and Afromestizo identity, lamenting the fact that their history has been distorted or largely forgotten. Local food and festival celebrations are also highlighted.

6. Bobby Vaughn's Black Mexico Home Page, Afro Mexicans of the Costa Chica, mirrored here on Mexico Connect with his kind permission.

Many common garden flowers originated in Mexico

by Tony Burton

Many common garden flowers were developed from samples collected in Mexico by a German botanist financed by Britain's Horticultural Society.

323

Karl Theodor Hartweg (1812-1871) came from a long line of gardeners and had gardening in his genes. Born in Karlsruhe, Germany, on June 18, 1812, he worked in Paris, at the Jardin des Plantes, before moving to England to work in the U.K. Horticultural Society's Chiswick gardens in London. Keen to travel even further afield, he was appointed an official plant hunter and sent to the Americas for the first time in 1836. What was originally intended to be a three-year project eventually became a 7-year expedition.

By Hartweg's time, Europeans already knew that Mexico was a veritable botanical treasure trove, full of exciting new plants. For example, the humble dahlia, a Mexican native since elevated to the status of the nation's official flower, had already become very prominent in Europe.

Mexican cacti were also beginning to acquire popularity in Europe at this time.

The Horticultural Society saw both academic and financial potential in sponsoring Hartweg to explore remote areas of Mexico, and collect plants that might flourish in temperature climes such as north-west Europe.

And Hartweg was certainly the man for the job. He proved to be an especially determined traveler, who covered a vast territory in search of new plants. He collected representative samples and seeds of hundreds and hundreds of species, many of which had not previously been scientifically named or described. Orchids from the Americas were particularly popular in Hartweg's day. According to Merle Reinkka, the author of *A History of the Orchid*, Hartweg amassed "the most variable and comprehensive collection of New World Orchids made by a single individual in the first half of the [19th] century".

Shortly after arriving in Veracruz in 1836, Hartweg met a fellow botanist, Carl Sartorius (1796-1872), of German extraction, who had acquired the nearby hacienda of El Mirador a decade eariler. Sartorius collected plants for the Berlin Botanical Gardens. His hacienda, producing sugar-cane, set in the coastal, tropical lowlands, became the mecca of nineteenth century botanists visiting Mexico.

The world of plant collecting in those days was a relatively small world. Hartweg would later unexpectedly meet another famous botanist Jean Jules Linden on two separate occasions, once in Mexico and later in Columbia.

From 1836 to 1839, Hartweg explored Mexico, criss-crossing the country from Veracruz to León, Lagos de Moreno and Aguascalientes before entering the rugged landscapes around the mining town of Bolaños in early October 1837. In his own words, reaching Bolaños had involved "travelling over a mountain path of which I never saw the like before", one "which became daily work by the continual heavy rains." From Bolaños, Hartweg visited Zacatecas, San Luis Potosí (in February 1838) and Guadalajara, where he did not omit to include a detailed description of tequila making. From Guadalajara, he moved on to Morelia, Angangueo [then an important mining town, now the closest town of any size to the Monarch butterfly reserves], Real del Monte, and Mexico City, from where he sent a large consignment of plant material back to England. Hartweg then headed south to Oaxaca and Chiapas en route to Guatemala, Ecuador, Peru and Jamaica. He arrived back in Europe in 1843.

But he was soon back in the Americas. As emissary of what would prove to be the Horticultural Society's last organized expedition to the Americas, Hartweg left England on October 2, 1845 and reached Veracruz on November 13. He spent some days with his old friend Sartorius before traversing the country via Mexico City (early December) to Tepic, where he arrived on New Year's Day, 1846, to wait for news of a suitable vessel arriving in the nearby port of San Blas which could take him north to California. In the event he had to wait until May, so he occupied himself in the meantime with numerous botanical explorations in the vicinity, including trips to Compostela and the Tetitlán volcano, now better known as Ceboruco. Eventually, he sailed north to California, from where he sent further boxes of specimens back to England, including numerous plants which would subsequently become much prized garden ornamentals. During this trip, he also added several new conifers to the growing list found in Mexico. It is now known that Mexico has more of the world's 90+ species of pine (Pinus) than any other country on earth. This has led botanists to suppose that it is the original birthplace of the entire genus.

Disagreements about his remuneration and expenses caused Hartweg to return to Europe, sever his links with the Horticultural Society, and resettle in Germany in 1848. The Society library still houses three substantial volumes of correspondence and documents pertaining to Hartweg's trips. Karl Theodor Hartweg died in Baden, Germany, on February 3, 1871. In an obituary, one of Hartweg's closest friends, William Swale, severely criticized the Horticultural Society for the disgraceful treatment of Hartweg meted out by some of its senior members.

It took several years for the boxes and boxes of material sent back to England by Hartweg to be properly examined, cataloged and described. Many of the samples from his early trip were first described formally by George Bentham in Plantae Hartwegianae, which appeared as a series of publications from 1839 to 1842. Among the exciting discoveries were new species of conifers, such as Pinus hartwegii, Pinus ayacahuite, P. moctezumae, P. patula, Cupressus macrocarpa, and Sequoia sempervirens. Hartweg's collecting prowess is remembered today in the name given to a spectacular purple-flowering orchid, Hartwegia purpurea, which is native to southern Mexico.

Numerous garden plants derive directly from plants Hartweg sent back to Europe. These included Salvia patens (a blue flowering member of the mint family) which became the ancestor of modern bedding salvias, the red-flowering Fuchsia fulgens, ancestor of a very large number of Fuchsia cultivars, and the red-flowering Zauschneria californica, commonly known as California fuchsia.

Sources:

Elliot, Brent. "The adventures of Hartweg", The Garden, November 2004, 868. London: Horticultural Society.

Hartweg, Karl Theodor. "Journal of a mission to California". Journal of the Horticultural Society. London, England. In several parts: 1846, 180-185, 1847, 121-125, 187-191, and 1848 217-228.

Hartweg, Karl Theodor. "Notes of a visit to Mexico, Guatemala and Equatorial America, 1836 to 1843, in search of plants and seeds for the Horticultural Society of London. London, England": Transactions of the Horticultural Society, vol. 3, 1848, 115-162.

Reinikka, Merle A. *A History of the Orchid*. Timber Press. 1995.

The Thanksgiving and Christmas turkey originated in Mexico.

by Tony Burton

Strange but true; the bird now so closely associated with many festive meals is a direct descendant of the wild turkeys still found in many parts of Mexico. How is it possible that a Mexican bird acquired the name turkey?

Wild Turkey, Meleagris gallopavo

The most likely explanation derives from the fact that the merchants who traded in the Middle Ages between the Middle East and England were based in the Turkish Empire and hence known as "Turkey merchants". Turkey merchants are believed to have introduced the guinea fowl, a native of Madagascar, to European dinner tables.

Later, the larger New World bird, the present-day turkey, was brought back to Spain by the conquistadors. The rearing of New World birds gradually spread to other parts of Europe and North Africa. The Turkey merchants capitalized on the new opportunity, and began to supply the new birds instead of the guinea fowls to the English market, and the rest is history.

The first use in English of the word "turkey" to describe the bird dates back to 1555. By 1575, turkey was already becoming the preferred main course for Christmas dinner. Curiously, the Turkish name for the turkey is Hindi, which is probably derived from "chicken of India", perhaps based on the then-common misconception that Columbus had reached the Indies.

Mexico's wild turkeys had been domesticated by pre-Columbian Indian groups long before the Spanish conquistadors arrived. Several archaeological sites provide tantalising clues as to precisely how turkeys were reared. One such site is Casas Grandes in the northern state of Chihuahua, an area where modern, large-scale turkey-rearing is an important contributor to the local economy.

Corn

According to Ernst and Johanna Lehner, corn, which also originated in Mexico, was misnamed as Turkish corn at the same time, and for much the same reason. Europeans first saw corn, called maize or mahiz by the indigenous people, when Columbus and his followers arrived in the New World. They took samples back to Spain at the very end of the 15th century.

It quickly became an important crop, successfully cultivated throughout the continent. Sixteenth century herbalists in Europe called the new plant by various names, including Welsh corn, Asiatic corn, Turkish wheat and Turkish corn. The latter name was the most usual, since they believed that the grain had been brought into central Europe from Asia by the Turks, who had introduced dozens of other products from the east into Europe at about the same time.

The Turks themselves called the crop "Egyptian corn"; the Egyptians called it "Syrian sorghum"... The German botanist Hieronymus Bock, in his *New Kreüterbuch* or herbal in 1546, remained on the fence, calling it "foreign corn". Given the confused terminology, perhaps it is not surprising that, to quote Ernst and Johanna Lehner, "It took Spanish botanists more than 50 years to convince other European herbalists that corn was American." Corn was given its botanical name, Zea mays, by Carl von Linné in the 18th century.

Potatoes

Alongside turkey and/or corn at Thanksgiving and Christmas, the humble yet versatile potato is often eaten. That, too, was introduced to Europe from Mexico. I have written about the connections between Mexico, the potato, and the Irish migration to North America following the potato famine of the early 19th century.

But did you also know that potatoes were originally sold in Spain on the strength of claims that they could cure impotence, at prices up to two thousand dollars a kilo?

Nowadays, potatoes in one form or another are virtually ubiquitous - from mashed or baked or potato salad, to French fries and the quintessentially Québécois variation of poutine (fries, curds and gravy).

The first Thanksgiving

My esteemed colleagues Don Adams and Teresa Kendrick have presented a strong case that the very first Thanksgiving celebration by Europeans in North America was held not in the U.S. at all, but in Mexico, on April 30, 1598.

This date certainly precedes the claims of Plimoth Plantation, Massachusetts, site of the 1621 thanksgiving, and negates the latter's claim to be the birthplace of Thanksgiving. One curious historical footnote is that the feast on that occasion apparently did not include either turkey or potatoes!

Pumpkin Pie

And how could you have pumpkin pie without the pumpkin? All varieties of pumpkin, whatever their size and shape, belong to the Cucurbita genus. While there are some doubts about the precise origin of the wild forms of pumpkin, they were certainly being cultivated in Mexico as long ago as 5500 B.C. and were an integral part of the daily diet of many Indian groups. The use of "pumpkin" in English can apparently be traced back to 1547. For many people, pumpkins are eternally associated with both Thanksgiving and with Halloween.

Christmas Poinsettias

Putting menu details to one side, Christmas in North America would not be complete without the finishing splash of color provided by another Mexican native: the Poinsettia.

This beautiful plant, with its colorful bracts, has become indelibly associated with the season. Most people who buy indoor pots of Euphorbia pulcherrima, commonly known in Spanish as Flor de Noche Buena (Christmas Eve Flower), probably do not realize that the plant in its native habitat grows as high as a small tree. Poinsettia, its English name, honors Dr. Joel R. Poinsett, a U.S. diplomat who served in Mexico in the 1820s. While most poinsettias have modified leaves or bracts that are scarlet- or vermilion-colored, other varieties have pink or even white bracts.

So, wherever you are this festive season, keep your eyes open for Mexican influences...

Many traditional Thanksgiving and Christmas dinners would simply not be the same were it not for a few key ingredients from Mexico!

Sources:

Lehner, Ernst & Lehner, Johanna. *Folklore and Odysseys of Food and Medicinal Plants.* New York: Tudor Publishing Company. 1962.

Don Adams and Teresa A. Kendrick. "Don Juan de Oñate and the First Thanksgiving". Don Mabry's Historical Text Archive. Retrieved on 2008-07-13.

Elizabeth Armstrong (2002-11-27). "The first Thanksgiving", Christian Science Monitor. Retrieved on 2008-07-13.

Online Etymology Dictionary. Acessed 2008-07-13.

Consuelo Velázquez and "Bésame mucho"

by Tony Burton

The song "Bésame mucho" (Kiss me a lot) was written by a young Mexican woman who had never been kissed.

This article is a tribute to Consuelo Velázquez, who died January 22, 2005, at the age of 84.

Consuelo Velázquez was one of Mexico's best known modern songwriters. She wrote her most famous song—"Bésame mucho"—before her 20th birthday. When asked, years later, whose love had inspired the powerful lyrics, she replied that she had written it before she had ever been kissed, and said that the entire song was a "product of imagination".

Quite some imagination! The song has been translated into more than 20 languages, and been sung in many different styles, by dozens of artists ranging from The Beatles, Frank Sinatra, Wes Montgomery, The Morton Gould Orchestra, Andy Russell, Pedro Vargas, Linda Ronstadt, Valentino's Sax, Diana Krall and Plácido Domingo to Sammy Davis Jr., Magdalena Zárate, José Carreras, Joao Alberto, Elvis Presley and Mexican heart-throb Luis Miguel.

Words of "Bésame mucho" (Consuelo Velázquez)

Bésame, bésame mucho,
Como si fuera esta noche la última vez.
Bésame, bésame mucho,

329

Que tengo miedo perderte,
Perderte otra vez.

Quiero tenerte muy
Cerca, mirarme en tus
Ojos, verte junto a mí,
Piensa que tal vez
Mañana yo ya estaré
Lejos, muy lejos de ti.

Bésame, bésame mucho,
Como si fuera esta noche la última vez.
Bésame mucho,
Que tengo miedo perderte,
Perderte después.

Unofficial English translation:

Kiss me, Kiss me a lot,
As if tonight were the last time.
Kiss me, kiss me a lot,
Because I'm afraid of losing you,
To lose you again.

I want to have you very close
To see myself in your eyes,
To see you next to me,
Think that perhaps tomorrow
I already will be far,
very far from you.

Kiss me, Kiss me a lot,
As if tonight were the last time.
Kiss me, a lot,
because I'm afraid of losing you,
To lose you later.

Consuelo Velázquez was born in Ciudad Guzmán, Jalisco, on August 21, 1920, but grew up in Guadalajara. She began playing piano when she was 4, gave her first public recital at age 6, and moved to Mexico City in her teens to attend the National Conservatory and the Palace of Fine

Arts. She became a concert pianist and started writing popular songs shortly afterwards, while overseeing classical music programs for the pioneering radio station XEQ.

"Bésame mucho"(Kiss me a lot) was first recorded in 1941 (by Emilio Tuero and Chela Campos) and became a huge Big Band hit during the Second World War. In 1999, the song, the only Mexican song ever to have topped the U.S. hit parade for 12 straight weeks, was declared the "Song of the Century" at a Univisión event in Miami, Florida.

In addition, "Bésame mucho" featured in several movies, including "A toda máquina" (1951), "The moon over Parador" (1988), "Sueños de Arizona" (1993), and "Moskva Slezam ne Verit", a Russian movie which won the 1980 Oscar for Best Foreign Film.

"Bésame mucho" brought fame and numerous awards to Consuelo Velázquez, including a Special Citation of Achievement Award from the U.S. Broadcast Music Incorporated. Invited to Hollywood to meet the legendary Walt Disney, she found him to be "nice, kind and respectful." Velázquez agreed to work in Disney's "The Three Caballeros". During the filming of this movie, Rita Hayworth stopped by and insisted on meeting Velázquez.

According to her close friends, Consuelo Velázquez remained a gentle, humble person throughout her life, often telling anecdotes about her life as if she was talking about someone else. She continued to play the piano most afternoons until well into her 80s.

Among other songs that she wrote that were popular in their day are "Yo no fui" (sung most famously by Pedro Infante), "Anoche", "Al nacer este día", "Aunque tengas razón", "Déjame quererte", "Pensará en mí", "Amar y vivir", "Que seas feliz" (interpreted recently by Luis Miguel), "No me pidas nunca", "Chiqui", "Volverás a mí", and "Cachito". When she died, she had only just finished another song—"Por el camino"—written especially for Luis Miguel's next album.

Consuelo Velázquez, "Consuelito", can rightfully be considered Mexico's greatest ever female composer. Her life and her songs will be remembered with great affection by music-lovers everywhere for years to come.

Que descansa en paz - May she rest in peace.

To contact Tony Burton, you can email him at: *tonyburton@pacificcoast.net*

18 MEXICAN AND YUCATECAN HOLIDAYS & TRADITIONS

If you are building a life for yourself in Mérida, you are well advised to get to know a few of the holidays and traditions that make this such a special place. Let's start with food, and work our way to the special traditions in Mérida that are some of the pleasures of being down here.

Traditional Yucatecan Dishes

Yucatecan food has evolved from a wide range of influences, from Maya cuisine, to dishes from the Middle East, Spain and the Dutch. It is a unique style and is very different from what most people consider "Mexican" food. Some of the "regional" dishes that are popular all over the peninsula include:

Poc Chuc, a Maya version of a classic grilled pork dish.

Salbutes and Panuchos. Salbutes are soft, cooked tortillas with lettuce, tomato, turkey, and avocado on top. Panuchos feature fried tortillas filled with black beans, and topped with turkey or chicken, lettuce, avocado and pickled onions. Habanero chiles accompany most dishes, either in solid or purée form, along with fresh limes and corn tortillas.

Queso Relleno is a "gourmet" dish featuring ground pork inside of a carved edam cheese ball served with tomato sauce.

Pavo en Relleno Negro (also known locally as Chilmole) is turkey meat stew cooked with a black paste made from roasted chiles, a local version of the mole de guajalote found throughout Mexico. The meat soaked in the black soup is also served in tacos, sandwiches, and even in panuchos or salbutes.

Sopa de Lima is a lime soup with a chicken broth base often accompanied by shredded chicken or turkey and crispy tortilla.

332

Papadzules. Egg "tacos" bathed with pumpkin seed sauce and tomatoes. This is one of the few vegetarian Maya dishes.

Cochinita Pibil is a marinated pork dish and by far the most renowned from the Yucatecan food.

Bul keken (Mayan for "beans and pork") is a traditional black bean and pork soup. The soup is served in the home on Mondays in most homes. The soup is usually served with chopped onions, radishes, chilies, and tortillas.

Brazo de reina (Spanish for "The Queen's Arm") is a traditional tamal dish. A long, flat tamal is topped with ground pumpkin seeds and rolled up like a roll cake. The long roll is then cut into slices. The slices are topped with a tomato sauce and a pumpkin seed garnish.

Please note the one, quintessential spice found everywhere: *Achiote!* This is the most popular spice in the area. It is derived from the hard annatto seed found in the region. The whole seed is ground together with other spices and formed into a reddish seasoning paste, called *recado rojo*. The other ingredients in the paste include cinnamon, allspice berries, cloves, Mexican oregano, cumin seed, sea salt, mild black peppercorns, apple cider vinegar, and garlic. The most popular hot sauce, "El Yucateco," is made in Mérida, Yucatán. Hot sauces in Mérida are usually made from the indigenous chiles in the area which include: Chile Xcatik, Chile Seco de Yucatán, and Chile Habenero.

Día de los Muertos

Día de los Muertos, or **Day of the Dead,** throughout much of the Catholic world, especially in Latin America, is a time to celebrate life by remembering loved ones who have died. Friends and family members gather to clean and decorate graveyards and visit cemeteries offering prayers for the dead, set up devotional altars in their homes where they make offerings of food and drink to the deceased and gather to tell stories about ancestors, family lore, and recall loving anecdotes of friends and family who have died. Here's what you need to know to participate in this colorful and life-affirming tradition that honors those we've known and loved, but have passed from this life.

In Yucatán, Day of the Dead has a very distinct Maya sensibility to it that sets it apart from other celebrations around the country when it comes to food. "Hanal Pixán" in Yucatec Maya means "food of souls," and throughout the Yucatán, Day of the Dead is referred to as "Hanal Pixán" by the Maya. There are specific dishes associated with these festivities.

The quintessential dish is the "mucbipollo," which means "buried chicken." Very similar to tamales, it is made of corn dough and wrapped in banana leaves, but unlike regular tamales, it is prepared in a larger dish. In the countryside, it is baked in an underground pit. Many families in Mérida have place orders for their "mucbipollos" with local restaurants, and there always seems to be someone in the neighborhood who specializes in making them for friends and acquaintances.

Day of the Dead nomenclature:

Los angelitos: Young children who have died.

Calavera: Skulls. Often made out of sugar and placed on *ofrendas* (offering altars) or eaten as candy.

Ceras: Candles lit to guide the souls of the departed.

Ofrenda: Altars often decorated with flowers, photos, trinkets and food in honor of deceased souls.

Pan de muerto: Sweet bread often baked into buns shaped like bones and eaten with hot chocolate or set on ofrendas.

Papel picado: Paper cut into elaborate patterns and used for decorations or on ofrendas.

Retablos: Small devotional artwork.

Answer to the often-asked questions, **What's up with the skulls? Why are there so many skulls and skeletons?** Because that's these are iconography preferred by the First Peoples, which have been incorporated into mainstream Latin American societies.

Firecrackers

What a great tradition!

Yes, it can be startling at times to hear firecrackers going off in the distance—especially when so many people are on edge about "violence" in Mexico.

In many parts of Mexico, it's customary for young men to propose engagement to their girlfriends at gatherings—family reunions, or when out with friends. And it's customary for the young man's friends to be ready for the moment when she says "Yes." How? With firecrackers nearby to celebrate the engagement!

It's also customary to have special events when there's a piñata—and the beaten up piñata, once it has been emptied of candy and treats, to be destroyed with firecrackers, as if to say good riddance. In fact, many Yucatecans celebrate New Year's Eve with a piñata in the shape of an old man, symbolizing the Old Year, and it really gets a thrashing since the Old Year never quite lived up to its promise. It's customary for the next day to destroy the piñata carcass on the sidewalk with firecrackers. So don't be surprised if on January 1st there are scores of old piñatas being blown up with firecrackers all over town by neighborhood youngsters. Good riddance to all the unmet expectations, right?!

Bombas!

In Spanish, "bomba" means an explosive, as in a car bomb; and it also means a pump, as in the pump for a well. In the Yucatán, "bomba," believe it or not, is also a naughty limerick!

Oh, yes, the Maya are culturally *very* randy, and double-entendres are part of everyday speech. So it only makes sense that, when they learned Spanish, they realized that Spanish is a very poetic language that lends itself to very naughty limericks. If you're not familiar with dirty poems, consider the Irish tradition of raunchy limericks. Here is one:

> *There once was a fellow McSweeny*
> *Who spilled some gin on his weenie*
> *Just to be couth*
> *He added vermouth*
> *Then slipped his girlfriend a martini*

Normally, the Maya will tell their limericks during public dances, where, for instance, a man and a woman are dancing and they suddenly stop. He tells a limerick, the audience shouts, BOMBA amid laughter and then the dancing resumes. Bookstores around town sell small booklets with dozens of raunchy bombas, which is really a great way to impress friends with your "cultural immersion"!

Here are three popular, rather mild, limericks—and for those who don't speak Spanish, get someone in your Spanish class to help you!

Bomba!
Tienes la cara bonita,
Tus hombros estan muy bien,
Me gusta tu cinturita,
Y lo que sigue también!

Bomba!
Quisiera ser zapatito
Y estar en tu lindo pie
Para mirar un poquito
De lo que el zapatito ve!

Bomba!
La mujer de don Wilfrido
Anda buscando un buen socio
Porque dice que el marido
No le atiende su negocio!

Now you know the kinds of jokes you'd hear if you were able to eavesdrop in Mérida's central market—and you can imagine how scandalized the Spanish missionaries were centuries ago when they encountered such a magnificently bawdy society as that of the Yucatec Maya!

Mexico's Flag

In Mexico, as in most countries, the flag is revered. It is protected by law, not only the flag itself, but its imagery. In fact, the flag, as well as the Coat of Arms, or *escudo nacional*, and the National Anthem are considered *símbolos patrios*, or patriotic symbols, of the nation, and it is against the law to desecrate them.

The flag itself consists of three vertical bands. One in green, the other in white and the last one is red. Mexican schoolchildren are taught to respect the "verde, blanco y colorado." Mexico's Coat of Arms, portraying an eagle resting on a pear cactus with a snake held in its beak and talons, which is based on an Aztec myth, is in the center of the white band. The proportions of the flag are 4:7.

The current flag was adopted in 1968, which is a slight variation of the flag first used in 1821. There have been few changes in the flag, principally reflecting changes in the Coat of Arms. The original meaning of the colors was that the green represented Independence, the white stood for religious faith, and the red was symbolic of the intermixing of the European and First Peoples of Mexico. This was changed by President Benito Juárez, whose was in office 1858 to 1872. His liberal government secularized Mexican society. Green today represents hope, white stands for unity and red is symbolic of the blood of fallen heroes who have defended the nation.

Mexico's Coat of Arms is the most distinctive feature of the Mexican flag. Legend has it that the Aztecs, a nomadic people from northern Mexico, established themselves in the Valley of Mexico when a prophecy was fulfilled. The Aztecs, who were also known as the "Mexica," pronounced "meh-shee-ka," believed that Huitzilopochtli, their God of War, had ordered them to build their city—Tenochtitlán—where they would come upon an eagle devouring a serpent while resting on a prickly pear cactus. Unfortunately for the Aztecs, they came upon such a scene in an inhospitable area of the Valley of Mexico, a series of swamps and marshes amid three lakes.

But in fulfillment of their beliefs, they set about to dredge the swamps and lakes, and build a city in the center of the Valley of Mexico. The resulting metropolis, with pyramids and temples amid a series of canals would, centuries later, remind the Spanish of Venice.

Flag Day is February 24, a national holiday celebrated with civic ceremonies throughout the nation that are solemn and joyous. Viva Mexico!

Gremios

What are "Gremios"?

Each fall, beginning in September, there are a series of religious processions through the streets in all the neighborhoods throughout the Historic Center. These are known as "los gremios," or "the guilds." They trace their origin to Medieval Europe, and the first one is September 14 at the Cathedral on the Main Square. At 9 AM in the morning the Christ of the Blisters is removed from its sanctuary and there is a mass to commence the Guild Season at precisely 11 AM.

From September 27 through October 17 there will be scores of processions, with various saints and virgins honored through celebrations. The origin, of course, stems from the belief that different saints offered protection for various trades. There are patron saints who watch over bakers, market stall vendors, shoemakers, teachers, homemakers, taxi cab drivers, carpenters, and so forth. Each profession, like a union, reserves a day and time when they will make a pilgrimage to honor their profession's patron saint.

The procession consists of pilgrims, usually accompanied by a small band, and young men with fireworks—holding banners and often times carrying their saint aloft. The women tend to wear impeccable Maya dresses—white huipiles with beautiful embroidery. The men often wear crisp guayabera shirts. So it goes for about three weeks until October 17, when at 11 AM a procession returns the Christ of the Blisters to its rightful spot, and mass is celebrated.

This tradition dates back to 1654 and is the longest, continuously celebrated Guilds in Mexico.

Here's a breakdown of the processions, by date and trade:

September processions:
27-28, Construction workers
28-29, Small business owners
29-30, Supplicants of Christ
30-1 October, Mirror, aluminum and glass workers

October processions:
1-2, Shoemakers
2-3, Seamstresses and embroiderers
3-4, Taxi drivers
4-5, Painters
5-6, Mechanics and ironworkers
6-7, Carpenters
7-8, Women
8-9, Business owners
9-10, Shop owners
10-11, Shop owners and workers
11-12, Teachers and students
12-13, Bakers
13-14, Train workers
14-15, Trinket stall owners and employees
15-16, Professionals
16-17, Market stall vendors

For more information call the Archdiocese: (999) 928-6131.

Mardi Gras–Carnaval

Mérida celebrates Mardi Gras to the fullest. It has, in fact, the third-largest Mardi Gras in the nation. (Only the ones in Veracruz and Mazatlán are bigger.) That said, be prepared for a week of festivities and parades, all leading up to a huge street party where revelers are out and about in full revelry.

Mardi Gras was held along Paseo de Montejo but beginning in 2014 it is being relocated to the State Fair Grounds (Xmatkuil because it has grown so large and so popular. In recent years it has become somewhat unruly. Compared with Mardi Gras in Rio de Janeiro, Brazil or New Orleans in the U.S., people in Mérida keep their wits about them—and there is a great deal less public drunkenness and disorderly conduct than one normally associates with such public displays of excess. But it still is a time when it seems the entire city goes a bit crazy—and that's crazy in a good way.

How popular is Mardi Gras? Consider this: The City maintains a full-time office to coordinate all activities associated with "el Carnaval." For more information, city government maintains a website dedicated exclusively to the Mardi Gras.

Here it is: *www.merida.gob.mx/carnaval/index.html*

Mexican Holidays

January 1: New Year's Day

January 6: Founding of Mérida

February 7: Constitution Day

March 21: Birthday of Benito Juárez

March-April: Holy Week

April 30: Day of the Child

May 10: Mother's Day

September 16: Independence Day; Feast Day for Mérida's Christ of the Blisters

October: Festival of Fall

November 1: Day of the Innocents

November 2: Day of the Dead & Hanal Pixan

December 12: Day of the Virgin of Guadalupe

December 24: Christmas Eve (Nochebuena)

December 25: Navidad (Christmas Day)

Buen Provecho & Social Politeness!

There will come a time when you will be sitting at a restaurant and someone you know will be across the room. If they approach you, either on their way in or their way out, or come directly to your table to say hello, they might very well say "Buen provecho," when they either pass by, or take their leave.

What does that mean? Two simple words, really, but they are loaded with meaning. It's easy to say it's the Spanish equivalent of "Bon Appetit," or "Guten Appetit," but these fall short in comparison. In Spanish it conveys the hope that the meal is pleasing and enjoyable—and that it is beneficial to your health.

It's such a gracious expression that sometimes complete strangers will say it to each other, when one is leaving a restaurant and passes by a table that is being served. Get in the habit of using it, since it's seen as a mark of good breeding and civility.

And speaking of social politeness, take these recommendations from our friends at Mexperience.com to heart:

"Politeness, patience and tolerance in situations, however frustrating they may appear, is always appreciated and, indeed, ultimately rewarded in Mexico. Conversely, a display of impatience, anger, frustration or lack of general respect in formal or informal situations tend to fall on 'deaf ears' when dealing with most people in Mexico; ...the ultimate outcome in a situation could be made worse for you through deliberate obstruction or total rejection of your wishes, ...as a reaction to what is deemed your impoliteness."

And ...

"Personal space: Mexicans tend to stand closer to each other than in the US and Europe. It may be off-putting at first, if you are used to having two feet or more of 'air' between you and other people (and especially those of the same gender as you), but in Mexico it's quite common for people to stand and converse with each other a foot or less away from each other, regardless of gender. Stepping back too far may be taken as a sign of mistrust."

And …

"If you invite someone to eat out, it is assumed (and expected) that you will settle the bill. Splitting the bill is not done in Mexico and, indeed, suggesting it should be done is considered rude and uncouth. The invitee(s) will always offer to pay: this is a social grace, and one that should always be politely declined. If you are invited out for a meal you, too, should offer to pay, and then gratefully accept the decline of your offer."

19 PHILANTHROPY & NON-PROFIT ORGANIZATIONS

If an organization solicits a donation from the public, but cannot provide an official receipt that is accepted by Mexico's federal tax and revenue agency, known as the Secretaria de Hacienda y Credito Público, or SHCP, it is violating the law. Mexican law is very clear that solicitation from the **public at large** can only be made by bona fide nonprofit organizations duly authorized to solicit donations and issue tax-deductible receipts. "Civil Associations," or "asociaciones civiles," can **receive** donations, but not through **public** fund-raising activities, and their receipts are not accepted as tax-deductible donations. Protect yourself from scams.

This is a list of bona fide non-profit organizations duly authorized by the SHCP to solicit donations **from the public** and issue tax-deductible receipts. The list may not be complete, so one way to make sure that an organization is authorized to solicit donations is to ask for an official receipt—"un recibo fiscal." **EVERY** organization authorized to solicit donations from the public **MUST** give you such a receipt, and if they cannot do so, then they are soliciting donations unlawfully!

Authorized Nonprofit Organizations Operating in the State of Yucatán

Albergue del Anciano en Progreso, A.C.

Albergue de San Vicente de Mérida, A.C.

Asilo de Ancianos, Señor de la Misericordia, A.C.

Alas al Vuelo, A.C.

Amanecer Nuevamente, A.C.

Amigos del Macay, A.C.

Apoyo a los Valores Humanos, A.C.

Aprendamos Juntos, A.C.

Asilo Brunet Celarain, A.C.

Asociación de Ayuda Alimenticia para Personas de Escasos Recursos Económicos, A.C

Asociación Cultural Teotepec, S.C.

Asociación para la Equinoterapia, A.C.

Asociación Hacia Todos los Caminos, A.C.

Asociación Mexicana de Ayuda a Niños con Cáncer Peninsular, A.C.

Asociación Mexicana para la Comunicación y Superación de las Personas con Discapacidad Auditiva, A.C.

Asociación Mexicana de Esclerosis Tuberosa, A.C.

Asociación Yucateca de Lucha contra el Autismo y Otros Transtornos del Desarrollo, A.C.

Asociación Yucateca de Padres de Familia Pro-Deficiente Mental, A.C.

Asociación Yucateca Pro-Deficiente Auditivo, A.C.

Avelino Montes Linaje, A.C.

Ayuda a la Mujer Embarazada, A.C.

Banco de Alimentos de Mérida, A.C.

Banco del Vestido, A.C.

Bien Cimentado, A.C.

Biocenosis, A.C.

Caballeros Kadosh, A.C.

Cáritas de Yucatán, A.C.

Casa para Ancianos Desamparados La Divina Providencia, A.C.

Casa Infantil El Roble, A.C.

Centro de Atención a Madres Solteras de Yucatán, A.C.

Colegio América de Mérida, A.C.

Centro Asistencial para la Superación de la Mujer en la Familia, A.C.

Comunidad Coox Meyaj, A.C.

Centro de Comunicación y Servicios Sociales, A.C.

Centro Comunitario Yutsil, A.C.

Comité de Desarrollo Integral, A.C.

Centro de Desarrollo Integral Enséñame a Caminar por la Vida, A.C.

Centro de Educación Especial La Luz de un Nuevo Amanecer, A.C.

Centro Escolar Miguel Alemán, A.C.

Centro de Investigación Científica de Yucatán, A.C.

Centro Loyola de Mérida, A.C.

Centro Social El Porvenir, A.C.

Centro Universitario Montejo, A.C.

Club Especial Ayelem, A.C.

Colegio Mérida, A.C.

Colegio Montejo, A.C.

Colegio Peninsular, A.C.

Colegio Teresa de Avila de Tizimín, A.C.

El Comienzo de un Nuevo Viaje, A.C.

Comunidad Vicentina de Mérida, A.C.

Convicción Social, A.C.

Cottolengo de Yucatán, A.C.

Daré de Mérida, A.C.

Dispensario María Soledad, A.C.

Educación Peninsular, A.C.

Educarte, A.C.

Escuela Jeanne de Matel, A.C.

Escuela Joaquín Peón, A.C.

Educación Profesional Peninsular, A.C.

Escuela Vasco de Quiroga, A.C.

Fundación Alborada, A.C.

Fundación de Apoyo Infantil Yucatán, A.C.

Fundación Banco del Vestido, A.C.

Fundación Bepensa, A.C.

Fundación para el Bienestar Natural, A.C.

Fundación CHI´K´AK´NAB para la Conservación de la Biodiversidad, el Desarrollo Sustentable y la Cultura, A.C.

Fundación Cultural Macay, A.C.

Fundación Emanuel de Mérida, A.C.

Fundación García Lavín, I.B.P.

Fundación Guadalupe Basteris de Molina, A.C.

Fundación Gruber Jez, A.C.

Fundación Grupo Abraham, A.C.

Fundación Kuri, A.C.

Fundación Mexicana para la Salud Capítulo Peninsular, A.C.

Fundación México-Libanesa, A.C.

Fundación Nicolás Urcelay, A.C.

Fundación Nicolás Xacur Slaimen, A.C.

Fundación de Orientación Holística, A.C.

Fundación Plan Estratégico de Mérida, A.C.

Fundación Progreso Yucatán, A.C.

Fundación Roche, A.C.

Fundación por la Salud en Yucatán, A.C.

Fundación Siqueff Millet, A.C.

Fundación de la Universidad Autónoma de Yucatán, A.C.

Fundación Valentina Arrigunaga Peón, A.C.

Fundación Yucatán, A.C.

Grupo de Apoyo a Pacientes Traumatizados y Ortopédicos, A.C.

Grupo Kerigma, A.C.

El Hombre sobre la Tierra, A.C.

Institución Asistencial, A.C.

Instituto José Pablo Rovalo Azcue, A.C.

Impulso Universitario, A.C.

Impulsora del Colegio Jenaro Rodríguez Correa, A.C.

Inter Universidad del Sureste, A.C.

Jesús de la Misericordia, A.C.

Joven Ballet de Mérida, A.C.

Luisa María Clar, A.C.

Mano Amiga Yucatán Conkal, A.C.
Mérida Itzáes Yucatán, A.C.

El Milagro de la Vejez, A.C.

Motolinía de Mérida, A.C.

Museo de la Canción Yucateca, A.C.

Niños y Crías, A.C.

Oasis de San Juan de Dios, A.C.

Organización de Servicios y Ayuda para la Navidad de los Enfermos, A.C.

Pastoral del Amor, A.C.

Patrimonio Peninsular, A.C.

Patronato de la Escuela de Educación Especial Roberto Solís Quiroga, A.C.

Patronato de Hogares Juveniles, A.C.

Patronato para la Orquesta Sinfónica de Yucatán, A.C.

Patronato Pro Historia Peninsular de Yucatán, A.C.

Patronato Peninsular Pro Niños con Deficiencia Mental, A.C.

Patronato Vida Humana Integral, A.C.

Pronatura Península de Yucatán, A.C.

Protección de la Joven María Suárez Molina, A.C.

Púrpura Plastika Fundación Cultural para el Desarrollo y la Expresión Artística, A.C.

Proyección Valor, A.C.

Red de Ecoturismo de Yucatán, A.C.

Refugio para Ancianos, A.C.

El Renacer del Mayab, A.C.

Serfam, A.C.

Sol y Luna, A.C.

Tras una Sonrisa, A.C.

Universidad del Mayab, S.C.

Universidad Marista de Mérida, A.C.

Ven Vive Convive, A.C.

Vida y Familia de Mérida, A.C.

Vive y Trasciende, A.C.

Voluntarias Vicentinas, A.C.

The Danger of the Hapless Altruist

This is a big country. This is an important country.

Far too many Americans make the mistake of thinking, when they move to Mexico, that they have moved to the same country as it was portrayed in the 1950s, that of a nation making the transition from an agricultural society to a modern, industrial one. If you think of Mexico as a backwards, unsophisticated nation, then you have to readjust your thinking.

Mexico is one of the most important nations in the world. It's a member of the G-20, which means that it is in top percentile of nations in the world. The World Bank, the International Monetary Fund and the CIA World Factbook each rank Mexico as the 14th largest economy on the planet.[4] When it comes to social programs, it has one of the most comprehensive social welfare systems anywhere in the hemisphere—only Canada has more social programs. Every conceivable concern is looked after, from an aggressive (and very successful) HIV education and prevention

program, to a thorough and comprehensive health care system, to tough child-welfare programs, to pioneering environmental protection agencies. The peso, Mexico's currency, is one of the most stable in the world, often used in a basket of currencies by the IMF to support other central banks. This is a country that strives, albeit imperfectly and not always successfully, with providing for the general welfare.

Yes, given its resources and its population, many people fall between the cracks. Of Mexico's population of 110,000,000 people, just fewer than 80,000,000 are active participants in the nation's social welfare programs. That leaves 30,000,000 living in the "informal economy," as it is euphemistically called. For comparative purposes, 1 in 7 Americans rely on food stamps to feed their families, and in the largest American city, New York, 1 in 4 children live below the federal poverty line. No country addresses all of the needs of its people, but Mexico is diligent in working towards that end.

If you think that this is a country with no laws or legal institutions, a kind of place reminiscent of some Hollywood movie where it's the "Wild, Wild West," then you are in for a surprise. Mexico is one of the most bureaucratic nations in the hemisphere—it rivals France when it comes to official paperwork! And it rivals the Scandinavian countries when it comes to its aspirations for being a "nanny state." In fact, international agencies—from the World Bank to the International Monetary Fund—continue to remind Mexico that is has to "streamline" its bureaucracy if it wants to become more competitive in the global economy.

If you thought that the Instituto Nacional de Migración (INM) had a lot of paperwork for issuing an FM2 or FM3 visa or the new immigration documents, or that the Comision Federal de Electricidad (CFE) required lots of documentation before it opened an electric account in your name, that's a taste of the level of scrutiny applied to every facet of life in Mexico.

---

[4] See: en.wikipedia.org/wiki/List_of_countries_by_GDP_(nominal)

Mexico, in many ways, is a pioneering society. In December 2010, for instance, Yucatán State government announced the formation of an Office of Climatic Change (Oficina de Cambio Climático), with a $35 million peso budget, and which would work to coordinate efforts with the state governments of Campeche and Quintana Roo, in order to understand and mitigate the effects of climatic changes throughout the peninsula. If this isn't a progressive and proactive place, than what is?

The reason it's important to understand this about Mexico is to prevent you from making mistakes that many English-speaking expats make: they look around, and since they can't speak the language, or understand how Mexcian society is organized, they presume that if they don't see it, it's not there. And then, with good intentions, they go about creating a *parallel* initiative, one without the political or societal foundation for enduring success.

It is always advisable to work within the **established** system. Become **informed**. Find out if there are organizations or government agencies already working on the issue about which you are passionate, and then see how you can contribute. Look at the breathtaking variety of nonprofit organizations already up and running in Yucatán State and you are sure to find something about which you are passionate.

You will be welcomed, but if you ignore the established groups, and launch an expatriate-led initiative that excludes the existing organizations, you will be marginalized. As with most charitable endeavors, a bit of soul-searching is always in order. Ask yourself this: Are you trying to give to the community around you, or are you attempting to ameliorate a disappointment in your life? The answer will determine the place from which you are coming when you reach out and those around you.

Expatriates Contribute to Mexico's Charitable Organizations

By Anne McEnany

Due to the value that expatriate Americans place on their voluntary service as a way to forge a sense of belonging in their adopted communities, the degree of volunteerism, charitable giving, and civic engagement is potentially greater among U.S. retirees in Mexico than those residing in the U.S.:

• Respondents not only give in Mexico, but continue to give in the U.S. as well. Almost 70% of respondents reported contributing financially to Mexican charitable organizations, with over half (53%) reported donating over $100, sometimes significantly more, including over 4% that gave over $2,500 annually.

• Over 51% of those surveyed continue to contribute to U.S. charities back in their communities of origin.

• Relatively few of these donors receive a tax deduction in the U.S. or Mexico for their gifts (15%).

• Nearly 60% of respondents volunteer their time to a charitable cause in Mexico and over 29% volunteer at least once a week or on a regular basis. Respondents engage in a wide range of volunteer activities, most prominently with education-focused charities, community projects, and the environment.

• U.S retirees in Mexico volunteer because of their strong sense of social responsibility and desire to make a difference in their adopted communities. Survey respondents reported that their volunteer efforts increase their sense of belonging in Mexico, and contribute to an increased sense of community among local neighbors and friends.

• 42% of American retirees surveyed are actively involved in at least one or two Mexican charities in their adopted communities, while another 11% are affiliated with more than three

Source: "U.S. Retirement Trends in Mexico's Coastal Communities," International Community Foundation, Webiste: *www.icfdn.org*.

Five Organizations to Stay Away From! (in our opinion)

The following organizations have been known to solicit donations from the public, primarily targeting American expatriates, but do not appear on the official list compiled by the SHCP. In other words, these organizations have targeted the expat community to solicit donations without having met the legal requirements under Mexican law. Be careful: **Amigos de Artesanos Nuevos de Yucatán (AANY), Brazos Abiertos, Inc., Fundación BAI, A.C., Mérida English Language Library (MELL),** and **Mérida Verde.**

The reasons?

Under Mexican law, nonprofit organizations must be registered with Hacienda (SHCP) and be authorized to solicit donations from the public.

348

If an organization is not able to provide you with *Recibos Fiscales* (Official Receipts), they are not authorized to be soliciting donations from the public. And, in consequence, they are engaged in fraud. There are also rules governing how funds are handled. For instance, it's illegal to ask donors to send money to bank accounts in foreign countries, since all funds raised in Mexico for charitable organizations must be deposited directly into Mexican bank accounts. No funds raised for charitable purposes can leave Mexico as well. This means that all monies raised in Mexico for charitable purposes in Mexico must remain in Mexico.

These organizations do not comply with legal requirements:

Amigos de Artesanos Nuevos de Yucatán (AANY). Consider that in an email sent to contributors, Joan Farrell instructed donors that, "When you have your donation ready just e-mail me and we will find an easy way for you to get it to us, either by deposit in a US account …" This constitutes money laundering and fraud under Mexican laws. Imagine if a group of Mexicans showed up in, say, Chicago, announced they wanted to help local artists and then asked that you send your donation to their bank account in Mexico City. What? AANY has asked donors to send money to bank accounts in the U.S. while claiming to be doing charitable work in Mexico.

Brazos Abiertos, Inc. has never been authorized to operate in Mexico. This was a scam and the two ringleaders, José Solis and John Truax, fled to the U.S. once their scam was exposed. Ellen Fields and James Fields who, thorugh Yucatan Living, promoted this scam, alo fled Mexico.

Fundacion BAI, A.C., a new version of the Brazos Abiertos scam, is run by Carlos Cabrera with the help of local expats who want to continue the fun little scam they had going on. Suffice it to say that if you asked for a *Recibo Fiscal* what you will get is one hundred and one excuses why their paperwork has not been processed.

Mérida English Language Library is so poorly run—and not properly licensed—that when their director emptied the library's bank account of *almost half a million pesos*, the library could do nothing about it—since those funds were raised in violation of Mexican law. Before you make a donation, ask for a *Recibo Fiscal* and see what excuse they offer.

Mérida Verde, founded by Julie Hoover as an environmental organization, soon became her own Political Action Committee (PAC) which caused a furor when she held, on May 29, 2011, a news conference to *denounce* Mérida city government. Taking political positions and adopting political advocacy programs, remain forbidden activities for foreigners. Remember, foreigners are prohibited from running any Political Action Committees (PAC).

Part VI

Almost Paradise ...

20 ATTORNEYS & PUBLIC NOTARIES

Dealing with a Mexican Attorney

When it comes to hiring an attorney, many of whom are also Public Notaries, the Mérida Consulate advises U.S. citizens:

How to Deal with Your Foreign Attorney:
a) Find out the attorney's qualifications and experience.
b) Find out how the attorney plans to represent you. Ask specific questions and expect the attorney to explain the legal process in the country concerned, as well as the legal activities planned on your behalf, in language that you can understand. Have your attorney analyze your case, giving you the positive and negative aspects and probable outcome. Be honest with your attorney. Tell the attorney every relevant fact in order to get the best representation of your interests. Do not fail to ask how much time the attorney anticipates the case may take to complete.
c) Find out what fees the country charges and what fees are expected. Some attorneys expect payment in advance; some demand payment after each action taken, refusing to proceed until they are paid. Others may take the case on a percentage basis, collecting a pre-arranged percentage of the monies awarded by a foreign court.
d) Ask that your attorney keep you advised of the progress your case according to a pre-established schedule. Remember your responsibility to keep your attorney informed of any new developments in your case. Request copies of all letters and documents prepared on your behalf.
e) Do not expect your attorney to give a simple answer to a complex legal problem. Be sure you understand the technical language contained in any contract or other legal document prepared by your attorney.

In addition to the comments made by the U.S. Consulate there is also another consideration that is very, very important. As someone moving to Mérida, you are moving into an established community. Think what would happen if you, for instance, moved from New York to Cleveland. Arriving in Cleveland, you enter an established community where people know each other, often for several generations, and know "the lay of the land." As someone moving in, how long will you be here? Forever, or for a few years?

No one knows, but the people who are established in Cleveland are more likely to remain in Cleveland, whether you stay or go.

In other words, do you know the relationships that your attorney has with others in Mérida? Are you certain that, for instance, if you hire an attorney to represent you in purchasing a house that, in a what-a-small-world moment, it turns out that your attorney knows the seller's attorney, or the seller, or the seller's family?

Mérida is a city of a million people, but it can also resemble a small town. Be aware that there may be conflicts of interest arising from social, business or family relationships and connections. Be mindful that there may be conflicts of interest. Make sure that your attorney has *your* best interests at heart. Make sure that your attorney does not favor the other party—conscientiously or unconscientiously—because of existing relationships. If you have any doubts, it might be a good idea to hire a different attorney to look over the paperwork before you go forward.

These kinds of conflicts of interest are human, and more likely to occur when you are in a situation in which you are moving into an existing community where people have been here for generations.

Heed this advice: Never assume that the attorney you hire is exempt from a conflict of interest or unconscious bias that will undermine his or her ability to represent your interests fully.

With this in mind, here is a list of the attorneys in Mérida compiled by the State Department in Washington, D.C. for providing to American citizens in Mérida.

Please remember that choosing an attorney is a serious matter, and it is advisable that you consult with people you know and trust. Conversely, it is always a good idea to ask an attorney for two or three references from American or Canadian citizens for whom they have offered services.

In compiling this list, only attorneys who comply with State Department criteria are included here.

Mérida

Lic. Salvador Augusto Avila Arjona

Address: Calle 20 #203 by 29, Colonia García Ginerés, Mérida, Yucatán, 97070
Telephone: (999) 920-1133 (phone and fax)
Mobile: (999) 947-1727
Email: avila@racabogados.com.mx
Languages: Speaks Spanish and fluent English.
Specializes in: Contracts, corporations, criminal law, estates, foreign investments, immigration, marketing agreements, obtaining civil documents such as birth and death certificates, patents/trademarks/copyrights, theft/fraud/embezzlement. Masters Degree in corporate law at Anahuac University in 2005. Has practiced law for 20 years, experience in Yucatán, Campeche, Quintana Roo, Nuevo Leon, and Mexico City. Professional license number 4563411, issued on September 13, 2005.

Lic. Raúl Ballote Pantoja

Address: Calle 62 #313-A between Calle 35 and 37 Street, Centro, Mérida, Yucatán
Telephone: (999) 920-2011 ext.104
Mobile: (999) 947-1832
Email: raul@raulballote.com
Languages: Speaks Spanish and Full command of English. Limited French—Reading ability.
Specializes in: Contracts, corporations, foreign investments, immigration, real estate law. Certified legal Translator and Notary. Has practiced law for more than 20 years, experience in Yucatán, Campeche, and Quintana Roo. Professional license number 188243, issued on June 21, 1971. Lawyer registry number 3016, issued on March 6, 1996.

Lic. Luis Miguel Ceballos Capetillo

Address: Calle 20 #203-A by 29 Street, Colonia García Ginerés. Mérida, Yucatán, 97070
Phone and Fax: 999-920-1133
Mobile: 998-100-0873
Email: ceballos@racabogados.com.mx
Languages: Speaks Spanish and fluent English.
Specializes in: Contracts, corporations, criminal law, estates, foreign investments, investment, immigration, marketing agreements, obtaining civil documents such as birth and death certificates, patents/trademarks/copyrights, theft/fraud/embezzlement, notary law.

Notary and Translator. Has practiced law for 13 years, experience in Campeche, Yucatán, and Quintana Roo. Professional license number 2490012, issued on 1997.

Lic. Jaime Uriel Pacheco Torres

Address: Calle 58 #526-E between Calle 55 and 57 Street, Fracc. Las Granjas, Mérida, Yucatán, 97197
Telephone: (999) 941-2571
Mobile: (999)163-9602
Email: jaime0712@hotmail.com
Languages: Spanish, Limited English
Specializes in: Auto/accidents, banking/financial, contracts, corporations, criminal law, government relations, insurance, investment, patents/trademarks/copyrights, theft/fraud/embezzlement. Has practiced law for 8 years, experience in Yucatán, Campeche, Tabasco, and Quintana Roo. Professional license number 6024403, issued on June 24, 2009.

Lic. José Ignacio Puerto Gutiérrez

Address: Calle 25 #159 by 30 Street, Colonia García Ginerés, Mérida, Yucatán, 97100
Telephone: (999) 920-3050 (phone and fax)
Mobile: (999) 900-3260
Email: ipuerto@puertoypino.com
Languages: Speaks Spanish and fluent English.
Specializes in: Banking/financial, civil damages, collections, contracts, corporations, criminal law, estates, foreign investments, government relations, investment, immigration, labor relations, marketing agreements, marriage/divorce, patents/trademarks/copyrights, taxes, theft/fraud/embezzlement. Masters Degree in corporate law at Yale University in 1991. Has practiced law for 21 years, experience in New York City, Mexico City and Yucatán. Professional license number 1656658, issued on May 4, 1992. Lawyer registry number 2698, issued on August 17, 2000.

Lic. Mauricio Arturo Rojano Romero

Address: Calle 20 #203-A by 29 Street, Colonia García Ginerés, Mérida, Yucatán, 97070
Telephone: (999) 920-1133 (phone and fax)
Mobile: (999) 910-0464
Email: rojano@racabogados.com.mx
Languages: Speaks Spanish and fluent English.

Specializes in: Contracts, corporations, criminal law, estates, foreign investments, immigration, marketing agreements, investment, obtaining civil documents such as birth and death certificates, patents/trademarks/copyrights, theft/fraud/embezzlement, notary law. Has practiced law for 15 years, experience in Yucatán, Campeche and Quintana Roo. Professional license number 2170137, issued on September 26, 1995.

Valladolid

Lic. Salvador Augusto Avila Arjona

Address: Calle 20 #203 by 29 Street, Colonia García Ginerés, Mérida, Yucatán, 97070
Telephone: (999) 920-1133 (phone and fax)
Mobile: (999) 947-1727
Email: avila@racabogados.com.mx
Languages: Speaks Spanish and fluent English.
Specializes in: Contracts, corporations, criminal law, estates, foreign investments, immigration, marketing agreements, obtaining civil documents such as birth and death certificates, patents/trademarks/copyrights, theft/fraud/embezzlement. Masters Degree in corporate law at Anahuac University in 2005. Has practiced law for 20 years, experience in Yucatán, Campeche, Quintana Roo, Nuevo Leon, and Mexico City. Professional license number 4563411, issued on September 13, 2005.

Lic. Raúl Ballote Pantoja

Address: Calle 62 #313-A between Calle 35 and 37 Street, Centro, Mérida, Yucatán, 97000
Telephone: (999) 920-2011 ext.104
Mobile: (999) 947-1832
Email: raul@raulballote.com
Languages: Speaks Spanish and Full command of English. Limited French—Reading ability.
Specializes in: Contracts, corporations, foreign investments, immigration, real estate law. Certified legal Translator and Notary. Has practiced law for more than 20 years, experience in Yucatán, Campeche, and Quintana Roo. Professional license number 188243, issued on June 21, 1971. Lawyer registry number 3016, issued on March 6, 1996.

Lic. Jaime Uriel Pacheco Torres

Address: Calle 58 #526-E between Calle 55 and 57 Street, Fracc. Las Granjas, Mérida, Yucatán, 97197
Telephone: (999) 941-2571

Mobile: (999)163-9602
Email: jaime0712@hotmail.com
Languages: Spanish, Limited English
Specializes in: Auto/accidents, banking/financial, contracts, corporations, criminal law, government relations, insurance, investment, patents/trademarks/copyrights, theft/fraud/embezzlement. Has practiced law for 8 years, experience in Yucatán, Campeche, Tabasco, and Quintana Roo. Professional license number 6024403, issued on June 24, 2009.

Lic. José Ignacio Puerto Gutiérrez

Address: Calle 25 #159 by 30 Street, Colonia García Ginerés, Mérida, Yucatán, 97100
Telephone: (999) 920-3050 (phone and fax)
Mobile: (999) 900-3260
Email: ipuerto@puertoypino.com
Languages: Speaks Spanish and fluent English.
Specializes in: Banking/financial, civil damages, collections, contracts, corporations, criminal law, estates, foreign investments, government relations, investment, immigration, labor relations, marketing agreements, marriage/divorce, patents/trademarks/copyrights, taxes, theft/fraud/embezzlement. Masters Degree in corporate law at Yale University in 1991. Has practiced law for 21 years, experience in New York City, Mexico City and Yucatán. Professional license number 1656658, issued on May 4, 1992. Lawyer registry number 2698, issued on August 17, 2000.

Lic. Mauricio Arturo Rojano Romero

Address: Calle 20 #203-A by 29 Street, Colonia García Ginerés, Mérida, Yucatán, 97070
Telephone: (999) 920-1133 (phone and fax)
Mobile: (999) 910-0464
Email: rojano@racabogados.com.mx
Languages: Speaks Spanish and fluent English.
Specializes in: Contracts, corporations, criminal law, estates, foreign investments, immigration, marketing agreements, investment, obtaining civil documents such as birth and death certificates, patents/trademarks/copyrights, theft/fraud/embezzlement, notary law. Has practiced law for 15 years, experience in Yucatán, Campeche and Quintana Roo. Professional license number 2170137, issued on September 26, 1995.

Cancún, Quintana Roo

Lic. Ivan Itzmael Aldave Vázquez

Address: Boulevard Kukulkan, Manzana 52, Lote 18-12, Km. 12 J-2 Zona Hotelera, Cancún, Quintana Roo
Telephone: (998) 176-8180 / 82
Mobile: (998) 100-2007
Email: ialdave@aldaveabogados.com
Languages: Speaks Spanish and fluent English.
Specializes in: Banking/financial, civil damages, collections, contracts, corporations, foreign investments, insurance, investment, immigration, marketing agreements, marriage/divorce, patents/trademarks/copyrights, taxes. Has practiced law for 21 years, experience in Mexico City and Quintana Roo. Professional license number 1948644, issued on June 8, 1994.

Lic. Raúl Ballote Pantoja

Address: Calle 62 #313-A between Calle 35 and 37, Centro, Mérida, Yucatán, 97000
Telephone: (999) 920-2011 ext.104
Mobile: (999) 947-1832
Email: raul@raulballote.com
Languages: Speaks Spanish and full command of English. Limited French—Reading ability.
Specializes in: Contracts, corporations, foreign investments, immigration, real estate law. Certified legal Translator and Notary. Has practiced law for more than 20 years, experience in Yucatán, Campeche, and Quintana Roo. Professional license number 188243, issued on June 21, 1971. Lawyer registry number 3016, issued on March 6, 1996.

Lic. Humberto Baquedano Parra

Address: Real de Minas, Casa 8-A, Supermanzana 45, Manzana 2, lote 2, Cancún, Quintana Roo
Telephone: 998-843-5881, 998-848-0482
Mobile: 998-100-2737, 998-577-3250, 998-842-0639
Email: h_baquedano@hotmail.com
Languages: Speaks Spanish, fluent English, and French 80%.
Specializes in: Adoptions, auto/accidents, child custody, civil damages, collections, contracts, corporations, criminal law, government relations, marriage/divorce, narcotics, obtaining civil documents such as birth and death certificates, theft/fraud/embezzlement. Has practiced

law for 20 years in all Yucatán Peninsula. Professional license number 2170143, issued on November 22, 2005.

Lic. Luis Miguel Ceballos Capetillo

Address: Calle 20 #203-A by 29 Street, Colonia García Ginerés, Mérida, Yucatán 97070
Phone and Fax: 999-920-1133
Mobile: 998-100-0873
Email: ceballos@racabogados.com.mx
Languages: Speaks Spanish and fluent English.
Specializes in: Contracts, corporations, criminal law, estates, foreign investments, investment, immigration, marketing agreements, obtaining civil documents such as birth and death certificates, patents/trademarks/copyrights, theft/fraud/embezzlement, notary law. Notary and Translator. Has practiced law for 13 years, experience in Campeche, Yucatán, and Quintana Roo. Professional license number 2490012, issued on 1997.

Lic. Juan José Corona Barssé

Address: Reno #45, Supermanzana 20, Manzana 20, Cancún, Quintana Roo
Telephone: 998-884-3437, 998-884-5717
Mobile: 998-100-2604
Fax: 998-884-5393
Email: jj@coronabarsse.com and jjcb@prodigy.net.mx
Languages: Speaks Spanish and fluent English.
Specializes in: Contracts, corporations, foreign investments, investment, immigration, and real estate. Notary and Translator. Has practiced law for 30 years, experience in Mexico City and Quintana Roo. Professional license number 978223, issued on May 3, 1985.

Lic. Fernando Doblado Rueda

Address: Avenida Nader #28-1, Primer Piso Edificio Popolna, Supermanzana 2, Cancún, Quintana Roo
Phone/Fax: (998) 898-0306, 998-898-1422
Email: fdr@asd.com.mx
Languages: Speaks Spanish and fluent English.
Specializes in: Aeronautical/Maritime, banking/financial, collections, contracts, corporations, foreign investments, government relations, investment, immigration, marketing agreements, patents/trademarks/copyrights, taxes, real estate. Has practiced law for 25 years in Quintana Roo. Professional license number 1402683, issued on October 9, 1989.

359

Lic. José Guillermo González Lomeli

Address: Seccion las Luciernagas, Supermanzana 17, Manzana 4, Lote 44, Avenida Contoy, Cancún, Quintana Roo
Telephone: (998) 884-4575
Fax: (998) 884-4531
Mobile: (998) 846-4921 and (998) 577-7398
Email: memolomeli2010@hotmail.com
Languages: Speaks Spanish, good English, and Italian.
Specializes in: Auto/accidents, child custody, contracts, corporations, criminal law, foreign investments, government relations, investment, immigration, labor relations, marriage/divorce, narcotics, obtaining civil documents such as birth and death certificates, patents/trademarks/copyrights, theft/fraud/embezzlement. Translator at court. Has practiced law for 13 years in Quintana Roo. Professional license number 4577834, issued on October 10, 2005.

Lic. Ernesto Che Gutiérrez Pérez

Address: Avenida Bonampak, Supermanzana 4, Manzana 6, lote 38-A, Office B, Cancún, Quintana Roo
Telephone: 998-892-7897
Mobile: 998-865-5999
Email: Cancun-lawyer@hotmail.com
Languages: Speaks Spanish, good English, and good French.
Specializes in: Adoptions, auto/accidents, child custody, collections, civil damages, contracts, corporations, criminal law, estates, foreign claims, foreign investments, government relations, insurance, investment, immigration, labor relations, marketing agreements, marriage/divorce, obtaining civil documents such as birth and death certificates, patents/trademarks/copyrights, taxes, theft/fraud/embezzlement, tourism law. Has practiced law for 27 years, experience in Mexico City, Puebla, Nayarit, Jalisco, Morelos, and Estado de Mexico. Professional license number 1958854, issued on July 12, 1994.

Lic. Andres Labarthe Sánchez

Address: Robalo #15, Supermanzana 3, Cancún, Quintana Roo
Telephone: 998-898-3547
Mobile: 998-100-1485
Email: alabarthe@gmail.com
Languages: Speaks Spanish and fluent English.

Specializes in: Child custody, contracts, corporations, estates, foreign claims, foreign investments, government relations, investment, immigration, labor relations, marriage/divorce, obtaining civil documents such as birth and death certificates, patents/trademarks/copyrights, taxes, trust and real estate consulting. Notary and Translator. Masters Degree in Corporate law. Has practiced law for 14 years, experience in Mexico City, San Luis Potosi, and Quintana Roo. Professional license number 2712797, issued on September 9, 1998.

Lic. José Roberto López Villa

Address: Ave. Nichupté 9 - C, Supermanzana 15, Cancún, Quintana Roo 77500
Phone/Fax: 998-884-9119
Mobile: 998-241-2879
Email: jrlopezvilla11@yahoo.com.mx
Languages: Speaks Spanish, fluent English.
Specializes in: Civil damages, contracts, corporations, criminal law, foreign investments, investment, marketing agreements, marriage/divorce, narcotics, taxes, theft/fraud/embezzlement. Can provide services as translator and notary. Has practiced law for 20 years, experience in Mexico and Panama. Professional license number 1535941, issued on January 25, 1991.

Lic. Francisco Javier Lozano Aceves

Address: Reno #34, Lote 13, Manzana 19, Supermanzana 20, Cancún, Quintana Roo, 77500
Telephone: 998-887-0350
Mobile: 998-577-2448
Email: lozanoab@prodigy.net.mx
Languages: Speaks Spanish and fluent English
Specializes in: Banking/financial, contracts, corporations, estates, foreign claims, foreign investments, government relations, investment, immigration, labor relations, marketing agreements, marriage/divorce, obtaining civil documents such as birth and death certificates, patents/trademarks/copyrights, real estate expert, time share contract cancelations. Masters Degree in Civil law. Has practiced law for 22 years, experience in Jalisco and Quintana Roo. Professional license number 1377263, issued on February 19, 1990.

Lic. Gabriel Marin González

Address: Robalo #15, Supermanzana 3, Cancún, Quintana Roo
Telephone: 998-898-3547

Mobile: 998-842-0022
Email: maringab@prodigy.net.mx
Languages: Speaks Spanish and good English.
Specializes in: Child custody, civil damages, contracts, corporations, estates, foreign claims, foreign investments, government relations, investment, immigration, labor relations, marriage/divorce, obtaining civil documents such as birth and death certificates, patents/trademarks/copyrights, taxes, trust and real estate consulting. Notary and Translator. Masters Degree in Corporate law. Has practiced law for 15 years, experience in Toluca and Quintana Roo. Professional license number 3010827, issued on July 12, 2007.

Lic. Jaime Uriel Pacheco Torres

Address: Calle 58 #526-E between Calle 55 and 57 Street, Fracc. Las Granjas, Mérida, Yucatán 97197
Telephone: (999) 941-2571
Mobile: (999)163-9602
Email: jaime0712@hotmail.com
Languages: Spanish, Limited English
Specializes in: Auto/accidents, banking/financial, contracts, corporations, criminal law, government relations, insurance, investment, patents/trademarks/copyrights, theft/fraud/embezzlement. Has practiced law for 8 years, experience in Yucatán, Campeche, Tabasco, and Quintana Roo. Professional license number 6024403, issued on June 24, 2009.

Lic. Angel Prieto Palmeros

Address: Retorno de la Paz #41, Super manzana 50, Manzana 20, Cancún, Quintana Roo 77533
Telephone: 998-251-7010, 998-872-3732
Mobile: 998-137-8545
Fax: 998-848-0020
Email: prietoangel@yahoo.com
Languages: Speaks Spanish, fluent English, and limited Portuguese.
Specializes in: Adoptions, auto/accidents, banking/financial, child custody, civil damages, collections, contracts, corporations, criminal law, estates, foreign claims, foreign investments, government relations, insurance, investment, immigration, labor relations, marketing agreements, marriage/divorce, obtaining civil documents such as birth and death certificates, patents/trademarks/copyrights, theft/fraud/embezzlement. Has practiced law

for 19 years, experience in Philadelphia, Veracruz, and Quintana Roo. Professional license number 3619832, issued on August 14, 2002.

Lic. José Ignacio Puerto Gutiérrez

Address: Calle 25 #159 by 30, Colonia García Ginerés, Mérida, Yucatán 97100
Telephone: (999) 920-3050 (phone and fax)
Mobile: (999) 900-3260
Email: ipuerto@puertoypino.com
Languages: Speaks Spanish and fluent English.
Specializes in: Banking/financial, civil damages, collections, contracts, corporations, criminal law, estates, foreign investments, government relations, investment, immigration, labor relations, marketing agreements, marriage/divorce, patents/trademarks/copyrights, taxes, theft/fraud/embezzlement. Masters Degree in corporate law at Yale University in 1991. Has practiced law for 21 years in New York City, Mexico City and Yucatán. Professional license number 1656658, issued on May 4, 1992. Lawyer registry number 2698, issued on August 17, 2000.

Lic. Mauricio Arturo Rojano Romero

Address: Super Manzana 27, Manzana 1, Lotes 7 and 8, Avenida Palenque by Xpuhil, Edificio Nerja, Apt. 11, Cancún, Quintana Roo
Telephone: (998) 884-8542
Fax: (998) 884-0678
Mobile: (999) 910-0464
Email: rojano@racabogados.com.mx
Languages: Speaks Spanish and fluent English.
Specializes in: Contracts, corporations, criminal law, estates, foreign investments, immigration, marketing agreements, investment, obtaining civil documents such as birth and death certificates, patents/trademarks/copyrights, theft/fraud/embezzlement, notary law. Has practiced law for 15 years in Yucatán, Campeche and Quintana Roo. Professional license number 2170137, issued on September 26, 1995.

Lic. Luis Alfredo Francisco Ramirez García

Address: Mojarra 2, Super Manzana 3, Cancún, Quintana Roo
Telephone: (998) 884-1406, 887-2416
Fax: (998) 884-1406
Mobile: (998) 897-1552

Email: luisalfredoramirez@hotmail.com
Languages: Speaks Spanish and good English.
Specializes in: Contracts, corporations, criminal law, investments, immigration, marriage/divorce, theft/fraud/embezzlement, time share contract cancelation. Has practiced law for more than 33 years in Mexico City and Quintana Roo. Professional license number 411355, issued on September 8, 1976.

Lic. Eutiquio Alejandro Salas Castillo

Address: Calle Venado #25, Supermanzana. 20-M, Manazana 19, Edif. 2, Planta Baja, Cancún, Quintana Roo
Telephone: (998) 887-7065, 887-8983
Fax: (998) 884-1053
Mobile: (998) 845-8841
Email: esalas@solissalasabogados.com
Languages: Speaks Spanish and good English.
Specializes in: Adoptions, banking/financial, child custody, civil damages, collections, contracts, corporations, criminal law, foreign claims, foreign investments, insurance, investment, immigration, labor relations, marriage/divorce, obtaining civil documents such as birth and death certificates, patents/trademarks/copyrights. Has practiced law for 14 years in Yucatán and Quintana Roo. Professional license number 2490031, issued on June 23, 1997.

Lic. Patricio de la Peña Ruiz de Chávez

Address: Calle Granada #30, SM 2-A, Cancún, Quintana Roo
Phone: 998-887-9368
Mobile: 998-147-1603
Fax: 998-887-9368
Email: ppr@salasconsultores.com, ppr@dlpytrujillo.com
Languages: Speaks Spanish and good English
Specializes in: Civil damages, corporations, criminal law, labor relations, marriage/divorce, obtaining civil documents such as birth and death certificates. Has practiced law for nine years in Nuevo Leon and Quintana Roo. Professional license number 5311673, issued on October 24, 2007.

Lic. Augusto Rivero Bolio

Address: AVENIDA Tulum #49 and #51, int. 101, SM.22, Centro. Cancún, Quintana Roo

Telephone: (998) 251-2553

Fax: (998) 251-2553

Mobile: (998) 136-3273

Email: augustorb@hotmail.com, *cancelyourtimeshare@hotmail.com*

Languages: Speaks Spanish and fluent English.

Specializes in: Auto/accidents, collections, contracts, corporations, criminal law, foreign claims, foreign investments, Government relations, insurance, investment, immigration, marketing agreements, obtaining civil documents such as birth and death certificates. Has practiced law for 12 years in Nuevo Leon and Quintana Roo. Professional license number 2770690, issued on November 24, 1998.

Campeche, Quintana Roo

Lic. Jaime Uriel Pacheco Torres

Address: Calle 58 #526-E between Calle 55 and 57 Street, Fracc. Las Granjas, Mérida, Yucatán 97197

Telephone: (999) 941-2571

Mobile: (999)163-9602

Email: jaime0712@hotmail.com

Languages: Spanish, Limited English

Specializes in: Auto/accidents, banking/financial, contracts, corporations, criminal law, government relations, insurance, investment, patents/trademarks/copyrights, theft/fraud/embezzlement. Has practiced law for 8 years, experience in Yucatán, Campeche, Tabasco, and Quintana Roo. Professional license number 6024403, issued on June 24, 2009.

Lic. José Ignacio Puerto Gutiérrez

Address: Calle 25 #159 by 30, Colonia García Ginerés, Mérida, Yucatán 97100

Telephone: (999) 920-3050 (phone and fax)

Mobile: (999) 900-3260

Email: ipuerto@puertoypino.com

Languages: Speaks Spanish and fluent English.

Specializes in: Banking/financial, civil damages, collections, contracts, corporations, criminal law, estates, foreign investments, government relations, investment, immigration, labor relations, marketing agreements, marriage/divorce, patents/trademarks/copyrights, taxes, theft/fraud/embezzlement. Masters Degree in corporate law at Yale University in 1991. Has practiced law for 21 years in New York City, Mexico City and Yucatán. Professional license number 1656658, issued on May 4, 1992. Lawyer registry number 2698, issued on August 17, 2000.

If you have additional questions, contact the appropriate division of the Office of Citizens Services at:

Department of State
SA-29, Fourth
2201 C Street NW
Washington, D.C. 20520
Telephone: (202) 647-5226

Important Notice:

The Editor and authors assume no responsibility or liability for the professional ability or reputation of, or the quality of services provided by, the preceding persons or firms. The list above was made available by the U.S. State Department, which compiled it.

21   DOCTORS

As a new resident of Mérida, one of the great surprises you will find is the excellent number of doctors available. What's more, you will be taken aback at the "bedside" manner of Yucatecan physicians. The level of caring is astounding, and the level of human interaction is, for most Americans, exceptional. From my own experience, I can tell you that housecalls, follow-up visits and consultations by phone after an office visit are considered normal in Mexico. A physician will go out of his way to drop by your home to make sure you're doing fine, as a courtesy. A call in the middle of the night will be answered, and if necessary, the doctor will drive over to see you.

The professionalism and personal courtesies are sincere, and wonderful. Part of it, of course, is the nature of Latin American culture, where there is a greater emphasis on personal relationships. The other aspect, of course, is the pride and seriousness with which doctors and physicians view their profession in Latin America: They are here to provide an essential service to the community, and to do so honorably. Many Americans I know in town time and again tell me wonderful things about their doctors here, and my experience has been nothing short of exceptional.

This is a list of doctors and physicians that have complied with requirements set by the State Department in Washington, DC for being recommended to Americans living in Mérida. It is by no means exhaustive, and you are always well advised to ask others for recommendations, but here is a good starting list for your consideration.

Doctors listed by Specialties

GENERAL PRACTITIONERS

Dr. Humberto Angulo Cortés, (Eng 50% /Spa); **Telephone:** (999) 926-3078. CENTRO MÉDICO LAS AMÉRICAS. Calle 54 #365, by Avenida Pérez Ponce, Centro, Mérida

Dr. Eduardo Mena Arana, (No Eng); **Telephone:** (999) 925-8233. CLÍNICA DE MÉRIDA, Avenida Itzáes #242, Colonia García Ginerés, Mérida

ALLERGISTS

Dr. Jorge Carlos Bolaños Ancona, (Eng 50%); **Telephone:** (999) 925-8385. CLÍNICA DE MÉRIDA, Avenida Itzáes #242, Colonia García Ginerés, Mérida

CARDIOLOGISTS

Dr. Sergio A. Villareal Umana, (Eng / Spa); **Telephone:** (999) 926-6348. EDIFICIO ANEXO (CENTRO MÉDICO LAS AMÉRICAS). Calle 54 #365, by Avenida Pérez Ponce, First Floor C Room 9, Centro, Mérida

Dr. David Arjona Canto, (Eng / Spa); **Telephone:** (999) 925-4487. CLÍNICA DE MÉRIDA, Avenida Itzáes #242, Colonia García Ginerés, Mérida

Dr. Joaquin Jimenez Noh, (Eng / Spa); **Telephone:** (999) 925-4976. CLÍNICA DE MÉRIDA, Avenida Itzáes #242, Colonia García Ginerés, Mérida

Dr. Salvador Padilla Morales, (Eng / Spa); **Telephone:** (999) 926-2367. CENTRO MÉDICO LAS AMÉRICAS. Calle 54 #365, by Avenida Pérez Ponce, Centro, Mérida

Dr. Carlos Wabi Dogre, (Eng / Spa); **Telephone:** (999) 925-6255. CLÍNICA DE MÉRIDA, Avenida Itzáes #242, Colonia García Ginerés, Mérida

DERMATOLOGISTS

Dr. Roger Enrique Pérez Pérez, (Eng / Spa); **Telephone:** (999) 925-9976. CLÍNICA DE MÉRIDA, Avenida Itzáes #242, Colonia García Ginerés, Mérida

Dra. María Rosa Rivero Vallado, (No Eng); **Telephone:** (999) 925-8406. CLÍNICA DE MÉRIDA, Avenida Itzáes #242, Colonia García Ginerés, Mérida

DENTISTS

Dr. Carlos Alayola Montañez Orthodontics Specialist, (Eng / Spa); **Telephone:** (999) 923-5380 928-5939. Calle 60 #387-B by Calle 43, Centro, Mérida

Dr. Javier Cámara Patrón, (Eng / Spa); **Telephone:** (999) 925-3399. Calle 17 #170 by Calle 8 and 10 Street, Colonia García Ginerés, Mérida

Dr. Rolando Peniche Marcín, (Eng / Spa); **Telephone:** (999) 926-4434. CENTRO MÉDICO LAS AMÉRICAS. Calle 54 #365, by Avenida Pérez Ponce, Centro, Mérida

Dra. Ana Leticia Morales Vera, (Eng / Spa); **Telephone:** (999) 928-6810. Calle 6 #489 by Calle 17 and 19 Street, Colonia GARCÍA GINERÉS, Mérida

Dr. Rafael Alonso Dominguez, (Eng / Spa); **Telephone:** (999) 920-2461. CENTRO ESTETICO ODONTOLOGICO. Avenida Cupules #74. POR 6 & 8 Colonia García Ginerés, Mérida

ENDOCRINOLOGISTS

Dr. Hugo Laviada Molina, (Eng / Spa); **Telephone:** (999) 925-8233. CLÍNICA DE MÉRIDA, Avenida Itzáes #242, Colonia García Ginerés, Mérida

Dr. Mario Barrero Estrada, (No Eng); **Telephone:** (999) 920-1037. CENTRO MÉDICO PENSIONES, AVENIDA BARRERA VÁZQUEZ #215-A, Colonia Pensiones, Mérida

GASTROENTEROLOGISTS

Dr. Francisco Rivero Maldonado, (No Eng); **Telephone:** (999) 925-4776. CLÍNICA DE MÉRIDA, Avenida Itzáes #242, Colonia García Ginerés, Mérida

GENERAL SURGERY

Dr. Miguel Fernandez Martínez, (Eng / Spa); **Telephone:** (999) 943-7070. STAR MÉDICA, Calle 26 #199 between Calle 15 and 7 Street, FRACC. Altabrisa. 404, Mérida

Dr. Luis Alberto Navarrete Jaimes, (Eng / Spa); **Telephone:** (999) 920-0949. CLÍNICA DE MÉRIDA, Avenida Itzáes #242, Colonia García Ginerés, Mérida

GYNECOLOGISTS

Dra. Catalina Aldana de Mendez, (Eng / Spa); **Telephone:** (999) 943-2694. STAR MÉDICA, Calle 26 #199 between Calle 15 and 7 Street, FRACC. Altrabrisa. Mérida

Dr. Manuel Mendez Arceo, (Eng / Spa); **Telephone:** (999) 943-1344. STAR MÉDICA, Calle 26 #199 between Calle 15 and 7 Street, FRACC. Altabrisa, Mérida

Dr. José Pereira Carcano, (Eng / Spa); **Telephone:** (999) 925-6819. CLÍNICA DE MÉRIDA, Avenida Itzáes #242, Colonia García Ginerés, Mérida

Dr. Luis Jesús Rodriguez Bolio, (Eng / Spa); **Telephone:** (999) 925-3998. CLÍNICA DE MÉRIDA, Avenida Itzáes #242, Colonia García Ginerés, Mérida

INTERNAL MEDICINE

Dr. Sergio A. Villareal Umana, (Eng / Spa); **Telephone:** (999) 926-6348. EDIFICIO ANEXO (CENTRO MÉDICO LAS AMÉRICAS). Calle 54 #365, by Avenida Pérez Ponce, Centro, Mérida

Dr. Antonio Briceño Vargas, (Eng / Spa); **Telephone:** (999) 925-0868. CLÍNICA DE MÉRIDA, Avenida Itzáes #242, Colonia García Ginerés, Mérida

NEUROLOGISTS

Dr. Ruben Dario Vargas García, (Eng / Spa); **Telephone:** (999) 925-7508. CLÍNICA DE MÉRIDA, Avenida Itzáes #242, Colonia García Ginerés, Mérida

ONCOLOGISTS

Dr. Delio Ceballos Bojorquez, (Eng / Spa); **Telephone:** (999) 925-8333 and (999) 925-5499. CLÍNICA DE MÉRIDA, Avenida Itzáes #242, Colonia García Ginerés, Mérida

OPHTHALMOLOGISTS

Dr. Adolfo Baqueiro Díaz, (Eng /Spa); **Telephone:** (999) 925-3253. CLÍNICA DE MÉRIDA, Avenida Itzáes #242, Colonia García Ginerés, Mérida

Dr. Alberto Cáceres Peniche, (Eng /Spa); **Telephone:** (999) 925-4152. CLÍNICA DE MÉRIDA, Avenida Itzáes #242, Colonia García Ginerés, Mérida

Dr. Alejandro Millet Molina, (Eng /Spa); **Telephone:** (999) 925-6944. CLÍNICA DE MÉRIDA, Avenida Itzáes #242, Colonia García Ginerés, Mérida

ORTHOPEDISTS

Dr. Luis Mario Baeza Mezquita, (Eng /Spa); **Telephone:** (999) 926-2154. CENTRO MÉDICO LAS AMÉRICAS. Calle 54 #365, by Avenida Pérez Ponce, Centro, Mérida

Dr. Felipe Eduardo Camara Arrigunaga, (Eng / Spa); **Telephone:** (999) 943-6202 and (999) 43-7202. STAR MÉDICA, Calle 26 #199 between Calle 15 and 7 Street, FRACC. Altabrisa, Mérida

Dr. Herbe Rivero Maldonado, (Eng / Spa); **Telephone:** (999) 920-1658. CLÍNICA DE MÉRIDA, Avenida Itzáes #242, Colonia García Ginerés, Mérida

Dr. Eduardo Muñoz Menéndez, (Eng / Spa); **Telephone:** (999) 925-4865. CLÍNICA DE MÉRIDA, Avenida Itzáes #242, Colonia García Ginerés, Mérida

Dr. Javier Pasos Novelo, (Eng / Spa); **Telephone:** (999) 926-2009. CENTRO MÉDICO LAS AMÉRICAS. Calle 54 #365, by Avenida Pérez Ponce, Centro, Mérida

OTORRINOLARINGOLOGISTS

Dr. Miguel Baquedano Sauri, (Eng / Spa); **Telephone:** (999) 925-5034. CENTRO ESPECIALIDADES MEDICAS, Calle 60 #329-B by Calle 35 and Avenida Colón, Mérida

Dr. Juan José Castellanos Dorbecker, (Eng / Spa); **Telephone:** (999) 943-2991. STAR MÉDICA, Calle 26 #199 between Calle 15 and 17 Street, FRACC. Altabrisa, Mérida

Dr. Sergio Ivan Díaz Esquivel, (No Eng); **Telephone:** (999) 926-4278. CENTRO MÉDICO LAS AMÉRICAS. Calle 54 #365, by Avenida Pérez Ponce, Centro, Mérida

PEDIATRICIANS

Dr. Gregorio Cetina Sauri, (Eng / Spa); **Telephone:** (999) 925-7056. MEDICA ITZÁES ESPECIALIDADES, Avenida Itzáes #252 by Calle 29, Mérida

Dr. Carlos Lara Navarrete, (No Eng); **Telephone:** (999) 926-2920. CENTRO MÉDICO LAS AMÉRICAS. Calle 54 #365, by Avenida Pérez Ponce, Centro, Mérida

Dr. Enrique Ortegón Ruiz, (Eng / Spa); **Telephone:** (999) 925-9944. CLÍNICA DE MÉRIDA, Avenida Itzáes #242, Colonia García Ginerés, Mérida

PNEUMOLOGISTS

Dr. Nicolas Hernandez Flores, (Eng / Spa); **Telephone:** (999) 925-8218. CLÍNICA DE MÉRIDA, Avenida Itzáes #242, Colonia García Ginerés, Mérida

Dr. Javier Torre Bolio, (Eng / Spa); **Telephone:** (999) 926-8589. CENTRO MÉDICO LAS AMÉRICAS. Calle 54 #365, by Avenida Pérez Ponce, Centro, Mérida

PSYCHIATRISTS

Dr. Roberto Carrillo Ruiz, (Eng / Spa); **Telephone:** (999) 944-7347. Calle 15 #251-1 between Calle 36 and 38 Street, FRACC. Campestre. Mérida

Dr. Arsenio Rosado Franco, (Eng / Spa); **Telephone:** (999) 920-1644. Avenida Colón #199A by Calle 24, Colonia García Ginerés, Mérida

UROLOGISTS

Dr. Jorge Carlos Aviles Rosado, (Eng / Spa); **Telephone:** (999) 926-2745. CENTRO MÉDICO LAS AMÉRICAS. Calle 54 #365, by Avenida Pérez Ponce, Centro, Mérida

Dr. Jorge Navarrete Fernandez, (Eng / Spa); **Telephone:** (999) 920-1986. CLÍNICA DE MÉRIDA, Avenida Itzáes #242, Colonia García Ginerés, Mérida

MEDICAL EMERGENCIES

Dr. Juan José Falcón Arias, (Eng 50% /Spa); **Telephone:** (999) 920-4040, EXT 116. CENTRO ESPECIALIDADES MEDICAS, Calle 60 #329-B by Calle35 and Avenida Colón, Colonia García Ginerés, Mérida

State Department Advice on Finding a Doctor

Where can I find a list of physicians in the country I plan to visit?

- For detailed information on physicians abroad, the authoritative reference is The Official ABMS Directory of Board Certified Medical Specialists, published for the American Board of Medical Specialists and its certifying member boards.

- U.S. embassies and consulates abroad maintain lists of hospitals and physicians, many of which are posted on the embassy or consulate web site.

Important Notice:

The Editor and authors assume no responsibility or liability for the professional ability or reputation of, or the quality of services provided by, the preceding doctors and physicians. The list above was made available by the U.S. State Department, which compiled it.

SCHOOLS, COLLEGES, UNIVERSITIES AND RESEARCH CENTERS

The city of Mérida has 244 preschool institutions, 395 elementary, 136 Junior High School (2 years middle school, 1 high), 97 High Schools and 26 Universities/Higher Education facilities and research centers.

As a result, Mérida has emerged as an educational powerhouse in southeastern Mexico. It's not uncommon to find students from other states, particularly from neighboring Quintana Roo, but also foreign countries enrolled in schools here. There are students from Cuba, Costa Rica, Venezuela, Belize as well as post-graduate research students from the United States, Canada, the United Kingdom, Spain, Italy and Korea enrolled in the city's schools.

An increasing number of American and Canadian expatriates are moving to Mérida with their school-age children, or are having children (American-Mexicans!) here. And, of course, a good number of young adults are pursuing college and graduate-level courses, which is a phenomenon that is contributing to the diversity of campus life in Mérida. What follows is a list of schools that have expatriate students enrolled.

Schools, Kindergarten through High School (Preparatorias)

American School

Phone: (999) 941-9371
Address: Calle 3B #244, between Calle 20 and 18 Street
Colonia Xcumpich
Levels: Kinder and Primaria

Centro Educativo Palmerston

Phone: (999) 944-5457
Address: Calle 21 #144
Levels: Kinder, Primaria

Centro Educativo Renacimiento (CER)

Phone: (999) 944-4808
Address: Calle 33 #468, between Calle 10 and 14 Street
Fraccionamiento Montebello
Levels: Primaria, Secundaria and Preparatoria
Website: *www.cerenacimiento.edu.mx*

Colegio Americano

Phone: (999) 928-5509

Address: Calle 72 #499, between Calle 59 and 61 Street
Centro
Levels: Primaria, Secundaria and Preparatoria
Website: www.americanomerida.edu.mx

Colegio Iberoamericano de Mérida, A.C.

Phone: (999) 925-2712 and (999) 925-3112
Address: Avenida Colón #196-A , between Calle 12 and 14 Street
Colonia García Ginerés
Levels: Kinder, Primaria, Secundaria, Preparatoria
Website: www.iberoMérida.com

Colegio Peninsular Roger's Hall

Phone: (999) 944-5364
Address: Calle 21 #131 (a short distance street from Office Depot)
Levels: Kinder, Primaria, Secundaria, Preparatoria

Educrea

Phone: (999) 925-7931
Address: Calle 23 #209, between Calle 30 Street and Avenida Itzáes
Levels: Kinder, Primaria, Secundaria, Preparatoria
Website: www.educrea.com.mx

Escuela Modelo

Phone: (999) 927-9833 and (999) 927-9944
Address: Calle 56-A #444 (Paseo de Montejo)

Levels: Primaria, Secundaria and Preparatoria
Website: www.modelo.edu.mx

Instituto Cumbres (for Boys)

Phone: (999) 944-4090
Address: Calle 5 by Calle 18 S/N ("S/N" stands for "Sin Número," or "without a number") Glorieta Cumbres
Levels: Primaria, Secundaria, Preparatoria

M.J. International

Phone: (999) 984-3939
Address: Calle 66 #618-C, between Calle 77 and 79 Street
Levels: Kinder, Primaria

Saint Patrick's

Phone: (999) 948-0985
Address: Calle 31 #144
Colonia Mexico
Levels: Kinder

Centro Educativo Piaget, A.C.

Calle 33 #140, between Calle 20 and 22 Street
Colonia Chuburná.
Levels: Kinder, Primaria, Secundaria and Preparatoria
Website: www.piaget.edu.mx/index2.htm

These are state institutions offering higher education

Universidad Autónoma de Yucatán (UADY)
Escuela Superior de Artes de Yucatán (ESAY)
Instituto Tecnológico de Mérida (ITM)
Universidad Tecnológica Metropolitana (UTM)
Universidad Pedagógica Nacional
Escuela Normal Superior de Yucatán (ENSY)
Universidad Nacional Autónoma de México (UNAM)

These are the more important private institutions for higher education

Centro de Estudios Superiores CTM (CESCTM)
Colegio de Negocios Internacionales (CNI)
Universidad Anáhuac Mayab
Universidad Marista
Universidad Modelo
Universidad Interemericana para el Desarrollo (UNID)
Centro Educativo Latino (CEL)
Universidad Interamericana del Norte
Centro Universitario Interamericano(Inter)
Universidad Mesoamericana de San Agustin (UMSA)
Centro de Estudios de las Américas, A.C. (CELA)
Universidad del Valle de Mexico (UVM)
Instituto de Ciencias Sociales de Mérida (ICSMAC)
Universidad Popular Autónoma de Puebla, Plantel Mérida (UPAEP Mérida)

Mérida has several national research centers of renown. They include–

Centro de Investigación Científica de Yucatán (CICY)
Centro de Investigaciones Regionales Dr. Hideyo Noguchi, dependent on the UADY, which conducts biological and biomedical research.

Centro INAH Yucatán, dedicated to anthropological, archaeological and historical research and preservation.
Centro de Investigacion y de Estudios Avanzados CINVESTAV/IPN

23 Nutrition, Yoga & Personal Trainers

Do you recall that it was mentioned that the median temperature in the Yucatán peninsula was hotter than it is in the Arabian peninsula?

If you don't, then think about it now. It can be hot, and that means that your diet and nutrition needs to reflect the reality of living in the tropics. Unless you are moving to Mérida from Hawaii, the Desert cities near Death Valley in California, the American Southwest or South Florida, there is no place in the United States that compares with the heat in this part of the world.

This is simply the way it is, and it probably requires a few lifestyle changes for you, from being more conscious of drinking more fluids, to changing your exercise regime to early morning or late afternoons, evenings or nights. It also means you have to eat more fruits and vegetables, and refrain from indulging in as much alcohol, tobacco, and fatty foods as you might otherwise be used to consuming. A good recommendation, of course, is to have a complete physical once a year. Tell your regular physician of the heat in Mérida, so he or she can make any necessary adjustments to the medications, if any, that you take.

In recent years, "wellness retreats" in Yucatán have focused on nutrition and improving one's quality of eating and lifestyle choices. "Boot camp" retreats that help to detoxify the body and teach you how to eat again have grown in popularity. One leading American nutritionist from San Diego conducts intensive two-week retreats where participants learn to become reacquainted with their bodies, food, think about nutrition as part of their daily lives and adopt habits that improve one's health, well-being and psychological outlook on life.

Acclimatization

Acclimatization is the physiologic and psychological adjustment to a new environment. In terms of heat acclimatization, this can be something as dramatic as moving from a cool, dry climate to a hot, humid one, or simply adjusting from spring to summer.

Some of the physiologic adaptations during heat acclimatization include: reduced heart rate, core temperature, and utilization of muscle glycogen, as well as increased blood flow to the skin, plasma volume, and work time until exhaustion. Well-conditioned athletes have a higher heat tolerance than sedentary people, as regular exercise creates "internal heat stress" and thus pre-acclimatizes athletes to some degree.

Heat acclimatization usually takes 10 to 14 days, although 75% of the adaptations are believed to occur within the first five days. Exercise sessions during the acclimatization process should be shorter and less intense, gradually building up to normal by the end of the two week period.

Source: www.personalbestnutrition.com

Gyms and Health Clubs

The great thing about Mérida is that if offers a wide variety of gyms, from a no-frills place with antiquated equipment, something straight out of a movie about boxers and boxing in the 1950s, to state-of-the-art facilities that offer cappuccinos and espresso bar at the coffee station, along with yoga and massage services. A good number of expatriates were members of gyms back home, and many others find that joining now is not only much more affordable, but less intimidating that the health clubs in the U.S.

Here is a list of gyms and health clubs around town that count on expatriates as members.

Thunder Gym

Calle 86 #476-K (Avenida Itzaes, between Calle 49 and 51 Street, Centro
Telephone: (999) 289-4238
This gym, with state-of-the-art equipment fills up at night with young Meridians who are serious about working out and hanging out. An increasing number of younger expats are joining and the emphasis of the club is focused on serious exercise and serious training; members routinely participate in body-building competitions and sporting events. With an active presence on social media, the only drawbacks or criticisms center around the small parking lot and the music played over the sound system, which often clases with what patrons are listening to on their iPhones whil e on the machines.
Hours:
Monday-Friday: 5:00 AM to 10:00 PM
Saturday: 5:30 AM to 10:00 PM
Sunday: 7:00 AM to 7 PM
Facebook: https://www.facebook.com/ThunderGymMID

Boscos

Calle 61 #550, between Calle 70 and 72 Street, Centro

Telephone: (999) 928-1380

This place is a relic from the 1950s. What a mess, but a charming, no-frills mess. Concentrating on free weights and ancient weight machines, this place is *mixto*, meaning co-ed. (There's a women's area on the second floor.) The gym has lockers and showers, and a good number of muscle-bound body builders are always hanging around. You have to remind yourself that you get what you pay for: $20 pesos for a day pass; $200 pesos for a month membership.

Hours:
Monday-Friday: 5:30 AM to 9:30 PM
Saturday: 5:30 AM to 3:00 PM
Sunday: 7:00 AM to 12 PM

Exersite Fitness Center

Plaza Altabrisa
Calle 7 #451, Local 73
Fracc. Altabrisa
Telephone: (999) 167-9257
Website: *www.exersite.com.mx*

At the other extreme is this state-of-the art health club that rivals anything you could expect either in Los Angeles or Miami. This mixto health club also has quite a number of activities for children, who are well supervised. The facilities include squash courts, a swimming pool, yoga, Pilates, and training for everything from men's cycling to children's Jazzercise classes. There are steam rooms, sauna, and rooms set aside for varied classes as aerobics to ballroom dancing to boxing classes. Their website is astounding at the number of activities that are offered, and its membership reflects the solidly middle- and upper middle-class of Yucatecan society.

Hours:
Monday-Friday: 6:00 AM to 10:00 PM
Saturday-Sunday: 8:00 AM to 3:00 PM

Mérida Sports Center

Kilometro 12 Carretera Mérida—Progreso, Residencia Xcanatun

To say this is a state-of-the-art health club does not do it justice. This is, by far, a world class facility, a health club and sports center so large, comprehensive and with all the modern amenities, that it has its own full-service spa. It could be beamed to Los Angeles or Miami and it would rival anything anywhere in the world. That it is on the highway to Progreso itself tells you much: it caters to an exclusive clientele that can spend just over $100 USD a month for basic membership. There are more classes that can be listed in this description, and the best recommendation is to visit their website, and then drive on over. If you are serious about health clubs, and just as serious about sweating in the company of the city's privileged and elite, than this is the club for you. Their facilities rival anything you've every seen that's available today—

except for one small detail: It doesn't have a heliport, like a certain health club in Sao Paulo, Brazil has!

Hours:
Monday-Thursday: 6:00 AM to 11:00 PM
Friday: 6:00 AM to 10:00 PM
Saturday: 8:00 AM to 6:00 PM
Sunday: 9:00 AM to 4:00 PM
Website: *www.meridasportcenter.net*

North Gym Center

Calle 56 #496, between Calle 59 and 61 Street, Centro
This is a modern facility, with free weights, weight and resistance machines and a good number of cardio equipment and treadmills. A *mixto* health club, it attracts women because of its spinning and cardio classes, as well as the popular dance courses that range from salsa to Jazzercise. There is a sunning lounge on the roof, but this is for women only.
Hours:
Monday-Friday: 6:30 AM to 9:00 PM
Saturday: 7:00 AM to 3:00 PM
Closed Sunday

SporTec Muscle Factory

Calle 22 #113, between Calle 13 and 15 Street
Colonia San Antonio Cinta
Telephone: (999) 948-4640
With a high-tech name like this, you have certain expectations, but these are mistaken if you presume it's a place for body builders. On the contrary, it is a modern, *mixto* facility with as much cardio equipment as weight training machines and free weights. The place features modern locker rooms, a studio for aerobics, Pilates and spinning classes. There is a snack bar featuring healthful beverages and juices, and the place is fully air conditioned.
Hours:
Monday-Friday: 6:00 AM to 10:00 PM
Saturday: 7:00 AM to 3:00 PM
Closed Sunday

WW Gym

Calle 30 #99, between Calle 19 and 21 Street
Colonia Mexico
Telephone: (999) 944-4739
This *mixto* facility is the only one in Mérida that features an Olympic-size swimming pool. It is enormous, with studios dedicated exclusively to certain activities: one studio for spinning classes,

another for yoga, and another for aerobics. The cardio room has two dozen treadmills, and the weight training room has state-of-the-art machines. The free weight room has a good number of weights, but it is the least frequented room, which indicates that while a *mixto* facility, more women then men are members. The health club offers a dizzying array of dance classes from Salsa to traditional Latin. A good number of members are women whose children attend the Roger's Hall school across the street, and they work out with their friends before school lets out for the day, meaning that lunch is being prepared back home by their cooks. Yes, its membership comes from the more privileged segment of Yucatecan society.

Hours:
Monday-Friday: 6:00 AM to 10:00 PM
Saturday: 7:30 AM to 2:00 pm.
Closed Sunday

Xtreme Body Gym

Calle 50 #55, Local 10
Plaza Montejo
Fracc. Francisco de Montejo

Located in a middle-class neighborhood, this is a small facility, with minimal cardiovascular equipment, but a respectable selection of weight resistance equipment. A mixto facility as well, it does not currently have yoga or Pilates classes. Its membership reflects the neighborhood, and there are few expatriates as members, apart from a number of Cuban and Lebanese expatriates.

Hours:
Monday-Friday: 7:30 AM to 9:00 PM
Saturday: 8:00 AM to 2:00 PM
Closed Sunday

Additional Gyms

Over the past three years, however, it needs to be noted that many expatriates have moved to many of the "Colonias"—neighborhoods—far from Centro.

As a result, many are looking for health clubs and gyms in other areas outside "Gringo Gulch." Here is a list of facilities that may be near your home. Most of these, however, are for locals, meaning that there may not be English-speaking staff.

On the other hand, most of these facilities offer exceptional membership value. Most also specialize in certain activites, whether it is weight training, kickboxing or cardiovascular programs. It's best to visit the facilities themselves. Keep in mind the truth about Mérida: Gyms located in the north and northeast sections of the city attract a more monied crowd of patrons than gyms located in the southern and southeastern areas of the town.

The Gym
Calle 30 360 x 59 y 61
Colonia San Antonio Cucul
Tel.: (999) 285-7591

Excess
Calle 85 x C Colonias S/N
Col. San Antonio Kaua IV
Tel.: (999) 983-1482

Pumping Iron
Calle 22 # 436, between
Calle 49 and 49-A Street
Colonia Juan Pablo II
Tel.: (999) 285-8326

Hypoxi
Calle 43-A 214
Colonia Francisco de
Montejo
Tel.: (999) 927-4228

Gimnasio Almali
Calle 114 #459-A
Colonia Bojórquez
Tel.: (999) 912-1646

Pilates Reformer Mérida
Calle 13 123, between
Calle 24 and 26 Street,
Privada Real
Colonia Mexico
Tel.: (999) 944-6438

Top Body Sports Club
Calle 5-100 S/N, San
Antonio
Colonia San Antonio
Tel.: (999) 944-4840

Bio Sport
Calle 15 #355
Colonia San Damian
Tel.: (999) 987-0272

Fitness Club
Calle 1-B & Calle 2- B #64-
A
Colonia Montecristo
Tel.: (999) 943-1067

Gym Biceps
Calle 62 #480-A
Colonia Centro
Tel.: (999) 928-6391

North Gym
Calle 28 #346
Colonia Emiliano Zapata
Norte
Tel.: (999) 948-1081

Sportivos Gym
Calle 10 #415
Colonia Díaz Ordaz
Tel.: (999) 944-6882

Corpus Pilates
Calle 44 #445, between
Calle 21 and 23 Street,
Local 4-B
Colonia Residencial Los
Pinos
Tel.: (999) 254-0910

Curves
Calle 17 #97 by Calle 20,
Local 5

Colonia Plaza Veinte
Tel.: (999) 948-3254

Club Heymo
Calle 10 #410
Colonia Díaz Ordaz
Tel.: (999) 944-3111

Ferraez Gym
Calle 103 #518-H
Colonia Delio Moreno
Cantón
Tel.: (999) 239-8441

Intense Sport Club
Calle 36 #310, between
Calle 111 and 113 Street
Colonia Francisco Villa
Puerto
Tel.: (999) 576-7316

Gimnasio Milton Ghio
Calle 37 #507-A
Colonia Centro
Tel.: (999) 925-3847

Slim Gym
Calle 21 #268 S/N
Colonia Miguel Alemán
Tel.: (999) 927-9267

Mr. Muscle
Calle 120-A #353
Colonia Yucalpeten
Tel.: (999) 945-1214

**Pilates Reformer Life
Styles**

Calle 36 328, between
Calle 45 and 47 Street
Colonia Benito Juárez
Norte
Tel.: (999) 271-7983

Renex Fitness Center
Calle 21 #300 Altos,
between Calle 48 and 50
Street
Colonia Roma
Tel.: (999) 183-0499

Pumping Iron
Calle 22 #436, between
Calle 49 and 49-A Street
Colonia Juan Pablo II
Tel.: (999) 285-8321

Spin Rush
Av 117 Local 2, between
Calle 36 and 38 Street
Colonia Villa Poniente
Tel.: (999) 177-8361

Motion Fitness
Calle 32 #339
Planta Baja Plaza
Palmeras
Colonia San Ramón Norte
Tel.: (999) 285-8855

Personal Trainer

There are several personal trainers and martial arts instructor in Mérida, but the one who is American is Philip Geerts. If you are not confident in your Spanish, you might prefer a native English-speaking trainer.

Philip Geerts
Telephone: (999) 151-9734
Website: *www.meridatrainer.com*
Email: *phil.geerts@yahoo.com*

Massages

There are a good number of masseurs and masseuses in Mérida, but the two who continue to get great reviews from expatriates are Mexian masseuses:

Leticia Salazar
Masseuse
Telephone: (999) 294-3855
Cell: (999) 340-5288
Email: *Spa.Merida@hotmail.com*

Célida Padilla
Masseuse
Coqui Coqui & Spa Boutique Catherwood
Facebook: https://www.facebook.com/hatzaha.natura/about
Telephone: (999) 908-6802
Email: *hatzahanatura@gmail.com*

Massage Clinic

The Lakini Massage Clinic, for women only, has established itself as an exceptional massage center. Under the direction of Lorena Scafidi, a holistic approach is followed:

Lorena Scafidi
Lakini Massage Clinic
Plaza Los Laureles
Calle 21 #120 by Calle 24, Local 15
Colonia Mexico
Telephone: (045) 551-374-7605
Email: *lorena@lakini.mx*

Website: *www.lakini.mx*

Yoga

There are a good number of yogis in Mérida, and Mérida is emerging as a yoga retreat destination in its own right. Clauda Guerrero of Semilla Yoga is completely fluent in English and Spanish and she has trained and taught throughout Mexico and in the United States. Emily Navar is an American, but she is located in Izamal, a nearby city an hour or so northeast of Mérida. There are other yoga centers, but the clients are primarily Yucatecans and Mexicans, and the classes are primarily conducted in Spanish.

Semilla Yoga

Claudia Guerrero
Calle 15 #210 between Calle 24 and 26 Street
Colonia García Ginerés
Telephone: (999) 920-5361
Website: *www.semillayoga.com.mx*

Centro VIRYA 2011

Calle 14 #85 by Calle 5
Colonia San Antonio Cinta
Telephone: (999) 127-9810
www.meridayoga.com

Yoga Para Ti

Calle 26-A #313, between Calle 43 and 45 Street
Fracc. Montealban
Telephone: (999) 444-166

Cin Maya

Cin Maya
Calle 31 #280, between Calle 18 and 20 Street
Colonia García Ginerés
Telephone: (999) 955-1115 and (999) 970-0214
Email: *cinmaya-merida@hotmail.com*

Hotel Macan Ché

Emily Navar and Alfred Rordame
Izamal, Yucatán
Telephone: (988) 954-0287

Email: *macanche@gmail.com*
Web: *www.macanche.com*

Dance & Self Expression

Self-expression through dance and interpretative movement has found a place in contemporary Mérida and there is one excellent place for learning contemporary dance, improvisation, hip-hop and yoga techniques.

Centro Tum Aka'T

Tum Aka'T Studio & Residence
Calle 51 #475-A, between Calle 52 and 54 Street, Centro
Telephone: (999) 923-1852
Email: *tumakat@gmail.com*
Website: *www.tumakat.com*

Massage & Adult Swimming Schools

As the holistic and wellness movements flourish in Mérida, so has interest in continuing education for adults. There are several schools dedicated to offering certification for swimming, massage, physical therapy, aromatherapy and wellness retreat management.

Escuela de Masaje

Escuela de Masaje Tulum
Telephone: (999) 924-4821
Email: *escueldemasaje@yahoo.com.mx*
Website: *www.escuelade-masaje-tulum.com*

Swimming Classes

Centro Deportivo Bancario
Telephone: (999) 943-0550
Email: *info@natare.com.mx*
Website: *www.natare.com.mx*

Yucatán Polo Club

There are now enough avid polo players in Yucatán to merit a proper club. If you are interested in polo, you might want to check this organization to see if it's a match.

Website: *www.yucatanpoloclub.mx*

386

Canine Clubs

There are two canine clubs in Mérida. If you are a member of the American Kennel Club, it's well worth the effort to look into either (or both) of these organizations: Club Manada Canina de Yucatán and the Club Canino Mérida de Yucatán. World-class breeding is provided by Criadero Itaboca (more information on page 391).

Facebook: *https://www.facebook.com/clubmanadacanina*
Facebook: *https://www.facebook.com/Club.Canino.Yucatan*

Dog shows take place several times a year and participants come from all over Mexico, the U.S. and Central America. These are conducted by the Club Expositor Canófilo de Yucatán. For more information, please contact:

Yussiff F. Farah Dzib
Address: Calle 23 #215
Colonia Jardines de Pensiones
Mérida, Yucatán, México
Telephone: (999)-9877472

Dogs Aficionados

Mérida is a city of dog lovers.

In recent years all kinds of dog-friendly companies and clubs have opened up. There are hotels that welcome dogs and restaurants that serve canines and their human companions!

The world-renowned company, Harry Barker, which makes high-end products for dogs, from leashes to dog beds, is now sold in town. Do note that in the Mayan language, "pek," pronounced "peh-ehk," means dog. That's why many dog-friendly ventures are named "Pek" or "Peek" in town.

So, if you love dogs, here is a list that is bound to be invaluable:

Peek Park
Parque Paseo Verde
Calle 28, between Calle 7 and 9 Street
Fracc. Juan Pablo II, Segunda Etapa
Telephone: (999) 182-2800

Website: www.peekpark.org

Club Manada Canina de Yucatán
Calle 55, between Calle 14 and 16 Street
Fraccionamiento del Parque
Youtube video:
https://www.youtube.com/channel/UCr0DBgqqNT4Q_OygXtOn9VA

Club Canino de Merida
Calle 60 Norte, between Calle 21 and 23 Street
Colonia Chuburná de Hidalgo
Telephone: (999) 981-4297 and (999) 981-0739
Website: *http://tienda.zoomania.com.mx/general*

Best Veterinarians in Mérida

Zoomania
Calle 20 #207, between Calle 27 and 29 Street
San Pedro Cholul
Telephone: (999) 358-0545
Facebook: https://www.facebook.com/eljardincanino/info/?tab=overview

Pet Grooming and Sitting Service

El Jardin del Canino
Calle 20 #207, between Calle 27 and 29 Street
San Pedro Cholul
Telephone: (999) 358-0545
Facebook: https://www.facebook.com/eljardincanino/info/?tab=overview

Dog Friendly Restaurants and Bistros

Ki' Ool Bistro
Calle 59 #572, between Calle 72 and 74 Street
Telephone: (999) 151-6266
Facebook: *https://www.facebook.com/KiOOL-Comida-Saludable-305035616360146/timeline*

Peek Restaurant
Calle 57b #647, between Calle 10 and 12 Street

Telephone: (999) 576-4518
Facebook:
https://www.facebook.com/PeekFoodRestaurant/info/?tab=overview

Dogs Rescue and Assistance

Peke Pets
Facebook: https://www.facebook.com/pekepets/timeline
Email: *Pekespets@gmail.com*

Harry Barker

Canine Couture / Couture Canino
Harry Barker items are available at The Shop / La Tienda
Calle 59 #572, between Calle 72 and 74 Street
Website: *www.casa-catherwood.com*
Email: *info@casa-catherwood.com*

24   HEALTH CARE, HEALTH INSURANCE & MEDICAL TOURISM

The careful reader will have noticed that one of the complaints about Mérida is that it is brutally hot in the summer. For expatriates who are living in Mérida year-round, this is a serious concern. It can wear on your physical being, and heat exhaustion is not uncommon. As we age, our bodies are more sensitive to the heat, and more care is required. In the subtropics and tropics alike, plenty of fluids, a good night's sleep, eating healthful foods and moderate exercise are the key ingredients to remaining healthy.

It's no wonder that healthy Yucatecans are up bright and early (some before the crack of dawn!) and walking briskly in the parks and sports stadiums, getting in their cardiovascular workouts before the sun rises. It's also common to see them in the fruit markets, buying whatever happens to be in season for a healthful breakfast that is nutritious—while being environmentally responsible. What does that mean? That it makes sense to enjoy a ripe mango that was harvested from someone's backyard for breakfast, than it is to buy imported strawberries that were picked—when not fully ripe!—and then flown thousands of miles to end up in a grocery store.

One of the great things about Mérida is that, if you set your mind to it, it is possible to have one of the healthiest and most nutritious diets you can possibly imagine, where fruits and vegetables are grown in small towns, outside the industrial agricultural business. The same goes for the fish, poultry, and pork that are sold in the commercial local neighborhood *mercados*. Almost everything is free range and raised without vaccines, growth hormones, and humanely.

With that in mind, it's a good time to begin to assess your health, since this will determine how best you go about staying healthy—and in some cases, becoming healthy. If you are unfamiliar with how to assess where you stand, so to speak, when it comes to your own health, the best thing to do, of course, is to get a physical.

It is also a good idea to find a local doctor with whom you feel comfortable. The chapter on doctors has a list of exceptional physicians in Mérida, as well as dentists. It's also important to find a hospital that is close to your home or with which you are satisfied. You can be confident in the world-class medical facilities in town. Mérida has a good number of regional hospitals and medical centers. All of them offer full services for the residents of Mérida. The Regional Hospitals provide services for residents of outlying communities of Yucatán State, as well as patients from neighboring states of Campeche and Quintana Roo.

What Expats Say About Mexico's Health Care System

By Anne McEnany

As the number of retirees increases in the United States and abroad, so too does the pressure to secure adequate and affordable healthcare for them. Already, the majority of Americans residing in Mexico obtain some health care services in Mexico, particularly dental care, lower-cost prescription drugs, and routine medical exams.

• 55% of U.S. retirees now living in Mexico were concerned about access to health care when making the decision to relocate.

• 70% of respondents indicated that health care was affordable and accessible in Mexico. Almost 61% stated that the quality of available health care in Mexico was comparable to the U.S.

• The majority of U.S. retirees in Mexico's coastal communities would be considered active retirees. Less than 2% reported receiving home care or assisted living services in Mexico although over 25% have considered assisted living options in Mexico.

• 73% of respondents kept their health insurance in the U.S. and 17% of those individuals also had insurance in Mexico. Over 10% of respondents had no health insurance, while 7% had health insurance only in Mexico.

• 57% of respondents return to the U.S. for health care or medical procedures, but over 32% do not.

• Retirees living close to the U.S-Mexico border are most likely to procure regular health care services in the United States with over 72% doing so. This compares to those Americans living in Riviera Maya and Puerto Vallarta/Riviera Nayarit that had lower return rate by comparison, 40% and 47% respectfully.

• 79% of U.S retirees would favor a pilot program to provide Medicare reimbursability to U.S. retirees living in Mexico.

• Although less than 2% of respondents currently have home care in Mexico, many more are considering their long-term options for "aging in place" in their adopted communities in Mexico.

• Mexico remains a country more suited for active retirees. Currently Mexican coastal communities do not have adequate assisted living, nursing home facilities or have considered handicap accessible land use policies to promote U.S. retirees "aging in place."

Source: "U.S. Retirement Trends in Mexico's Coastal Communities," International Community Foundation, Webiste: *www.icfdn.org*.

Advice from the State Department on Health Insurance

Why should I be concerned about medical coverage abroad?

• The Social Security Medicare Program does not provide coverage for hospital or medical costs outside the United States.

• Many health insurance plans do not provide coverage overseas. Those that provide "customary and reasonable" hospital costs abroad may not pay for your medical evacuation back to the United States which can cost $10,000.00 and up depending on your location and medical condition.

• Many foreign doctors and hospitals require payment in cash prior to providing service.

• Uninsured patients may be refused service.

• Countries with socialized medicine may not provide full services to non-residents.

• Payment of hospital and other expenses abroad is the responsibility of the traveler.

• Some countries require tourists to carry accident or travel insurance. Check the Country Specific Information for the countries you plan to visit for detailed information.

Can the U.S. government assist me if I become disabled overseas?

• If an American becomes ill or is seriously injured abroad, a U.S. consular officer can assist in locating appropriate medical services and informing family or friends.

- If necessary a consular officer can also assist in the transfer of funds from the United States.

- Payment of hospital and other expenses is the responsibility of the traveler.

What questions should I ask my health insurance company?

- Does this insurance policy cover emergency expenses abroad such as returning me to the United States for treatment if I become seriously ill?

- Does this insurance cover high-risk activities such as parasailing, mountain climbing, scuba diving and off-roading?

- Does this policy cover pre-existing conditions?

- Does the insurance company require pre-authorizations or second opinions before emergency treatment can begin?

- Does the insurance company guarantee medical payments abroad?

- Will the insurance company pay foreign hospitals and foreign doctors directly?

- Does the insurance company have a 24-hour physician-backed support center?

- Senior citizens may wish to contact the American Association of Retired Persons for information about foreign medical care coverage with Medicare supplement plans.

Private Hospitals

Mérida has one of the most prestigious medical faculties in Mexico under the direction of the Universidad Autónoma de Yucatán. Mérida's proximity to U.S. cities of Miami and Houston allow local doctors to cross-train and practice in both countries. As a result Mérida is one of the best cities in Mexico in terms of health services availability. There is a rapidly-expanding "medical" tourism industry, where foreigners are coming to Mérida for medical and dental treatment at significantly lower prices that are available in their home countries. It is an important regional health care center, one that rivals Miami in its facilities and attention to patients. Indeed, Mérida is emerging as an important "medical tourism" destination for people from the U.S. and Canada who wish to have medical treatment, procedures and dental work done at reasonable costs provided at world-class facilities. There are several companies that now cater specifically to this niche market and can take are of all the details necessary for medical treatment to be performed here. There are several health clubs dedicated to seniors and a good number of assisted living centers with bilingual staff. In addition there are tour companies that specialize in trips for the "over 50" crowd, with itineraries that accommodate specific needs of elder travelers.

But for resident expatriates, you really aren't tourists since you live here. It's nevertheless important to be current on medical facilities available, healthy living and the kinds of insurance that are available to you. First, it's always good to know the hospitals in town, private and public.

Clínica de Mérida

Avenida Itzáes #242
Colonia García Ginerés
Telephone: (999) 942-1800
Emergencies - Adults: Ext. 1141 & 1142, **Children:** Ext. 1123
Intensive Care - Adults: Ext. 1122, **Children:** Extx 1235
Website: *www.clinicademerida.com.mx/DEP.html*

Star Médica

Calle 26 #199 by Calle 15 and 17 Street
Colonia Altabrisa
Telephone: (999) 930-2880, **Emergencies:** Ext. 5
Website: *www.starmedica.com/default.asp?seccion=150*

Centro de Especialidades Médicas (CEM)

Calle 60 #329-B by Calle 35 and Avenida Colón
Colonia Alcalá Martín
Telephone: (999) 920-4040
Emergencies: Ext. 111
Website: *www.cemsureste.com/cem_index.htm*

Centro Médico de las Américas (CMA)

Calle 54 #365
Centro
Telephone: (999) 926-2111
Emergencies - Adults: Ext. 127 or phone 927-2199, **Children:** Ext. 512
Website: *www.centromedicodelasamericas.com.mx/directorio.php?Offset=0*

Centro Médico Pensiones (CMP)

Calle 7 #215-A
Colonia Pensiones
Telephone: (999) 925-8019, **Emergencies:** Ext. 106
Website: *www.hospitalcmp.com/index.htm*

Hospital Santelena

Calle 14 #81, by Calle 5 and 7 Street
Colonia San Antonio Cinta
Telephone: (999) 943-1333, **Emergencies:** Ext. 135
Website: *www.hosantme.medicosmerida.com*

Public Hospitals:

Hospital Agustin O'Horán

Avenida Itzáes by Avenida Jacinto Canek
Centro
Telephone: (999) 924-0749
Director: Dr. José Rafael Pacheco

Hospital Regional de Alta Especialidad

Km 8.5 Carretera Mérida-Cholul s/n, Colonia Maya Mérida
Telephone: (999) 924-7600
Website: *www.hraeyucatan.salud.gob.mx*

Cruz Roja Mexicana

Avenida Quetzacoalt #104
Centro
Telephone: (999) 983- 0233

Centro de Salud Pública

Calle 72 #463, between Calle 53 and 55 Street
Centro
Telephone: (999) 928-6185

Clínica Materno-Infantil "María José"

Calle 53 #484 by Calle 54 and 56 Street
Centro
Telephone: (999) 928 5325

IMSS (Instituto Mexicano de Seguro Social, or Mexican Institute of Social Security)

H. G. P. Torre de Especialidades Mérida CMN Yucatán
Calle 34 by 41 #439, Ex-Terrenos El Fénix
Colonia Industrial
Telephone: (999) 922-56-0601, and for emergencies (999) 922-5656 Ext. 4102

Hospital Benito Juárez IMSS

Avenida Colón by Avenida Itzáes
Colonia García Ginerés
Telephone: (999)925-0831 and for emergencies (999) 925-0866 ext. 2553

Whether private or public, all hospitals are required by law to treat people in the emergency room regardless of what, if any, insurance they have, or their legal status in the country. No one can be turned away. Additionally, the Hospital O'Horan has state-of-the-art facilities for treating people living with HIV and AIDS.

Personal Health Insurance

In addition, you will need to have some sort of health insurance—unless you are prepared to self-insure. Be aware that Americans citizens and permanent aliens who are enrolled in Medicaid and Medicare in the United States will find that neither program pays for health coverage while in Mexico. There are a few trial programs and exchange pilot initiatives but these tend to be concentrated on the U.S.-Mexico border, such one between San Diego and Tijuana. The U.S. military has also been working on administering healthcare coverage for U.S. veterans living in Mexico.

Here is how the American Association of Retired Persons (AARP) addresses the current situation:

"Experience has been gained in Mexico, however, showing that a less ambitious program, the military's Tricare Standard coverage, can operate there and ensure reasonable coverage for retirees living there and delivery of medical and hospitalization services at a cost saving compared to scheduled Medicare costs in the USA. The experimental program there was administered by the Wisconsin Physicians Service. It was not only effective; it has encouraged the adoption of medical standards recognized as meeting Medicare criteria, in Mexico."

It is expected that sometime in the course of this new decade, some Medicare programs will be available in Mexico.

In the meantime, there are three general approaches to securing health insurance in Mexico. First is to secure private insurance, either from an U.S. company that offers health insurance to Americans living overseas. The second is to secure health coverage from a private Mexican health insurance company. The third is to enroll in Mexico's public health program, which allows

396

foreigners in Mexico with an FM2 or FM3 visa, or the new immigration documents, to participate in the national healthcare program available nationwide.

Please note that throughout 2013 Mexico streamlined its immigration categories, and this will impact how other federal agencies and programs enroll expatriates. For up-to-the-minute information on these changes, please visit the Instituto Nacional de Migración's website for the latest news: *www.inami.gob.mx*.

Health Insurance from American and Canadian Companies

Expat Global Medical

This is from their Mission Statement:
Since 1992 our companies have been insuring people all over the globe. Affordable, comprehensive health and medical insurance coverage for expatriates. If you are planning to live abroad, outside your country of normal residence, your government or regular health insurance plan will not cover you. The Expatriate health insurance plan is designed for Expatriates who are no longer covered under a basic health insurance plan, or individuals who are awaiting other insurance coverage in the country in which they intend to reside.

J.W. McGee & Associates

J.W. McGee & Associates
106 Keswick Drive, 1st Floor
Advance, NC 27006
Telephone: (336) 998-9583 (This is a U.S. area code)
Email: *john@expatglobalmedical.com*
Website: *www.expatglobalmedical.com*

American Express (Aetna Global Benefits)

This is from their Mission Statement:
If you are looking for a first-class expatriate health insurance product with excellent service, contact American Express worldwide health insurance. We have a wide range of health insurance programmes that have been developed specifically for expatriates over many years. Our expat health insurance products can provide you with some of the best cover available - as one of our policyholders, you can rest assured that we will always be at hand to help if you have an accident or fall ill while you are overseas

American Express

American Express Goodhealth Worldwide (Global) Limited
c/o Aetna Global Benefits
4630 Woodland Corporate Blvd.
Tampa, FL 33614
Telephone: (866) 545-3252 (Toll-free, inside USA only) or (813) 775-0220
Email: *AmericasServices@aetna.com*
Website: *www.worldwidehealthplan.com/Expatriate_health_insurance.asp*

Expat Financial

This is from their Mission Statement:
Expat Financial offers several different international health insurance plans for expatriates of any nationality across the world. We offer plans from several different insurance companies that are designed for foreign nationals (expats) living outside the country for which they hold a passport or any local national living outside US or Canada. We also offer excellent service before and after you purchase your international health insurance plan.

Expat Financial (Canada)

Expat Financial
c/o TFG Global Insurance Solutions Ltd.,
#216 - 2438 Marine Drive
West Vancouver, BC V7V 1L2
Canada
Telephone: (800) 232-9415 (Toll-free, inside the USA and Canada)
Email: *info@tfgglobal.com*
Website: *www.expatfinancial.com*

Health Insurance from Mexican Companies

In Mérida, there are several Mexican companies that offer health insurance plans for expatriates. These have a wide selection of plans, and once you know what is available from companies in the U.S. and Canada for expatriates in Mexico, you will have a good idea of what you can expect to pay.

Here are three, two with offices in Mérida, and Met Life Mexico, the largest insurer in the country.

Allianz

Calle 13 #120 between Calle 28 and Paseo de Montejo, Colonia Buenavista
Telephone: (999) 927-2260

For health insurance, email: *seguros@allianz.com.mx*
Website: *www.allianz.com.mx*

GE Seguros (in the process of becoming HDI Seguros)

Calle 60 #289, between Calle 23 and 25 Street, Colonia Alcalá Martín
Telephone: (999) 920-7215
For health insurance, ask for Julileta Morales
Website: *www.hdi.com.mx*

GNP

Calle 16 #97, Colonia Mexico
Telephone: (999) 944-6334
For health insurance, ask for Adriana González
Website: *www.gnp.com.mx*

La Peninsular Seguros

Calle 58-A #499, between Calle 29 and 33 Street, Centro
Telephone: (999) 920-2329
For health insurance, ask for María Esquivel
Website: *www.lapeninsular.com.mx*

Met Life Mexico

Manuel Ávila Camacho 32
Pisos SKY, 14 al 20 y PH
Colonia Lomas de Chapultepec, C.P. 11000
Delegación Miguel Hidalgo
México, D.F.
Telephone: (555) 328-7000
Email: *contacto@metlife.com.mx*
Website: *www.metlife.com.mx*

Health Insurance from the Mexican Government

The final option is to sign up for Mexico's national health care program. The **Instituto Mexicano del Seguro Social**, known as **IMSS**, now offers a program that allows foreign residents to join the national health care system. IMSS is the largest health care system in the Spanish-speaking world and it offers medical services for everyone at reasonable rates.

IMSS has established two offices where foreigners can sign up for health insurance. Depending on the coverage you choose, the premiums range from $1,000 pesos to $3,000 pesos annually—that's $80 USD to $250 USD!

This is from their Mission Statement:

The Mexican Sociay Security (Health Care) Institute has a legal mandate derived from Article 123 of the Political Constitution of the United States of Mexico. Its mission is to be the basic instrument of social security (health care), established as a public service of national nature for all workers and their families. This means that the increase in the population coverage is pursued as a constitutional mandate, with a social approach.

If you live north of Calle 59, you have to apply in person with your FM2 or FM3, and three copies of the entire passport:

IMSS (Pensiones)

Calle 7 #432, between Calle 32 and 34 Street
Colonia Pensiones

If you live south of Calle 59, you have to apply in person with your FM2 or FM3, and three copies of the entire passport:

IMSS (Serapio Rendon)

Calle 42 Sur #999, between Calle 127-A and 131 Street
Colonia Serapio Rendon

Once the paperwork has been processed, you will be assigned to a "primary" IMSS clinic. At that time you will be issued your Carnet, which is a small booklet, which is a record of your visits. Upon your first visit, you will be assigned a general practioner, who will be your primary care physician. Normally, you will then be scheduled for a complete physical, just to have a record of your health, medical history and the medications you are currently taking. At that time, your primary care physician may refer you to specialists within the IMSS system.

Going forward, all visits to the IMSS clinic are free, since they are covered by your premium. The good news is that you now have affordable health care. The bad news is that Mexico's IMSS does not allow you the choice in doctors assigned to you. Hundreds of American expatriates, however, have taken advantage of this program, and most report that they are pleased with the services they receive and the care offered to them.

For more information, visit the website for IMSS: *www.imss.gob.mx/English.*

How Obamacare Affects American Expats in Mexico

There are the five things every U.S. expat living in Mexico needs to know about Obamacare and its impact your taxes due the IRS In 2014, the Affordable Care Act, more commonly known as Obamacare, went into effect. In consequence, there has been confusion among Americans concerning how Obamacare affects them. This confusion extends to U.S. expats living in Mexico and around the world. To understand more fully how U.S. taxes for expats will be affected—or not—below are the five things that, as an American citizen living in Mérida, you need to know about Obamacare.

1. Many U.S. Expats are Exempt, But Not All

As a rule, Americans living overseas are exempt from the Obamacare regulations if they are considered legal residents of another country. This means you would need to comply with Mexico's laws for being a legal resident and satisfy the U.S. requirements for being an expat under the IRS code. To meet these criteria and be considered an expat, you must meet one of the two residency tests:

The Physical Presence Test. To meet this test, one must earn income in a foreign country and be physically present outside of the U.S. for 330 days of any 365-day period.

The Bona Fide Residence Test. To be considered a bona fide resident of another country, such as Mexico, one must live outside of the U.S. for at least one year and have no intentions of returning to the United States permanently.

If one qualifies for the Foreign Earned Income Exclusion, meaning that one complies with one of the two residency tests mentioned above, then one is *not subject to the provisions of Obamacare*.

2. Non-Resident Aliens in the U.S. are Exempt

When you are considered a non-resident, then you are exempt from Obamacare's provisions. Should you remain in the U.S. long enough to be considered a resident, however, one will be then required to obtain the minimum essential coverage as required by law. Otherwise, one will be subject to the so-called "Obamacare tax." This is a penalty leveled by the IRS It is based on a prorated penalty for each month in a tax year that one does not have required coverage.

Do remember that Obamacare applies to "applicable individuals" who are lawfully present in the U.S. As a general rule, once one returns to the U.S. for three months or longer, one is considered lawfully present and must comply with the mandate. Penalties for failing to comply, however, are included with the taxpayer's return for the year in question. In other words, should a resident or non-resident alien have no U.S .filing requirement in a given year, there is no way to enforce the penalty. In this case, noncompliance becomes a non-issue.

It is important to bear in mind that having health coverage under a foreign healthcare policy does not exempt one from the provisions of Obamacare. The minimum essential coverage does not, in fact, refer to the level of benefits a plan provides one may have while living in Mexico. The minimum requirement, under U.S. law, is based on the plan being a "qualifying U.S. plan." This means that a qualifying policy must be issued in the U.S. and one must be a resident of the state in which the coverage was issued.

What is the minimum essential coverage required by Obamacare? Following are the specifics of what is considered an acceptable healthcare policy:

- Employer-sponsored coverage (including COBRA coverage and retiree coverage)
- Coverage purchased in the individual marketplace, including a qualified health plan offered by the Health Insurance Marketplace, more commonly known as an Affordable Insurance Exchange
- Medicare Part A coverage and Medicare Advantage plans
- Most Medicaid coverage plans
- Children's Health Insurance Program (CHIP) coverage
- Certain types of veterans health coverage administered by the Veterans Administration
- TRICARE
- Coverage provided to Peace Corps volunteers
- Coverage under the Nonappropriated Fund Health Benefit Program
- Refugee Medical Assistance supported by the Administration for Children and Families
- Self-funded health coverage offered to students by universities for plan or policy years that begin on or before December 31, 2014
- State high risk pools for plan or policy years that begin on or before December 31, 2014 (for later plan or policy years, sponsors of these programs may apply to HHS to be recognized as minimum essential coverage)

Minimum essential coverage does not include insurance plans only offering limited benefits, such as coverage only for vision care or dental care. It does not include Medicaid covering only certain benefits such as family planning. It does not include state Workers' Compensation or Disability policies.

3. U.S. Expatriate Health Plans

American expats who purchase a U.S. expatriate health plan are exempt from Obamacare. The government noted that such plans face complex details, and as such, these plans are considered to be in compliance with the law and fully-insured expatriate plans are determined to provide the minimum essential coverage for I.R.S purposes. This currently applies to plans through December 31, 2015. After that date the I.R.S. will issue new guidelines. This exemption for expatriate healthcare plans applies to plans where the "primary insured" resides outside the U.S. for at least six months of the plan year.

4. Short-Term Contractors Are Not Exempt

Please not that short-term overseas contractors fall into an Obamacare gray area, known as an Obamacare gap. Contractors may not qualify as being a bona fide expat because they are not overseas long enough, but at the same time, they may not be able to purchase an acceptable U.S. healthcare policy through the exchange because they don't currently reside in a specific U.S. state.

What are the penalties for failing to comply with the provisions of Obamacare? Her are the penalties for 2014, 2015, and 2016:

2014: The GREATER of $95 USD per adult and $47.50 USD per child, up to a maximum of $285 USD for a family, OR 1% of your family income, for income over and above the filing threshold

2015: The GREATER of $325 USD per adult and $162.50 USD per child, up to $975 USD for the family, OR 2% of your family income, for income over and above the filing threshold

2016 and beyond: The GREATER of $695 USD per adult and $347.50 USD per child, up to $2,085 USD for the family, OR 2.5% of your family income, for income over and above the filing threshold

5. If You Move Back to the U.S. then you are granted a window of time to enroll

If an American expat returns to the U.S., he or she is granted 60 days to obtain coverage that meets the minimum requirements under the law. Remember that having coverage for only one day in a specific month is considered coverage for the *whole* month. This means you have, in fact, almost three month to enroll in a healthcare plans that is right for you.

For the most part, most American expats in Mérida will meet the Physical Presence test and be exempt from Obamacare. Others may not, especially the "snow birds" that only spend the winter months in Mérida. For those that are exempt, be mindful of your travels back to the U.S. If one spends even 36 days in the U.S. throughout the course of a calendar year, are not only is one subject to Obamacare, but one will also lose your eligibility for the Foreign Earned Income Exclusion. This could increase taxes significantly. Having provided this overview of Obamacare, should you have any questions about how you qualify as an American expat, please seek the advice of a tax professional who can determine your residency status and help you plan.

Beyond Health Care

There's more health care than eating right, a list of hospitals and health insurance. There's also the pursuit of happiness. So here are a few ways expatriates are pursuing better health through the pursuit of happiness.

Gym for Seniors

Right in the heart of the "north" part of Mérida one finds a state-of-the-art gym designed for people over the age of 50. There are no excuses about gyms are filled with young ladies listening to Beyonce on the treadmills, or muscle-building young men dropping weights on the floor!

Seniors Gym

Calle 19 #88, by Calle 32
Colonia Campestre
Telephone: (999) 944-5427
Website: *www.fisiocare.com.mx*

Sex and the Expat

We all know that a healthy sex life is an integral part of a healthy lifestyle, right? Fortunately, many expatriates are married, or have partners, a fact that solves the question of sex (or not!).

But that's not the case for everyone, of course. Many widows, widowers, divorced people or singles end up becoming expatriates in Mérida. There are several scenarios that play themselves out. First, for some reason, a disproportionate number of gay men end up relocating to Mérida. Some joke that since there is so much remodeling and redecorating to be done in the city's Historic Center, they flock down here to be "creative." Of course this plays to stereotypes, but it can't be denied that there are lots of gay expatriates in town.

Gay men in Mérida have their own culture, insular, and self-affirming, which may or may not be a good thing, depending on one's perspective. A disproportionate number of gay men, for example, are clients of male hustlers in town, and they often fall victim to the kind of crimes familiar with that kind of lifestyle. (Gringo Gultch is filled with boring gossip about the misadventures of expatriate gays and local hustlers, which in many ways is a throwback to the 1940s and 1950s when "rough trade" dominated gay life in the United States. Two American pedophiles were slain in 2012, both by the teenagers they had raped over a period of years, Jerry

Sandusky-style.) Gay women, on the other hand, have always been more circumspect and sophisticated in their community, and it is often the case that they make a much more easy transition to the woman-centered community of Mérida's lesbians.

Second, the world being what it is, straight men are the most fortunate: There are plenty of single, straight expatriate women and local women who covet foreigners, giving them ample choices. (Again, stereotypes prevail, and Yucatecan and Mexican women think, rightly or wrongly, that foreign men are more willing to be "equals" in their relationships.) Whether this is true or not, it is astounding to see how many American and Canadian men in town, well into their 50s and 60s, are with Mexican and Yucatecan women, decades younger, and starting new families.

Third, there are the familiar challenges that women face the world over. As a result, straight female expatriates have the most difficult time finding their groove. There are simply not enough straight male expatriates to go around, and most female expatriates are not sufficiently fluent in Spanish to carry on romantic relationships with Mexican or Yucatecan men. That isn't to say that there is an emerging "subculture" of Latin Lovers out there—Mexican and Yucatecan men who fancy themselves Casanovas, and who enjoy seducing expatriate women. Oh, yes, word has gotten out to the point that there is an expression in Mérida for the Single Expatriate Woman: "Gringas muertas por pingas." It may sound crass and unkind—"Gringas dying for dick"—but that's the perception out there.

And this leads to a warning: **Beware the Gigolo**, regardless of nationality, since there have been cases of wonderful middle-aged women being taken advantage of by men with ulterior motives. In one notorious case, one expatriate found herself waking up alone one morning—the love of her life gone back to Philadelphia, after he empited her bank account of almost $50,000 USD. If it weren't bad enough that a good number have had their bank accounts emptied, what can mend a broken heart? For women of all ages, "Sex and the Single Female Expat" requires constant vigilance!

Sports Facilities

Mérida has a good number of sports facilities and nationally-ranked professional teams in baseball, soccer and basketball. There are wonderful opportunities to enjoy these facilities, to join informal leagues and to make life-long friends in pick-up basketball games, participating in baseball matches, and finding a friend to play a court sport. In the early mornings, many of these parks are filled with avid "brisk" walkers getting in their cardio exercise first thing in the morning before the heat of the day arrives.

Sports facilities include:

- **Estadio Salvador Alvarado** in the north
- **Unidad Deportiva Kukulcán** (with the major Soccer Stadium Carlos Iturralde, Kukulcán BaseBall Park and Polifórum Zamná multipurpose arena)
- **La Inalambrica Sports Complex**, in the west (with archery facilities that held a world series championship)
- **Unidad deportiva Benito Juárez García**, in the northeast.
- **Gimnasio Polifuncional**, where professional basketball team Mayas de Yucatán plays for the Liga Nacional de Baloncesto Profesional de México (LNBP) representing Yucatán.

Nationally-Ranked Teams

Team Name/Sport	League
Leones de Yucatán, Baseball	Liga Mexicana de Béisbo
F.C. Itzáes, Soccer Mérida F.C., Soccer	I Segunda División de México Liga de Ascenso de México
Mayas de Yucatán, Basketball	Liga Nacional de Baloncesto Profesional de México

A Note for Friends of Bill W.

There are three English-language AA meetings. The Mérida English Library hosts one on Tuesdays at 5:30 PM, Thursdays at 7:00 PM, and on Sundays at 5:30 PM. In addition, the Mérida English Language Library hosts an Al-Anon meeting on Wednesdays at 5:30 PM. Use Google to find the most up-to-the-minute locations in town.

Adventure Travel and the Elder Expat

It's good to know that Mexico's culture of respect for age extends to expatriates! There are few places that where a travel tour company does wonderful business designing adventure travel for those who are active and retired. **Aguilar & Lord** is a travel agency that specializes in mature travelers.

This is from their Mission Statement:

"Aguilar & Lord — and the December 2010 trip to the Yucatán — came about as a result of our own experience traveling though the Yucatán with an older family member; someone who loves learning about new places and people, but who wasn't looking for a rugged trek through the jungle. It was the beginning of March. She had escaped the cold of a New England winter and come to spend a little time with us in Mexico to get the chill out of her bones. After a couple of days of relaxing by the beach, we packed our bags and set out to explore."

Set out to explore by contacting them at their website: *www.aguilarandlord.com.*

Medical Tourism in Mérida

Medical Tourism in Mexico

"Mexico is experiencing an increase in medical tourists and this year [2010] the number will comfortably exceed the 50,000 in 2009, says *Health Digital System* (HDS). Between January and September of this year, 44,512 foreigners checked in to Mexican hospitals, 25 percent more than the 35,610 who did so during the same period in 2009. Last year, some 50,000 foreign patients were treated in Mexico and each one spent an average of $13,000 per week on medical care, for a total of $650 million, according to an HDS study.

HDS expects this sector to continue growing and that in two years it will generate revenues of about $1.2 billion. The good quality of care and the low charges, which are about half the equivalent medical costs in the USA, spurs foreign patients to come to be treated in Mexican hospitals. Most come from the United States and Canada for everything from regular checkups to dental and cosmetic surgery, and more recently there has been an increase in those seeking major surgery. Jaime Cater of HDS says, 'Mexico has managed to increase the development of its health system and in private hospitals as well as federal ones emphasis is being decisively placed on strengthening this type of tourism.'"

Source: *http://www.imtj.com/news/?entryid82=254700*

Medical Tourism in Mérida: A Diplomat's Testimonial

"Where would we go if something serious were to happen? When I asked other expats about their healthcare experiences here in the Yucatán Peninsula, Mérida was consistently mentioned and with positive comments too. I have always been partial to using hospitals that are near to teaching institutions. Again, Mérida fits the bill.

The need did arise one evening when I had an appendicitis attack. I threw a few items in a bag and made the long trek to Mérida. I arrived at the emergency room of Star Médica Hospital, and was seen by the emergency room physician in less than five minutes. A prompt examination and a few tests and my suspicions were confirmed. They called in a surgeon and I was in surgery shortly after my arrival. (The surgeon was actually sitting in a chair outside of the operating suites, waiting for me.)

I only spent one additional night in the hospital. I was in a spotlessly clean private room with nice artwork on the walls. The surgeon was trained in the U.S. and his care was excellent and personal. He gave me his personal cell phone number and made arrangements for me to have my sutures removed back in Mahahual. The hospital staff was attentive without interrupting my rest and recovery.

The cost for emergency room, emergency room physician, all tests, surgeon, operating suite and two nights in the hospital - $3,000 USD. That was my deductible when I lived in the U.S.!

A reason I picked Star Médica was due to positive things I heard from other expats. It always makes you feel a little better when you run a doctor's name by someone. I have come to appreciate how really good health care can be here in Mérida," Kevin Graham, U.S. Counsel Warden, and proprietor of Costa Maya Living Real Estate.

This is a rather succinct explanation why Mérida is emerging as one of the most important destinations for Medical Tourism in Mexico. There are many reasons American and Canadian patients are choosing Mérida as a destination-of-choice when it comes to securing medical and dental services. Consider the "driving" factors of the medical tourism industry in general, and then the reasons why Mérida is now among the premier destinations for medical and dental services to people from around the world.

Medical Tourism Drivers & the Five "A" Factors

By Dr. Prem Jagyasi

Why do patient travel for Medical services? What are the key factors driving this industry? Primarily there are five major factors involved in decision making process of medical tourist. I call them the "5 A Factors." They are Affordable, Accessible, Available, Acceptable and Additional.

Affordable

An American proverb says "the laughter is the best medicine." An American person says "it's medicine cost that brings tears." If medical disorder brings discomfort then treating such disorder brings problems full of discomfort. The developed world is experiencing serious problems for the cost of medical services. Millions of uninsured patients seek affordable care. This factor is key factor for the emerging industry.

Available

Many patients travel because the medical treatment not available in their local areas. This type of travel is known as "need factor travel" which makes medical tourist to opt for best available option.

Accessible

Many developed countries have care available for patients, but because of high demand the treatment and care are not accessible. In some countries, patients have to wait for six to twelve months for a surgery, hence patient search for easy accessible care.

Acceptable

Few patients travel because "medical services" are acceptable abroad. Services might be affordable, available and accessible but are not acceptable because of religious, political and social reasons. It is hard to define ethical value of such services.

Additional

This is the most important and extensive factor of all. Many patients travel because they receive additional benefits by making use of treatment abroad. It could be better care, modern technology, latest medicine, better hospitality, personalized care or privacy among others. This factor provides some sort of additional benefits to patients which is better comparable to home country.

The five above factors are the major ones which are driving patients to seek treatment abroad. Similarly, the evolution of medical tourism industry involves five key drivers.

For more information, see: *www.medicaltourismmag.com/article/defining-medical-tourism-another-approach.html*

Medical Tourism in Mérida—The Pros and the Cons

By Elizabeth Arnott

For many years, the private health system in Mérida, Yucatán has been of the highest standard and has a wide range of specialties. Savvy Americans and Canadians have been coming for years to take advantage of the much cheaper costs of medical treatment compared with back home. ... Most of the doctors and surgeons have studied at the University of Yucatán (UADY) which has the reputation for having one of the finest medical schools in Mexico. Many of these doctors go on to study in America and Europe, and return with highly advanced skills and up-to-date technology.

Another aspect of medical tourism in Mérida is the excellent level of dentistry. Dentists have studied in Mérida and then completed post-graduate study in the States. They have all the facilities necessary from basic check-ups to every conceivable form of dental work.

The Pros:

* The first major consideration is that it is so much cheaper than back home.
* Doctors are highly qualified and up-to-date.
* Hospitals are very well equipped, and comfortable.
* If your doctor needs you to have an analysis or X-rays, they can be arranged immediately, within the same building.
* Most doctors speak excellent English.
* Appointments can be made quickly. You do not have to wait months to see your specialist. Usually you can call and be seen on the same day.

The Cons:

* You are in a foreign country, far from your family and loved ones. ... Ideally you would come with a companion, who could stay in a hotel close by, to be near you for moral support and make sure that everything goes according to your wishes.
* Post treatment recovery. Until your doctor releases you from his care, all the follow-up checks have been made, and you feel ready to fly back to your own country, you will need to find comfortable accommodation for your recuperation period. Mérida has an enormous range of hotels from five-star, through boutique hotels, to the humble bed and breakfast.

To read Elizabeth Arnott's complete article, see: *http://EzineArticles.com/6470663*.

Medical Tourism Hospitals and Operators in Mérida

With this background, following are the four premier hospitals providing Medical Tourism services to foreigners. This means that these hospitals are familiar with the kinds of procedures many foreigners want; their staffs are prepared to deal with English-speaking patients; and their doctors meet stringent international medical training and certification for the procedures which they are performing.

Clínica de Mérida

Avenida Itzáes #242
Colonia García Ginerés
Telephone: (999) 942-1800
Website: *www.clinicademerida.com.mx/DEP.html*

Star Médica

Calle 26 #199 by Calle 15 and 17 Street
Fraccionamiento Altabrisa
Telephone: (999) 930-2880
Website: *www.starmedica.com/default.asp?seccion=150*

Centro de Especialidades Médicas (CEM)

Calle 60 #329-B by Calle 35 and Avenida Colón
Colonia Alcalá Martín
Telephone: (999) 920-4040
Website: *www.cemsureste.com/cem_index.htm*

Centro Médico de las Américas (CMA)

Calle 54 #365
Centro
Telephone: (999) 926-2111
Website: *www.centromedicodelasamericas.com.mx/directorio.php?Offset=0*

Medical Tourism Operators

There are several companies specializing in conducting "medical tourism" for English-speaking foreigners in Mérida. These companies have relationships with doctors, clinics, hospitals and can make arrangements for accommodations, insurance payments, and follow-up care. As with everything else, it is the responsibility of the patient to vet properly each tour operator. The publisher provides the following information as a public service, and neither endorses these operators, nor are there any financial relationships of any nature with either one.

Health Star Medical Tourism

Health Star Medical Tourism has offices in St. Paul, Minnesota and has been working in Mérida for several years. They specialize in the following procedures:

411

- Orthopedics, including hip and knee surgeries, **hip replacement**, partial or total knee replacement, shoulder, elbow, ankle and foot surgeries

- Angiology, including **CCSVI liberation surgery** for MS patients, jugular angioplasty, treatment of lymphatic disease, and aortic and endovascular disease

- Orthodontics and **Dentistry**, including endodontic procedures, crowns, root canals, bridges, implants as well as aesthetic and prosthetic dentistry

- **Plastic and cosmetic surgery**, including breast augmentation, face- and neck lift, tummy tuck, liposuction, and rhinoplasty

- **Cardiology**, including pacemakers, coronary angioplasty, MS liberation procedures, and stem cell implantation for angiogenesis

- Gastrointestinal surgery, including **bariatric lap band surgery**, hysterectomy, and surgeries for stomach, colon and abdominal cancer

- **Urology**, including kidney stone removal, surgery of kidney and bladder cancer, and laparoscopic surgery

Health Star Medical Tourism
2211 Knapp Street
St. Paul, MN 55108
Telephone: (651) 225-0598
Email: *info@healthstarmedicaltourism.com*
Website: *www.healthstarmedicaltourism.com*

Medical Traveler Yucatán

Medical Traveler Yucatán's is a medical tourism company whose mission is "committed to providing the global patient with the highest quality medical care through a seamless, economical, and successful healthcare experience." They specialize in the following procedures:

WEIGHT LOSS / BARIATRIC
- Laparoscopic Gastric Bypass
- Intragastric Balloon

GASTRO-ENTEROLOGICAL
- Gall Bladder
- Hernia
- Colonoscopy

412

- Endoscopy
- Colorectal Surgery
- Laparoscopic Surgery

SURGICAL ONCOLOGY
- Breast, Head, Neck

CARDIOVASCULAR / CARDIOLOGY
- Coronary Artery Bypass
- Angioplasty
- Valve Replacement
- Diagnostic (Electrocardiogram, Echo, Catheterization)
- Congenital Heart Disease

Medical Travel Yucatán
Calle 26 #199 between Calle 15 and 17 Street
Fraccionamiento Altabrisa
Telephone: 011 52 (999) 143-3432 (Calling from the U.S.)
Canada Telephone: (416) 604-7165
Email: *info@medicaltraveleryucatan.com*
Website: *www.medicaltraveleryucatan.com*

Plastic Surgery & Fertility Clinics

As part of the growing medical tourism industry in Mérida, there are now a number of plastic surgeons. Whether it is liposuction or breast augmentation, Botox or rhinoplasty, Mérida is becoming an important destination for affordable surgery. In addition, there is a world-class fertility center that provides state-of-the-art facilities and treatments for couples trying to conceive and carry a pregnancy to full term.

Plastic Surgery: Clínica Colón

Dr. Fernando Muñoz
Avenida Colón #199, by Calle 26
Colonia García Ginerés
Telephone: (999) 920-2121
Website: *www.clinicacolon.com*

Fertility Center: Instituto Vida

Dr. Antonio Gutiérrez
Avenida Colón #204-D, between Calle 24 and 26 Street
Colonia García Ginerés

Telephone: (999) 925-2120
Website: *www.institutovidamerida.com*

25   GAY AND LESBIAN MÉRIDA

It can be safely said that the vast majority of expatriates moving to Mérida come from societies whose principle religious traditions derive from the three Abrahamic faiths: Judaism, Christianity and Islam. These three religions take dim views of same-sex relations. In the Torah and Leviticus (18:22) call same-sex relations an "abomination." Leviticus is also one of the books in the Christian Bible. In the Qu'ran (Koran), we find, "The Prophet, peace and blessings of Allaah be upon him, said: 'If a man has sexual relations with another man, they are both guilty of zina (adultery), and if a woman has sexual relations with another woman they are both guilty of zina (adultery).'"

Other religious traditions also take dim views of homosexuality. The three major faiths of Indian origin—Hinduism, Buddhism and Sikhism—discourage or forbid engaging in same-sex relations.[5] Further East, the same biases are found. In the Taoic religions, homosexuality is not viewed as being a path to human fulfillment, and it is discouraged as vacuous. (As recently as the 1970s Maoist China condemned homosexuality as a form or mental illness.)

This religious disapproval has also shaped secular views of homosexuality, the point being that gays and lesbians encounter various forms and degrees of biases and bigotries, and the struggle for acceptance is a continuing one.

That said, many expatriates look at Mexico, realize that it is a deeply Catholic society, and make the assumption that the dim views of homosexuality that inform Catholic teachings dominate.

Yes and no.

Officially, Mexicans are taught that homosexuality is to be frowned upon, and that it violates Biblical teachings. But in practice, there are two trends that mitigate homophobia in society at large. The first is secular: the Mexican belief that one should mind one's own business. "Uno no se debe meter en vidas ajenas," meaning "One should not meddle into other people's affairs," is a saying that often-repeated in Mérida's homes—just as one is about to dish gossip about

---

[5] See: Gyatso, Janet (2003). *One Plus One Makes Three: Buddhist Gender Conceptions and the Law of the Non-Excluded Middle*, History of Religions. 2003, no. 2. University of Chicago Press.

somebody. As a result there is a very strong cultural aversion to passing judgment on others, one of the traits that makes Yucatecans such good neighbors, and it promotes a healthy "live and let live" attitude.

The other factor is cultural: the ambivalence about same-sex relationships among the Maya. This is consistent with the world views of the First Peoples throughout the continent, where gay and lesbian sexual relations are not normally condemned. In recent years, much scholarly work has been undertaken to explore the view of homosexuals as being "two-spirited" people throughout the pre-Columbian societies of the Americas, especially among North American First Peoples.

Among the Maya, for instance, some deities, such as God K, are bisexual, depicted as having relations with women in some places, and with men in others. The Moon Goddess, which became closely associated with the Virgin Mary during the Colonial period, was represented as bisexual![6]

The social organization of homosexuality is vastly different among the Maya, and these cultural views offer greater acceptance than what normally finds in other areas of Mexico. It's not often appreciated by foreigners, but **throughout Mexico, the Yucatán is seen as a place—whether one admires it or ridicules it—where there is a kind of hedonism that encourages libertine sexual expression**. While certain cultural norms prevail for everyone—*public displays of overt sexuality are frowned upon regardless of sexual preference*—it's possible to see age-appropriate couples if not walking hand-in-hand, then at least arm-in-arm, without raising eyebrows.

With this background, it's not difficult to imagine why Mérida is a place where gays and lesbians let their guards down and enjoy greater social acceptance and freedoms.

Gay Mérida

If many associate "Mexico" with "macho," then Mérida is perhaps the least "macho" city in the entire country, and this is meant as a compliment, regardless of sexual orientation. There are few places in the world where one sees men holding their children, fathers kissing their kids, men helping women with the grocery shopping, or assisting their elderly parents at restaurants in such loving and unselfconscious ways.

---

[6] For more information, see: *From Moon Goddesses to Virgins: The Colonization of Yucatecan Maya* Sexual Desire, by Pete Sigal, University of Texas Press, 2000; and *The Construction of Homosexuality*, by David Greenberg, University of Chicago Press, 1990.

The cultural gentleness of the Maya, which is evidenced in any small town you visit, where people gather around a baseball field, or the local market, is remarkable. And this gender-neutral division of social responsibilities extends to tolerance for gay and bisexual men. It would be misleading to say that there is no social stigma to being gay in Mérida, but there is far less hostility than foreigners tend to presume. Yes, a slightly inebriated man dressed in high heels pretending to be Tina Turner walking down the street will get looks, and a few chuckles, but he is almost likely to be left alone, by passersby or the local police alike.

And if you have any doubts about the tolerance in Mérida for gays and lesbians, then Mérida's Carnival should put anxieties to rest, since the number of gays on the floats resembles a cross between Mardi Gras in New Orleans and Folsom Street Fair in San Francisco. If you are curious, there are a dozen or so videos on YouTube depicting various Gay and Lesbian marchers during Pride in Mérida. (Go to YouTube.com and search "Marcha Lésbico Gay Mérida Yucatán—2009" to see the video clips.)

And Mexico itself is very progressive. In recent years same-sex marriage has been legalized (in Mexico City) and so have same-sex adoptions. Mexico's Supreme Court ruled in August 2010 that gays and lesbians in Mexico must be afforded the same rights as heterosexuals. (In August 2010, Mexico became the 11th country in the world to provide LGBT people equal access to marriage, joining the Netherlands, Belgium, Portugal, Spain, Canada, South Africa, Iceland, Norway, Sweden, and Argentina.) As a result, there's now a new confidence among gays and lesbians. The ascendance of the homophile community in Mexico, interestingly, coincides with the influx of gay and lesbian expatriates not only from the U.S. and Canada, but Europe and South America, meaning that over the past decade the GLBTQ communities have grown more diverse and disparate.

Still, several observations can be made to offer guidance. As is often the case, gay men are more visible in the community than are lesbians and Mérida is no exception. From the Main Square (Zócalo) north along Calle 60 to the Peón Contreras Theater, the Cafés, parks and outdoor restaurants are favorites among gay men. Other places that remain popular are the Internet cafés along Calle 61. Mérida, however, being a city of almost a million people, not everyone cares to frequent a four-city block area, and the scores of places in the Colonias where local gay men gather. In the past decade a more popular way of connecting is through social networking.

Places to stay

Casa Mexilio

Calle 68 #495, between Calle 57 and 59 Street

Centro
Website: *www.casamexilio.com*

Los Arcos B&B

Calle 66 #408-B, between Calle 49 and 51 Street
Centro
Website: *www.lorarcosmerida.com*

Casa Lorenzo

Calle 41 #516-A, between Calle 62 and 64 Street
Centro
Website: *www.lacasalorenzo.com*

Bars

Gay bars and discos are located along the highway that encircles the city. If you don't have a car, they are a short cab ride from downtown.

Pride Disco

Anillo Periferico Mérida-Campeche
(200 meters from the Uman Bridge near the airport)
Telephone: (999) 947-9874
Open: Thursday - Sunday
Website: *www.pridedisco.com*
The bar opens at 10 PM, has a drag show every night, caters primarily to gay men, but is frequented by a good number of lesbians.

Scalibur

Calle 4-B #308, by 39-A Street
Colonia San Camilio II
Telephone: (999) 108-2046
Open: Thursday - Sunday
Website: www.myspace.com/scalibur_cabare_Mérida
The bar opens at 11 PM, has a drag show every night. There is a Tea Dance on Saturday and Sunday, beginning at 2 PM

Milk Gay Club

Kilometro 0.3, Carretera Mérida-Cancún
Telephone: (999) 101-0492
Open: Thursday - Sunday

Website: *www.milkgayclub.com*

The bar opens at 10 PM, has both a stripper show and a drag show every night. Straight women also attend, most of whom arrive with their girlfriends, since they like to see muscle boys stripping on stage. Features Sunday Tea Dances.

Angel Luz Club

This club has two locations.
Anillo Periferico Mérida-Campeche, Kilometro 7
Open: Thursday - Sunday
Website: *www.angeluzclub.com.mx*
The bar opens at 10 PM, has a drag show every night.
The other location is across from the Post Office in Itzimná, Colonia Itzimná

Foxxy's

Periferico Oriente, 30 meters towards Tixkokob
Telephone: (999) 988-1466
Open: Wednesday - Sunday
Website: *www.foxxys.mx*
The bar opens at 8 PM, has both a stripper show and a drag show every night.

Cafés and Scenes

Café La Habana

Calle 59 #511-A, between Calle 60 and 62 Street, Centro

Café Chocolate

Calle 60 #442, by 49 Street, Centro

Café El Hoyo

Calle 62 #491, between Calle 59 and 61 Street, Centro

Amaro Restaurant

Calle 59 #507, between Calle 60 and 62 Street, Centro
Centro

Gran Hotel Café

Calle 60 #496, between Calle 59 and 61 Street, Centro

Sorbeteria Colón

North side of the Main Square (Calle 61, between Calle 60 and 62 Street), Centro

Mérida Gay Facebook Community

www.facebook.com/pages/GAY-MERIDA/94476241897

Travel Agents Specializing in Gay Travel to Yucatán

Helena Iorio
HMI Travel Consulting
Website: *www.hmitravelconsulting.com*
Email: *HMItravelconsulting@gmail.com*
Telephone: 781-475-2005

Lesbian Mérida

What can you say about a Mexican city of a million people that elected a lesbian mayor over a decade ago?

You go, girl!

As is often the case around the world, lesbians are more discreet and have lower visibility compared to gay men. All it takes, however, is a simply a stroll around town to notice that female energy that abounds. But, it's one thing to see Packers and Princesses everywhere, and quite another to make contact with them. That there are no lesbian bars, however, should not discourage you: kitty punchers and vagitarians abound in the cafés around town, and there are three time-tested ways of making contact.

For casual interactions, it's best to frequent one of the cafés, galleries and museums favored by the lesbian community, as well as getting recommendations on events about town from the women who are the owners of Casa Ana.

The other defining characteristic of Mérida's lesbian community, as is seen by the high profiles women have in the political life of the Yucatán, is to reach out to certain groups that are non-profit organizations headed by, or staffed with, a high number of distinguished and accomplished lesbians. It is refreshing to see half a dozen or so very high-profile and active nonprofit organizations, which work in environmental, special education, women's health and child welfare organizations that are run by lesbians. Whenever these organizations have events, scores of attendees are lesbians. In fact, in the same way that gay men dominant events such as the opening night of a symphony concert or an opera, lesbians figure prominently in the city's nonprofit sector, where they are executive directors, program directors and managers of some of the city's most important NGOs working in the fields of health, education and environment. Ask around about local charities and organizations, and check their websites.

420

Then there are online resources. More than 225 Mérida lesbians are "friends" of "Solteras Less Mérida," meaning "Mérida Single Lesbians." It wouldn't hurt to become a friend and make contact with a few women before your visit. Obviously, if you know some Spanish that will help. But bear in mind that there is no shortage of Mexicans who want to improve their English by practicing with a native-English speaker! The benefit of this online community is that it allows you to establish contact with as many self-identified Mérida lesbians as you'd like to, and there's no reason why you can't set up to meet for coffee, or drinks, or a meal before you arrive—or once you are in town. As is the case with just about everyone else, Yucatecans are very proud of their city, of the Maya civilization and of their history. Most welcome nothing more than the opportunity to be gracious and helpful and to show you around town. And what could be better than having a new friend show you around town? Go ahead, there's absolutely nothing wrong with flowmancing via Facebook in Mérida!

It bears repeating: Without having to spend time drinking in bars, it's quite possible to become part of Mérida's lesbian community. From making a few introductions casually over Facebook, hanging out at some of the cafés and coffee shops where local lesbians hang out, or making an effort to reach out to some of the prominent and socially active lesbians heading important NGOs in town, one thing you will find is that this is a very nonjudgmental society, where women face few obstacles and little discrimination in living their lives on their own terms.

What *Pink Choice* says about Mérida

For the gay and lesbian traveler, the good news is that Mérida is fairly safe place to visit because it is a close knit community and there simply isn't any place to run. It has the lowest crime rate in the whole of Mexico. Traffic is chaotic, particularly downtown and as most of the streets are one way, getting around by car is definitely challenging. ... Mérida is nothing like Cancún or Playa del Carmen. If you want to experience Mexican culture while staying relatively close to the Caribbean Sea then Mérida is a great place to go. The city is a wonderful blend of a colonial city and a cosmopolitan destination. The central main plaza of Mérida is a great base, from where you can visit cathedrals and churches, Maya ruins, museums, haciendas and cenotes, shops and the local theaters.

Travel Agents Specializing in Lesbian Travel to Yucatán

Helena Iorio
HMI Travel Consulting
Website: *www.hmitravelconsulting.com*

Email: *HMItravelconsulting@gmail.com*
Telephone: 781-475-2005

Places to Stay

The following are lesbian-owned businesses, or are places where local lesbians frequent.

B&B and Hotels

Casa Ana

Calle 52 #469, between Calle 51 and
53 Street
Centro
Website: www.casaana.com

Hotel Casa del Balam

Calle 60 #488, by 57 Street
Centro
www.casadelbalam.com

Bars

Pride Disco

Anillo Periferico Mérida-Campeche
(200 meters from the Uman Bridge near the airport)
Telephone: (999) 947-9874
Website: www.pridedisco.com
The bar opens at 10 PM, has a drag show every night, caters primarily to gay men, but is frequented by a good number of lesbians.

Cafés and Hangouts

Café Chocolate

Calle 60 #442, by Calle 49 Street, Centro

Café Organico

Centro Comercial Colón, Local 1-C
Calle 33-D and Reforma Avenue
Colonia García Ginerés

Amaro Restaurant

Calle 59 #507, between Calle 60 and 62 Street, Centro

Gran Hotel Café

Calle 60 #496, between Calle 59 and 61 Street, Centro

Sorbeteria Colón

North side of the Main Square (Calle 61, between Calle 60 and 62 Street)

Places Favored by Lesbians

Museum of the City

Calle 56, between Calle 65 and 65-A Street
Hours: Tuesday—Saturday, 9 AM to 8 PM
Sundays, 9 a.m to 2 PM
Free admission

Mérida Lesbian Blog

www.lesgaradio.blogspot.com

Mérida Lesbian Facebook Community

www.facebook.com/pages/Solteras-Less-merida/106226992763453

Mérida GLBTQ Community Resources

Mérida has a gay and lesbian magazine called MID-OPEN. "MID" is the airport code for the city, and OPEN is about openly affirming one's identity. The magazine's motto is "In Mérida Things Change." The Facebook page has almost 3,000 "Likes," from the spectrum of Mérida's GLBTQ communities. The Facebook's Wall has everything from public endorsements from Mérida's mayor to the GLBTQ community to information on upcoming drag shows.

Website: *www.mid-open.com*
Facebook: *www.facebook.com/pages/MID-OPEN/100808197394*

Gay Pride Celebrations

Gay Pride is celebrated the last week in June.

26   U.S. Taxes and Voting

If you are an American citizen or a resident alien who is living in Mérida, you still have to comply with both your legal obligations to the IRS and (for citizens) your civic duty to vote. Yes, Uncle Sam wants you to file a tax return, and your mother wants you to vote!

Taxes for U.S. Citizens and Resident Aliens Abroad

If you are a U.S. citizen or resident alien, the rules for filing income, estate, and gift tax returns and paying estimated tax are generally the same whether you are in the United States or abroad. Your worldwide income is subject to U.S. income tax, regardless of where you reside.

When to File

If you reside overseas, or are in the military on duty outside the U.S., you are allowed an automatic 2-month extension to file your return until June 15. However, any tax due must be paid by the original return due date (April 15) to avoid interest charges. If you are unable to file your return by the due date, you can request an additional extension to October 15 by filing Form 4868 before the return due date. However, any payments made after June 15 would be subject to both interest charges and failure to pay penalties.

Where to File

If you are a U.S. citizen or resident alien (Green Card Holder), and you live in a foreign country or you are a non-resident alien, mail your U.S. tax return to:

Department of the Treasury
Internal Revenue Service Center
Austin, TX 73301-0215

Estimated tax payments should be mailed with form 1040-ES to:

Internal Revenue Service
P.O. Box 660406

Dallas, TX 75266-0406

Taxpayer Identification Number

Each taxpayer who files, or is claimed as a dependent on, a U.S. tax return will need a social security number (SSN) or individual taxpayer identification number (ITIN). To obtain a SSN, use form SS-5, Application for a Social Security Card. To get form SS-5, or to find out if you are eligible for a social security card, contact a Social Security Office or visit Social Security International Operations. If you, or your spouse, are not eligible for a SSN, you can obtain an ITIN by filing form W-7 along with appropriate documentation.

Exchange Rates

You must express the amounts you report on your U.S. tax return in U.S. dollars. If you receive all or part of your income or pay some or all of your expenses in foreign currency, you must translate the foreign currency into U.S. dollars. Taxpayers generally use the yearly average exchange rate to report foreign-earned income that was received regularly throughout the year. However, if you had foreign transactions on specific days, you may also use the exchange rates for those days. Exchange rates can be found at www.oanda.com. Yearly average currency exchange rates for most countries can be found at Yearly Average Currency Exchange Rates.

Please note that the U.S. dollar strengthened significantly against all major currencies beginning in the Fall 2014. The U.S. dollar-Mexican peso exchange rate jumped from 14.75 pesos to the U.S. dollar in mid-2015 to over 17.75 pesos to the U.S. dollar by the time 2016 rolled around. That's a significant appreciation of the U.S. dollar vis-à-vis the Mexican peso. Enjoy it while it lasts throughout 2016!

How to Get Tax Help

The IRS Office in Philadelphia provides international tax assistance. This office is open Monday through Friday from 6:00 AM to 11:00 PM EST and can be contacted by:

Telephone: (215) 516-2000 (not toll-free)
Fax: (215) 516-2555

Mail: Internal Revenue Service
P.O. Box 920
Bensalem, PA 19020
USA

Voter Registration & Voting for American Citizens in Mérida

This information is provided by the State Department, Washington, D.C. for American citizens in Mérida:

"U.S. citizens overseas are eligible to participate in primary, run-off, and special elections that occur throughout the year, as well as the general elections in November. A calendar of election dates is available on the Internet at www.fvap.gov/pubs/primarycal.html. You should register to vote and/or request absentee ballots as early in the year as possible to ensure that you will receive all ballots for which you are eligible.

The following is the basic absentee voting process:

1. You complete an application form, available from any U.S. Consulate, and send it to local election officials in the U.S.
2. The local official approves your request, or contacts you for further information
3. The local official sends you an absentee ballot
4. You vote the ballot and send it back in time to meet your state's deadline

If the ballot receipt deadline is drawing near, and you have not yet received the blank ballot from local officials, you can download an emergency ballot, write in the names of the candidates and the offices for which they are running, and send it back in time to meet your state's ballot receipt deadline. Registration and ballot request procedures and deadlines vary by state.

There may be late changes to your state's voting calendar, procedures or deadlines. When these occur, the Federal Voting Assistance Program (FVAP) will issue a News Release.

The official US Government website for overseas absentee voting assistance is the Federal Voting Assistance Program website at www.fvap.gov/. It has a wealth of information about absentee voting, including the downloadable absentee ballot application (SF-76, Federal Post Card Application, or FPCA), state-specific instructions for completing the form, links to or contact numbers for state and local officials, and the downloadable emergency ballot.

To register to vote and to request an absentee ballot, download the Federal Post Card Application at *www.fvap.gov/pubs/ofwab.pdf*. You can also obtain this form from overseas American citizens groups or from the U.S. Embassy/Consulate. Fill it out and send it in, following the guidelines for your state. A postage-paid envelope template, valid if you are using the U.S. postal system, is available at *www.fvap.gov/pubs/returnenvelope.pdf*.

Each state has different voting procedures. Information about your state's procedures is available at *www.fvap.gov/links/statelinks.html*. Information about your state's deadlines to register and vote, as well as calendar of election dates, is available at *www.fvap.gov/pubs/primarycal.html*.

States sometimes make last-minute changes. There may be late changes to your state's voting calendar, procedures or deadlines. When these occur, the Federal Voting Assistance Program (FVAP) will issue a News Release. News Releases are available at *www.fvap.gov/pubs/releases.html*.

Be an educated voter. Non-partisan information about candidates, their voting records, and their positions on issues is widely available and easy to obtain via the Internet. Use the links appearing on the Federal Voting Assistance Program website at *www.fvap.gov/links/electionlinks.html*, or choose any one of several search engines to locate articles and information.

The Voting Assistance Officer at the U.S. Embassy in Mexico City is available to answer questions about absentee voting. To contact the Voting Assistance Officer, call (55) 5080-2000 x 4131 or send an email to *ccs@usembassy.net.mx*.

Overseas Americans may contact Democrats Abroad, Republicans Abroad or other American citizens groups or organizations for absentee voting information, or for assistance in registering to vote or to request absentee ballots. Additionally, the Voting Assistance Officer at the U.S. Consulate in Mérida is available to answer questions about absentee voting. To contact the Voting Assistance Officer, send an email to: *Meridacons@state.gov*.

Again, we strongly encourage you to begin this process as soon as possible. Should questions or problems occur, you would still be able to address them in time to vote in your state's primary and general elections."

If you want to be informed of changes in tax or voting laws, be advised that several times a year officials from the U.S. Embassy in Mexico City travel to Mérida to conduct public awareness seminars and consult with American citizens and resident aliens. The Consulate in Mérida has a schedule for upcoming visits.

27 GENERAL SERVICES: EMERGENCY, POLICE, FIRE, POST OFFICES & MORE

General Contact Numbers

General Emergency Numbers

General Emergency: 066 from land line, or 113 from a cell phone
Mérida Police Department: (999) 942-0060
Mérida Federal Police Department: (999) 946-1203
Mérida Fire Department: (999) 924-9242 or (999) 923-2971
Red Cross (Cruz Roja): (999) 924-9813
Green Angel Roadside Assistance: (999) 983-1184
Consumer Protection Agency: (999) 923-2323
Federal Consumer Protection Agency: 01-800-468-8722 (ask to speak to an English language operator, or visit their **Website:** www.profeco.gob.mx/english.htm)Immigration (Instituto Nacional de Migracion): (999) 925-5009

Utilities

JAPAY (Water): (999) 930-3450
CE (Electricity): 071
Telmex (Phone): 01-800-123-0000

Hospitals

CEM Hospital, Calle 60 and Avenida Colón (across from Hyatt Hotel): (999) 920-4040
Clínica de Mérida, Avenida Itzáes #242, (near the Donde factory): (999) 925-4508
CMA, Calle 54 & Pérez Ponce, (near Wal-Mart) (Emergency room and Hospital): (999) 926-2111
Star Médica Hospital, Calle 26 #199 and 15 Street, Colonia Altabrisa: (999) 930-2880, (Ext. 5 for emergencies)

Ambulances

Red Cross (Cruz Roja) Free Ambulance: 065, or (999) 924-9813
Alfa Ambulance Service (serves Star Médica): (999) 924-1322
Sami Ambulance Service: (999) 925-4048

Taxis

EconoTaxi: (999) 945 0000
Taxi Santa Ana: (999) 928-5600
TaxiMetro: (999) 922-7575

Animal Rescue

Animal Rescue (AFAD): 044 (999) 947-6319 (This is a cell phone)

Visitor Information

For a comprehensive listing of current events, pick up a copy of "**Explore Yucatán**," readily available at most hotels, car rental, and tourist agencies. It's free of charge and has the most comprehensive, objective, and useful visitor information, along with a comprehensive guide to monthly events. It is also available online at *www.revistaexplore.com*.

Post Offices

Mérida Post Offices

Calle 53 #468, between Calle 52 and
54 Street, Centro
Telephone: (999) 928-5404

Calle 65 by Calle 56 Street, Centro
Telephone: (999) 928-5404

Calle 72 #389 (Avenida Reforma) by
Calle 37 Street, Centro
Telephone: (999) 920-2106

Calle 20 #99-G, between Calle 19
and 21 Street, Colonia Chuburná de
Hidalgo
Telephone: (999) 981-3833

Calle 59 #300 by 50 Street, Colonia
Cordemex
Telephone: (999) 944-1112

Calle 95 #504 by Calle 62

Colonia Delio Moreno Canton
Telephone: (999) 928-5225

Calle 28 #224 (Avenida Pérez Ponce),
between Calle 21-A and 26 Street,
Colonia Itzimná
Telephone: (999) 927-1323

Calle 24 #440, between Calle 41 and
43 Street, Colonia Las Brisas
Telephone: (999) 986-3048

Calle 5 #432 by 48 Street, Colonia
Pensiones
Telephone: (999) 987-0840

Calle 50 #441, between Calle 57 and
59 Street, Colonia Pacabtun
Telephone: (999) 982-1826

Progreso Post Office

Calle 81 #150, between Calle 78 and 80 Street
Telephone: (969) 935-0565

Postal Service Website: *www.sepomexyuc.gob.mx/oficinas.html*

General Information about Yucatán

Population (2010)
Total 1,945,840
Rank 21st
Density 49.1/km2 (127.2/sq mi)
Density rank 17th

Time zone
Central Standard Time, (UTC-6)
Summer (DST) CDT (UTC-5)

Postal code for Centro 97000

Telephone Area Codes
• 969 • 985 • 986 • 988 • 991 • 997 • 999

Elevation
10 m (33 ft)
Major Airport:

Manuel Crescencio Rejón International Airport
IATA Code: MID
Internet Access:

All public parks and squares are equipped with free Wi-Fi. Most in the Historic Center also have kiosks with electrical outlets for recharging batteries for laptops and cellphones.

Air Ambulance & Med-Evac Companies

U.S.-based Companies

STAT AIR INTERNATIONAL - AIR AMBULANCE

Telephone: (800) 557-5911 or
(619) 754-6550
Fax: (619) 754-6153
www.statair.com

TRINITY AIR AMBULANCE INTERNATIONAL

Lauderdale by the Sea, FL 33308
Telephone: (954) 771-7911
Fax: (954) 771-4882
www.trinityairambulance.com

AIR COMPASSION

(866) 270-9198
001- (883)-270-9198
www.aircompassionamerica.org

ADVANCED AIR AMBULANCE

Miami, FL
(800) 633-3590 / (305) 232-7700
www.flyambu.com

AIRMD AIR AMBULANCE SERVICES

Clearwater, FL
(800) 282-6878 / (727) 530-7972
www.airmd.net

AIR AMBULANCE PROFESSIONALS

Fort Lauderdale, FL
(800) 752-4195 / (954) 491-0555
www.airambulanceprof.com

AIR RESPONSE

Orlando, FL
(800) 631-6565 / (303) 858-9967
www.airresponse.net

CRITICAL AIR MEDICINE

San Diego, CA
(800) 247-8326 / (619) 571-0482

U.S. Embassy, Consulates and Consular Agencies in Mexico:

Embassy Location:
The U.S. Embassy is located in Mexico City at Paseo de la Reforma 305, Colonia Cuauhtemoc.
Telephone from the United States: 011-52-55-5080-2000
Telephone within Mexico City: 5080-2000
Telephone long distance within Mexico 01-55-5080-2000
Website: *mexico.usembassy.gov/eng/main.html*

U.S. Consulates

Ciudad Juárez:

Paseo de la Victoria 3650

Telephone: (656) 227-3000

Guadalajara:

Progreso 175, Colonia Americana
Telephone: (333) 268-2100

Hermosillo:

Calle Monterrey 141 Poniente,
Colonia Esqueda
Telephone: (662) 289-3500

Matamoros:

Avenida Primera 2002 and Azaleas
Telephone: (868) 812-4402

Mérida:

Calle 60 #338 K between Calle 29
and 31 Street, Colonia Alcalá Martín
Telephone: (999) 942-5700

Monterrey:

Avenida Constitución 411 Poniente
Telephone: (818) 047-3100

Nogales:

Calle San José, Fraccionamiento "Los
Alamos"
Telephone: (631) 311-8150

Nuevo Laredo:

Calle Allende 3330, Colonia Jardin
Telephone: (867) 714-0512

Tijuana:

Avenida Tapachula 96, Colonia
Hipodromo
Telephone: (664) 622-7400

Consular Agencies

Acapulco:

Hotel Continental Emporio, Costera Miguel Alemán 121 - Local 14
Telephone: (744) 484-0300 or (744) 469-0556

Cabo San Lucas:

Blvd. Marina Local C-4, Plaza Nautica, Centro
Telephone: (624) 143-3566

Cancún:

Blvd. Kukulcán Km 13 ZH Torre La Europea, Despacho 301
Telephone: (998) 883-0272

Cozumel:

Plaza Villa Mar en El Centro, Plaza Principal, 2nd floor, Locales 8 and 9
Telephone: (987) 872-4574

Ixtapa/Zihuatanejo:

Hotel Fontan, Blvd. Ixtapa
Telephone: (755) 553-2100

Mazatlán:

Hotel Playa Mazatlán, Playa Gaviotas 202, Zona Dorada
Telephone: (669) 916-5889

433

Oaxaca:

Macedonio Alcalá #407, Interior 20
Telephone: (951) 514-3054 or (951) 516-2853

Piedras Negras:

Abasolo 211, Local 3, Centro
Telephone (878) 782-5586 or (878) 782-8664.

Playa del Carmen:

The Palapa, Calle 1 Sur, between Avenida 15 and Avenida 20
Telephone: (984) 873-0303

Puerto Vallarta:

Paseo de Los Cocoteros 85 Sur, Paradise Plaza—Local L-7, Nuevo Vallarta, Nayarit
Telephone: (322) 222-0069

Reynosa:

Calle Monterrey 390, Esq. Sinaloa, Colonia Rodríguez
Telephone: (899) 923-9331

San Luis Potosi:

Edificio "Las Terrazas", Avenida Venustiano Carranza 2076-41, Colonia Polanco
Telephone: (444) 811-7802 or (444) 811-7803

San Miguel de Allende:

Dr. Hernandez Macias 72
Telephone: (415) 152-2357

Veterinary Services

If it's true that "you can judge a country by the way they treat their animals," there's something to be said about Mérida. The Autonomous University of Yucatán, or UADY, opened its new world-class, state-of-the-art veterinary hospital in September 2011 at a cost of $1.1 million USD. Located in Colonia of San José Vergel, minutes from downtown, this facility rivals any veterinary hospital in Latin America or the U.S. In addition, it is great to know that there are government facilities dedicated to protecting animal welfare. There are also private nonprofit organizations that work to find homes for pets, as well as conduct workshops to provide free services to pets.

Bilingual Veterinarians:

Pets & Company

Sandra Milena Leguizamón
José Encarnación Muñoz
Address: Calle 17 #222, Suite 2, by Calle 20, Colonia Jardines del Norte, Mérida, Yucatán
Telephone: (999) 943-7787
Email: *info@petsandcompany.com*
Website: *www.petsandcompany.com*

Veterinary Association

For expatriates, the Asociación de Médicos Veterinarios Especialistas en Pequeñas Especies de Yucatán, A. C. (AMVEPEY), is a nonprofit organization that can direct you to a bilingual veterinary doctor close to you. For more information, you can contact the AMVEPEY:

AMVEPEY

Website: *www.amvepey.com*

Adopt-a-Pet:

To adopt a pet, Silvia Cortés operates a sanctuary for dogs in need of a loving home. Her organization, Evolución Yucatán, continues to win praise from the expatriates.
Silvia Cortés, Director
Evolución Yucatán
Email: *slv_cc@hotmail.com*
Website: *evolucionyucatan.com*

Responsible Dog Breeders

Mérida is home to Criadora Itaboca, a world-class dog breeding company, that exports dogs all over Mexico, the U.S. and as far away as Russia and Malaysia. Trained in Brazil, Felipe Xacur Baeza, complies with the norms established by the American Kennel Club and aims to preserve and improve the breeds to which he is dedicated.

Criadora Itaboca

Felipe Xacur Baeza, Director
Calle 16 #213 by Calle 13, Fracc. Vista Alegre, Mérida, Yucatán
Telephone: (999) 943-0148
Email: *faxcur@itaboca.com*
Website: *www.itaboca.com*

28   If There Were a "Better Business Bureau" in Mérida ...

There is no "Better Business Bureau" in Mexico as it is understood in the United States. By that we mean a non-governmental organization that receives complaints from the public and advocates on behalf of the aggrieved consumer and offers ratings on local businesses.

Mexico, however, does have a federal agency to protect consumers. It does not rank companies on the basis of complaints filed against them. But it is a proactive federal agency that receives praise from the Mexican public as being diligent, honest, and effective. If you encounter any consumer problem, PROFECO may be the place to go to file a complaint if you have exhausted your recourse by contacting the company directly. PROFECO's services are free of charge; they operate a national toll-free number and have a very comprehensive website.

Mexico's Procuduria Federal del Consumidor, or PROFECO, has an English-language website designed to help individuals, regardless of nationalities, protect their rights as consumers. PROFECO's website offers this advice:

WELCOME

Welcome to the Federal Attorney's Office of Consumer (PROFECO) web site. This portal contains basic information on the PROFECO in English. ... Mexico is the second Latin-American country with a Federal Law of Protection to the Consumer and the first one in creating an Attorney's office. The Mexican experience is important, especially for the countries that [are beginning to employ] protection of the rights of the consumers. On February 5, 1976, the Federal Law of Protection to the Consumer enriches the social rights of the Mexican people, which for the first time established rights for the consuming population and believes a specialized agency in the proxy of justice in the sphere of the consumption. There were conceived from the National Institute of the Consumer and the Federal Attorney's office of the Consumer, this one as [an] organism decentralized of social service, juridical personality and own patrimony with functions of administrative authority entrusted to promote and protect the interests of the consuming public.

MISSION

To promote and to protect the rights of the consumer, to foment intelligent consumption and to arbitrate the equity and juridical safety in the relations between suppliers and consumers.

VISION

To be an effective institution in the promotion of a culture of intelligent consumption and in the application of the law.

AIMS OF THE PROFECO

To protect the rights of the consumer.

To promote the rights of the consumer.

To foment a culture of intelligent consumption.

To arbitrate the equity in the relations of consumption.

To arbitrate the juridical safety in the relations of consumption.

For more information, their website is: *www.profeco.gob.mx/english.htm*

If there were a "Better Business Bureau" in Mérida!

There is no "Better Business Bureau" in Mérida and consumer protection agencies do not publish a list of companies that have complaints filed against them. As a result, be mindful, that based on years of living in Mérida, expatriates are more likely to be scammed not by locals but by other expatriates. All we are saying is **CONSUMER BEWARE!**

With this caveat, here is a list of companies to approach with caution. —*Eduviges Montejo*

Henry Ponce Architects

Henry Ponce has used his fluent English to ingratiate himself in the expat community emerging as a "star" architect. In consequence, over the years his fees have skyrocketed and his designs have become cookie-cutter. Despite what expats tell you, he is not "famous." Outside Mérida, few know who he is and his designs have only garnered a Silver prize in one national competition. When you encounter someone who boasts a "Henry Ponce design" that person is either a naïf or blind. Indeed, if you want to boast a design by an architect of true national and international recognition who lives in Mérida, avail yourself to Salvador Reyes.

Website: *http://www.henryponce.com/*

Urbano Rentals

Run by two displaced New Yorkers, John Powell and Josh Ramos, complaints continue to be voiced about this property management and rental company. There are two kinds of gripes. First, renters who arrive and find that nothing has been prepared so their holiday is interrupted by plumbers, electricians, and the cable guy coming in to take care of things that should have been taken care of before they arrived for their stay. Second, property owners complain that their homes were used, without their permission, to host parties or were included in "house tours" while they were away.

Website: *http://www.urbanorentals.com/*

Malena Peón Art

Individuals who commission paintings have expressed regret at the delivery time and the quality of the art created. Malena Peón Vega de Martínez, interestingly, was a Board Member of the Mérida English Library when her husband, José Martínez, was president of that organization and embezzled more than $450,000 Mexican pesos from the library. Malena Peón and José Martínez were ousted from the library board. Both are persona non grata for their theft of library funds and betrayal of the trust of established expats.

Website: *http://malenapeon.com/*

Mexico International Real Estate

Mitch Keenan's decision to renounce his U.S. citizenship was met with disbelief and outrage by the overwhelming majority of the expat community. To turn your back on the nation of one's birth was seen as something that bordered on treason. In consequence, his company fell into disfavor, which only accelerated after several real estate agents associated with his firm fled Mérida after their participation in sex tourism activities were disclosed. To this, add that, under his watch as a Board Member, the Mérida English Library was plundered by its president. Hi failure to exercise oversight further hostility towards him.

Website: *www.mexintl.com/*

Los Dos Cooking School

Anyone can call himself anything he wants, but the title of "Chef" is technically reserved for someone who graduated from a culinary school. In the U.S., the American Culinary Federation (ACF) confers certification that allows an individual to use the title "Chef" for professional purposes. This is why even television personalities, such as Rachel Ray and Martha Stewart, call themselves "cooks" and never use the title of "chef." David Sterling calls himself "chef" although he never even attended any culinary school anywhere for a single semester; his formal education is in interior design. This speaks volumes about him, his skills, and his culinary "school."

Website: *http://los-dos.com/*

More detailed information on consumer scams appears at:
http://mesoamerica-foundation.org/meridascams.html

29 End of Life Issues: Wills, Assisted Living Options & Caring for a Terminally Ill Loved One

In Samuel Butler's classic, *The Way of All Flesh*, the reader is reminded of each person's mortality, since that is part of the cycle of life. It is a masterful work, one that traces four generations of a family that attempts, often in vain, to find happiness. The novel does ask readers to contemplate the nature of mortality, and end of life issues. It would be easy to point out that none of the characters lived in Mérida! No wonder they're miserable! So it is for expatriates in Mérida. There will come a time when an important decision will have to be made: to remain in Mérida, or to return home.

Traditionally, there have been two scenarios played out. There are expatriates who, once they reach a certain stage in life and can no longer comfortably or capably live on their own, avail themselves to their adult children, siblings or other relatives back home. Often times, arrangements are made for them to return to assisted living centers in the U.S., or to nursing homes. When this happens, the chapter of their lives living in Mérida is meticulously closed up, and they leave for the twilight of their time back in their home country. The other is to make arrangements to remain in Mexico, through a network of friends and institutional relationships forged during their time living in Mérida. There are some who, for lack of family, or the desire to remain far removed from the travesties of the elder healthcare industry in the U.S., decide to remain in Mérida.

Whichever course is right for you—should I stay or should I go?—it's important to have a will and written instructions that clearly, legally and *bilingually* spell out your wishes. Just because you live in Mérida doesn't mean you won't get hit by the proverbial bus!

There's another point to consider: Since 2000 there has been rapid and strong growth of assisted living communities in Mérida, as well as nursing homes. Many are a fraction of the costs back in the U.S. or Canada, and they offer far superior person-to-person individualized care, from both physicians and staff. This is fast-becoming a popular option. How popular? Consider this: To assist the expatriate community, the State of Yucatán commissioned an opinion poll to help determine if government-assistance is required in creating a retirement community for Americans citizens living in Mérida, which would include an assisted living center.

That said, if you have a will in English, and you should, it is well worth having a summary of it translated and notarized by either a Mexican Public Notary or the U.S. Consulate public notary services, just in case. Quick! If the proverbial bus *were* to hit you now, do you want your body shipped back to your home country, or do you want to be cremated in Mérida? How would the coroner's office know your wishes?

With this in mind, the following is a first-person account of a couple that decided to remain in Mérida while the husband cared for the terminally-ill wife. After this account, the procedures for handling a death in Mérida are discussed.

Elder Care Options in Mérida

by Eduviges Montejo

Elder care options are somewhat limited in Mérida because of longstanding traditions of family home care. In other words, care for the elderly is normally provided by their children and/or members of the extended family. In the past two decades, however, some private care facilities have emerged which may meet the needs of foreign residents.

The **Residencia Josefina Montes**, as its name implies, is a private residence much in demand among Yucatecan women of the upper classes. It was founded some twenty years ago and consists of a large modern building in Colonia México Oriente with landscaped courtyards for recreation and relaxation, library and TV rooms. The dormitory rooms are either single or double and there are a handful of two-room suites available. All rooms have private bath. There is limited parking for residents cars.

The **Residencia Josefina Montes** is exclusively for women and provides certain residential services such as:

1) Meals (breakfast in the rooms, lunch and dinner in the communal dining room at specific times only and served in bedrooms in demonstrated cases of illness or disability).

2) Daily room cleaning.

3) Clean bed linens and towels provided on a weekly basis.

4) All utilities including hot water. Residents are allowed TV sets, small size refrigerators and A/C equipment in their rooms. The cost of the use of A/C is charged to the resident on a monthly basis.

The facility does not provide elder care such as bathing, dressing, moving, and medical attention. Residents in need of any of the above types of care need to arrange for them directly through private nurses or caretakers, independently from the residence. Furthermore, the Josefina Montes is owned and administered by an order of Roman Catholic nuns and, although everyone may be accepted regardless of religious affiliation, a certain amount of the organized activities relate to religious feasts and observances.

The place is clean, well kept, airy, and very comfortable. The interaction among residents is friendly and congenial. It should be emphasized that the nuns manage the place efficiently but do not provide care. Although some residents are fluent in English, only Spanish is spoken by management and staff. Room availability is limited because of high demand. The cost of a private room and services should run well less than US$1,000 a month. Admittance limited to women under 72 years of age and in reasonable health but once you are a resident if your health deteriorates you may stay.

Another choice is the **Casa Aurea** located in Colonia México on the edge of Itzimná. This is a full service nursing home comprising two houses and one annex in the main property, and a second facility about one mile away. All rooms are considered doubles but it is possible for a single individual to rent a full room. It is a co-ed facility. Residents range from elderly in excellent physical health who simply wish to live independently of their families to the frail elderly in need of round the clock care. There is male and female nursing staff 24/7 and care is offered as needed. A team of doctors associated with the home is on call. Transportation to Star Médica and Clínica de Mérida is provided in case of emergencies. There is no age limit for admittance.

All rooms have a private bath, hot water, TV, wireless internet, choice of SKY or cable programming and nice furnishings which including shades, curtains, and bedspreads. Bed linens and towels are provided but at an additional cost as is laundering of personal items. There are gardens for outdoor use.

Meals are served in the communal dining room but it is possible to be served in one´s room. Meals are adjusted to individual circumstances, i.e. liquefied for elderly unable to swallow whole foods.

The administration and some nurses speak English. The home has residents from Europe, Canada and the United States as well other areas of Mexico and, of course, Yucatán.

The cost of a room is around $2,000 USD a month but it can be shared with another resident. Additional information can be found under Casa Aurea in the Internet.

A third option is to arrange for in house medical care through a geriatric specialist who supervises a team of nurses. Such person is Dr. Xail Pérez Medina who can be reached at (999) 271-2413 (cell phone). Her office is on Calle 47 #418 by 66 Street in Centro. She has cared for IWC members in the past and is recommended by the respective families. The main advantage of in home care is that it is totally personalized and one-on-one and that the patient and the family can control all the aspects.

The Final *Adios*

Every expatriate who decides to remain in Mérida until death do you part, would be wise to:

1. Have an original and a copy of his or her birth certificate on hand, along with an official, notarized, translation of that birth certificate.

2. Have an official translation of your will, notarized, and on hand.

These two documents will save those taking care of the final details of your affairs much easier, especially when navigating through the bureaucracy that surrounds death.

The first step in all of this, of course, requires that you take the initiative and, how shall we put it? Yes, you need to die. Having done that, your part is done. But what of those who now have to deal with your physical remains and disposing of your worldly possessions?

Here is a breakdown of what happens:

If you died at a clinic, or hospital, or at the scene of an accident, or at home with others by your bedside, chances are that a doctor is involved in the matter. If you died in your sleep, alone, then someone will have to find your body.

Once you die and your body is found, whoever is present, notifies a doctor. If you are an American citizen, someone should also contact the U.S. Consulate to report the death of an American in Mexico.

The doctor confirms the death and fills out one document: Certificado de Defunción which is an official document from the Secretaria de Salud del Estado de Yucatán, which confirms that the person died in the State of Yucatán.

This certificate, along with an original and notarized translation of the birth certificate, is taken to a funeral home. If the death occurred in a medical facility, the staff calls a funeral home ahead of time.

The staff at the funeral home examines the birth certificate, the notarized translation, and the Certificado de Defunción to make sure everything is in order. Arrangements are made for the body to be picked up.

The funeral home will assign a staff member to assist you in going to the Registro Civil, on Calle 65 between Calle 64 and 66 Street, to register the death. Once the information is entered into the Registro Civil's computer, an Official Death Certificate is issued. This grants the funeral home the legal authority to make arrangements for the disposal of the body—cremation, burial in Mexico, or arrangements to ship the body overseas. Ask for at least three copies of the Official Death Certificate since it will expedite things along the way.

The funeral home will then notify the Municipal Crematorium, the cemetery or the next of kin for instructions. If the body is to be cremated or buried in Mexico, there will paperwork associated, along with the fees (and payment of those fees), for either cremation or opening and closing of the tomb. If the body is to be shipped overseas, airlines have their own offices that are in charge of shipping human remains.

The final step is filling out forms at the U.S. Consulate, and returning the passport to consular personnel. The U.S. Consulate will issue a "Report of the Death of an American Citizen Abroad," which, in essence, confirms the legality of all the Mexican paperwork, which is necessary for the next of kin to be able to execute the will, and handle legal matters in the United States. The Consulate will automatically inform all U.S. agencies, such as the Social Security Administration, Veterans Affairs, and so forth, of your death. One **final note that applies to women:** If your name, because of marriage, is different in your passport than it is on your birth certificate, this will complicate matters. Please make sure you have a document from a Notario Público explaining that "Mary Smith" is the same person as "Mary Doe" since Ms. Mary Doe became Mrs. Mary Smith when she married Mr. John Smith.

Have a wonderful afterlife, or reincarnation!

MEXICAN EMBASSIES AND CONSULATES IN THE U.S. AND CANADA

USA

Alaska

Anchorage

610 "C" Street Suite A-7, Anchorage, Alaska 99501
Telephone: Tel (907) 334-9573 * Fax (907) 334-9673

Arkansas

Little Rock

3500 South University Avenue, Little Rock, AR, 72204
Telephone: (501) 372-6933 * **Fax:** (501) 372-6109

Arizona

Douglas

1201 F Avenue, Douglas, AZ 85607
Telephone: (520) 364-3142 * **Fax:** (520) 364-1379

Nogales

571 N. Grand Ave., Nogales, AZ 85621
Telephone: (520) 287-2521 * **Fax:** (520) 287-3175

Phoenix

1990 W. Camelback, Suite 110, Phoenix, AZ 85015
Telephone: (602) 242-7398 * **Fax:** 242-2957

Tucson

553 S. Stone Ave., Tucson, AZ 85701
Telephone: (520) 882-5595 * **Fax:** (520) 882-8959

Yuma

298 S. Main Street, Yuma, AZ 85364
Telephone: (928) 343-0066 * **Fax:** (928) 343-0077

California

Calexico

408 Herber Ave., Calexico, CA 92231
Telephone: (760) 357-4132 * **Fax:** (760) 357-6284

Fresno

2409 Merced Street, Fresno, CA 93721
Telephone: (559) 233-3065 * **Fax:** (559) 233-6156

Los Angeles

2401 W. Sixth Street, Los Angeles, CA 90057
Telephone: (213) 351-6800 * **Fax:** (213) 351-2114

Oxnard

3151 West Fifth Street, Oxnard, CA 93030
Telephone: (805) 984-8738* **Fax:** (805) 984-8747

Sacramento

1010 8th Street, Sacramento, CA 95814
Telephone: (916) 441-3287 * **Fax:** (916) 441-3146

San Bernardino

293 North "D" Street, San Bernardino, CA 92401
Telephone: (909) 889-9836 * **Fax:** (909) 889-8285

San Diego

1549 India Street, San Diego, CA 92101
Telephone: (619) 231-8414 * **Fax:** (619) 231-4802

San Francisco

532 Folsom Street, San Francisco, CA 94105
Telephone: (415) 354-1700 * **Fax:** (415) 495-3971

San José

540 North First Street, San José, CA 95112
Telephone: (408) 294-3414 * **Fax:** (408) 294-4506

Santa Ana

828 N. Broadway Street, Santa Ana, CA 92701-3424
Telephone: (714) 835-3069 * **Fax:** (714) 835-3472

Colorado

Denver

5350 Leetsdale Drive, Suite 100, Denver, CO 80246
Telephone: (303) 331-1110 * **Fax:** (303) 331-1872

District of Columbia

Washington (Embassy of Mexico)

1911 Pennsylvania Ave., N.W., Washington, D.C., 20006
Telephone: (202) 736-1000 * **Fax:** (202) 234-4498

District of Columbia (Consulate)

2827 16th. Street N.W., Washington D.C., 20009-4260
Telephone: (202) 736-1000 * **Fax:** (202) 2344498

447

Florida

Miami

5975 S.W. 72nd Street, Miami, Florida 33143
Telephone: (786) 268-4900 * **Fax:** (786) 268-4895

Orlando

100 W. Washington Street, Orlando, FL 32801
Telephone: (407) 422-0514 * **Fax:** (407) 422-9633

Georgia

Atlanta

2600 Apple Valley Rd, Atlanta, GA 30319
Telephone: (404) 266-2233 * **Fax:** (404) 266-2302

Idaho

Boise

720 Park Boulevard, Suite 260, Boise, Idaho, 83712
Telephone:(208) 343-6228 343-6237 * **Fax:** (208) 343-6237

Indiana

Indianapolis

39 west Jackson Place, Suite 103, Indianapolis, IN 46225
Telephone:(317) 951-0005 * **Fax:** (317) 951-0006

Illinois

Chicago

204 S. Ashland Ave., Chicago, IL 60607
Telephone: (312) 738-2383 * **Fax:** 312-491-9072

Louisiana

New Orleans

901 Convection Center Boulevard, Suite 119, New Orleans, LA 70130
Telephone: (504) 528-3722

Massachusetts

Boston

20 Park Plaza, Suite 506, Boston, MA 02116
Telephone: (617) 426-4181 * **Fax:** (617) 695-1957

Michigan

Detroit

645 Griswold Ave. Suite 1700, Detroit, MI 48226
Telephone: (313) 964-4515 * **Fax:** (313) 964-4522

Minnesota

Saint Paul

797 East 7th Street, Saint Paul, MN 55106
Telephone: (651) 771-5494 * **Fax:** (651) 772-4419

Missouri

Kansas City

1600 Baltimore, Suite 100, Kansas City, MO 64108
Telephone: (816) 556-0800 * **Fax:** (816) 556-0900

Nebraska

Omaha

3552 Dodge Street, Omaha, NE 6811
Telephone: (402) 595-1841-44 * **Fax:** (402) 595-1845

Nevada

Las Vegas

330 S. 4th Street, Las Vegas, Nevada 89101
Telephone: (702) 383-0623 * **Fax:** (702) 383-0683

New Mexico

Albuquerque

1610 4th Street NW, Albuquerque, NM 87102
Telephone: (505) 247-4177 * **Fax:** (505) 842-9490

New York

New York

27 East 39th. Street, New York, NY 10016
Telephone: (212) 217-6400 * **Fax:** (212) 217-6493

North Carolina

Charlotte

P.O. Box 19627, Charlotte, NC 28219
Telephone: (704) 394-2190

Raleigh

336 E. Six Forks Rd, Raleigh, NC 27609
Telephone: (919) 754-0046 * **Fax:** (919) 754-1729

Oregon

Portland

1234 S.W. Morrison, Portland, OR 97205
Telephone: (503) 274-1450 * **Fax:** (503) 274-1540

Pennsylvania

Philadelphia

111 S. Independence Mall E, Suite 310, Bourse Building, Philadelphia, PA 19106
Telephone: (215) 922-4262/3834 * **Fax:** (215) 923-7281

Texas

Austin

200 E. Sixth Street, Suite 200, Austin, TX 78701
Telephone: (512) 478-2866 * **Fax:** (512) 478-8008

Brownsville

724 E. Elizabeth Street, Brownsville, TX 78520
Telephone: (956) 542-4431 * **Fax:** (956) 542-7267

Corpus Christi

800 N. Shoreline Blvd. Suite 410, North Tower, Corpus Christi, TX 78401
Telephone: (512) 882-3375 * **Fax:** (512) 882-9324

Dallas

8855 N Stemmons Freeway, Dallas, TX 75247
Telephone: (214) 252-9250 ext. 123 * **Fax:** (214) 630-3511

Del Rio

2398 Spur, Del Rio, TX 78840
Telephone: (830) 775-2352 * **Fax:** (830) 774-6497

Eagle Pass

2252 E. Garrison Street. Eagle Pass, TX 78852
Telephone: (830) 773-9255 * **Fax:** (830) 773-9397

El Paso

910 E. San Antonio Street, El Paso, TX 79901
Telephone: (915) 533-3644 * **Fax:** (915) 532-7163

451

Houston

4507 San Jacinto Street, Houston, TX 77004
Telephone: (713) 271-6800 ext 1400 * **Fax:** (713) 271-3201

Laredo

1612 Farragut Street, Laredo, TX 78040
Telephone: (956) 723-6369 * **Fax:** (956) 723-1741

McAllen

600 S. Broadway Ave., McAllen, TX 78501
Telephone: (956) 686-0243 * **Fax:** (956) 686-4901

Presidio

Juárez Ave.Y 21 de Marzo Street, Presidio, TX 79845
Telephone: (423) 229-2788 * **Fax:** (423) 229-2792

San Antonio

127 Navarro Street, San Antonio, TX 78205
Telephone: (210) 271-9728 * **Fax:** (210) 227-7518

Utah

Salt Lake City

155 South 300 West 3rd floor, Salt Lake City, Utah 84101
Telephone: (801) 521-8503 * **Fax:** (801) 521-0534

Washington

Seattle

2132 Third Ave., Seattle, WA 98121
Telephone: (206) 448-3526 * **Fax:** (206) 448-4771

CANADA

Alberta

Calgary

Suite 1100-833 4th Avenue SW
Calgary, Alberta T2P 3T5
Telephone: (403) 264-4819 * **Fax:** (403) 264-1527

British Columbia

Vancouver

Suite 411-1177 West Hastings Street, 4th Floor
Vancouver, B.C. V6E 2K3
Telephone: (604) 684-1859 * **Fax:** (604) 684-2485

Ontario

Ottawa (Embassy of Mexico)

45 O'Connor Suite 1500
Ottawa, Ontario K1P 1A4
Telephone: (613) 233 8988 * **Fax:** (613) 235 9123

Toronto

199 Bay Street, Suite 4440, Commerce Court West
Toronto, Ontarip M5L 1E9
Telephone: (416) 368-1847 * **Fax:** (416) 368-8141

Quebec

Montreal

2055 rue Peel, Suite 1000,
Montreal, Québec, H3A 1V4
Telephone: (514) 288 2502 y (514) 288 2707 * **Fax:** (514) 288 8287

CPSIA information can be obtained
at www.ICGtesting.com
Printed in the USA
LVOW09s0019031116
511449LV00025B/415/P

9 781939 879226